Praise for INFORMative Assessment . . .

For too long, instruction has been an act separated from assessment for middle school and high school mathematics teachers. In *INFORMative Assessment*, Joyner and Bright provide a remarkable road map for the seamless blending of these two high-impact teacher responsibilities. They offer discussion protocols, tools, and clear examples of teacher practice within a well-defined and research-affirmed ongoing cycle of teacher and student reflection. *INFORMative Assessment* is just that—a must-read that will *inform* the deep and successful practice of every teacher and teacher team!

> —Timothy D. Kanold, Past President, National Council of Supervisors of Mathematics

With all the attention on large-scale accountability tests, we need to keep our eye on the most important kind of assessment of all: formative assessment. In this easy-to-read resource, Joyner and Bright combine expert wisdom with sound research and practical advice, delivering exactly the tools every teacher needs to make sure students learn the math they need to learn.

> —Cathy L. Seeley, author of *Faster Isn't Smarter* and *Smarter Than We Think*

There are not enough usable materials for secondary teachers about teaching and student learning. *INFORMative Assessment* helps fill this void, emphasizing how important it is to know what students are thinking. Joyner and Bright ask teachers to reflect on questions about their beliefs, an essential step for moving to a stage where formative assessment can help students learn mathematics in a meaningful way.

> —Mary M. Lindquist, Past President, National Council of Teachers of Mathematics

INFORMative Assessment is an excellent resource for teachers, helping them think more about the seamless relationship that should exist between instruction and assessment. It supports teachers in taking the action steps called for in National Council of Teachers of Mathematics' (NCTM) *Principles to Actions: Ensuring Mathematical Success for All* (2014) as well as connecting to the eight mathematics teaching practices of NCTM. Moreover, *INFORMative Assessment* makes explicit connections to the content standards and the standards for mathematical practice of the Common Core State Standards for Mathematics.

> —Marilyn E. Strutchens, Emily R. and Gerald S. Leischuck Endowed Professor and Mildred Chesire Fraley Distinguished Professor, Auburn University, Alabama

INFORMative Assessment

Assessment

[Formative Assessment Practices to Improve]

MATHEMATICS ACHIEVEMENT

MIDDLE AND HIGH SCHOOL

Jeane M. Joyner

George W. Bright

Foreword by Steve Leinwand

Math Solutions
Sausalito, California, USA

Math Solutions
One Harbor Drive, Suite 101
Sausalito, California, USA 94965
www.mathsolutions.com

Library of Congress Cataloging-in-Publication Data
Names: Joyner, Jeane M. | Bright, George W.
Title: Informative assessment : formative assessment practices to improve mathematics
   achievement, middle and high school / Jeane M. Joyner, George W. Bright;
   foreword by Steve Leinwand.
Other titles: Informative assessment
Description: Sausalito, California : Math Solutions, [2016] | Type size
   difference in title emphasizes word Inform. | Includes bibliographical
   references and index.
Identifiers: LCCN 2015033262| ISBN 9781935099451 | ISBN 1935099450
Subjects: LCSH: Mathematics—Study and teaching (Middle school) |
   Mathematics—Study and teaching (Secondary) | Middle school Teachers—Training of. |
   High school teachers—Training of. | Mathematics teachers—Training of.
Classification: LCC QA39.3 .J69 2016 | DDC 510.71/2—dc23
LC record available at http://lccn.loc.gov/2015033262

Executive Editor: Jamie A. Cross
Production Manager: Denise A. Botelho
Cover Design: Lisa Delgado and Company
Interior Design: MPS Limited
Composition: MPS Limited

Printed in the United States of America.
1 2 3 4 5 6 7 8 9 10   31   25 24 23 22 21 20 19 18 17 16

A Message from Math Solutions

We at Math Solutions believe that teaching math well calls for increasing our understanding of the math we teach, seeking deeper insights into how students learn mathematics, and refining our lessons to best promote students' learning.

Math Solutions shares classroom-tested lessons and teaching expertise from our faculty of professional development consultants as well as from other respected math educators. Our publications are part of the nationwide effort we've made since 1984 that now includes

- more than five hundred face-to-face professional development programs each year for teachers and administrators in districts across the country;
- professional development books that span all math topics taught in kindergarten through high school;
- videos for teachers and for parents that show math lessons taught in actual classrooms;
- on-site visits to schools to help refine teaching strategies and assess student learning; and
- free online support, including grade-level lessons, book reviews, inservice information, and district feedback, all in our Math Solutions Online Newsletter.

For information about all of the products and services we have available, please visit our website at *www.mathsolutions.com.* You can also contact us to discuss math professional development needs by calling (800) 868-9092 or by sending an email to *info@mathsolutions.com.*

We're always eager for your feedback and interested in learning about your particular needs. We look forward to hearing from you.

*To Meg, James, and the other students
who helped us make this work come alive*

Contents

(continued)

Contents

Foreword

Few phrases in our teaching lexicon are used more often and meant to convey as many ideas and practices as *formative assessment.*

To some, formative assessment is simply the exit slip task expected of students near the end of most lessons. To others, it is as broad as any non-high-stakes summative assessment administered to students. It is fascinating to hear the exact same "benchmark" assessment referred to as "formative" in one school district and "summative" in another. I've heard some educators narrowly, but simply and consistently, consider quizzes to be formative and tests to be summative, while others argue that every question a teacher asks students, whether orally or in writing, is a type of formative assessment. Still others contend that formative assessment is merely an essential component of effective instruction and should be called "assessment" in the first place because its purpose is to monitor and adjust ongoing *instruction.*

I tend to believe, in alignment with the authors of this wonderful guide to these issues, that as we teach, we assess, and, as we assess, we teach— that is, formative assessment and instruction are two sets of interconnected processes representing two sides of the same coin. Formative assessment is an intentional and systematic process used by teachers and students during instruction that provides feedback to adjust ongoing teaching and learning in order to improve students' achievement of intended instructional outcomes.

Meanwhile those who have endured "PD on FA" learn that according to the appropriately dubbed gurus of formative assessment, Paul Black and Dylan Wiliam, "We use the general term *assessment* to refer to all those activities undertaken by teachers—and by their students in assessing their own learning—that provide information to be used as feedback to modify teaching and learning activities. Such assessment becomes *formative assessment* when the evidence is actually used to adapt the teaching to meet student needs." To which any teacher next asks, "OK, but *how?*"

It is into this cacophony of opinions and beliefs that Jeane Joyner and George Bright dare tread. They cut through the haze and present a practical, coherent, and INFORMative guide to the many aspects of using formative assessment to enhance the effectiveness of teaching and raise student achievement in mathematics. But, like so many other research-affirmed practices, formative assessment tends to be much more common at the elementary level than at middle school and high school where far too many mathematics classes continue to cling to the process of teaching by telling, showing, and practicing, with far too little regard to actual student learning. Perhaps there just hasn't been the same push to incorporate these practices into one's teaching or perhaps there hasn't been adequate guidance or there is a perception that this is just another add-on for which there isn't enough time. Regardless of the reasons, in this comprehensive resource, Joyner and Bright tackle the matter specifically at the middle and high school levels. In doing so, they provide middle and high school teachers with a professional nudge, clear pedagogical guidance, and a slew of readily adaptable examples.

As one delves into the resource and into effective formative assessment, one finds a constellation of themes that emerge to truly help us inform our practice.

Clarity of learning goals. How do we measure or monitor anything if the learning goal isn't clear? Joyner and Bright give us insightful guidance and examples for focusing our learning goals.

Meaningful, and often rich, tasks. What specific tasks can we use to gather evidence of learning or the lack thereof? Joyner and Bright offer a range of great tasks, from simple to rich, and they model how these tasks can be effectively used.

Prior knowledge and misconceptions. Why would we teach what our students already know and how do we address common misconceptions in our teaching? Joyner and Bright show how formative assessment is a critical tool for determining the degree of prior knowledge and the extent of common misconceptions that persist even after effective instruction.

Questions. How do we stimulate student thinking and elicit the depth of student understanding? Joyner and Bright offer insightful and easy-to-adapt strategies to sharpen our questioning.

Intentional listening. How do we honor student answers and use these answers to foster deeper learning? Joyner and Bright's chapter on this topic is a perfect reading for a professional learning community discussion.

Making inferences. How do we interpret and make use of students' oral and written work? This is the heart of formative assessment—using what we hear and see to strengthen student learning—and Joyner and Bright give us a range of insights and practical techniques for making appropriate inferences, including differentiating among correct, incomplete, and incorrect work.

Providing actionable feedback. What exactly do we say or write to students to move them toward full and complete understanding? Once again, Joyner and Bright walk us through a process and a set of techniques for doing exactly this, including using additional questioning in place of merely telling.

Classroom culture. Finally, how do we institute a classroom culture that supports the kind of openness and inquisitiveness that support learning? Joyner and Bright end this resource with a set of guidelines and practices that need to be inculcated in every middle school and high school mathematics classroom.

These overarching themes are introduced early in this resource and captured in the following six decision-making strategies, which form the backbone of the book.

Teachers must make decisions:

- about what students already know (use starter questions, pre-assessments, class discussions, and concept maps);
- about what to teach (guided by state standards and/or Common Core State Standards for Mathematics and learning progressions);
- as students respond to instruction (provide additional examples, facilitate group or class discussions, give specific feedback to individuals, and reteach);
- that support student learning (continue to probe students' thinking and modify instruction related to critical content);
- from reflecting on data (use alternative multiple-choice format, portfolios, and anecdotal records); and
- about evaluating learning (evaluations might be through grading and using daily informal assessments to inform instruction).

Every chapter provides incredibly useful guidance and examples to help all teachers make these decisions.

In summary, our individual and collective improvement of practice entails shifts in mindsets, pedagogical knowledge, better tasks and questions, and a professional culture that reinforces good daily teaching practice. The chapters that follow offer a great first step on this journey.

—STEVEN LEINWAND
AMERICAN INSTITUTES OF RESEARCH

How to Use This Resource

INFORMative Assessment is a road map that will help you move forward on the journey toward incorporating formative assessment seamlessly into your planning and delivery of instruction. It will also assist you in knowing how to provide feedback to students and in establishing routines that support greater engagement by students. In reading this resource and engaging in its reflections, you will gain a foundational understanding of formative assessment as an INFORMative process.

Because different teachers have different interests, experiences, and skills, different parts of the resource may seem relatively more important or relatively more compelling. Some teachers will be most interested in student self-assessment (Chapter 7). Others may decide to think more carefully about refining learning targets and clarifying what achievement looks like (Chapter 3). Still others have an interest in using questions to probe students' thinking (Chapters 4 and 8).

One premise of this resource is that learning is generative for teachers as well as students. Just as students must make sense of the mathematics they are learning, teachers are successful in implementing formative assessment to the extent that formative assessment practices and strategies make sense to them and are congruent with their beliefs.

> **Assessment Tip** ✓
>
> What is most likely to improve the quality of mathematics education for all students is the thoughtful shifts that teachers make during daily instruction to understand students' thinking and use that knowledge to make decisions.

Generativity refers to individuals' abilities to continue to add to their understanding. When individuals learn with understanding, they can apply their knowledge to learn new topics and solve new and unfamiliar problems. When individuals do not learn with understanding, each new topic is learned as an isolated skill, and the skills they have learned can only be used to solve problems explicitly covered by instruction. (Franke et al. 2001, 655–56)

The INFORMative Assessment Model

Throughout this resource you'll find a model for formative assessment. It illustrates ways that decisions about teaching and learning are connected; the chapters address the parts of the model, both individually and in combination. For more on this model, see Chapter 1.

The Chapters: An Overview

Chapter 1: In this chapter you will think about your own beliefs and actions as an introduction to INFORMative assessment. The chapter then tackles the question "What is INFORMative assessment?" and gives you a road map for starting to think about formative assessment in your classroom. The chapter introduces the INFORMative Assessment Model and concludes with an illustration of the use of INFORMative assessment in a classroom.

Chapter 2: Teachers make hundreds of decisions each day that impact students' learning. This chapter addresses the "Decisions: Next Steps" part of the model by identifying strategies for supporting the decisions about "next steps."

Chapter 3: This chapter takes a deeper look at the "Clear Learning Targets" part of the model. Mathematics instruction includes learning targets that involve facts, concepts, and procedures. This chapter emphasizes the importance not only of planning instruction with clear learning targets and criteria for success in mind but also of sharing that information with students.

Chapter 4: This chapter begins a discussion of the "Tasks, Questions, and Assessments" portion of our model. Teachers are able to learn a great deal about students' thinking through class discussions and targeted questions. This chapter identifies opportunities for oral assessments that occur during a typical mathematics class.

Chapter 5: This chapter continues the discussion of the "Tasks, Questions, and Assessments" part of the model for INFORMative assessment. Students' written work is a primary source of information about students' mathematical understanding. Characteristics of quality formative assessment tasks, examples of debriefing these tasks, and strategies for gathering information about student's thinking from their written work are the focal point of this chapter.

Chapter 6: Tasks lie at the heart of both instruction and assessment. This chapter expands the discussion of "Tasks, Questions, and Assessments" and highlights the importance of rich tasks in engaging students at different levels of sophistication and in moving students' thinking toward the goals of instruction.

Chapter 7: This chapter focuses the "Student Self-Assessment and Responsibility" component of the model. It is important to create an environment that encourages greater student responsibility. Strategies are identified for engaging students in self-assessment and moving students toward working like mathematicians.

Chapter 8: This is the first of two chapters related to the "Inferences and Feedback" portion of the model. There are many purposes for classroom questions. This chapter focuses on using questions to make inferences about what students understand and the logic behind students' answers.

Chapter 9: Feedback can be powerful in supporting student learning. Chapter 9 continues the discussion of the "Inferences and Feedback" portion of the model and focuses on converting inferences into actionable feedback.

Chapter 10: This chapter reviews key elements of assessment as instruction and instruction as assessment, especially as those elements connect with the model for INFORMative assessment. There are illustrations of teachers' uses of these ideas to make instruction more effective so that students learn more. The chapter ends with a reminder that the use of formative assessment is an ongoing journey.

The Reflections

As you read this resource we invite you to reflect repeatedly on your own beliefs and decisions as well as to encourage reflective practices among students that will help them take greater responsibility for their own learning. Remember that teaching is not a "performance art," with the teacher doing the performing and the students acting as the audience for the teacher's performance. Effective teaching, especially effective teaching that includes formative assessment, requires interactions among students and the teacher. Teachers have to manage these interactions, but students must also be active participants. We invite you to make a commitment to implement INFORMative assessment to enhance the long-term success of your students. At the end of each chapter there are opportunities for you to relate assessment strategies and examples to your own classroom. There is also a place for you to reflect on your thinking about formative assessment.

Learn More...
INFORMative assessment helps teachers and students become partners in the support of students' learning.

The Common Core State Standards for Mathematics

The mathematics examples used in this resource illustrate expectations set forth in the Common Core State Standards for Mathematics (CCSSM). CCSSM addresses both content standards and Standards for Mathematical Practice, and the discussions of mathematics examples attend to both kinds of standards. INFORMative assessment and Mathematical Practices (MP) seem to reinforce each other; one mutual purpose is to help students develop, and reflect on, their understanding of key mathematics ideas. All teachers are impacted by external tests, such as statewide end-of-grade tests, assessments tied to Common Core State Standards, or national tests that students take for admission to college. However, in spite of these external pressures, the ultimate goal of instruction is to help students master the mathematics outlined in state-approved standards.

┌─ **Learn More…** ─┐
More information about CCSSM is provided in Chapter 2.

To learn more about the Common Core State Standards for Mathematics, visit corestandards.org.

Let's Get Started!

INFORMative Assessment is targeted for teachers of mathematics in grades 7–12 and is organized to help teachers develop skills at using formative assessment. Faculty "book clubs," mathematics department members, and professional learning communities can use the chapters as a basis for discussions. Pre-service teachers can use the ideas to help them plan lessons with probing questions and to make sense of discussions with students. Professional development providers, such as district mathematics supervisors or university faculty, can use the ideas to create professional development workshops that will help teachers work together to better understand both the principles of formative assessment and ways of implementing those principles in classrooms. We hope you will join us on the journey to implement INFORMative assessment in your instruction.

Acknowledgments

Like all educators, we have benefited greatly from watching and interacting with teachers whose creativity and commitment to excellence make them our valued colleagues. We have also benefited from the writings of numerous researchers and authors who have been willing to put their ideas out for public scrutiny. We are grateful for all these opportunities to enrich our own understanding by examining the thinking of others.

The student work and classroom examples are composites of what we have seen during our interactions with students and teachers. We hope our perceptions accurately display the work of all those people, though we take full responsibility for any errors or misinterpretations that may have crept into our descriptions. Of course, the names that we have used in those composites are pseudonyms.

To Jamie Cross and Denise Botelho we say thank you for guiding us in crafting a manuscript that communicates clearly and is a pleasure to read. Finally, we thank our families and colleagues who encouraged us along the way.

—JEANE M. JOYNER AND GEORGE W. BRIGHT

Reflections

The following is a listing of all the Reflections in this resource. These reflections, found at the end of each chapter, give you the opportunity to relate assessment strategies and examples to your own classroom.

Classroom Scenarios

Throughout this resource, we offer examples from lessons that illustrate INFORMative practice in action; we call these sections "A Closer Look" and hope they are helpful in supporting your implementation of formative assessment in your classroom.

(continued)

(continued)

Section I

What Is INFORMative Assessment?

Beginning an Assessment Journey

What we believe affects how we teach, and how we teach affects what and how our students learn. In this chapter you will think about your own beliefs and actions as an introduction to INFORMative assessment. The chapter then tackles the question, "What is INFORMative assessment?" and gives you a road map for starting to think about formative assessment in your classroom. The chapter introduces the INFORMative Assessment Model and concludes with an overview of the rest of the resource.

Decisions: Next Steps ↔ Clear Learning Targets

INFORMative Assessment Model

Inferences & Feedback

Tasks Questions Assessments

Student Self-Assessment & Responsibility

Overview

Our Beliefs Versus Our Actions

Have you ever heard anyone say something like . . .

I believe in having students share their ideas. We just don't have time for extended conversations because we have so much content to cover.

Or

I believe in the use of technology to help students make sense of mathematics, but there is not enough time to teach them how to use software effectively. I model this technology rather than have students use it themselves.

Or

Open-ended questions do give more information about what students know, but I have so many students that I can't score all those questions each week. And the state tests are multiple-choice anyway, so why bother?

All teachers want what is best for their students; no teacher wants to make decisions that impede student learning. In an ideal world, teachers collaborate with each other to plan lessons and assessments, discuss student work, and have strong support from parents and school leaders. Learning targets are clear and resources are plentiful. Students and teachers have a vision of the mathematics that students are learning and what accomplishment looks like. In these situations, we feel empowered and students are likely to flourish.

In reality, however, many teachers work more in isolation, with little time for planning and collaboration with colleagues. We may feel alone in articulating specific learning targets and establishing what student performance will look like when the goals are accomplished. Because we feel the pressures of state standards and tests, we may believe we must use similar measures throughout the year to "prepare" students for the high-stakes assessments. In these situations teachers often make instructional decisions without a clear understanding of the peculiar logic or the misunderstandings behind student answers. The results of such a system are instructional decisions that may not support student learning.

Are My Beliefs and Actions Congruent?

What we believe has an impact on the things we do in our classrooms; after all, what we say and do will always impact our students. What we do, and what we believe about what we do, reflects our knowledge of mathematics, our understanding of students' interests and mathematics thinking, and our awareness of resources. What are some fundamental beliefs you have about teaching and learning? Complete the chart in "Reflection 1–1: My Beliefs About Teaching and Learning" (see page 19). First, record your beliefs. What do you feel strongly about related to teaching and learning? Next, write down an example for how each belief "plays out" in your classroom. And finally, reflect on the "match" between each belief and the example you gave for that belief. Do your actions match what you believe? Do this before continuing to read; here is an example to help you get started:

Reflection 1–1
My Beliefs About Teaching and Learning
Page 19

A fundamental belief about teaching and learning:	An example of how that belief plays out in my classroom:	The "match" (1 = LOW to 10 = HIGH) between the belief and the example:
Students need to learn key mathematics concepts.	I use weekly quizzes to see if students are learning the content.	8, because my students know how much they know from their quiz scores.

Look at your reflection chart as a whole. What matches are there between what you believe and what is happening in your classroom? When we say we believe something but our day-to-day actions model something different, no matter how good our intentions, our actions are what most often shape the effects on students.

Beliefs about how students learn influence the kinds of mathematics tasks we select for instruction as well as for assessment. Based on an observational study of a national sample of more than 350 mathematics and science lessons in grades K–12, Weiss and colleagues concluded that higher-quality instruction occurs when teachers ask questions that help students not only make sense of the mathematics they are learning but also at the same time help teachers understand what their students know (Weiss et al. 2003). That is, a belief that students can make sense of mathematics is critical for high-quality instruction. This kind of instruction is the essence of merging instruction with formative assessment. In short, the tasks we choose and the questions we ask make a difference in students' opportunities to learn.

What Is INFORMative Assessment?

┌─ **Learn More...** ─┐
"Formative assessment is a tool that teachers use to measure student grasp of specific topics and skills they are teaching. It's a 'midstream' tool to identify specific student misconceptions and mistakes while the material is being taught."
—"Where in the World Are Formative Tests? Right Under Your Nose!" (Kahl 2005, 11)

Formative assessment is a collection of strategies for gathering evidence about students' thinking both before and during instruction and then making informed instructional decisions to guide students' learning. Every assessment can potentially inform instruction; however, assessments become *INFORMative* when they positively influence instructional decisions. This frequently involves collecting and analyzing students' oral and written work in order to make inferences about their thinking. This process is discussed in Chapters 4 and 5. Since teachers' instructional decisions grow out of their inferences about students' thinking, it is critical that both those inferences and the feedback we give students be based on information that is as accurate as possible. We discuss this in depth in Chapters 8 and 9.

Formative assessment relies on interactions between a teacher and students. The interactions required for formative assessment often suggest the need for changes in the roles of the teacher and students. Teachers purposefully establish and share learning targets and criteria for success; plan activities, discussions, and questions that elicit evidence of students' understanding; and provide feedback to students about students' responses. Students attend to the targets and the criteria for demonstrating learning of these targets, serve as resources for each other, and take greater responsibility for their own learning.

The word *assessment* comes from Medieval Latin *assessus*, "to sit beside." Merriam-Webster gives one definition of *formative* as "capable of alteration by growth and development" (merriam-webster.com/dictionary/formative). Putting these two ideas together, we can create a mental image of a teacher moving throughout the classroom, stopping by individuals' desks, and talking with students about the mathematics they are doing. Rather than the teacher spending the majority of the time telling, the teacher is spending more time listening. Students tell about how they solved a problem and talk about what they are not sure of. Their written work and their conversations become assessments that INFORM us of their learning. The term *INFORMative assessment*, then, is used to emphasize the fact that formative assessment provides INFORMATION to teachers about students' thinking so that instruction can be better aligned to the needs of those students.

The journey toward the goal of better understanding student thinking can take many paths. Just as students in the same classroom learning a new mathematics concept bring different backgrounds to their tasks, we come to ideas of INFORMative assessment with different experiences and levels of expertise.

Part of the journey is doing what we just did—thinking about how our beliefs and actions are connected. INFORMative assessment provides the tools that teachers need to understand how students think about key mathematics ideas so that instruction can be targeted to the needs of those students. The result of well-implemented INFORMative assessment, then, is implementation of instructional strategies and practices that better support student learning, so that students learn more mathematics than they have in the past and achieve at higher levels.

The Research

The implementation of formative assessment has for many years been recognized as a very powerful way to increase students' learning.

> Black and Wiliam (1998) conclude from an examination of 250 research studies on classroom assessment that "formative assessment does improve learning"—and that the achievement gains are "among the largest ever reported for educational interventions." . . . In other words, if mathematics teachers were to focus their efforts on classroom assessment that is primarily formative in nature, students' learning gains would be impressive. These efforts would include gathering data through classroom questioning and discourse, using a variety of assessment tasks, and attending primarily to what students know and understand. (Wilson and Kenney 2003, 55)

Assessment Tip ✓

The goal of INFORMative assessment is to generate INFORMATION for us as teachers about students' thinking.

Learn More ...

"The important point is that one must acknowledge that what students learn is not necessarily what the teacher intended, and it is essential that teachers explore students' thinking before assuming that students have 'understood' something."
—"Keeping Learning on Track: Classroom Assessment and the Regulation of Learning" (Wiliam 2007b, 1069)

INFORMative Assessment Versus Summative Assessment

Formative and summative assessments serve different purposes. Summative assessments are evaluative and may or may not influence instruction. Given at the end of units, grading periods, semesters, or courses, summative assessments are likely to be end points for particular mathematics goals. In contrast, INFORMative assessment—the ongoing monitoring of students' understanding—guides decisions about what to do next to support students' learning. It helps teachers differentiate next steps, especially when next steps need to be different for different classes. Whether a teacher decides to ask probing questions of individual students and give them feedback or assign a related task or facilitate further discussion on the topic, formative assessment is used to help students learn. Stiggins and Chappius (2006) refer to this as assessment *for* learning rather than assessment *of* learning. Assessment *of* learning tends to be evaluative; it is a summing up of achievement of individual students and the class. Assessment *for* learning provides information that is used right away to influence instructional decisions and provide feedback to students. Both formative and summative assessments are necessary, but formative assessments support learning as it is taking place. Assessment *for* learning is continuous monitoring and responding in a timely manner.

Learn More…

"An assessment of a student is formative if it shapes that student's learning."
—"Formative Assessment: Getting the Focus Right" (Wiliam 2006, 284)

In the conclusions to a review of literature, Black and Wiliam stated first, that formative assessment was beneficial for all students, with benefits for low achievers being even greater than for other students, and second, that the achievement gap was diminished, while the overall achievement level was increased (Black and Wiliam 1998). More recent research (Wiliam 2007b) has helped to reinforce and refine these conclusions.

Five Strategies for Effective Formative Assessment

In a Research Brief published by the National Council of Teachers of Mathematics (NCTM) in 2007, Dylan Wiliam (2007a) suggests five strategies for effective formative assessment; those strategies are paraphrased here and are addressed in varying ways in later chapters. In particular, examples of the use of INFORMative assessment focus heavily on aspects of the second strategy.

The Research: Five Strategies for Effective Formative Assessment

- Clarifying learning targets along with criteria for success and making sure that students understand these targets and criteria

- Managing classroom discussions, activities, and tasks that allow students to show what they know

- Providing actionable feedback to students that moves their learning forward

- Helping students become more responsible for their own learning

- Helping students become resources for each other

Learn More …

The Research Clip associated with this Research Brief is available for members at http://tinyurl.com/ogb9osp. The Research Brief appears in full as an appendix in *INFORMative Assessment: Formative Assessment to Improve Math Achievement, Grades K–6* (Joyner and Muri 2011).

It is equally important for us to understand that implementing formative assessment will affect us as teachers. It takes considerable effort to change practices so that formative assessment becomes part of the normal routines. Research studies rarely attempt to measure teachers' effort; however, we have seen teachers become reinvigorated as they have struggled productively to learn how to use formative assessment. Teachers tell us that they can see changes in students' learning that had previously been "invisible." Seeing those changes makes teachers excited about being even more helpful in promoting learning. It is frustrating to work hard and see no effect. But when teachers work hard and can document changes in students' learning, those changes serve as positive reinforcement for teachers to continue to work hard. Teacher renewal is one of the unexpected, but wonderful, effects of implementation of formative assessment.

The INFORMative Assessment Model

Figure 1–1 is a model for formative assessment. This model reinforces and formalizes the description of "what is INFORMative assessment?" It illustrates ways that decisions about teaching and learning are connected. It is helpful to remember that each arrow in the model points in two directions; these arrows also could connect each cell with each of the other cells. The model provides coherence to the ideas throughout this

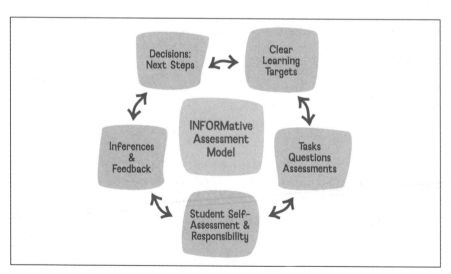

FIGURE 1-1. INFORMative Assessment Model for Teaching and Learning

resource. Each part of the model may be viewed as a "point of entry" for using formative assessment to INFORM what you do in the classroom every day.

We use the model in each chapter to help organize our discussion of formative assessment as it relates to the focus of that chapter. As you read the chapters, always keep in mind that "an assessment of a student is formative if it shapes that student's learning" (Wiliam 2006, 284). The purpose of INFORMative assessment is to provide you with enough information about students' learning so that you can adjust instruction to meet the needs of students where they are in their development of mathematics understanding. We hope that the model provides you with a tool for reflecting on your understanding of specific aspects of formative assessment.

┌─ **Learn More** ... ─┐
"Assessment for learning is any assessment for which the first priority in its design and practice is to serve the purpose of promoting student learning."
—"Working Inside the Black Box: Assessment for Learning in the Classroom" (Black et al. 2004, 10)

Moving Through the Model

Teachers' inferences about students' thinking lead to decisions about next steps, which is the first part of the model we look at. We discuss six specific decision-making strategies in Chapter 2, with emphasis on revealing students' prior knowledge and students' misconceptions. Decisions that teachers might make include proceeding as planned, altering the next task, reteaching an important idea, providing more practice on a skill, or rearranging groupings of students. Any of these decisions might better align instruction with the needs of students. Although discussion begins in Chapter 2, decision making is so crucial to planning and delivery of effective instruction that it continues through all the chapters.

Instructional planning typically begins by identifying the content to teach; that is, identifying clear learning targets (Chapter 3). Then the tasks, questions, and assessments that teachers choose to use create opportunities for learning (Chapters 4, 5, and 6). Indeed, most of instructional time is associated with this part of the model. Teachers' choices should support students' engagement with critical ideas and provide an environment in which students reveal the depth of their understanding. This support happens when teachers engage in intentional listening and use questioning to probe students' thinking (Chapter 4), develop skill at interpreting students' written work (Chapter 5), and choose rich tasks to engage students with important mathematics ideas (Chapter 6).

If students are to become lifelong learners, they need to develop strategies for self-assessment and responsibility (Chapter 7). Teachers can support this development by regularly incorporating expectations for student self-assessment into instruction.

Students do not simply tell teachers everything they know; rather, teachers have to make inferences about the correct or incorrect knowledge that students have stored in their minds (Chapter 8). Those inferences help determine the feedback that teachers give to students to help them understand mathematical ideas as well as to identify misconceptions that might have been developed (Chapter 9). Teachers' skill at making inferences and providing feedback is dependent, in part, on teachers' content knowledge, the curriculum materials being used, and the technology that is available for both teachers and students to use.

Finally, it is important to think about how to continue to refine our understanding of formative assessment (Chapter 10). In the final chapter, we look at the ways that two teachers are using INFORMative assessment principles in their instruction. These examples will help you to plan next steps for continuing the journey to incorporate INFORMative assessment into your instruction.

⌐ Learn More... ⌐
"A good assessment makes a good teaching activity, and a good teaching activity makes a good assessment."
—"Performance Assessments: Political Rhetoric and Measurement Reality" (Shavelson, Baxter, and Pine 1992, 22)

Merging Instruction and Assessment: How Lesson Planning Fits with the INFORMative Assessment Model

Formative assessment, by its very nature, happens along with instruction. As we teach, we assess; and as we assess, we teach. Instruction and formative assessment are seamlessly merged. We propose six practices for how to merge instruction and assessment; that is, how to view assessment as instruction and instruction as assessment (see page 13).

These six practices are an elaboration of more-or-less standard lesson-planning practices, but those elaborations are critical for successful implementation of INFORMative assessment. Setting clear learning targets has always been part of instructional planning, but it is also important to identify how students will be expected to demonstrate

Merging Instruction and Assessment: How Lesson Planning Fits with the INFORMative Assessment Model

1. Identify a clear learning target along with criteria for determining how students can demonstrate achievement of that target.

2. Identify prior knowledge and misconceptions that need to be addressed, possibly through administering a pre-assessment.

3. Choose tasks, based on the information about prior knowledge, that seem likely to move students toward attainment of the learning target.

4. Support students as they engage in the chosen tasks, encouraging students' self-assessment and peer interaction.

5. Debrief students' work on the tasks, engaging students in group and class discussions.

6. Administer a post-assessment to determine the level of students' achievement, reflect on the results, and determine what to do next.

Learn More...
These practices are explored further in Chapters 2 through 10.

that learning. Then, what students already know relative to the learning targets needs to be assessed, either before the lesson begins or at the beginning of the lesson. As students work on instructional tasks and debrief their work, there will be further determination of the progress that students are making toward achieving the learning targets. Teachers have opportunities here to adjust the tasks or pose additional tasks to keep students moving forward.

Comparing the results of pre- and post-assessments is one way to determine what students have learned from the instruction. Results of a post-assessment reflect the status of thinking at the end of instruction, but they may not be an accurate measure of learning. Instruction is informed by a teacher's interpretation of the results of a pre-assessment, and the effects of that instruction are measured by the growth of students' thinking from the pre- to the post-assessment.

> To be effective, these [formative assessment] strategies must be embedded into the day-to-day life of the classroom and must be integrated into whatever curriculum scheme is being used. That is why there can be no recipe that will work for everyone. Each teacher will have to find a way of incorporating these ideas into her or his own practice, and effective formative assessment will look very different in different classrooms. It will, however, have some distinguishing features. Students will be thinking more often than they are trying to remember something, they will believe that by working hard they get smarter, they will understand what they are working towards, and they will know how they are progressing. The teachers will ensure that students understand what it is that they are meant to be learning, they will be collecting evidence frequently about the extent of students' progress towards the goal, and they will be making frequent adjustments to the instruction to better meet the learning needs of the students. (Wiliam 2007b, 1091)

Assessment Tip ✓

Balancing the need to cover content and to help students learn is never easy, but clear information about what students know can focus instruction so that it is effective and efficient.

Coverage of Content Versus Learning of Content

Teachers are under great pressure to "cover" content; testing is perhaps the greatest of these pressures. University admission tests expect that particular content will be taught to secondary students, and these expectations, along with CCSSM and states' standards, drive the nature of standards for high school mathematics. Teachers often find themselves in the position of deciding whether it is more important to cover content or to take the time needed to help students learn whatever is being taught. Balancing these two issues is never easy, but having clear information about what students know can help focus instruction so that it is both effective and efficient. INFORMative assessment generates this information.

Effective Use of Instructional Time

Using formative assessment results can often suggest different, and more effective, use of instructional time. For example:

- Homework assignments can be structured to assess students' thinking or to activate prior knowledge, and the debriefing of homework can "set up" the lesson.

- The ratio of "lecture" to class discussions can be altered so that students' thinking, rather than the teacher's thinking, is made more public.

- The relative frequency of different kinds of questions can be altered to help students develop deeper understanding or to become better at self-assessment.

Teachers need to be sure that whatever decisions they make about the use of time are consistent with both the broad goals for learning and the specific learning targets for individual lessons. This does not mean that every lesson should involve a complex task that addresses multiple standards or that skill lessons are never appropriate. It becomes more important for teachers to work together to identify common misconceptions related to mathematics they are about to teach and plan how time can best be used, even though individual teachers will always need to use their best professional judgments to adjust those decisions to match the needs of particular groups of students.

"Reflection 1–2: Connecting the Model with My Assessment Practices" (see page 20), provides an opportunity for you to identify the aspects of formative assessment you are currently incorporating into your instruction and instructional planning. Think about questions or concerns you have about formative assessment and aspects of the model that you want to explore further.

Reflection 1–2

Connecting the Model with My Assessment Practices

Page 20

→ A Closer Look

Mr. Singh's Use of INFORMative Assessment with *Similar Triangles*

Learn More...
Throughout this resource we offer examples from lessons that illustrate INFORMative practice in action; we call these sections "A Closer Look" and hope they are helpful in supporting your implementation of formative assessment in your classroom.

The following task illustrates how one teacher, Mr. Singh, uses a classroom task as formative assessment to support greater depth of learning.

Task: Similar Triangles

The figure below shows two right angles. The length of AE is x and the length of DE is 40. Find the value of x. Show your work.

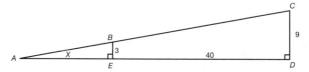

Source: National Center for Education Statistics, U.S. Department of Education, National Assessment of Educational Progress (NAEP). Released NAEP item, geometry, grade 8, short constructed response, 2007-8M11, #13.

Three student solutions are shown in Figure 1–2. All three solutions display understanding that this is a proportional reasoning situation and that

Jarell	Ming	Wendy
$\dfrac{9}{3} = \dfrac{40+x}{x}$ $9x = 120 + 3x$ $6x = 120$ $x = 20$	$\dfrac{9}{3} = \dfrac{40+x}{x}$ $9x = 120 + x$ $8x = 120$ $x = 15$	$\dfrac{9}{3} = \dfrac{40}{x}$ $9x = 120$ $x = 13\frac{3}{9} = 13\frac{1}{3}$

FIGURE 1–2. Three Student Solutions

a proportion can be used to generate the solution. Jarell and Ming start out on the right path, but Ming seems to make an error in solving the proportion. Wendy displays possible confusion about the labeling of some parts of the diagram.

One focus of formative assessment is to identify what parts of students' thinking are correct and can be used to build deeper mathematical understanding and what parts are incorrect and require reorganization or reconceptualization. From students' solutions, Mr. Singh makes some preliminary inferences about what his students know. This helps Mr. Singh prepare questions for a class discussion. The class discussion in turn helps Mr. Singh validate his inferences.

During the class discussion, Mr. Singh asks the students questions to probe their thinking. He poses the first question to Wendy. (See Figure 1–3.)

> **Assessment Tip** ✓
>
> Questions provide information about students' thinking and serve the purpose of helping all students deepen their understanding. Planning questions for a productive discussion involves knowing what mathematics should be put before the group and what follow-up questions might be used to highlight that information. For more on questions, see Chapter 4.

Question	Why Ask?	Possible Responses	Follow-Up Question	Why Ask?
What are the end points of the base of the larger triangle?	to determine if Wendy is misinterpreting segment ED as the base of the larger triangle	A and D	How long is that base?	to determine if students recognize that the length of the base is $x + 40$ rather than 40
		E and D	Can you trace with your finger the sides of the larger triangle?	to determine what shape students are focusing on
What parts of the two triangles are corresponding parts?	Setting up a correct proportion depends on identifying corresponding parts of the similar triangles.	the two vertical sides	Are there other pairs of corresponding parts?	to determine if the other legs in the triangles are recognized as corresponding parts
		the legs of the right triangles	Can you be more specific?	to determine if the legs can be paired off correctly

FIGURE 1–3. Sample Questions for a Class Discussion

Keep in mind that there is not one set of right questions to ask; following are some other questions Mr. Singh could have posed to probe students' thinking in this scenario.

- What are the end points of the base of the smaller triangle?
- What are the lengths of the legs of the smaller triangle? The larger triangle?
- Can you pair off corresponding parts in more than one way?
- What do you have to be careful about when you pair off corresponding parts?
- How do you know that the two triangles are similar?

Developing skill at asking questions when debriefing students' solutions is critical for effective implementation of formative assessment. Some questions can be created during instructional planning, but many questions have to be developed "on the fly." Follow-up questions have to respond to the specifics of what students say or write. In Chapters 8 and 9 we further explore ways in which good questions may lead to greater validity in our inferences and strengthen the feedback we provide for our students.

INFORMing My Practice

As you read about INFORMative assessment, we invite you to reflect on your own beliefs and decisions as well as to encourage reflective practices among students that will help them take greater responsibility for their own learning. Remember that teaching is not a "performance art," with the teacher doing the performing and the students acting as the audience for the teacher's performance. Effective teaching, especially effective teaching that includes formative assessment, requires interactions among the teacher and students. Teachers have to manage these interactions, but students must also be active participants. We invite you to make a commitment to implementing INFORMative assessment to enhance the long-term success of your students. We've provided "Reflection 1–3: INFORMing My Practice: Beginning an Assessment Journey (see page 21) as a place for you to record your thinking.

Reflection 1–3

INFORMing My Practice: Beginning an Assessment Journey

Page 21

Reflection 1–1: My Beliefs About Teaching and Learning

A fundamental belief about teaching and learning:	An example of how that belief plays out in my classroom:	The "match" (1 = LOW to 10 = HIGH) between the belief and the example:
1.		
2.		
3.		
4.		

Reflection 1-2: Connecting the Model with My Assessment Practices

1. Examine the INFORMative Assessment Model. What aspects of formative assessment do you currently incorporate into your instruction and instructional planning? What questions or concerns do you have about formative assessment?

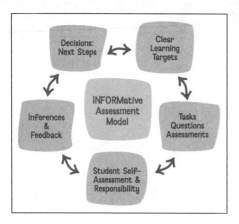

2. The task that follows could be posed to students at different grades. First read the task and think about how you would solve it. How do you think your students would solve it? What aspects of those solutions would you want to discuss with students? Explain.

Task: Similar Triangles

The figure below shows two right angles. The length of AE is x and the length of DE is 40. Find the value of x. Show your work.

Source: National Center for Education Statistics, U.S. Department of Education, National Assessment of Educational Progress (NAEP). Released NAEP item, geometry, grade 8, short constructed response, 2007-8M11, #13.

Reflection 1-3: INFORMing My Practice: Beginning an Assessment Journey

Think about the chapter you just read. Use this space to record your ideas.

Ideas about beginning an assessment journey:

Ideas I envision becoming a more important part of my practice:

Questions I have:

Frustrations/concerns I have:

Section II

What Will I Assess?

Key Strategies for Making Decisions About "Next Steps"

As teachers, our instructional decisions about "next steps" influence the extent of students' engagement with mathematics ideas and the depth of students' knowledge. Because these decisions directly impact what students learn, exploring them is a critical part of the INFORMative assessment journey. This chapter highlights the "Decisions" component of the INFORMative Assessment Model and discusses learning progressions as a way to think about how students learn mathematics. The chapter illustrates six key strategies that inform our decisions about "next steps."

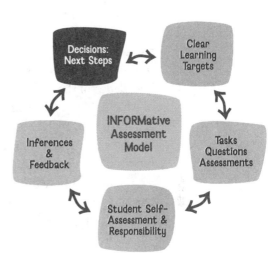

Overview

Six Decision-Making Strategies

As teachers, we make many instructional decisions each day. Some of these decisions are made during the initial planning of a unit and specific lessons. These include deciding what content will be taught, identifying what students already know about this content, choosing tasks, and determining assignments. But many decisions are made "in the moment" during class. We must decide when we need to repeat something, whether we need to provide additional examples, when students are ready for a different challenge, and so on. As teachers our decisions are always based on a combination of our knowledge of the mathematics we are expected to teach and our perceptions of what students know and can do. Decisions about tomorrow's instruction are made within the context of both long-term goals and adjustments to lessons as we teach. Think for a moment about the multiple decisions you make related to mathematics lessons.

Each component in our model for INFORMative assessment prompts teachers to make decisions and provides a glimpse into the complexity of good teaching. (See Figure 2–1.)

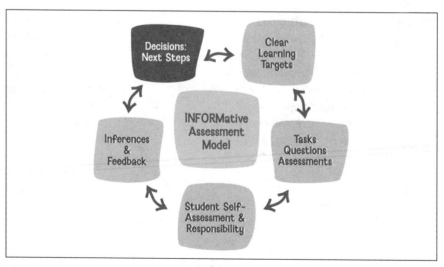

FIGURE 2-1. INFORMative Assessment Model for Teaching and Learning

The model illustrates the recursive nature of teachers' decision making. Just as fractals may be thought of as reduced copies of the whole, planning and teaching daily lessons mirror the process of planning and teaching larger units.

While each of us might describe the decisions we make related to teaching and learning in slightly different ways, this chapter focuses on six areas of decision making where INFORMative assessment assists in supporting both the teacher and the student. These decisions occur at different points in the INFORMative Assessment Model. Because the decisions are interrelated, we continue these discussions in later chapters.

Six Decision-Making Strategies

1. Make decisions about what students already know (use starter questions, pre-assessments, class discussions, and concept maps).

2. Make decisions about what to teach (guided by state standards and/ or Common Core State Standards for Mathematics and learning progressions).

3. Make decisions as students respond to instruction (provide additional examples, facilitate group or class discussions, give specific feedback to individuals, and reteach).

4. Make decisions that support student learning (continue to probe students' thinking and modify instruction related to critical content).

5. Make decisions from reflecting on data (use alternative multiple-choice format, portfolios, and anecdotal records).

6. Make decisions about evaluating learning (evaluations might be through grading and using daily informal assessments to INFORM instruction).

Strategy 1: Make Decisions About What Students Already Know

Learning takes place when we incorporate new ideas with what we already know. *Making sense* means examining facts, concepts, and procedures in light of what already has meaning to us and adjusting our thinking to incorporate the new ideas.

If students' prior knowledge is not considered in planning instruction, too much time may be allocated to dealing with ideas and skills that most students either are not prepared to learn or already understand, resulting in too little time available for dealing with content that students need to struggle with and make sense of. Classroom management issues sometimes arise when instruction repeats what students already know, causing students to become bored and tune out. Similarily, when students lack a grasp of background knowledge for new instruction and feel they have no chance of being successful, they may decide that not trying is better than failing.

It is important for students always to make connections. Helping students make connections between new knowledge and existing understandings is a continual process; however, making connections is especially crucial at the beginning of a unit. If students do not make connections to previous understanding, their learning is likely to be fragmented and superficial. One of the reasons that students do not learn mathematics deeply is that they do not "see" how key ideas are related. Their knowledge is fragile so they have difficulty knowing what mathematics concepts are relevant for solving a particular problem or task or how to connect mathematics ideas. These instructional "traps" can to a large extent be avoided when we identify what students know or do not know and then use that knowledge to tailor instruction to the needs of the students. When teachers use formative assessment to expose cracks in students' understanding, instruction can be modified to help students fill in those cracks and create richer mathematics understanding.

Formative assessment can also reveal information about how well students remember what they were previously taught and how they connect what they remember to current instruction.

There are many tools teachers can use as a way to help make connections and pinpoint what students already know about the subject of instruction. These tools serve a formative assessment function by helping reveal what students remember. On the following pages, we focus on using four of these tools: starter questions and tasks, pre-assessments, class discussions, and concept maps.

Assessment Tip ✔

What students remember can be called *residual knowledge.*

Assessment Tip ✔

Instruction that assists students in building a schema (i.e., a structure of well-connected knowledge) supports students as they move from being a novice to becoming proficient in doing mathematics.

Tools for Guiding Decisions About What Students Already Know

1. Starter Questions and Tasks

2. Pre-assessments

3. Class Discussions

4. Concept Maps

Use Starter Questions and Tasks

One strategy for gathering useful information about students' prior knowledge is to begin class with a "starter" question or task that encourages students to recall what they know about specific content. That is, begin with a question or a short task to help activate prior knowledge.

Starter questions can be posted for students to begin working on as they enter the classroom or posed by the teacher as a way to begin the instruction for the day. They are a preamble to the main lesson and should take only five or so minutes. However, this is five minutes packed with

Assessment Tip ✔

If students lack flexibility and do not make connections, every problem is new; it's crucial to activate students' prior knowledge.

potential! Students engage with the content right away, recalling what they know from previous experiences, while the teacher gathers information about the range of understanding in class relative to the day's lesson. Starter questions and tasks help students remember mathematics that they may not have thought about recently or may not immediately think is relevant, and teachers get critical information about students' residual knowledge.

A starter task might be very broad: *Make a list of everything you know about angles.* Here the teacher is listening for use of models and vocabulary. Or it might be more focused: *Which of these examples does not show a linear equation? Why do you say that?* Here the teacher is looking for overgeneralizations or common mistakes. Sometimes teachers direct students to collaborate with a partner and then share their discussions about the starter question. The following task could be used in this way.

Task: Height of Water in Beakers

The graph shows how the height in Beaker X varies as water is steadily dripped into it. Show the height-volume relationships for Beakers C and D.

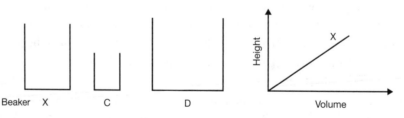

Source: *The Language of Functions and Graphs* (Swan et al. 1985, 22[94].) Used with permission.

Starter questions and tasks that allow for a variety of responses are more likely to engage a range of students than are questions that have only a single answer. Part of the challenge for us as teachers is finding ways to interest, support, and engage most, if not all, students in our classes. The ways that a teacher fields students' responses is critical. The thinking behind responses needs to be respected, even if those responses are mathematically incorrect. Starter questions and tasks can remind students of things they have previously learned, bring mathematical vocabulary into the conversation, and help set the stage for connecting things they know with the new instruction the teacher has planned.

Getting All Students to Respond

Formative assessment strategies to activate prior knowledge will only be effective if we as teachers can get students to respond to questions and tasks. There are different ways for encouraging responses—for example, think, pair, share; partner discussions; and written responses on index cards that a teacher can examine very quickly. We need to consider carefully the approaches that seem most appropriate for each group of students. It is especially important to accept responses from typically reticent students; doing so can encourage those students to contribute more in the future. Sometimes a "heads up" about the lesson for tomorrow as students are leaving class is all the encouragement needed. For example, *Lucinda, be thinking about what you know about symmetry. We will be talking about this tomorrow.* The comment provides an opportunity for Lucinda to be prepared to join the conversation the next day. Including all students in discussions over time is an important equity outcome.

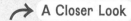 A Closer Look

Mr. Parulski's Starter Questions with *Lines of Symmetry*

When Mr. Parulski began a unit on congruence in high school geometry, he wanted to assess what students remembered from middle school instruction on transformations. He began with starter questions to assess students' knowledge of symmetry:

For the entire set of CCSSM standards on congruence in high school geometry see CCSS.MATH .CONTENT.HSG .CO.A.1–A.5; B.6–B.8; C.9–C.11; D.12–D.13.

Task: Lines of Symmetry

1. *How many lines of symmetry does a square have? Show them by sketching an appropriate square along with all of its lines of symmetry.*

2. *How many lines of symmetry does a 3-by-5 rectangle have? Show them by sketching an appropriate rectangle along with all of its lines of symmetry.*

3. *How many lines of symmetry does a parallelogram have if its base is 5, its height is 2 and it has a 60° angle? Show them by sketching an appropriate parallelogram along with all its lines of symmetry.*

Some students responded correctly to all three tasks, but others failed to draw all lines of symmetry for the square and some included incorrect lines of symmetry for the rectangle and the parallelogram. (See Figures 2–2 and 2–3.) The students' knowledge was not as sophisticated as Mr. Parulski had hoped.

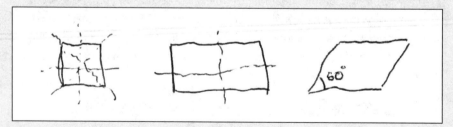

FIGURE 2–2. One Student's Correct Solution for Mr. Parulski's Tasks

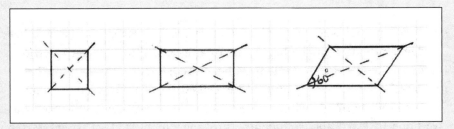

FIGURE 2-3. Incomplete or Incorrect Solutions for Mr. Parulski's Tasks

Mr. Parulski decided to review basic information early in the unit, asking students to define "line of symmetry" and then helping them connect that to the more formal notion of "reflection across a line" as an operation in transformation geometry.

Mr. Parulski: What does a line of symmetry tell us about a figure?

Shawn: If the two halves are the same.

Lisa: If the figure can be folded.

Mr. Parulski: Lisa, what do you mean by "folded"? Can I fold any shape?

Lisa: If the two parts match up.

Shawn: That's what I said.

Mr. Parulski: If a figure has a line of symmetry, what actions can you do so that the figure looks the same afterward?

Lisa: Fold it.

Shawn: But that makes it look like only half of the shape.

Lisa: Yeah, right.

Shawn: If we slide it or turn it, it wouldn't look the same, but if we flip it, it will look the same. Isn't that what symmetry means?

Mr. Parulski: Flipping a figure over a line is called a reflection across that line.

Then Mr. Parulski posed the three tasks again with the alternate, more sophisticated terminology (e.g., *How many lines of reflection are there for a parallelogram with a 60° angle?*). Having students talk about their understanding of symmetry helped students correct and connect their conceptualization of symmetry and reflections.

Assessment Tip ✓

Gather information about students' prior knowledge through "starter" questions and warm-ups.

Traditional warm-up tasks are often used to review skills or to get students' attention at the beginning of a lesson. When starter questions focus on bigger ideas, they may be more effective for helping bring students' prior knowledge into a brief class discussion. If we become more attuned to listening to what students say and to planning in advance what we hope to learn about students' thinking during a discussion, starter questions can provide assessment information for our further planning and at the same time focus students' attention on what they already know about the content, that is, activating their prior knowledge. Conversations with colleagues might be a good way to begin to create a list of appropriate starter questions for any particular unit of content. Consider using "Reflection 2–1: Making Decisions About What Students Already Know: Starter Questions and Tasks" (see page 57) with your colleagues or on your own as you plan your next lesson. In Chapter 4 we talk more about engaging questions that are designed to bring students into discussions in a manner similar to the way in which starter questions help them to make connections.

Reflection 2–1

Making Decisions About What Students Already Know: Starter Questions and Tasks

Page 57

Use Pre-assessments

Pre-assessments are another strategy for gathering information about students' prior knowledge. Pre-assessments are sometimes formal diagnostic tests (discussed in more detail in Chapter 5) that are administered prior to instruction on a topic. Teachers need time to review and interpret the results of such tests. Pre-assessments can also be short informal tasks administered at the start of instruction (e.g., as a warm-up task at the beginning of a class) that are designed to reveal students' existing knowledge about a topic. Typically they consist of one or two related questions. All pre-assessments, however, are designed to give information prior to instruction. They can be used throughout the school year. It is important to think critically about the appropriate kinds of pre-assessments and how we can use them to inform instruction. Following are three considerations for guiding your use of pre-assessments.

Three Critical Considerations for Guiding the Use of Pre-assessments

1. Assessing students' understanding prior to instruction is valuable only if the information gathered is used purposefully.

2. Pre-assessment of students' understanding should be focused and specific to the immediate learning targets in order to provide the most useful information.

3. Diagnostic assessments, such as pretests, can be starting points, but there needs to be continual probing of students' thinking so that instruction can be adjusted to meet students' needs.

We can use our interpretation of students' responses on pre-assessments to make adjustments, sometimes on the spot, in the ways we approach instruction and to help students make connections between their prior knowledge and the content of instruction. Students' responses help us as teachers plan instruction that builds on what students know rather than asking them to engage in new material as if nothing previously learned is relevant. Consider the "A Closer Look" example on the following page.

→ A Closer Look

Mrs. Morehouse's Pre-assessment with *Mean and Median*

High school statistics goals assume that students understand the meaning of, techniques for computing, and applications of *mean*. Mrs. Morehouse used the following task as a pre-assessment to help reveal her students' understanding of mean and median.

Task: Mean and Median

There are four dogs. One of the dogs weighs 50 pounds. What is true? Explain.

A. The median could be 12, but the mean could not be 12.

B. The mean could be 12, but the median could not be 12.

C. Both the mean and the median could be 12.

D. Neither the mean nor the median could be 12.

E. There is not enough information to know.

Reflection 2–2

Making Decisions About What Students Already Know: A Pre-assessment Task

Page 58

Before reading about Mrs. Morehouse's students' work, turn to "Reflection 2–2: Making Decisions About What Students Already Know: A Pre-assessment Task" (see page 58). Identify which answer is correct and what your explanation would be. Consider what each incorrect choice might reveal about students' thinking.

When first reading the task, many students had questions about the format of the answer choices and the language of *could be*. One student asked if there was supposed to be more than one correct answer. Mrs. Morehouse suggested that students read and then reread the answer choices, explaining to themselves what each choice meant in the context of the problem. She also asked them to think about the difference in saying something "definitely is" and something "could be." This suggestion from Mrs. Morehouse was especially important for the students whose first language was not English, though it would apply equally to a wide range of students. When students do not understand the question being asked, their responses may not accurately reveal their mathematics knowledge. The students' questions revealed some potential lack of skill at interpreting subtle language. Probing students' understanding of language throughout lessons is an important strategy for helping them focus on the mathematics within lessons.

In scoring the item, Mrs. Morehouse found that seventeen of the twenty-four students chose answer A. However, few of the students' explanations contained thorough and accurate information. Two students chose C, and one chose D. This student stated, "Neither the mean nor the median could be 12 because there is nothing about 12 in the problem." Four students chose E. Most of these students merely repeated that there was insufficient information as their explanation, adding that you needed to know what the other dogs weighed to be able to answer the question. No students chose B. This task seemed to connect to students' understanding of mean and median, though it is not clear how students used that knowledge for this task.

Although 70 percent of the students chose the correct answer, Mrs. Morehouse was not satisfied that students had a depth of understanding of measures of central tendency. From the students' responses she inferred that most students could repeat a definition of mean and median, but they lacked a working knowledge that would allow them to accurately interpret data based on mean and median (i.e., a lack of precision). She suspected that students' knowledge was compartmentalized and not well connected to contexts. There are some characteristics of the context that make this task meaningful that she wanted students to notice; for example, the weight of each dog must be a positive number. Nothing in the statement of the task makes this notion explicit, so she felt it was important to discuss this issue. If the context had been about temperatures, then negative temperatures would be possible, and the solution (and answer) to the task would be different. Teachers must always be careful to be sure that the context for a problem is within students' experiences.

Assessment Tip ✓

Probing students' understanding of language throughout lessons is an important strategy for helping them focus on the mathematics within lessons.

Assessment Tip ✓

Sharing incorrect student work helps focus discussion on misconceptions within the classroom; however, as teachers we must be careful that the class cannot identify the student whose work is being shared.

Pre-assessments provide background information and help identify students' prior knowledge related to instruction. How we respond to that information will vary based on the students' responses, the goals of instruction, the time of year, and how easy it has been for students to achieve learning goals so far. Sometimes teachers make notes in order to follow up with individuals. Students whose understandings are inaccurate or incomplete may require a one-on-one conversation to clarify a misconception. Or, the decision might be to pull a small group aside prior to beginning the unit if it is clear that those students are not prepared (i.e., lack the prior knowledge) to be successful. Sometimes teachers reallocate the amount of time planned for different learning targets within the unit because the class as a whole has greater knowledge than was anticipated. One goal of pre-assessments is to reveal students' prior knowledge so that adjustments can be made to instruction to support students as they incorporate new ideas into their existing schema.

As teachers we have many options about how we will use data from pre-assessments. Mrs. Morehouse, from our earlier example, might have decided to use a starter question about measures of center to remind all students about mean, median, and mode. Or she could have asked students to explain what is correct or incorrect about each option in the multiple-choice question and how they should go about deciding which is the best response. Most of the responses discussed earlier suggest that mean and median were familiar terms for the students, so she could have begun the lesson with a focus on variability. For example, Mrs. Morehouse might have presented the following modification of the task:

Task: Mean and Median Modified

There are four dogs, one of which has a weight of 50 pounds. What are the weights of the other three dogs, if the median weight is 28 pounds? Is there more than one possible solution?

Whatever Mrs. Morehouse's decision about how to use the information from the pre-assessment, it provided her a window into students' prior knowledge. Take the following three critical steps into consideration when you gather information from a pre-assessment in your class.

Three Critical Steps for Gathering Information from a Pre-assessment

1. Think carefully about students' performance, both collectively and individually. If there is time, make notes about individual strengths and weaknesses. Are there clear "outliers" from the majority of the students? Some students may need specific interventions that involve preteaching, coaching, or different tasks; other students may not need the planned instruction and appear to be ready for opportunities to delve more deeply into the mathematics content.

2. Identify groups of students who exhibited similar misunderstandings, perhaps as shown by similar incorrect answers. This information may lead to temporary instructional groups to remediate those misunderstandings, especially if they are critical background for the mathematics of the next unit.

3. Make note of mathematics ideas that almost all students seem to understand. This information may help you either to rethink how you will allocate time spent on those ideas or to modify new tasks you plan to use.

Learn More...

See also "Reflection 2–5: Making Decisions About What to Teach: Assessing Prerequisite Knowledge," which is introduced under Strategy 2.

Pre-assessment Information Should Not Be a Secret!

Formative assessments can reveal students' thinking, but the information is beneficial only to the extent it is used by teachers to modify instruction or give feedback or by students to examine their ideas about the content. Information from pre-assessments should never be kept secret; it should be shared with students. Just as in planning instruction, as teachers we need to know clearly why we are giving any assessment task and what we hope to learn from the responses. Completing any assignment takes up students' time, and we do not want to waste their work.

Use Class Discussions

Sometimes a short class discussion can serve as a pre-assessment of what students already know. This will feel like a normal routine when students know they are expected to engage actively not only in their own learning but also in understanding each other's thinking. For example, at the beginning of a lesson on graphing parabolas, ask the class to think silently for two minutes about characteristics of graphs of linear functions. Then lead a short discussion and record items on the board. (See Figure 2–4.)

The discussion is an opportunity to listen to the language that students use and to note how that language might need to be improved to be more precise. The ideas in the list can also be used for comparing and contrasting similar notions for parabolas.

Characteristics of Graphs of Linear Functions
- The points can be put on a coordinate system.
- The graph is (x, y) points.
- The graph is a straight line.
- The graph has a slope, either positive, negative or zero.
- The slope shows whether the graph goes up, goes down, or stays the same.
- A vertical line is not a linear function.

FIGURE 2–4. Points from a Short Class Discussion Serving as a Pre-assessment

Use Concept Maps

A concept map is a graphic organizer that shows connections among big ideas and related information. Usually with a partner or in groups, students create a display of their current thinking about these connections. (See an example of a concept map in Figure 2–5.)

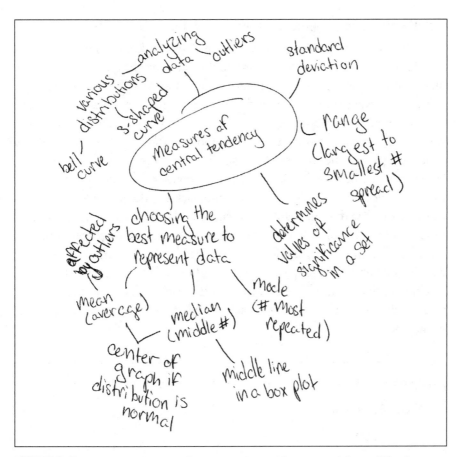

FIGURE 2–5. A Student-Created Concept Map on Measures of Central Tendency

The concept map can be added to, modified, or otherwise updated as understanding about the content increases. The initial concept map shows students' initial connections among ideas. Mrs. Morehouse, for example, could have asked students to create a concept map about measures of center as a pre-assessment task. Subsequent changes in a map allow us to monitor students' progress as instruction moves forward.

Strategy 2: Make Decisions About What to Teach

As teachers we incorporate what students already know into our second decision-making strategy: decisions about what to teach. These decisions are made with the recognition that students do not all learn at the same rate or in the same way; students bring different backgrounds to each lesson and often approach tasks in different ways. Some students grasp the underlying concepts of the mathematics and readily apply new ideas. Other students may believe they know the content and not even be aware of their misconceptions. Some students believe they can learn new mathematics content whenever their teacher introduces it. Other students lack confidence as mathematics learners and fear that they will not be successful. Thus, decisions about what to teach are based not only on knowledge of mathematics content but also on an understanding of individual differences and student motivations. Our decisions involve balancing the needs of individual students with the task of teaching each class as a whole. In this section we focus on two practices for making decisions about what to teach: using standards and using learning progressions.

Practices for Guiding Decisions About What to Teach

1. Use Standards

2. Use Learning Progressions

Assessment Tip ✔

"Standards define what students should understand and be able to do" (corestandards. org/Math/Content/ introduction/how-to- read-the-grade-level- standards/). Asking a student to understand something means asking a teacher to assess whether the student has understood it.

Use Standards

Standards influence teachers' choices about what tasks to ask students to complete, the relative emphasis placed on various aspects of mathematics, the amount of time spent on each topic, and the focus of questions that teachers pose to students. As teachers monitor students' work, they have to decide if students need more experiences with similar tasks, if reteaching with a different approach is required, or if it is "safe" to move on to the next topic or learning target.

Standards, Long-Term Goals, and Learning Targets

Standards as a whole provide the "big picture" of what is to be learned. Standards set expectations for what students should know and be able to do. Taken collectively, standards implicitly provide *long-term goals* of mathematics instruction. We explore, teach, and revisit these standards throughout a school year or even across multiple years. Taken individually, standards provide guidance for planning units of instruction and choosing daily *learning targets*; that is, objectives that we expect students to attain.

An example of a standard is "evaluate functions for inputs in their domains." An example of a learning target for this standard might be "Describe the similarities and differences of the domains for the square root function and the cube root function."

How well students are guided in moving along pathways from "not knowing" to a sophisticated understanding and use of content is a function of the clarity of teachers' learning targets and their identification of critical "building blocks" for the targets that should be assessed along the way. More detail about learning targets is provided in Chapter 3.

The complete standard is "Use function notation, evaluate functions for inputs in their domains, and interpret statements that use function notation in terms of a context" (CCSS.MATH .CONTENT.HSF.IF.A.2).

Standards documents provide "approved guidance" about what teachers need to teach and students need to learn; the Common Core State Standards for Mathematics is an example of such standards. CCSSM has been adopted by many states as the guide for mathematics instruction. Some states have added additional expectations; other states have modified and renamed the standards; and some states are using the standards as they are written. We use CCSSM as an example to stand for all kinds of state standards. CCSSM defines what students should understand and be able to do in mathematics. For example, the standards that follow form the first *cluster* within the "big idea," or *domain*, of "Interpreting Functions."

Understand the Concept of a Function and Use Function Notation

1. Understand that a function from one set (called the domain) to another set (called the range) assigns to each element of the domain exactly one element of the range. If f is a function and x is an element of its domain, then $f(x)$ denotes the output of f corresponding to the input x. The graph of f is the graph of the equation $y = f(x)$. (CCSS.MATH.CONTENT.HSF-IF.A.1)

2. Use function notation, evaluate functions for inputs in their domains, and interpret statements that use function notation in terms of a context. (CCSS.MATH.CONTENT.HSF-IF.A.2)

3. Recognize that sequences are functions, sometimes defined recursively, whose domain is a subset of the integers. *For example, the Fibonacci sequence is defined recursively by $f(0) = f(1) = 1$, $f(n+1) = f(n) + f(n-1)$ for $n \geq 1$.* (CCSS.MATH.CONTENT.HSF-IF.A.3)

Assessment Tip ✔

Real understanding comes when students can apply mathematics to novel situations.

The first standard in this list might serve as the long-term goal for multiple lessons that teach the relationship between domain, range, and shape of the graph of a function. Examples of functions in these lessons might include linear equations, parabolas, and step functions. Learning targets for individual lessons would need to support students in reaching this goal.

The importance of understanding the mathematical components of long-term goals as part of decision making about "next steps" is not to be underestimated. The "grain size" of long-term goals varies. For example, the grain size of goals for a unit is larger than the grain size of the learning targets for lessons within that unit. However, it is critical that teachers situate daily decisions within a "big picture" so that instruction focuses on in-depth mathematics learning rather than just checking off a list of discrete skills and facts to be mastered. Take a moment to think about your standards, long-term goals, and learning targets for this year. Answer the questions in "Reflection 2–3: Making Decisions About What to Teach: Standards and Learning Targets" (see page 60).

Reflection 2–3

Making Decisions About What to Teach: Standards and Learning Targets

Page 60

The Eight Standards for Mathematical Practice

Much of any public discussion about mathematics standards is typically focused on content standards. In addition to learning content, however, all students need to be mathematically literate. That is, they need to know the facts, concepts, and procedures of mathematics that will enable them to solve routine and nonroutine problems that arise in the workplace and in daily living.

They need to be able to *use* their mathematical knowledge to make judgments confidently and competently. This use of mathematics is captured in the eight Standards for Mathematical Practice.

The Eight Standards for Mathematical Practice

MP1. Make sense of problems and persevere in solving them.

MP2. Reason abstractly and quantitatively.

MP3. Construct viable arguments and critique the reasoning of others.

MP4. Model with mathematics.

MP5. Use appropriate tools strategically.

MP6. Attend to precision.

MP7. Look for and make use of structure.

MP8. Look for and express regularity in repeated reasoning. (CCSS.MATH.PRACTICE.MP1–8)

(continued)

The eight Standards for Mathematical Practice are part of the Common Core State Standards; see corestandards.org/Math/Practice/.

Learn More…

The Mathematics Assessment Project (MAP) Classroom Challenge "Interpreting Distance-Time Graphs" (map.mathshell.org/lessons.php?unit=8225) illustrates one way the content and practice standards can be incorporated into the same lesson.

(continued page from 45)

The heart of the Standards for Mathematical Practice is the way that they suggest how students should engage with mathematics content as they learn mathematics. These mathematical practices address the ways that students demonstrate their understanding of mathematics ideas and the ways that students learn both mathematics concepts and mathematics procedures. But it is the development of deep mathematical understanding that may be the most powerful way to connect mathematics content and mathematical practices.

As we discuss INFORMative assessment strategies in later chapters, we focus on the interplay of the Standards for Mathematical Practice with specific content standards. To begin your exploration of such, we encourage you to complete "Reflection 2–4: Making Decisions About What to Teach: The Eight Standards for Mathematical Practice" (see page 61).

Reflection 2–4

Making Decisions About What to Teach: The Eight Standards for Mathematical Practice

Page 61

Learn More…

"Teaching is a *contingent* activity. We cannot predict what students will learn as the result of any particular sequence of instruction. Formative assessment involves getting the best evidence about what students have learned and then using this information to decide what to do next."
—*Embedded Formative Assessment* (Wiliam 2011, 50)

Standards are not always complete; sometimes mathematics ideas that students need to learn are referenced only implicitly. As teachers we should be aware of this and use formative assessment to help determine if students are ready to learn the explicitly stated goals. So it is important, as a part of the lesson-planning process, to connect your knowledge of standards with your understanding of students' prior knowledge. Students' prior knowledge often will not encompass all the concepts and skills listed in prior grades' standards. It is important to identify possible gaps in students' understanding so that instruction can address these gaps. Choose a standard that you will be teaching within the next month and complete "Reflection 2–5: Making Decisions About What to Teach: Assessing Prerequisite Knowledge" (see page 62).

Use Learning Progressions

To successfully plan instruction that builds cohesive knowledge about important mathematics ideas, we need to develop a deep understanding not only of how mathematics ideas fit together and build on each other but also of how students typically learn key mathematics ideas. The ways students learn is often different from the ways ideas eventually become logically organized in mathematical explanations or in standards documents. Recognition of the differences helps structure decisions about "next steps" to address both short-term needs and long-term goals.

The notion of knowledge progressing along a pathway in a relatively predictable manner from less sophisticated to more sophisticated levels of understanding is described in different terms by different researchers (Clements and Sarama 2004; Confrey 2005; Heritage 2008b; Simon 1995). Science educators have often used the term *learning progressions* to describe this idea, while mathematics educators have often used the term *learning trajectories*. Although there are subtle differences in the ways that various researchers have defined these terms, we have chosen to use the term *learning progression* as our label for this idea. Understanding students' journey from novice to more expert in mathematics knowledge can help teachers plan lessons and assessments that target critical mathematics ideas. Although no one can specify a single set of skills and concepts to be taught through a prescribed set of tasks in a lockstep order, the idea of learning progressions provides a way to think about pathways that help teachers situate learning targets for individual lessons within a sense of long-term goals that are implicit in standards.

Reflection 2-5

Making Decisions About What to Teach: Assessing Prerequisite Knowledge

Page 62

Learn More...

See "Learning Trajectory Based Instruction: Toward a Theory of Teaching" (Sztajn et al. 2012) for a discussion of learning trajectory-based instruction as an integrated explanatory framework for teaching.

Learn More...

"Explicit learning progressions can provide the clarity that teachers need. By describing a pathway of learning they can assist teachers to plan instruction. Formative assessment can be tied to learning goals and the evidence elicited can determine students' understanding and skill at a given point."
—"Learning Progressions: Supporting Instruction and Formative Assessment" (Heritage 2008b, 2)

Learning Progressions: A Hiking Analogy

A learning progression has an analogy in the hikers' goal of walking the Appalachian Trail from Mount Katahdin in Maine to Springer Mountain in Georgia. Along that 2,175-mile trek there are places that are easy walking and mountains that are difficult climbs. In some places there are choices of side paths that will once again merge into the main trail. There are times when the guide determines the plans for a day and leads the hikers, and times when the hikers raise concerns and interests that cause the guide to negotiate and rethink the plans. The experienced guide may decide to have the hikers cut over the summit rather than take the long way around. Occasionally there are landslides that require unusual efforts to traverse. The guide may plan side trips because of wonderful views or interesting explorations of the environment. For part of the trail many miles may make a day's journey, and for other portions a day's journey may only be one mile. Along the way plans need to be made to reach certain shelters because there are not good places to camp or sources of supplies are scarce. Well-prepared guides take all of this into account in planning and leading hikers on the trip.

Assessment Tip ✓

Monitoring long-term goals is summative in nature, whereas monitoring learning targets for individual lessons is formative. Assessment of the attainment of these targets provides information to help keep learning on track.

Much like the guide in the hiking analogy, as teachers we keep standards in mind as we plan how to move our students toward mathematical achievement. There are many decision points that are influenced by our understanding of learning progressions. Long-term mathematics goals are often broad, but they can be successfully attained because of carefully planned tasks, discussions, and assessments along the way. With long-term goals in mind, we can use our knowledge of learning progressions to identify key concepts and skills that students need to develop and thus to know what is critical to assess.

A developmental progression spanning a longer period and tracing how concepts and skills build progressively can be organized into increments for instruction. However, if teachers know how learning moves forward or backward along a progression they have greater flexibility in planning for learning. In the case when all the learning goals of a unit of instruction have not been met, teachers can trace the threads of the concepts, identify subsequent opportunities along the progression when these concepts connect with later ones, and revisit them at this point. Alternatively, they might need to go further back in the progression to clear up misconceptions or to fill gaps in students' knowledge that are preventing them from meeting the goals of the unit. Additionally, a longer developmental trajectory enables teachers of students whose understanding outpaces that of their peers to focus instruction on developing their thinking to higher levels, which might be beyond that outlined in the unit. (Heritage 2008b, 11)

Strategy 3: Make Decisions as Students Respond to Instruction

Educators acknowledge that deciding what mathematics to teach and how to teach it are critical decisions that every teacher makes. Parallel to planning instruction, however, should be making decisions about what and how to monitor students' learning in an ongoing, formative manner. Formative assessment is likely to be most powerful during instruction because there is the opportunity for constant feedback; that is, the opportunity to make decisions as students respond to instruction.

The line between instruction and assessment blurs when we continually check for understanding and adjust our lessons. It makes sense to check for understanding and take action to address misunderstandings rather than wait until students have opportunities to practice misconceptions repeatedly. These actions might be thought of as early interventions that help to mitigate the need for future remediation. Assessing students' understanding in a timely manner is especially important for students who have not been successful with related mathematics content in the past and for students for whom English is not their primary language. Are students' incorrect responses the result of a misconception or not understanding the question posed by the teacher? Students may be responding correctly to a different question that they thought was being asked.

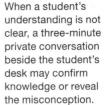

Assessment Tip ✔

Formative assessment is likely to be most powerful *during* instruction because there is the opportunity for constant feedback.

Assessment Tip ✔

When a student's understanding is not clear, a three-minute private conversation beside the student's desk may confirm knowledge or reveal the misconception.

Assessment Tip ✓

Continuous monitoring means that as teachers we interact with students to understand their thinking and intervene in ways that allow students to correct their misconceptions rather than solidify them.

Monitoring continuously and responding appropriately does not mean that teachers always intervene immediately and never encourage students to struggle with a task. Often learners do not internalize new knowledge in a single lesson, so repeated and long-term engagement with rich tasks is important for learning. Continuous monitoring means that as teachers we interact with students to understand their thinking and intervene in ways that allow students to correct their misconceptions rather than solidify them. It means that we engineer opportunities for students to struggle in productive ways and to self-correct whenever possible. Deciding what to do when students make errors is the professional decision-making part of "monitoring continuously and responding immediately."

Consider the *Octagon and Triangle* task that follows. The diagram contains an implicit condition; namely, that segment CB is an extension of the "bottom side" of the octagon.

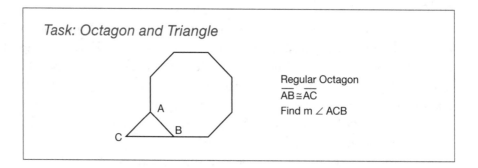

Task: Octagon and Triangle

Regular Octagon
$\overline{AB} \cong \overline{AC}$
Find m ∠ ACB

Learn More...

"If we can catch students' misunderstandings and confusion before they become habits, we can help students improve their learning both now and in the future."
—*Smarter Than We Think: More Messages About Math, Teaching, and Learning in the 21st Century* (Seeley 2014, 138)

Problems often unintentionally contain implicit conditions, and in this case, most students will accept this unstated condition without question. But teachers need to be watchful for these implicit conditions. Karen's solution demonstrates some knowledge upon which to build, but she also displays a misconception that needs to be addressed. (See Figure 2–6.) Stating that two of the angles have the same measure but identifying the pair incorrectly is not a mistake that we want her to practice again and again.

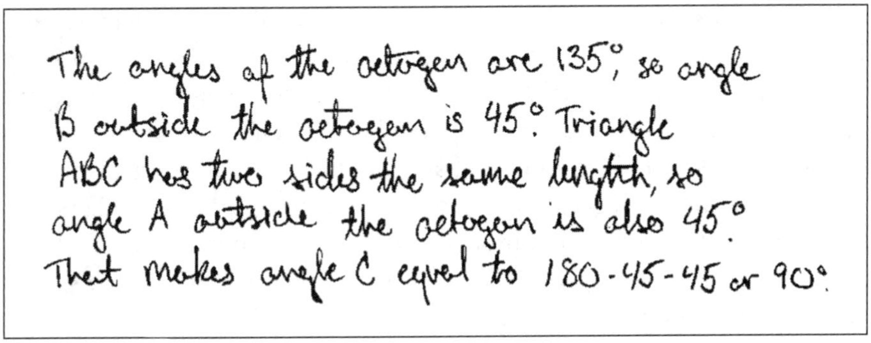

The angles of the octagon are 135°, so angle B outside the octagon is 45°. Triangle ABC has two sides the same length, so angle A outside the octagon is also 45°. That makes angle C equal to 180-45-45 or 90°.

FIGURE 2-6. Karen's Solution to *Octagon and Triangle*

Since student solution strategies and misconceptions on particular content tend to be similar from year to year, discussions with colleagues help us to be well prepared. Making a habit of thinking about tasks and problems through the lenses of the following four questions provides support for our moment-to-moment decisions.

Key Questions in Anticipating Students' Responses to Instruction

1. What do you think will be the most common solution to the problem?

2. How else *might* students solve the problem?

3. What errors might students make in solving the problem? What misconception is reflected by each error?

4. What thinking and reasoning do you *hope* students will exhibit?

Reflection 2-6

Making Decisions as Students Respond to Instruction: Anticipating Students' Responses

Page 63

Anticipating students' responses to a task is one way to improve skill at analyzing students' thinking. "Reflection 2–6: Making Decisions as Students Respond to Instruction: Anticipating Students' Responses" (see page 63) is an opportunity to think about students' responses to one task.

Decisions about the next lesson involve reflecting on previous work, identifying tasks and activities that build on that work, and connecting learning targets with standards. Teaching involves continually refining plans and asking, "What do I want my students to understand in tomorrow's lesson that will build on today's work and support the mathematics goals for the unit?" For example, if most of the students were successful in today's task of sorting scenario cards into proportional and nonproportional situations, tomorrow's learning target might be for students to identify which graphs show linear relationships that are proportional and which ones do not. That is, as teachers we always use what we have learned about students' thinking to make instructional decisions that will encourage and support even more learning.

Let's pick up where we left off with Mrs. Morehouse in "A Closer Look" on page 36. Mrs. Morehouse decided to share four student samples without names attached and have the class discuss what was correct in each explanation, what was incorrect, and what other information was needed for a quality response. This strategy brought students' ideas before the class and allowed her to raise the issue of context and pose questions to support and extend students' thinking. She accomplished two purposes. First, she could validate her hypotheses about the depth of students' knowledge. Second, she could highlight the elements of the context that students might have overlooked. We encourage you to think about what Mrs. Morehouse did. Complete "Reflection 2–7: Making Decisions as Students Respond to Instruction: Examining Student Work and Planning Discussions" (see page 66).

After the class discussion, Mrs. Morehouse decided to assign this follow-up task:

Reflection 2–7

Making Decisions as Students Respond to Instruction: Examining Student Work and Planning Discussions

Page 66

Follow-Up Task

Create a set of five positive numbers in which the median is 8 and the mean is 6.

This task was designed to reinforce the mathematics ideas that were central to the task. Mrs. Morehouse hoped that it would help students cement their understanding. Keep in mind that providing additional examples, facilitating group or class discussions, giving specific feedback to individuals, and reteaching are all strategies that we as teachers can use in responding continuously to students' learning.

Strategy 4: Make Decisions That Support Student Learning

To make decisions that support student learning, we need to continue to probe students' thinking and modify instruction related to critical content. We always have in the back of our minds what we want to accomplish in the next few weeks. We recognize that there are some understandings that are critical for long-term development of mathematics. Moving from additive reasoning to proportional reasoning is an example of one of those critical developments for middle school students. CCSSM recognizes the importance of ratio reasoning as well as other content.

> **Assessment Tip** ✓
>
> Teachers make *responsive decisions* when their instruction about what and how to teach is based on standards for the course, what students already know, and how students respond to instruction.

> Indeed, some of the highest priority content for college and career readiness comes from Grades 6–8. This body of material includes powerfully useful proficiencies such as applying ratio reasoning in real-world and mathematical problems, computing fluently with positive and negative fractions and decimals, and solving real-world and mathematical problems involving angle measure, area, surface area, and volume. (corestandards.org/Math/Content/note-on-courses-transitions/courses-transitions/)

When oral or written responses raise doubts about the depth of students' understandings or possible lingering misunderstandings, we question if the class is ready to move to new content. Before moving to a new learning target, it is important to determine if students' statements are "miscommunicated understandings" or "communicated misunderstandings"

(Bright and Joyner 2004). It may be necessary to change the next day's lesson or plan additional experiences in order to support student learning of critical content. As stated by Black and Wiliam (2009), "Practice in a classroom is formative to the extent that evidence about student achievement is elicited, interpreted, and used by teachers, learners, or their peers, to make decisions about the next steps in instruction that are likely to be better, or better founded, than the decisions they would have taken in the absence of the evidence that was elicited" (9).

Strategy 5: Make Decisions from Reflecting on Data

Every assignment that students complete generates data. When students respond in writing, their written work is "evidence" and can be scored, if necessary. For example, the "alternative multiple choice" format discussed in Chapter 9 provides written information about students' mathematical understanding and level of confidence about the correctness of that understanding. When students respond orally, we as teachers can create data by annotating students' answers or by remembering what students have said. For the purposes of INFORMative assessment, however, the important data are the responses themselves, not the scores that we might assign. These responses reveal the depth of students' understanding. Think about the differences in describing what a student knows based (a) only on grades in a grade book versus (b) responses to a variety of tasks included in a portfolio of student work versus (c) a thirty-minute personal conversation with that student about a couple of related mathematics tasks. INFORMative assessment strategies provide a mix of these kinds of data.

Sometimes orally generated data is limited. When a question is asked and the correct answer given by a student, it is important to recognize that there may be other students who might have answered differently had they been called on. During class discussions, cutting off conversations without getting a range of ideas on the table or probing students' thinking often results in some students' being left confused and others left with the impression that there is only one way to approach the mathematics. Rather than assuming that all students are making sense of a discussion or would have answered in a similar manner, we as teachers need to recognize that posing similar questions that address the same information gives a better picture of the knowledge of the class as a whole. By asking related questions, we avoid situations in which students make lucky guesses or only a few in the class grasp an idea. For example, Mrs. Morehouse might have asked any of these questions:

- *If the mean of 3 numbers is 14, what do you know about the sum of the numbers?*
- *If the mean of 3 positive numbers is 14, could the median be 12? Could it be 120?*
- *If the mean of 3 numbers is 14, could one of the numbers be –50?*

Using alternative multiple-choice format, portfolios, and anecdotal records are all ways to gather data to support our decision making.

Strategy 6: Make Decisions About Evaluating Learning

Evaluation of students' learning is a part of schooling and is critical for secondary students whose grades have the potential to influence the choices and opportunities they have following graduation. Different schools have different policies about the assignment of grades. However, it is daily assessments, formal and informal, that INFORM teachers about what students know and how well they are able to use their knowledge. For example, as students "construct viable arguments and critique the reasoning of others," teachers have powerful evidence to use in evaluating what students have learned.

"Constructing viable arguments and critiquing the reasoning of others" is the third Standard for Mathematical Practice in the CCSSM (CCSS .MATH.PRACTICE.MP3).

INFORMing My Practice

The discussion of standards and the examples in this chapter illustrate how formative assessment and instructional planning go hand in hand. We continuously make adjustments to lessons as we are teaching as well as decisions about tomorrow's instruction. These decisions are based on understanding long-term goals that are implicit in the standards. We ask ourselves questions such as these:

- Are the plans I made last week still appropriate?
- Did we accomplish what I had planned for today?
- Do we need to spend more time on today's learning target?
- How should I tie what we did in class today with tomorrow's lesson?
- What do I need to do to help students make the connections among the mathematics concepts and skills they are learning?

Formative assessments can reveal students' thinking; however, the information is beneficial only to the extent that it is used by teachers to modify instruction or give feedback or by students to examine their ideas about the content.

Like all teachers, we make hundreds of decisions each day. It is not realistic to think that even the most dedicated teacher can add two more hours into his or her day to implement formative assessment strategies. Rather, each of us needs to begin with what we believe will help us do a better job of teaching our students and what we can envision trying. Think about the ideas in this chapter related to decision making. We've provided "Reflection 2–8: INFORMing My Practice: Key Strategies for Making Decisions About 'Next Steps'" (see page 69) as a place for you to record your thinking.

Reflection 2–8

INFORMing My Practice: Key Strategies for Making Decisions About "Next Steps"

Page 69

Reflection 2–1: Making Decisions About What Students Already Know: Starter Questions and Tasks

Below are some possible starter questions for a lesson on *triangles*.

List everything that you know about *triangles*.

Write a definition for *triangle* and give examples of different kinds.

How is a *triangle* different from a *square* and how is a *triangle* similar to a *square*?

1. Write two more possible starter questions for a lesson on *triangles*.

2. Think about the mathematics focus of the next unit you plan to teach. Write some starter questions that you might use for one or two of the lessons in that unit.

3. What do you hope to learn from students' responses to these questions?

4. How well would your students engage with the starter questions? Explain.

Reflection 2-2: Making Decisions About What Students Already Know: A Pre-assessment Task

1. Mrs. Morehouse used the following pre-assessment to help reveal her high school students' understanding of mean and median. Read the task and think about how you would solve it.

> *Task: Mean and Median*
>
> *There are four dogs. One of the dogs weighs 50 pounds. What is true? Explain.*
>
> A. *The median could be 12, but the mean could not be 12.*
>
> B. *The mean could be 12, but the median could not be 12.*
>
> C. *Both the mean and the median could be 12.*
>
> D. *Neither the mean nor the median could be 12.*
>
> E. *There is not enough information to know.*

2. Complete the chart below:

Option	Correct or incorrect?	If correct, explain why. If incorrect, explain what mathematics error it represents.
A		
B		
C		
D		
E		

(continued)

Reflection 2-2: Making Decisions About What Students Already Know: A Pre-assessment Task (continued)

3. Explain the importance of "could" for understanding the mathematics of the choices.

4. Why would rereading the choices several times be a good strategy for students to employ?

Reflection 2-3: Making Decisions About What to Teach: Standards and Learning Targets

1. Think about the standards you are responsible for teaching this year. List two important ones.

2. Think about the most recent lesson that you taught to help students reach one of those standards. List the learning targets of that lesson.

3. How do the learning targets of that lesson align with the standard?

4. How did you help students understand both the learning targets of the lesson and the standard? What did you share with students about criteria for success?

Reflection 2-4: Making Decisions About What to Teach: The Eight Standards for Mathematical Practice

1. Review the eight Standards for Mathematical Practice (corestandards.org/Math/Practice/):

   1. Make sense of problems and persevere in solving them.
   2. Reason abstractly and quantitatively.
   3. Construct viable arguments and critique the reasoning of others.
   4. Model with mathematics.
   5. Use appropriate tools strategically.
   6. Attend to precision.
   7. Look for and make use of structure.
   8. Look for and express regularity in repeated reasoning.

2. Which practice is *most often* represented in your teaching? How does it show up in your teaching?

3. Which practice is *least often* represented in your teaching? What might you do to incorporate it more into your teaching?

Reflection 2–5: Making Decisions About What to Teach: Assessing Prerequisite Knowledge

1. Choose a standard that you will be teaching within the next month. Write it below.

2. List the prerequisite knowledge that students *must* have in order to attain this standard. Do not list everything you would *like* students to know, only the knowledge that they *must* know.

3. Create (or find) one or two tasks that you could pose to assess whether students have acquired the necessary prerequisite knowledge. Explain why your choices of tasks are good ones.

Reflection 2-6: Making Decisions as Students Respond to Instruction: Anticipating Students' Responses

Choose one of the three tasks below, or another task from your own instruction. Use the task to answer the four questions that follow.

Task: Height of Water in Beakers

The graph shows how the height in Beaker X varies as water is steadily dripped into it. Show the height-volume relationships for Beakers C and D.

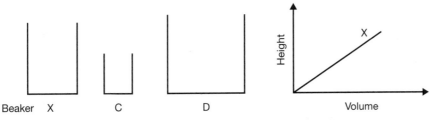

Beaker   X   C   D   Volume

Source: The Language of Functions and Graphs (Swan et al. 1985, 22[94])

Task: Octagon and Triangle

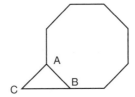

Regular Octagon
$\overline{AB} \cong \overline{AC}$
Find m $\angle$ ACB

(continued)

Reflection 2-6: Making Decisions as Students Respond to Instruction: Anticipating Students' Responses (continued)

Task: Journey to the Bus Stop

Every morning Tom walks along a straight road from his home to a bus stop, a distance of 160 meters. The graph shows his journey on one particular day.

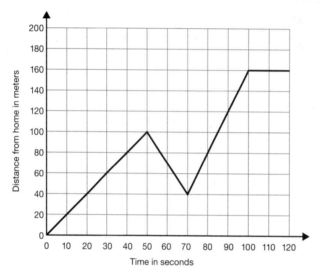

Source: From *Interpreting Distance–Time Graphs* (2015), map.mathshell.org/lessons .php?unit=8225, © Shell Centre, The University of Nottingham.

Describe what may have happened. You should include details like how fast he walked.

Are all sections of the graph realistic? Fully explain your answer.

(continued)

Reflection 2-6: Making Decisions as Students Respond to Instruction: Anticipating Students' Responses (continued)

1. What do you think will be the most common solution to the problem?

2. How else *might* students solve the problem?

3. What errors might students make in solving the problem? What misconception is reflected by each error?

4. What thinking and reasoning do you *hope* students will exhibit?

Reflection 2-7: Making Decisions as Students Respond to Instruction: Examining Student Work and Planning Discussions

Let's revisit the pre-assessment task Mrs. Morehouse used to help reveal her high school students' understanding of mean and median. Recall how you solved the task in Reflection 2–2.

Task: Mean and Median

There are four dogs. One of the dogs weighs 50 pounds. What is true? Explain.

A. The median could be 12, but the mean could not be 12.

B. The mean could be 12, but the median could not be 12.

C. Both the mean and the median could be 12.

D. Neither the mean nor the median could be 12.

E. There is not enough information to know.

Mrs. Morehouse decided to share four student samples without names attached and have the class discuss what was correct in each explanation, what was incorrect, and what other information was needed for a quality response (see "A Closer Look," page 36).

1. When we examine student work, we need to ask ourselves questions like those listed below. Analyze the students' responses by answering these questions.

   • What can I learn about the student's understanding of the mathematics in the task?

   • What misconceptions or incomplete understandings does the response indicate?

   • What follow-up questions do I want to ask the student?

   • What are the instructional implications from the student responses?

(continued)

Reflection 2-7: Making Decisions as Students Respond to Instruction: Examining Student Work and Planning Discussions (continued)

2. Complete the chart below.

Student Response	Analysis of the Response
a. If the median is 12, then the mean can't be 12 because there are smaller numbers so the mean is going to be smaller than 12.	
a is the answer. For the mean to be 12, the total weight of the dogs must be 48, and since dogs can't have negative weights, then the mean can't be 12. The median could be 12 if 3 of the dogs weighed 12 pounds or if only the 2 center ones averaged 12.	
a. If there are 4 dogs and 1 is 50 then mean cannot be 12 $1+1+1+50=53$ $4\overline{)53}$ = 13.25 ↑↑↗ lowest possible amount of other dogs $13.25 > 12$ But the median can 3, 4, 6, 50 $6 \times 4 = 24$ possible 12 → $2\overline{)24}$ = 12	
$3\frac{2}{6}$ $\frac{3}{2}$ $\frac{1}{6}$↑ c. There isn't 4 dog, one is 50 pounds, what are the weights of the other 3, to fine ~~and~~ mean you add all the "in this case, the weights" together and devide by the number of numbers which is 4. To find the median stack the numbers from least at the bottom to greatest at the top, then the one evenly in the middle is the median. median ↓ $\frac{5}{3}$ $\frac{1}{1}$	

(continued)

Reflection 2-7: Making Decisions as Students Respond to Instruction: Examining Student Work and Planning Discussions (continued)

3. Suppose you decided to have all four of these solutions shared in class. In what order would you have students present the samples? Why?

4. What mathematics ideas would you want to highlight with each sample?

Reflection 2–8: INFORMing My Practice: Key Strategies for Making Decisions About "Next Steps"

Think about the chapter you just read. Use this space to record your ideas.

Ideas about how I decide "next steps":

Changes in my thinking about INFORMative assessment:

Ideas I envision becoming a more important part of my practice:

Questions I have:

Frustrations/concerns I have:

3

Implementing Clear Learning Targets

As we briefly discussed in the previous chapter, one of the first tasks during planning is to identify the standards for the unit and to decide the learning targets for lessons. In this chapter, we take a deeper look at what a learning target is and consider the components that influence our choices of learning targets. We think about how to create clear learning targets, connect those learning targets to mathematical goals and assessment, and share learning targets with students in ways that communicate clearly what they are expected to accomplish.

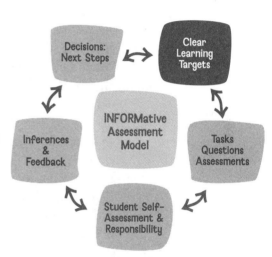

Overview

If You Don't Know Where You're Headed . . .

Once there was a little seahorse that swam through the ocean to seek his fortune. He was very proud of himself and the mission he was undertaking. Soon he met a sponge.

"Psst, hey, bud. Where are you going?" asked the sponge.

"I'm going to seek my fortune," replied the little seahorse very proudly.

"For two pieces of gold," said the sponge, "I will sell you these handy dandy flippers and you can zoom through the ocean twice as fast."

"Wow!" said the little seahorse as he paid his two pieces of gold. He put on the flippers and zoomed off into the ocean twice as fast.

Soon he met a clam. "Psst, hey, bud. Where are you going?" asked the clam.

"I'm going to seek my fortune," said the little seahorse very proudly.

"For ten pieces of gold," said the clam, "I will sell you this handy dandy scooter and you can zoom through the ocean five times as fast."

"Wow!" said the little seahorse as he paid his ten pieces of gold. He jumped on the scooter and zoomed off into the ocean five times as fast.

Soon he met a shark. "Psst, hey, bud. Where are you going?" asked the shark.

"I'm going to seek my fortune," said the little seahorse very proudly.

Cunningly the shark said, "I know a great shortcut. I will carry you and you can get there twenty times as fast." He opened his mouth and pointed inside.

"Wow!" said the little seahorse as he jumped on the handy dandy scooter and zoomed off into the shark's mouth, there to be devoured.

The moral of the story is, if you don't know where you are headed, you might end up someplace else and not even realize it (adapted from Mager 1962).

A major challenge at the beginning of a school year is figuring out where we are going. And like the flippers, scooter, and shark's supposed shortcut in this fable, we encounter many appealing resources. From pacing guides and teachers' guides in textbooks to collections of activities and worksheets—and an Internet that provides more sites than anyone has time to thoughtfully pursue—the overwhelming abundance of options makes it essential that we know where we're headed. In mathematics, one of the main ways we figure out where we're headed is by continually breaking down long-term goals into multiple learning targets.

What Are Learning Targets?

To address what learning targets are, we must first look at long-term goals. Implicit within the mathematics standards we are responsible for teaching are *long-term goals*. We explore, teach, and revisit these long-term goals throughout the school year or even over multiple years. Within each of these long-term goals there are likely to be multiple short-term *learning targets*; these learning targets are addressed in one or more lessons or in a short unit of instruction. (See Figure 3–1.)

A cluster of standards that might serve as a long-term goal and serve to help organize several standards is "Construct and compare linear, quadratic, and exponential models and solve problems" (CCSS.MATH.CONTENT .HSF.LE). Standards that could contribute to the attainment of this goal and

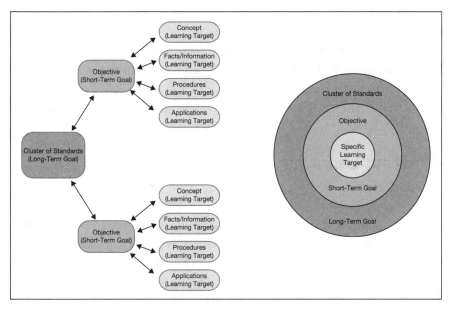

FIGURE 3–1. Two Models for Defining and Understanding Learning Targets Related to Short- and Long-Term Mathematical Goals

support the creation of learning targets include "distinguish between situations that can be modeled with linear functions and with exponential functions" (CCSS.MATH.CONTENT.HSF.LE.A.1); "construct linear and exponential functions" (CCSS.MATH.CONTENT.HSF.LE.A.2); and "observe . . . that a quantity increasing exponentially eventually exceeds a quantity increasing linearly [or] quadratically" (CCSS.MATH.CONTENT.HSF .LE.A.3). For the learning target "distinguish between situations that can be modeled with linear functions and with exponential functions," we would expect students to examine a situation to see whether there is a constant change function (i.e., linearly modeled) or whether the change was itself increasing or decreasing (i.e., exponentially modeled). For example, secondary students are at an age when it is important that they understand the different ways that interest rates are computed; simple interest is a linear situation, and compound interest is an exponential situation.

Long-term goals—the mathematical content to be introduced, developed, and eventually mastered by students—remind us of where we are headed. Clear learning targets break down these goals, help us articulate the steps along the way, define what evidence of learning will look like, and identify what we want to assess on a day-to-day basis.

When we communicate learning targets to students in language that they understand, we all share a vision of what constitutes achievement. By clearly articulating learning targets, we are able to sequence problems and sets of tasks with purpose, guiding students along productive paths that allow them to succeed with long-term goals.

Creating Learning Targets

Creating learning targets is the starting point not only for instructional planning but also for determining what is to be assessed and how it will be measured. Our choices at this stage determine, in large part, what students actually learn, so it is important that the targets be aligned with whatever standards are in place. The targets related to a particular standard need to encompass the range of mathematics knowledge identified by that standard. It's also important that the targets be *clear*—as unambiguous as possible so that appropriate measures of success can be designed. Choosing clear learning targets and then communicating those targets clearly to students will greatly increase the likelihood that students actually learn the mathematics that is intended to be learned.

A first step in creating learning targets is to consider different levels of thinking and types of knowledge. These considerations provide a context both for creating clear learning targets and choosing tasks to help students reach those targets.

Strategies When Creating Learning Targets

1. Recognize Different Levels of Thinking

2. Recognize Different Types of Knowledge

Strategy 1: Recognize Different Levels of Thinking

Looking at the verbs most frequently used in specifying learning targets reveals levels of thinking we expect students to master. The work of Bloom (1956) and Anderson and Krathwohl and their colleagues (2001) gives one framework for thinking about these verbs. (See Figure 3–2.)

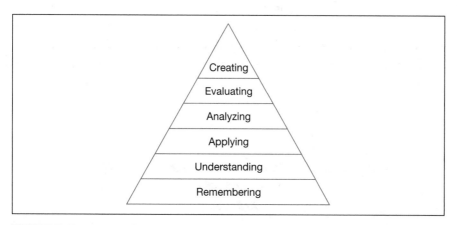

FIGURE 3–2. Bloom's Taxonomy Pyramid as Revised by Anderson and Krathwohl, eds. (2001), with Labels Changed from Nouns to Verbs

Each step or level of thinking has different verbs associated with it, some of which are listed here.

Levels	Verbs Associated with Different Levels of Thinking
Creating	Compose, Construct, Develop, Design, Invent, Model, Organize, Plan
Evaluating	Argue, Conclude, Critique, Evaluate, Generalize, Justify, Prove
Analyzing	Analyze, Classify, Compare, Contrast, Differentiate, Discriminate
Applying	Apply, Compute, Change, Choose, Select, Show, Solve, Use
Understanding	Demonstrate, Discuss, Explain, Illustrate, Restate, Summarize
Remembering	Count, Define, Describe, Draw, Identify, Label, List, Match, Name, Recall, Sequence, Tell, Write

Awareness of the verbs associated with different levels of thinking reminds us that there are often multiple levels of understanding within learning targets. The example that follows illustrates how different verbs might engage different levels of thinking and reveal different kinds of students' thinking.

Regular Polygons

Standard: "Given a rectangle, parallelogram, trapezoid, or regular polygon, describe the rotations and reflections that carry it onto itself" (CCSS.MATH.CONTENT.HSG.CO.A.3).

Learning target: "Identify rotations and reflections of regular polygons that carry each polygon onto itself."

Tasks:

- *Identify*, with sketches, all the rotations and all the reflections that carry each figure onto itself: regular quadrilateral (i.e., square), regular pentagon, regular hexagon, regular septagon.

- *Compare* the numbers of rotations with the numbers of reflections.

- *Write* a generalization to summarize your findings. *Explain* why your generalization will apply to a regular decagon.

Strategy 2: Recognize Different Types of Knowledge

In addition to considering levels of thinking when creating learning targets, we've found it helpful to consider different types of knowledge. Anderson and Krathwohl, along with their colleagues (2001), identified four types of knowledge: factual knowledge, conceptual knowledge, procedural knowledge, and metacognitive knowledge. We present a slightly different categorization of types of knowledge that has been useful in our own thinking when creating learning targets (Bright and Joyner 2004a). Following is a closer look at each of these knowledge types.

Six Types of Knowledge to Consider When Creating Learning Targets

1. Facts

2. Concepts

3. Skills and Procedures

4. Reasoning and Proof

5. Problem Solving and Applications

6. Confidence and Competence

Facts

A working knowledge of the specific meaning of mathematics vocabulary is an important learning target for students. There are different kinds of facts that are important to mathematical understanding; for example, names of mathematical objects like numbers, geometric figures, trigonometric functions, and standard units of measure. Facts like these are "socially negotiated"; that is, their labels and definitions are agreements that are standard across countries. As a result, we do not expect students to "discover" these names or "invent" them again. Rather, teachers provide that information. Definitions of terms and the names of those terms are at the factual level of thinking.

However, as teachers we have to decide how best to communicate this information to students, and what students already know will be a critical factor in making this decision. For example, in high school, the structure of complex numbers would not be "reinvented" by students. Rather, agreements among mathematicians about their structure would need to be communicated to students.

Recognizing the Precision of Mathematics Vocabulary

Mathematics vocabulary has specific meaning, even though the same words appear in everyday language. For example, what you do you think of when someone says, "table" or "similar" or "slope"? A table is furniture with a smooth, flat surface affixed to legs. Tables sometimes hold lamps or serve as places for people to eat. In mathematics, however, a table is an orderly arrangement of data, usually in rows and columns. And again, in everyday language a person might say that all triangles are similar because triangles are closed figures made of three line segments. But mathematically speaking, *similar* figures are those with the same angle measures and proportional sides. And while someone walking on a nature trail may think of a slope as a gently descending path, in mathematics, *slope* represents the degree of upward or downward slant.

There are some "facts" for which students develop understanding, such as basic number facts and values of trig functions for "benchmark" values, (e.g., $0, \frac{\pi}{2}, \pi$). One of the challenges of planning instruction is deciding which "facts" should be simply presented to students with explanations and which "facts" should be developed or derived as part of instruction. For example, for terms like *histogram* and *box plot*, the names and characteristics of these ideas need to be presented to students. But students need considerable experience both interpreting and constructing these types of graphs in order to internalize a deep understanding of how those graphs communicate meaning.

Assessment Tip ✓

One of the challenges of planning instruction is deciding which "facts" should be simply presented to students with explanations and which "facts" should be developed or derived as part of instruction.

When Thinking About Factual Knowledge in a Learning Target

- What vocabulary words need to be taught or reviewed?

- What factual knowledge is necessary for demonstration of competence for this target?

- Should critical factual knowledge be developed during the lesson or simply presented?

- What factual knowledge should students retain or internalize?

Turn to "Reflection 3–1: Recognizing Different Types of Knowledge as Part of Creating Learning Targets" (see pages 120–122) and complete the "Facts" row of the table using the questions to guide you.

Reflection 3–1

Recognizing Different Types of Knowledge as Part of Creating Learning Targets

Pages 120–122

Concepts

Concepts are "big ideas" that students need to embed firmly in their minds. All discussions of understanding in mathematics have acknowledged the importance of conceptual understanding.

Secondary school mathematics is grounded in important concepts, many of which are developed in elementary and middle school. If secondary students do not understand these ideas deeply, they are likely not to be successful. For example, proportional reasoning, equation solving, and geometry/trigonometry involve critical ideas needed for success in secondary school mathematics. Let's take a closer look at each of these in helping us create learning targets.

Recognizing Conceptual Knowledge: Proportional Reasoning

Students often leave elementary school with a mind-set toward additive thinking; however, success in high school algebra requires that students think proportionally. The following population growth task, which could be used with a variety of learning targets across middle school and high school, will help illustrate the difference in these two kinds of thinking.

Task: Population Growth

Over the course of a three-year period,

the population of Town A grew from 4,000 to 6,000,

the population of Town B grew from 40,000 to 60,000, and

the population of Town C grew from 400,000 to 402,000.

1. Which town grew the most? Justify your choice.

2. Which town grew the least? Justify your choice.

3. Which town likely changed the most during this three-year period? Justify your choice.

If students compute absolute differences, Town B shows the greatest growth, and Towns A and C show equal (and less) growth. However, if students compute relative (percentage) differences, Town A and Town B both grew by 50 percent, while Town C grew by only 0.5 percent. Students' responses to the first two questions will reveal whether they understand growth as an absolute or a relative term. Some

Learn More...

Sample lessons on proportional reasoning are available in *It's All Connected: The Power of Proportional Reasoning to Understand Mathematics Concepts, Grades 6–8* (Whitman 2011).

students, especially in middle school, will appear to be in a transition stage; they will not be sure whether absolute or relative comparisons are more appropriate. The third question is intended to help students focus on relative growth as an important factor. In particular, the residents of Town A are likely to perceive more change than residents of Town B, even though the growth rate for the two towns is the same.

Even many high school students are likely to be less-than-expert at proportional thinking, so assessing students' thinking can provide very important information for informing instructional planning. The role of proportional thinking in high school science courses is also important (Akatugby, Wallace, and Wallace 1999; Gabel and Sherwood 1983), so by working together, mathematics and science teachers can have a greater impact on students' proportional reasoning skills than either group alone.

Moving from additive reasoning to proportional reasoning does not happen instantly. It takes time and students may exhibit false starts during the process. We have to remember that when students are asked to reason about unfamiliar mathematics (e.g., a first introduction to trigonometric functions) they may revert to additive reasoning, even after they have demonstrated proportional reasoning in familiar contexts.

The kinds of thinking that students are willing and able to use will influence your choice of learning targets and the way that you plan lessons to help students attain those targets. Complete "Reflection 3–2: Recognizing Conceptual Knowledge When Creating Learning Targets: Proportional Reasoning" (see pages 123–124), first to reveal how your students use, or do not use, proportional reasoning and then to rethink clear learning targets for this critical mathematics understanding.

Assessment Tip

The kinds of thinking that students are willing and able to use will influence your choice of learning targets and the way that you plan lessons to help students attain those targets.

Reflection 3–2

Recognizing Conceptual Knowledge When Creating Learning Targets: Proportional Reasoning

Pages 123–124

REPRODUCIBLE

Recognizing Conceptual Knowledge: Equation Solving

In high school, we typically ask students to spend a large amount of time solving various kinds of equations, so helping students develop an understanding of "equation solving" is important. First, students need to distinguish between expressions and equations. An expression designates a value, either explicitly (e.g., 4 + 7) or implicitly (e.g., $2x - 5$). An equation is a statement that two expressions designate the same value. That is, each side of an equation is an expression, and the equals sign between them is used to show that those two expressions have the same value.

Sometimes students use the equals sign to connect their thoughts rather than to state the equality of two values. But that is a misuse of this critical symbol. For example, if you ask students to compute 7 more than the square root of 36, students may write:

$$\sqrt{36} = 6 + 7 = 13$$

Clearly, $\sqrt{36}$ does *not* equal 13, so mathematically, this "equation" is false, although it probably does reflect the students' stream-of-consciousness thinking. Some students will need repeated prompting to avoid writing strings of symbols that are mathematically incorrect.

In addition to becoming familiar with equations, students also need to understand "equation solving" as a process, and this is not a trivial idea. It involves a variety of aspects:

- Understanding the concept of an equation

- Knowing procedures for solving different kinds of equations

- Developing language for explaining these procedures

- Knowing when a solution has been reached

- Having the perseverance to engage in equation solving

Students need to know that $3x - 2 = 10$ and $3x = 12$ are equivalent equations (i.e., the solutions are the same), whereas, $x^2 = 49$ and $x = 7$ are not equivalent equations (i.e., the solutions are not the same). Taking the principal square root of both sides of an equation may not result in equivalent equations.

Students sometimes are distracted by the way symbols are written. For example, we have seen more than one student write the following:

$$12 = 3x - 3$$
$$15 = 3x$$
$$5 = x$$
$$x = 5$$

There is nothing incorrect in this string of equivalent equations, but the fact that the student had to turn $5 = x$ around to write $x = 5$ suggests that the student has an incomplete understanding of what it means to reach a solution. The "extra step" gives us important information about the student's thinking. This thinking may be the "high school analog" of the claim by young children that $7 = 3 + 4$ is "backward." For many young children, and indeed for some secondary school students, the equals sign is interpreted as a directive to write something down. We want high school students to be flexible enough in their thinking to recognize that $5 = x$ and $x = 5$ are really the same, as well as being equivalent. There is no need to write $x = 5$ when we've already written $5 = x$.

> **Learn More...**
>
> Cathy L. Seeley notes the need for "teaching for depth and understanding" as a critical part of effective instruction in Message 18, "Finishing Teaching: Covering Content Doesn't Cut It," in *Smarter Than We Think: More Messages About Math, Teaching, and Learning in the 21st Century* (2014, 131–36).

Recognizing Conceptual Knowledge: Geometry and Trigonometry

Mathematics concepts are always built out of a variety of other kinds of knowledge and skills. This is dramatically understood in geometry, where "point," "line," and "plane" are described intuitively but never formally defined. Geometry is built on these undefined terms. When identifying learning targets, it is important to attend to students' understanding of critical prerequisite ideas.

The ways that a concept is represented can be critical. In general, ideas can be represented with visual images, words (either written or oral), or symbols. Almost always, there are multiple ways to represent an idea. For example, historically sine, cosine, and tangent were often represented with "stand-alone" right triangles as the visual representation and ratios of pairs of sides of this triangle as the primary symbolic representations. Now the unit circle is a very common representation, with right triangles embedded in that unit circle; the coordinates of points on the unit circle take on values of the sine/cosine functions (CCSS.MATH.CONTENT.HSF.TF.A.4; CCSS.MATH.CONTENT.HSG.SRT.C.6–C.8). The following task might be used to help students reach this standard.

> ### Task: Equal Trig Values
>
> Use the unit circle to show $\sin(40°)$ and $\sin(220°)$. Explain why $\sin(40°) = -\sin(220°)$.

The two representations, stand-alone right triangles and the unit circle, are mathematically connected, and students are eventually introduced to both of them. But the choice of which one to begin with becomes a critical instructional decision. The first representation used to introduce a concept to students may significantly influence not only the way that students internalize that concept but also the subsequent flexibility that students have for using that concept. For example, the concept "mean of a set of data" is often introduced by showing students the algorithm for computing the mean. As a first experience, this has the potential for restricting the ways that students make sense of the significance of this concept (Mokros and Russell 1995). Teachers are often "stuck" with the representation used in their textbook, and choosing to use a different representation may take careful consideration and some extra instructional planning.

Assessment Tip ✔

Remember: The first representation used to introduce a concept to students may significantly influence not only the way that students internalize that concept but also the subsequent flexibility that students have for using that concept.

Students often compartmentalize mathematical ideas in their minds. This is most likely to happen when concepts and skills are learned in isolation, without important connections being made between previous knowledge and the new ideas that are the focus of particular instruction. Through teachers' careful planning and sequencing of learning targets, instruction helps students make these critical links, see connections between new content and prior learning, and avoid oversimplification of ideas. Sometimes students struggle because prior knowledge is not adequately learned, or because there is pressure for the teacher to "cover" content. In these environments students may *appear* to have learned the content, but a week later that "learning" seems to have evaporated. Students are more likely to learn and retain information if they make connections to prior knowledge. It's important to develop learning targets and teach concepts so that these connections are explicit.

Learn More...

In Chapter 4, we explore how questions can help reveal the depth of students' understanding, and in Chapter 6 we explore the use of mathematically rich tasks as a strategy for deepening students' understanding.

When Thinking About Conceptual Understanding
in a Learning Target

- What are some ways the concept might be represented?

- How are different representations connected?

- How should different representations be introduced to students?
  And in what order?

- What specific representations may be necessary for demonstration
  of competence for this target?

- What conceptual understanding should students retain or internalize?

Reflection 3-1

Recognizing
Different Types of
Knowledge as Part
of Creating Learning
Targets

Pages 120–122

Return to "Reflection 3–1: Recognizing Different Types of Knowledge as Part of Creating Learning Targets" (see pages 120–122) and complete the "Concepts" row of the table using the questions above to guide you.

Skills and Procedures

Many adults have memories of mathematics as mainly being the memorizing of specific sets of procedures. For example, we vividly remember being taught in high school a procedure for computing square roots by hand. We think it is appropriate for today's mathematics instruction to envision mathematics procedures as a component of "procedural fluency."

Learn More...

"Procedural fluency refers to knowledge of procedures, knowledge of when and how to use them appropriately, and skill in performing them flexibly, accurately, and efficiently."
—*Adding It Up*
(Kilpatrick, Swafford, and Findell 2001, 121)

Procedural Fluency Versus Procedural Awareness

There are some procedures that students might not be expected to be fluent with. For example, because of symbolic manipulation software, we might not expect students to be fluent on paper with multiplication of matrices, though we might expect them to be able to complete a simple example. Students need to know when to use this procedure and how to use technology to carry out the procedure; however, we might not expect them to be fluent themselves.

Procedures are like algorithms; that is, they are steps that, when followed correctly, always lead to the solution needed. High school geometry often includes attention to compass-and-straight-edge constructions. Each construction is a set of steps that will produce a particular figure (e.g., bisection of an angle); there is a specific order to the steps, and students are expected to carry out the steps in order. In general, if procedures are "learned" without understanding of how or why they work, students may mix up the steps or choose the wrong procedure for a particular task. For example, many mathematics teachers have experienced students using the wrong set of steps for solving the three kinds of "percent problems." If students understand the foundation for procedures, they are less likely to use an incorrect procedure, even though they may not always know how to solve every problem.

Procedural fluency that builds on conceptual understanding of operations is highlighted several times in CCSSM, for example, in the standard "Fluently add, subtract, multiply, and divide multi-digit decimals using the standard algorithm for each operation" (CCSS.MATH.CONTENT.6.NS.B.3).

Procedural Fluency and Symbolic Fluency

For secondary school mathematics, procedural fluency needs to be accompanied by "symbolic fluency"; that is, an ability to use symbols appropriately to represent quantities and to do symbolic manipulations appropriate for the level of mathematics being taught. Procedural fluency and symbolic fluency are analogous to number sense and symbol sense.

Symbolic fluency is not often discussed explicitly as a goal of secondary mathematics instruction, even though skill with symbolic manipulations seems frequently to take up a large amount of instructional time. We believe that symbolic fluency goes beyond symbol manipulation. It involves representing ideas with symbols and being able to reinterpret the meaning of symbolic solutions, once the symbol manipulation is complete. The use of symbols is critical for being able to think mathematically, so assessing how students think about and use symbols is important for instructional planning.

Assessment Tip ✓

Take time to probe students' understanding of the meaning and use of symbols.

Learn More...

"Fluency is not a simple idea. Being fluent means that students are able to choose flexibly among methods and strategies to solve contextual and mathematical problems, they understand and are able to explain their approaches, and they are able to produce accurate answers efficiently. Fluency builds from initial exploration and discussion of number concepts to using informal reasoning strategies based on meanings and properties of the operations to the eventual use of general methods as tools in solving problems."
—*Principles to Actions: Ensuring Mathematical Success for All* (National Council of Teachers of Mathematics 2014, 42)

"Perform operations with numbers expressed in scientific notation, including problems where both decimal and scientific notation are used," is a standard from the eighth-grade domain "Expressions and Equations" (CCSS.MATH. CONTENT.8.EE.A.4).

There are many skills and procedures that students need to understand; but some of these skills do not qualify as formal procedures. For example, solving even a simple linear equation is a skill, not a procedure. There are often multiple ways to find the solution, even though solving linear equations is often taught as if it were a well-defined procedure. Similarly, graphing of functions (either on paper, on a calculator, or with software) is a skill. That is, there are general guidelines for graphing, but the specific steps (e.g., determining the scale on the axes) have to be adjusted to meet the demands of the particular function and the particular task at hand.

Procedures in secondary school mathematics are often complex and involve a variety of fundamental concepts and skills. Consider the eighth-grade standard involving operations with numbers written in scientific notation: "Perform operations with numbers expressed in scientific notation, including problems where both decimal and scientific notation are used" (CCSS.MATH.CONTENT.8.EE.A.4). This standard seems straightforward, but it involves application of simple examples of the laws of exponents (e.g., $10^3 \times 10^4 = 10^{3+4} = 10^7$) as well as decision making about how to deal with values greater than 10 (e.g., $2.3 \times 10^3 + 9.8 \times 10^3 = 12.1 \times 10^3 = 1.21 \times 10^4$). Learning targets for this standard might include understanding the meaning of scientific notation, translating between decimal and scientific notation, and computing with numbers written in both decimal and scientific notation. Focusing on translating between decimal and scientific notation would help reveal important information about students' understanding of number sense. We might ask students, *Which is greater, 3.1 × 10³ or 31,000? Explain.* or *Which is greater, 3.1 × 10⁻³ or 0.00031? Explain.* Some students would rewrite the two numbers in each pair with a common format, but other students might reason by "visualizing" the sizes of the two numbers in each pair, for example, on a number line.

Providing Actionable Feedback on Procedural Errors

In examining students' incorrect solutions, it is important to recognize and acknowledge which parts of a procedure are correct and where the errors occur. For example, some students will make this error in dealing with exponents:

$$2.3 \times 10^3 + 9.8 \times 10^3 = 12.1 \times 10^6 = 1.21 \times 10^7$$

Most of this computation is correct, so "corrective action" should acknowledge those correct parts. Indeed the only incorrect element here is the adding of the exponents to get 10^6. By carefully attending to what students do correctly and what is incomplete or misunderstood, we can provide *actionable feedback* that is likely to positively impact the students' future work.

Learn More...

Actionable feedback is the subject of Chapter 9.

Assessment Tip

Separate what is correct from what is incorrect in students' solutions in order to provide actionable feedback and to target instruction.

Both algorithms, which always lead to a correct solution, and skills (at times, a "rule of thumb"), which may or may not lead to a correct solution, may need to be practiced, but the level of expertise at carrying out these procedures may be mitigated by available technologies. We have to think carefully about how much expertise is needed in order for students to be successful with both the current content and future content. We should not always demand complete facility before moving on to new content since students are able to refine their understandings through new experiences.

> ### When Thinking About Skills and Procedures in a Learning Target
>
> - Are there new procedures that students should learn? If so, what are they?
>
> - What steps are necessary to be written down as evidence that students understand a procedure they are using?
>
> - What other steps might students write down?
>
> - How much drill and practice should be provided during instruction?
>
> - What tasks or extensions will help students internalize procedures?

Reflection 3–1

Recognizing Different Types of Knowledge as Part of Creating Learning Targets

Pages 120–122

Return to "Reflection 3–1: Recognizing Different Types of Knowledge as Part of Creating Learning Targets" (see pages 120–122) and complete the "Skills and Procedures" row of the table, using the questions above to guide you.

Reasoning and Proof

Proof is often thought of only as "formal deductive proof," as illustrated by "two-column proofs" that have historically been used in high school geometry. However, here we think of reasoning and proof in a broader context, namely, the creation of convincing arguments. The essence of reasoning and proof is the creation of a "convincing argument." But *convincing* is not an absolute term; it is dependent on the level of mathematical thinking of the person who needs to be convinced and the person who is doing the convincing. The substance of a convincing argument made by a seventh grader would be very different from the substance of a convincing argument made by an eleventh grader in a pre-calculus course. Obviously, a convincing argument is only convincing to the extent that it is communicated to, and understood by, the person who needs to be convinced. Development of the language necessary for communicating convincing arguments needs to accompany instruction on proof. Assessment of students' development of increasingly sophisticated language as they progress through the grades is part of quality mathematics instruction.

Assessment Tip ✔

Assess students' development of increasingly sophisticated language as they progress through the grades.

Reasoning and Proof, the Standards for Mathematical Practice, and Learning Targets

For many people, reasoning and proof are the heart of mathematics expertise. In CCSSM, reasoning and proof are embedded in several of the Standards for Mathematical Practice; for example, *Reason abstractly and quantitatively* (MP2), *Construct viable arguments and critique the reasoning of others* (MP3), and *Look for and express regularity in repeated reasoning* (MP8). In *Principles and Standards for School Mathematics* (National Council of Teachers of Mathematics 2000) there is a standard of reasoning and proof, and in *Adding It Up* (Kilpatrick, Swafford, and Findell 2001) there is a strand of adaptive reasoning. Over many years, standards documents have recognized the importance of reasoning and proof, though the language in those documents has changed over time.

Learning targets tied to Standards for Mathematical Practice are as important as learning targets tied to content standards. Sometimes, learning targets, such as the examples listed below, relate Mathematical Practices and content.

- Explain how "dollars per pound" and "pounds per dollar" could each be used to compare "best buys" for dog food.

- Identify what characteristics of the denominator of a rational function indicate where that function might not be defined.

- Explain what the standard deviation tells you about a normal distribution.

Guiding students to become more articulate in explaining their reasoning is both a function of instruction and of feedback from assessments. Learning targets related to reasoning might need to focus on the completeness of arguments that students provide. These targets might need to be revised based on the performance of students on various tasks. Consider the following task:

Task: Thinking About Inequalities

Write two numbers that would make this number sentence true. Explain your choices.

54 < 3x

Following are three students' responses to the above task that was modified from an eighth-grade NAEP released item. The responses reveal some of the ways that students think about inequalities. Conversations can help them clarify their thinking.

Joan's answer is correct, along with an incomplete, but potentially correct, explanation. (See Figure 3–3.)

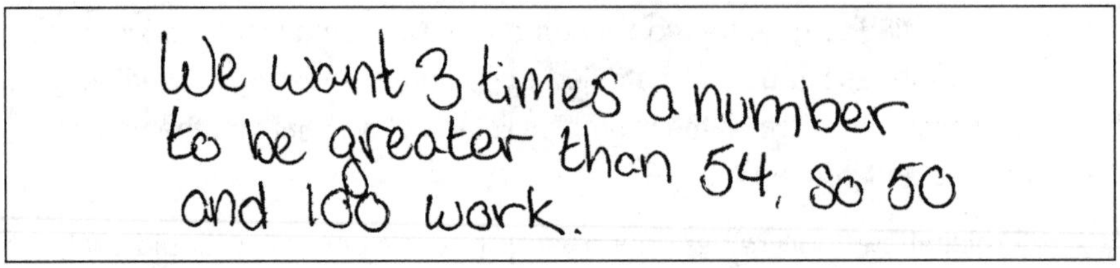

We want 3 times a number to be greater than 54, so 50 and 100 work.

FIGURE 3–3. Joan's Response to the *Thinking About Equalities* Task

> **Assessment Tip** ✓
> Encourage students to give complete explanations; they should not expect teachers to supply the missing parts of an explanation.

In order to accept the explanation as correct, teachers have to supply the remaining part of the explanation. It would have been better for Joan to complete the explanation by saying that 3 times 50 and 3 times 100 are each greater than 54. However, as teachers we need to be cautious about completing students' explanations. Students should be encouraged to give complete explanations; they should not expect teachers to supply the missing parts of an explanation.

Probing questions can help make the logic behind Joan's thinking explicit. Here is a way to show how one question could be used to begin a conversation. (See Figure 3-4.)

Teacher's Question	Why Ask?	Joan's Possible Responses	Teacher's Follow-Up	Rationale
Why do 50 and 100 work?	to be sure that Joan "sees" the complete logic	Each is more than 54.	50 isn't greater than 54, so can you say more?	to help complete the explanation
		3 times 50 is 150 and that is more than 54. Also for 100.	Oh, I understand that.	acknowledge correct reasoning

FIGURE 3-4. A Question to Probe Joan's Thinking

Notice that Joan says, "more than" in her response to the first question. In the follow-up question the teacher might use the more correct phrasing, "greater than."

Sam is almost correct; 18 is a solution for the equation, $54 = 3x$, rather than the inequality, $54 < 3x$. (See Figure 3-5.)

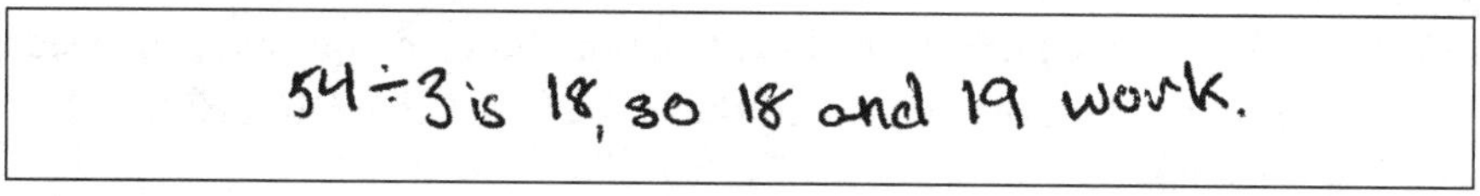

54 ÷ 3 is 18, so 18 and 19 work.

FIGURE 3-5. Sam's Response to the *Thinking About Equalities* Task

He provides no explicit explanation about why "18 and 19 work." A direct question is a simple way to get more information about Sam's thinking. (See Figure 3-6.)

Assessment Tip ✓

Questioning both incorrect and correct responses is likely to help students become better at self-monitoring their thinking.

Teacher's Question	Why Ask?	Sam's Possible Responses	Teacher's Follow-Up	Rationale
Why are 18 and 19 correct answers?	to draw a distinction between an incorrect and a correct answer	They both fit the inequality.	Can you show me how each one fits?	to help show that 18 is *not* a solution, but 19 is

FIGURE 3-6. A Question to Probe Sam's Thinking

Sam's reasoning might appear to be fairly clear, but sometimes students surprise us when they try to explain what they did. As teachers we should not "give away" too much information by focusing *only* on the incorrect part of the answer. If questions are posed only when a response is incorrect, students pick up on this pattern in questioning and often react to a question by assuming that their answer is incorrect. So it may be better to ask about both parts of the response. Questioning both incorrect and correct responses is more likely to help students become better at self-monitoring their thinking.

Mario seems to have solved the equation, but then applied the idea of "less than" to that solution, perhaps by thinking, "What numbers are less than eighteen?" (See Figure 3–7.)

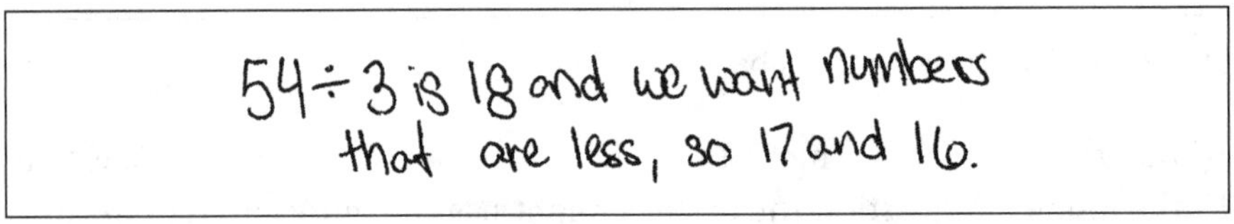

$54 \div 3$ is 18 and we want numbers that are less, so 17 and 16.

FIGURE 3–7. Mario's Response to the *Thinking About Equalities* Task

Questions could focus on the apparent conclusion that numbers less than eighteen are the solution set for this task. Knowing the solution to the equation could be part of a correct explanation; however, questioning needs to reveal exactly when Mario applied the idea of "less than" in his thinking. (See Figure 3–8.)

Teacher's Question	Why Ask?	Mario's Possible Responses	Teacher's Follow-Up	Rationale
Why are numbers less than 18 the correct choices?	to check the hypothesis about Mario's thinking	The inequality asks for numbers that are less.	Less than what?	to clarify the response
		The solution is 18 and we want numbers that are less.	What is the role of the "54"?	to help focus on the given inequality
		Oh, we want numbers less than 54.	What kinds of numbers?	to focus on 3 times *x*, rather than *x* alone

FIGURE 3–8. A Question to Probe Mario's Thinking

Helping students learn to reason is a critical part of secondary school mathematics instruction. Many times students are less than fully successful, and as teachers we have to be open to solutions to tasks that we might not have imagined during lesson planning. For students who struggle, tasks that have a context may help them identify the mathematics they need to use. Informal conversations with students about their responses will also help strengthen their skill in explaining their thinking. For the previous task, learning targets might include (a) understand that linear inequalities may have multiple solutions, (b) justify that particular values are actually solutions for a linear inequality, or (c) identify general strategies for justifying that a particular value is a solution for a linear inequality.

Reasoning and proof are complex mathematically, so it's no wonder the teaching of reasoning and proof is also complex to plan and deliver. Learning targets will often be tied to particular content, such as geometry, statistics, and modeling, but thinking generically can be a good way to crystallize some of the relevant issues. Turn to "Reflection 3–1: Recognizing Different Types of Knowledge as Part of Creating Learning Targets" (see pages 120–122) and complete the "Reasoning and Proof" row of the table, using the following questions to guide you.

Reflection 3–1

Recognizing Different Types of Knowledge as Part of Creating Learning Targets

Pages 120–122

When Thinking About Reasoning and Proof in a Learning Target

- What assistance can be provided (for example, questions or models) to students to help them become fluent in explaining their thinking and reasoning?

- What mathematics vocabulary, if any, should students use in making an argument?

- What role do examples or symbols play in creating a convincing argument?

- What would evidence of attainment of acceptable reasoning and proof look like?

Problem Solving and Applications

Problem solving builds on reasoning and proof; students have to "reason through" problem situations to identify the critical elements of those situations and then apply the mathematics that they know to create a solution. However, the mathematics actually needed for a solution may not be obvious upon initial reading of the problem. It is often helpful for students, first, to discuss the problem situation as a way to reveal the appropriate mathematics and second, to discuss possible solutions to determine the suitability of different mathematics ideas for creating an effective solution strategy. Discussion of completed solutions can help students internalize understanding of why particular mathematics ideas "fit" a given problem situation. Communication at all stages of problem solving, then, is a critical part of success.

Problem solving is frequently highlighted in standards documents, and the importance of problem solving is reinforced in research summaries. For example, *Adding It Up* includes a strand called *strategic competence*, which is described as the "ability to formulate, represent, and solve mathematical problems" (Kilpatrick, Swafford, and Findell 2001, 116).

Mathematics problems are sometimes set in contexts that involve mathematics ideas alone, without a real-world setting. Consider the following problems:

Task: Digits in a Decimal Expansion of a Fraction

What is the 105,687th digit in the decimal expansion of $\frac{1}{13}$?

Task: Common Factors of Two Numbers

If $\frac{a}{b}$ is a fraction in simplest form, show that $\frac{a^2}{b^2}$ and $\frac{a^3}{b^3}$ are also fractions in simplest form.

For the second task, high school students should be able to argue that if 1 is the only common factor of a and b, then 1 is also the only common factor of a^n and b^n for positive integer values of n. In particular, this is true for $n = 2, 3,$ or 4.

The questions in the table below illustrate how a teacher might begin to reveal students' thinking. This information would be useful for refining or extending the learning targets for this content. (See Figure 3–9.)

Teacher's Question	Why Ask?	Possible Responses	Teacher's Follow-Up	Rationale
If a/b is in simplest form, how are a and b related?	to be sure that students know that 1 is the only common factor.	There is no number that divides both.	What about 1?	to emphasize the need for precision in arguments
		You can't reduce the fraction.	Then how are a and b related?	to reemphasize that 1 is the only common factor
		They have no common prime factors.	Then how are a^2 and b^2 related?	to help generalize the idea of no common prime factors

FIGURE 3–9. Questions to Probe Students' Thinking About *Common Factors of Two Numbers*

Many pattern problems are also mathematics problems without a real-world context. Students are expected to reason from examples of the pattern; in the example that follows, students see the number of dots listed for each of the first few triangular numbers.

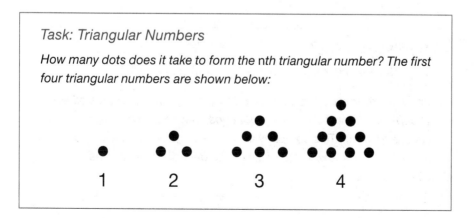

Task: Triangular Numbers

How many dots does it take to form the nth triangular number? The first four triangular numbers are shown below:

1   2   3   4

On the other hand, there are many mathematics problems set in real-world contexts. *Applications* is a term often used to designate these real-world problems, or simplifications of real-world problems. Applications involve problem solving, but they also require understanding of the context of the problem. The application that follows would require students to gather data and analyze them, probably using computer analysis software.

Task: Hand Spans by Gender and Age

Measure the hand spans and heights for boys and girls of different ages. How do age and gender affect the relationships?

Learn More...

There are many Web sites with data sets that can be used to construct applications; a few of our favorites are:

The Data and Story Library: http://lib.stat.cmu.edu/DASL/

Data Surfing on the World Wide Web: http://it.stlawu.edu/~rlock/datasurf.html

OzDASL (Australasian Data and Story Library): statsci.org/data/index.html

Measuring hand spans and heights requires that students use standardized measurement procedures and understand the role that measurement error would play in their conclusions.

Sometimes applications are structured around fictitious manufacturing situations, such as creating packaging for common objects. One example is the *Stacking Cups* lesson from Math Solutions (mathsolutions.com). In this application students need to generate data about the heights of cups stacked together and use those data to generate a pattern, or an equation, that can be generalized for a stack of fifty cups.

Task: Stacking Cups

You need: two different collections of 8 stacking cups

Problem: *Your class has been hired by a company that makes all kinds of cups of different sizes (foam hot cups, plastic cold cups, paper cold cups, and more). This company also makes holders for these cups, and it needs to know how tall to make the holders so that each one will hold 50 cups.*

The following chart displays some questions that might be used to determine how well students make sense of the context. (See Figure 3–10.)

Teacher's Question	Why Ask?	Possible Responses	Teacher's Follow-Up	Rationale
Is a stack of two cups twice as tall as one cup?	to determine if students see how the cups stack	No, part of the second one is inside the first.	How much taller is two cups?	to focus attention on the "lip" of the cup
		Yes, two is twice as much as one.	Can you show me?	to demonstrate the stacking

FIGURE 3–10. Questions to Probe Students' Thinking About the Context for *Stacking Cups*

Are Real-World Contexts a Must?

There is a trend in some educational circles to equate quality instruction only with lessons that have meaningful, real-world contexts. However, there are times when learning targets taught without a real-world context can be powerful if students focus on relationships among the mathematics ideas they are learning. Suppose the learning target is to know and use the formula for volume of a sphere. Rather than use a real-world context—*How much greater is the volume of a basketball than the volume of a baseball?*—one might use this task—*If sphere A has a diameter that is 2.5 times as great as the diameter of sphere B, what is the relationship between the volumes of those spheres?*

In the real-world example, there is a danger that students will get distracted by the process of measuring the diameters or radii of the basketball and baseball and lose focus on the key mathematics ideas. In the task that addresses mathematics without a real-world context, students might focus more on developing strategies for finding the solution in different ways, sharing how they thought about the task, suggesting alternative approaches, and hearing thinking that is sometimes congruent with and sometimes divergent from their own. It is during the debriefing of the task that much of the learning is taking place and students reveal their understanding of the underlying mathematics ideas.

The learning target "know and use the formula for volume of a sphere" was created from the eighth-grade standard "Know the formulas for the volumes of cones, cylinders, and spheres and use them to solve real-world and mathematical problems" (CCSS.MATH.CONTENT.8.G.C.9).

Problem solving and applications are important for development of mathematical expertise; however, applications (problem solving in real-world contexts) may be more motivating and engaging for many students. Of course, students need to have a clear connection to the real-world contexts. Problem solving and applications need to be presented to students so that they can begin to understand how mathematics ideas are developed with and without a real-world context. Learning targets, then, have to include attention to both types of contexts.

When Thinking About Problem Solving and Applications in a Learning Target

- What are the opportunities for students to use the mathematics with and without real-world contexts?

- How are the tasks structured so that students' solutions will demonstrate competence with problem solving and applications as well as competence with the underlying mathematics?

- Are there similar contexts, involving the same underlying mathematics, that can be used in assessing students' learning?

Reflection 3–1

Recognizing Different Types of Knowledge as Part of Creating Learning Targets

Pages 120–122

Turn to "Reflection 3–1: Recognizing Different Types of Knowledge as Part of Creating Learning Targets" (see pages 120–122) and complete the "Problem Solving and Applications" row of the table.

Confidence and Competence

Perhaps the most challenging type of knowledge to think about when creating learning targets and assessing success with those learning targets is confidence and competence. However, this may be one of the most important areas of expertise to develop in students. It is a sense of confidence and competence that encourages students to persevere when they do not immediately see how to complete a task or solve a problem. All teachers have had to deal with students who immediately raise their hands for help whenever they are asked to complete a task. Those students probably lack the confidence needed to figure out what to do on their own, and they may believe that they do not have enough competence to complete the task. If students are to become lifelong learners and to apply their mathematics knowledge to new problems, it is critical that they develop both confidence in their ability to do so and a sense of competence that they can be successful.

Adding It Up (Kilpatrick, Swafford, and Findell 2001) includes a strand called *productive disposition*, which is the "habitual inclination to see mathematics as sensible, useful, and worthwhile, coupled with a belief in diligence and one's own efficacy" (116). Confidence and competence are deeply connected to personal beliefs about the importance of diligence. It is important to develop students' perseverance in remaining engaged in mathematics problem solving long enough to generate solutions, or at least, attempts at solutions. In part this happens as a result of success in completing tasks, but those tasks have to be at an appropriate level of difficulty. If students encounter only problems that are simple and trivial, they will generalize that mathematics is not important, and when they face a challenging task, they are likely to give up. Students need to be successful with tasks that are solvable and that provide a sense of significant accomplishment when they are completed. Finding tasks that satisfy these two criteria can be, of course, challenging.

We believe that competence includes more than "strategic competence." Students need to develop competence with representations of concepts, with procedures, and with problem solving. We believe that it is also critically important for all students to develop confidence. In elementary school teachers often discuss and explicitly model "thinking about one's own thinking." This is critical in secondary school, though secondary teachers may be less explicit about metacognition because students have developed some self-awareness that accompanies age and experience. Teachers who include learning targets that incorporate metacognition as an expectation and attend to students' confidence as well as competence related to content goals are able to use formative assessment strategies such as feedback and think, pair, share to encourage students to examine their ideas and assess the quality of their work.

> **Learn More...**
>
> Cathy L. Seeley points out that sense making is one of the most crucial goals of mathematics instruction" in Message 45 of *Faster Isn't Smarter*, "Math Is *Supposed* to Make Sense!: The Most Important Mathematical Habit of Mind" (2015, 302–8).

Confidence, Competence, and the Common Core

It is interesting that the term *confidence* does not appear in the text of CCSSM. This is perhaps not surprising, since CCSSM is focused on content rather than affect. Attending to confidence, then, is a task for teachers.

The term *competence* appears once in CCSSM in a reference to *Adding It Up* (Kilpatrick, Swafford, and Findell 2001) and once in the introduction to the high school algebra section, where it is modified by the adjective *strategic*.

> An equation can often be solved by successively deducing from it one or more simpler equations. For example, one can add the same constant to both sides without changing the solutions, but squaring both sides might lead to extraneous solutions. Strategic competence in solving includes looking ahead for productive manipulations and anticipating the nature and number of solutions. (corestandards.org/Math/Content/HSA/introduction/)

Metacognition

Metacognition is the intersection of confidence and competence, a time when students' ideas about their own thinking come together to focus on what they know or do not know and how they can apply their own strategies for learning. Because metacognition involves the ability to evaluate one's own knowledge, skills, and learning, poor metacognition may lead students to be overconfident and make inappropriate decisions about the amount of study they need. Poor metacognition might also have the opposite effect in situations where students lack confidence in their abilities to be successful in mathematics.

We recognize that attending to confidence along with competence is a challenge for teachers who struggle with having enough time to provide opportunities for students to explore, discuss, and share their ideas in the context of learning all the mathematics for their grade or course. However, the payoff is worth the effort.

Learn More...

See Chapter 7 for discussion of student self-assessment.

When Thinking About Confidence and Competence in a Learning Target

- How will I allow for multiple entry points to engage all of my students?

- What will students need to do to be successful enough to build their confidence?

- How are there opportunities for using mathematics in familiar contexts as well as in more challenging, less familiar contexts?

- How does the criteria for success support students in self-assessing their progress toward learning?

Turn to "Reflection 3–1: Recognizing Different Types of Knowledge as Part of Creating Learning Targets" (see pages 120–122) and complete the "Confidence and Competence" row of the table, using the previous questions to guide you.

Reflection 3–1

Recognizing Different Types of Knowledge as Part of Creating Learning Targets

Pages 120–122

Connecting Learning Targets to Assessment

As we've learned, the first part of planning instruction using the INFORMative Assessment Model is often answering the question, "What is the learning target?" That is, what are students supposed to learn? Then tasks can be selected that will help students achieve the learning target. The levels of thinking and six broad types of knowledge previously discussed influence how we as teachers create learning targets and choose tasks. In addition to these considerations, we also need to think carefully about the question, "What evidence is acceptable as a demonstration of learning?" For example, what problems should students be able to solve, what terminology should students use, what procedures should students be able to carry out, and what are the key characteristics of convincing arguments? These considerations are particularly useful to help teachers know what to look for as students are working on tasks and responding to questions.

Consider the following questions when identifying what constitutes evidence of understanding and what common misconceptions students are likely to have.

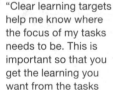

Assessment Tip

Think carefully about the question, "What evidence is acceptable as a demonstration of learning?"

Assessment Tip

"Clear learning targets help me know where the focus of my tasks needs to be. This is important so that you get the learning you want from the tasks you choose."
—Stacy Wozny, teacher

Thinking About Evidence of Understanding

- What are students able to do and to explain when they have acquired the conceptual and procedural knowledge related to the mathematics in the lessons?

- What mistakes do students typically make when the content is taught?

- What are students likely to say or do when they are "headed in the right direction" but have not yet solidified their understandings?

- What will be evidence of depth of learning?

Thinking about answers to these questions during the planning of lessons increases the likelihood that instruction will promote learning. As teachers, we have more sophisticated understanding of mathematics than students do, and it is sometimes difficult to remember how we were thinking as we learned mathematics. In our planning we have to be intentional about identifying expectations for students' performance and verbalizations. With this in mind, we explore two strategies for connecting learning targets to assessment.

Learn More...

"In other words, if teachers are specific about what content they want students to learn, they will likely be clear about how they will know when their students are achieving their learning goals, and when they are not."
—"Toward a Framework for Using Student Mathematical Representations as Formative Assessments" (Heritage and Niemi 2006, 271)

Strategies When Connecting Learning Targets to Assessment

1. Assess Students' Prior Knowledge

2. Choose Tasks to Promote Targeted Learning

Strategy 1: Assess Students' Prior Knowledge

Assessments are linked to learning targets through the tasks we ask students to undertake and the criteria set for accomplishing these tasks. Deciding how we will find out about students' prior knowledge related to a learning target is part of instructional planning. In Chapter 2 we discussed decisions about what students already know and elaborated on several tools for guiding these decisions. As you think about planning instruction with clear learning targets and assessing students' achievement of them, take a moment to look back at the discussion of these strategies on pages 26–55.

One of the standards from the "functions" conceptual area for high school is "Recognize that sequences are functions, sometimes defined recursively, whose domain is a subset of the integers. *For example, the Fibonacci sequence is defined recursively by $f(0) = f(1) = 1$, $f(n + 1) = f(n) + f(n - 1)$ for $n \geq 1$*" (CCSS.MATH.CONTENT.HSF.IF.A.3). The example provided as part of this standard helps to clarify the meaning of "recognize." The sample suggests

"Recognize that sequences are functions, sometimes defined recursively, whose domain is a subset of the integers. *For example, the Fibonacci sequence is defined recursively by $f(0) = f(1) = 1$, $f(n + 1) = f(n) + f(n - 1)$ for $n \geq 1$*" is part of the standards cluster "Understand the concept of a function and use function notation" (CCSS.MATH .CONTENT.HSF.IF.A.3).

that teachers might want to show a sequence and ask students to write a "recursive function" definition that generates the same set of numbers. As teachers we need to think carefully, however, about different ways that such a function might be described or defined.

Here is a learning target that might be posed as part of instruction for this standard: *Given a sequence of numbers, the student will define a function whose domain is the set of positive integers and whose range is the given sequence of numbers. As appropriate, the definition might include a recursively defined function.* Clarifying the kinds of numbers that would appear in the sequences would make this target even more precise; for example, positive integers or both rational and irrational numbers. The learning target specifies what students are supposed to do, and it suggests several kinds of prerequisite knowledge that might be pre-assessed; for example, knowing what it means to define a function and knowing what recursion is.

Instruction might begin with a pre-assessment to determine whether students understand the meaning of the term *recursive*. Perhaps the most obvious context is the Fibonacci sequence, {1, 1, 2, 3, 5, 8, 13, . . .}, where each entry is created by adding together the previous two numbers already listed. As teachers we need to keep in mind not only that the verb *recognize* is ambiguous but also that there are many contexts that would not require students to use recursion.

Strategy 2: Choose Tasks to Promote Targeted Learning

Deciding what tasks to pose depends on many factors, the most important being the mathematics focus of the learning target. Some tasks provide more opportunities for student thinking and reasoning than others, some tasks provide greater opportunities for multiple representations, and some tasks lend themselves to student collaboration to solve real-world problems. In Chapter 6 we discuss choosing mathematically rich tasks in detail. Here we remind ourselves of questions to be considered as part of task selection.

> **Learn More...**
>
> See Chapter 6 for a detailed discussion on choosing mathematically rich tasks.

Questions to Consider When Choosing Tasks Based on Learning Targets

- What do my students already know?

- How fluent are they with calculating?

- What technologies are available for them to use?

- How much algebra or geometry or statistics have students already studied?

- How fluent are they with "symbol manipulation"?

- How will I know from their performance whether students have attained the learning target?

- What evidence will I accept as indicative of reaching the learning target?

Suppose students were given this sequence:

$$1, 3, 9, 27, 81, \ldots$$

We recognize these values as powers of 3

$$3^0, 3^1, 3^2, 3^3, 3^4, \ldots$$

$$n\text{th term} = 3^{(n-1)}$$

but students might see this sequence recursively.

Each number is three times the previous number.

$$n\text{th term} = 3 \times (n-1)\text{th term}$$

Both characterizations are correct, and teachers need to think about how they can help students make connections between these two ways of thinking about the sequence. This might, for example, be an opportunity to build language about inductive reasoning.

Assessment Tip ✓

When creating learning targets, check to make sure you can describe the student performance that indicates learning.

Describing the kinds of student performance that indicate achievement of the learning target provides coherence between instruction and the assessments we use. We are better able to plan and carry out effective instruction when we can describe, and communicate to students, the kinds of behaviors that are acceptable as indicative of the learning that is desired. For example, if students are expected to use the Side Angle Side (SAS) theorem to prove congruence of triangles, then instruction should include examples of the kinds of tasks students are expected to solve and, at least in some cases, give students explicit directions to use this theorem.

There are almost always different ways that students could work toward attaining a given learning target. Some tasks involve knowledge of, and skill with, mathematics other than what is directly stated in the target. At times teachers choose to pose instructional tasks that ask for performance that goes beyond the basic performance needed to demonstrate mastery of a learning target. We encourage this, since it gives advanced students a chance to demonstrate their knowledge without requiring all students to achieve an advanced level of mastery. It also gives all students a chance to surprise teachers with the depth of their knowledge. When tasks are used in a formative manner, assessments can generate the information teachers need in order to recognize when students are ready for greater challenges and to know whether failure on a task is lack of attainment of the learning target or interference from lack of skill with other mathematics ideas.

Reflection 3-3

Connecting Learning Targets to Assessment: Communicating with Students

Page 125

Part of lesson planning is being able to describe evidence of attainment of a learning target. Complete "Reflection 3–3: Connecting Learning Targets to Assessment: Communicating with Students" (see page 125); this provides an opportunity for you to think about these issues for your own teaching.

Communicating Learning Targets to Students

When thinking about communicating learning targets, we like to consider both the teacher's and student perspectives. (See Figure 3–11.)

Teacher Perspective	Student Perspective
1. What are the learning targets?	1. What am I trying to learn?
2. How can I determine what the students are learning?	2. What do I understand and what do I still need to learn?
3. Where do I go next with instruction?	3. What help do I need to learn this?

FIGURE 3–11. Two Perspectives About Learning Targets

Because students need to know what the learning target is and the kinds of behaviors they must successfully demonstrate, teachers need to develop ways to communicate this information. We propose three strategies to keep in mind when communicating learning targets to students.

Three Strategies When Communicating Learning Targets to Students

1. Reword the Target to Student-Friendly Language

2. Give Students Mileposts

3. Support Students in Developing the Big Picture

Strategy 1: Reword the Target to Student-Friendly Language

When communicating learning targets to students, it is not sufficient simply to write the relevant standard on the board at the start of the class. Sometimes the standard *is* the learning target, but it is often the case that there will be several learning targets associated with a standard. Standards may give some sense of what is to be accomplished, but they are likely to use language that is more appropriate for teachers who already know the mathematics than for students who are still learning the mathematics.

For example, consider this sixth-grade standard on equations and inequalities from the students' point of view:

> Understand solving an equation or inequality as a process of answering a question: which values from a specified set, if any, make the equation or inequality true? Use substitution to determine whether a given number in a specified set makes an equation or inequality true. (CCSS.MATH .CONTENT.6.EE.B.5)

Rewording the standard using friendlier language may better communicate expectations to students. We have to be careful, though, always to use correct mathematics in whatever rewording we choose. One possible rephrasing is shown here:

> You need to solve a simple equation or inequality by finding numbers that can be used to make the equation or inequality true. Sometimes you will be given a set of numbers to choose from and sometimes you will have to identify the numbers yourself. You must explain how you found the correct numbers.

This rephrasing could be supplemented with examples, though care would be needed to insure that students do not misinterpret the examples as the *only* tasks that they need to be able to solve. It is important that the information communicated to students explicitly deals with mathematics ideas rather than the cosmetic aspects (e.g., showing all the steps) of whatever student work would be accepted as adequate performance.

Classroom Implications When Developing Partnerships with Students

- When students discuss solutions to open-ended problems or describe different ways to approach a task, assignments must have fewer problems.

- If students are to help establish criteria for success for different learning targets, they need opportunities to work with another student or with a group.

- When the emphasis is on scoring student work to identify what they have learned and what they still need to work on rather than scoring to assign a grade, it may mean redesigning the questions on the smaller quizzes we use throughout the unit and rethinking how we will provide feedback to students.

Strategy 2: Give Students Mileposts

One strategy for encouraging students to understand learning targets is for students to have mileposts along the path toward attainment. Mileposts might be learning targets or they might be mathematics tasks that students should be able to complete. Some students may not reach the learning target within the time set aside for instruction, and having mileposts allows them to monitor their own progress toward attainment of a target. The examples below show increasingly complex equations and inequalities that students might be expected to solve.

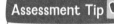

Assessment Tip

Showing students different levels of complexity of the same mathematics ideas allows students to self-monitor their progress.

Tasks: Equations and Inequalities Increasing in Complexity

$x + 4 = 6$ and $x + 4 > 6$

$3x = 12$ and $3x < 12$

$5x + 7 = 19$ and $5x + 7 < 19$

We are certainly *not* suggesting that all instruction be "compartmentalized" into segments that progress from the simplest cases to more challenging situations. Indeed, in tasks with equations/inequalities to solve there is considerable advantage to be gained by mixing various types of equations/inequalities within a lesson. However, both teachers and students need to have some way of assessing how far the students have come and how much

Learn More…

There is more discussion of self-monitoring in Chapter 7.

further they need to go. Students may be better able to self-monitor their progress if teachers show them the different levels of complexity of the same mathematics ideas. Better self-monitoring can lead to greater confidence about one's progress across time. If students can see their progress, they are more likely to assess their competence realistically.

Strategy 3: Support Students in Developing the Big Picture

While it is important that students recognize their progress related to specific learning targets, it is also important to help them see beyond the day-by-day improvement in their skill and expertise. They need to develop a "big picture" of the mathematics they are supposed to learn and identify how their knowledge both matches or falls short of this big picture. Students are not expected to read and internalize the mathematics standards for their state or district; however, as teachers we need to find ways of capturing the "sense" of the mathematics content to be learned in a given year or course and then communicating that to students.

Developing the Big Picture: The Common Core

The introductory paragraphs in CCSSM for each grade or set of high school standards can be used to support students in developing the big picture. For the Number and Quantity standards, one big issue is quantification. "[T]o find a good measure of overall highway safety, they might propose measures such as fatalities per year, fatalities per year per driver, or fatalities per vehicle-mile traveled. Such a conceptual process might be called quantification" (corestandards.org/Math/Content/HSN/introduction/). This statement will help students recognize that they are expected to develop understanding of a mathematics concept, and the example provides an illustration of what that concept might "look like" in a particular context.

Few teachers probably write lengthy learning targets in planning books. However, pausing to consider the importance of clarity of learning targets and to be explicit about why particular learning targets are chosen is likely to positively impact the quality of instruction. It is also important to select mathematics tasks carefully to match those clear learning targets. Those tasks should allow us to assess whether prerequisite knowledge is available in students' thinking as well as to judge the acquisition of the mathematics understanding outlined in the target. We close this chapter with two examples to reinforce these ideas.

> ┌ **Learn More...** ┐
> See Chapter 6 for a detailed discussion on choosing mathematically rich tasks.

 A Closer Look

Mr. Maples's Learning Target
for *Pythagorean Theorem*

Mr. Maples considered the CCSSM standard to "understand and apply the Pythagorean Theorem" (CCSS.MATH.CONTENT.8.G.B.8) to serve a dual purpose as a learning target: "Apply the Pythagorean Theorem to find the distance between two points in a coordinate system." He chose the following tasks to show different ways that students could work toward attaining this learning target. The tasks also required use of mathematical ideas that were not directly part of Mr. Maples's learning target. These ideas included simple computation skills, algebraic manipulation skills, and knowledge of geometric figures.

To decide what achievement should look like for the learning target, Mr. Maples made a judgment about how the prerequisite knowledge, or lack thereof, might interfere with students' being able to demonstrate mastery of the learning target. Mr. Maples's understanding of what his students could do was critical in choosing the kinds of tasks that his students needed to complete in order to demonstrate mastery of the learning target. When students fail to show mastery, teachers have to decide if that shows a failure to learn what was intended, reflects the interference of lack of prerequisite knowledge, or indicates students' lack of connections among relevant ideas.

>
> "Apply the Pythagorean Theorem to find the distance between two points in a coordinate system" is one of the eighth-grade geometry standards used to help students learn to understand and apply the Pythagorean Theorem (CCSS.MATH. CONTENT.8.G.B.8).

For this standard Mr. Maples considered tasks that go beyond the basic performance needed to demonstrate mastery of the learning target (i.e., use of Pythagorean Theorem). If Task 1 were the only kind of instructional task used, then some students might limit their understanding to this level. If more difficult tasks were used and discussed in class (e.g., Task 3), then students would likely find "test questions" (e.g., like Task 1) easy and would be more likely to be successful.

The Learning Target

Apply the Pythagorean Theorem to find the distance between two points in a coordinate system.

Task 1

Find the distance between (3, 5) and (–2, –7).

Mr. Maples needed to be intentional about his choices of numbers for Task 1. If the points were $(\frac{3}{4}, \frac{1}{2})$ and $(-\frac{2}{3}, -\frac{9}{11})$ the task would certainly be more difficult computationally; Mr. Maples thought about whether the increased difficulty is an important part of being able to document students' attainment of the learning target. On the other hand, if the points were (0, 5) and (0, 3) the task would probably be so easy that students would not even use the Pythagorean Theorem to compute the distance. He realized that choosing numbers that are "too easy" might interfere with the development of the appropriate understanding, and choosing numbers that are "too hard" might cause students to give up and not engage with the intended mathematics. He chose to use (3, 5) and (–2, –7) as appropriate for most of his students.

Mr. Maples also decided on this alternate task to pose to students who might need more of a challenge:

Alternate Task 1

Find y so that the distance between (3, 5) and (–2, y) is 2.

Since this task has no solution, some teachers might say that this was not a "fair" problem for Mr. Maples's students. However, some problems in the real world have no solution, and we believe it is important occasionally to present mathematics tasks that have no solution. Being able to explain why there is no numerical solution is actually a solution to the task!

Because Task 1 is a direct application of the use of the Pythagorean Theorem, Mr. Maples wanted to choose additional tasks that required students not to simply "do as I tell you to do." Task 2 encouraged Mr. Maples's students to imagine where five specific points might lie in the plane.

Task 2

Find five different points, each of which is 7 units away from (1, 9).

The request for *five* points in Task 2 is critical. Four points can be found without using the Pythagorean Theorem: (8, 9), (–6, 9), (1, 16), and (1, 2). Finding a fifth point, however, requires some application of the Pythagorean Theorem. Alternately, Mr. Maples knew he could simply eliminate the "four easy solutions" in the way he worded the task:

Alternate Task 2

Find a point that is 7 units away from (1, 9) but whose x-coordinate is not 1 and whose y-coordinate is not 9.

Choosing between Task 2 and Alternate Task 2 might depend on students' skill with language since the alternate task includes wording that is somewhat subtle. Both tasks require some "backward thinking" rather than direct application of the Pythagorean Theorem.

Task 3 goes beyond mere use of the Pythagorean Theorem to require use of knowledge of characteristics of different kinds of quadrilaterals. The additional knowledge required can reasonably be expected to be understood by most high school students.

> ### Task 3
>
> *The points (0, 6), (4, 0), (0, −6), and (−4, 0) are vertices of a quadrilateral. What kind of quadrilateral is it? Are there any points on the boundary of the quadrilateral that are 2 units apart?*
>
> > *If so, find a pair of points that are 2 units apart.*
> > *If not, explain why not.*
>
> *What is the maximum distance between pairs of points on the boundary of this quadrilateral?*

The quadrilateral is a parallelogram, and the maximum distance between two points would be the length of the longest diagonal, in this case 12, which could be found by inspection of the figure without use of the Pythagorean Theorem. This task illustrates one pitfall that sometimes happens when we try to make a task too accessible: we eliminate the need to use the intended mathematics. Mr. Maples recognized this potential weakness and realized this task could be made more appropriate by changing the coordinates of the vertices. For example, the points (1, 6), (4, 0), (−1, −6), (−4, 0) would make the task more appropriate.

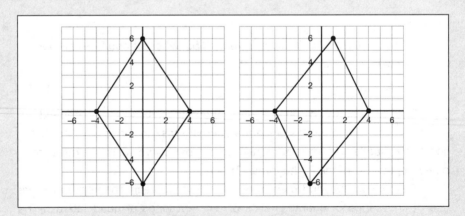

Choosing effective applications happens when teachers correctly recognize the mathematics that is embedded in those applications. Students then need to go beyond understanding the context of an application and recognize the mathematics that is required to create a solution.

→ A Closer Look

Mrs. Kolb Chooses a Learning Target for *Application of Pythagorean Theorem*

Mrs. Kolb wanted to push her students to become better at applying mathematics ideas that she was fairly certain they understood. She chose *The Umbrella* Task as an appropriate task for the learning target of "applying the Pythagorean Theorem." She began by asking students some questions about an umbrella in a box: "Think of what an umbrella looks like when it is folded up. Can you visualize that umbrella lying in a box? Now focus on the box. What is the longest umbrella that would fit inside your box? I want you to work in pairs and use your visualizations to help solve *The Umbrella* Task." Mrs. Kolb displayed the task on the whiteboard and asked students to begin work.

Task: The Umbrella

Find the length of the longest umbrella that can fit inside of a box whose interior dimensions are 6″ × 24″ × 32″.

Learn More…
"I first saw a task like *The Umbrella* over a decade ago in a professional development session conducted by Sid Rachlin, one of the authors of *Algebra I: A Process Approach*."
—Julie Kolb, teacher

Mrs. Kolb knew that if students recognized the underlying mathematics in this task as the Pythagorean Theorem, they would be ahead of the game in terms of generating a solution. When students work in groups to solve this task, conversations come naturally, and Mrs. Kolb had planned some ways to help students access the important mathematics information. If students struggle, an open box and a piece of string or masking tape give them tools to visualize the situation. As students work in groups, there are opportunities for them to critique one another's arguments and use representations to support their own solutions. Because the box is a rectangular prism, the debriefing discussion can include conversation about Pythagorean triples.

Some students tend to finish tasks such as this quickly because they recognize a solution path right away. Other students take much longer even

Learn More...

Cathy L. Seeley notes, "The most useful assessment results for influencing students' learning are those that are immediate and help students see for themselves whether they're headed in the right direction. So learning how to ask questions that push students' thinking is key, as well as knowing what to ask next based on a student's response" in Message 19, "How to Know What They Know: Assessing and Supporting Student Learning," in *Smarter Than We Think: More Messages About Math, Teaching, and Learning in the 21st Century* (2014, 137–44).

to understand the problem. Posing additional questions to those who answer the question right away for the class to discuss when everyone has finished extends the learning for all students. For example:

- *How high would the box (with base 24″ × 32″) need to be to hold an umbrella that is 42″ long? (Estimate before solving.)*

- *Maintaining a height of 6″, how long should the box be to hold a 42″ long umbrella?*

Different students are likely to identify three "common" solutions to the original task: 32-inch umbrella (the length of the box), 40-inch umbrella (the diagonal of the base of the box), and 40.4475-inch umbrella (the diagonal from a corner at the top of the 6-inch height to a corner on the opposite side of the bottom of the box). Each solution provides opportunities for students to explain their reasoning and provide a representation, either on paper or using a model. A question that might be posed at this point during the debriefing is, *Does it matter for your solutions how you visualize the box? That is, which dimensions form the base?* After discussion of the original task, the extension questions listed above are likely to be accessible to the majority of the students.

INFORMing My Practice

Mathematics, like all disciplines, has a body of knowledge from which ideas build, grow, and extend. Learning targets in mathematics should address all six types of knowledge: facts, concepts, skills and procedures, reasoning and proof, problem solving and applications, and confidence and competence. With clear learning targets, we are better able to plan, visualize, and describe for our students what they need to learn. With clear targets, we can be better prepared for moment-to-moment decisions as instruction moves forward. With clear targets, both students and teachers know "where we are headed." Good instruction begins with clear learning targets.

It is our responsibility always to keep the learning targets and their criteria for success in mind. For each unit, lesson, and assessment, we need to be able to articulate what we would like the student outcomes to be. By creating final assessments as we initially plan lessons, we are better able to be certain that our instruction is focused on a productive path. In planning a unit of instruction or creating daily lesson plans, three questions should guide our decisions about what and how to teach impending mathematics:

Three Questions About Learning Targets to Consider While Planning Lessons

- Am I clear about the learning targets for each day's lesson?

- Am I using ongoing assessment strategies to INFORM my daily planning?

- Am I prepared to communicate what I want my students to understand and to be able to do in terms that are meaningful and clear to them?

In the next two chapters our attention turns to techniques for revealing what students know. Chapter 4 deals with conversations and Chapter 5 deals with written work. Before leaving this chapter, turn to "Reflection 3–4: INFORMing My Practice: Implementing Clear Learning Targets" (see page 126) and record your thoughts about learning targets.

Reflection 3–4

INFORMing
My Practice:
Implementing Clear
Learning Targets

Page 126

Reflection 3-1: Recognizing Different Types of Knowledge as Part of Creating Learning Targets

Think about the different types of knowledge discussed on pages 77–103. The need to address different types of knowledge will influence your choices of learning targets. In the third column of the table, write two or three content examples of the type of knowledge specified in the first column. The questions in the middle column of the table are shortened versions of what was presented in this chapter; use them to help you think about the examples you write. Then answer the questions that follow the table.

Type of Knowledge	Questions to Prompt Reflections	Content Examples of Knowledge Type
Facts	• What vocabulary words need to be taught or reviewed? • Should critical factual knowledge be developed during the lesson or simply presented? • What factual knowledge should students retain or internalize?	
Concepts	• What are some ways each concept might be represented? • How should different representations be introduced to students? And in what order? • What conceptual understanding should students retain or internalize?	
Skills and Procedures	• Are there new procedures that students should learn? • What steps are necessary to be written down as evidence that students understand a procedure they are using? • What tasks will help students internalize procedures?	

(continued)

Reflection 3-1: Recognizing Different Types of Knowledge as Part of Creating Learning Targets (continued)

Type of Knowledge	Questions to Prompt Reflections	Content Examples of Knowledge Type
Reasoning and Proof	• What assistance can be provided to students to help them become fluent in explaining their thinking and reasoning? • What mathematics vocabulary, if any, should students use in making an argument? • What role do examples or symbols play in creating a convincing argument?	
Problem Solving and Applications	• What are the opportunities for students to use the mathematics with and without real-world contexts? • How are the tasks structured so that students' solutions will demonstrate competence with problem solving and applications as well as with the underlying mathematics ideas? • Are there different but similar contexts that might be used with students?	
Confidence and Competence	• How will I allow for multiple entry points to engage all of my students? • What will students need to do to be successful enough to build their confidence? • How do the criteria for success support students in self-assessing their progress toward learning?	

(continued)

Reflection 3-1: Recognizing Different Types of Knowledge as Part of Creating Learning Targets (continued)

1. Estimate the percentage of time this year you expect to spend (or you have spent) on each of the following categories. Remember that the percentages have to add to 100 percent.

Category	Facts	Concepts	Skills and Procedures	Reasoning and Proof	Problem Solving and Applications	Confidence and Competence
Percentage of Time						

2. Why is it important for your mathematics program to include all of these types of knowledge as well as to focus on developing students' confidence and competence?

Reflection 3-2: Recognizing Conceptual Knowledge When Creating Learning Targets: Proportional Reasoning

Proportional reasoning is critical for success in middle school and high school mathematics. Use the Population Growth task (see the next page) to help you document how well your students understand proportional reasoning. First read the task and think about how you would solve it, then do the following.

1. Choose one of your classes (at any grade level), and predict how many of your students would solve the *Population Growth* task correctly.

2. Administer the task and score the papers. Are you surprised at the results? Why or why not?

If you are not satisfied with students' performance, you may want to create and use one or more learning targets related to proportional thinking in the context of the content that you teach.

(continued)

Reflection 3-2: Recognizing Conceptual Knowledge When Creating Learning Targets: Proportional Reasoning (continued)

Date _____

Name _____

Task: Population Growth

Over the course of a three-year period,

> *the population of Town A grew from 4,000 to 6,000,*

> *the population of Town B grew from 40,000 to 60,000, and*

> *the population of Town C grew from 400,000 to 402,000.*

1. *Which town grew the most? Justify your choice.*

2. *Which town grew the least? Justify your choice.*

3. *Which town likely changed the most during this three-year period? Justify your choice.*

From *INFORMative Assessment: Formative Assessment to Improve Mathematics Achievement* by Jeane M. Joyner and George W. Bright. © 2016 by Math Solutions. Permission granted to photocopy for nonprofit use in a classroom or similar place dedicated to face-to-face educational purposes.

Reflection 3-3: Connecting Learning Targets to Assessment: Communicating with Students

1. Choose a long-term goal for your grade or course that you think is somewhat ambiguous. This goal might be one of the standards that you teach. Write it below and explain why it is ambiguous.

2. Write one or two learning targets that would clarify the intent of this long-term goal.

3. How would you communicate these learning targets to students?

4. Describe how you would know when students had satisfied one of your learning targets.

5. How would you communicate these requirements to students?

Reflection 3-4: INFORMing My Practice: Implementing Clear Learning Targets

Think about the chapter you just read. Use this space to record your ideas.

Ideas about the importance of clear learning targets:

Changes in my thinking about INFORMative assessment:

Ideas I envision becoming a more important part of my practice:

Questions I have:

Frustrations/concerns I have:

Section III

How Do I Assess?

Strategies to Support Oral INFORMative Assessments

It is helpful to remember that as teachers we are always gathering information, informally and formally, about our students. Focusing on INFORMative assessment, however, allows us to use the information we gather more strategically. In this chapter we focus on critical components of *oral* formative assessments—conversations, intentional listening, and questioning. Many different kinds of conversations occur during instruction, and we suspect that much of the learning about mathematics ideas happens during these conversations.

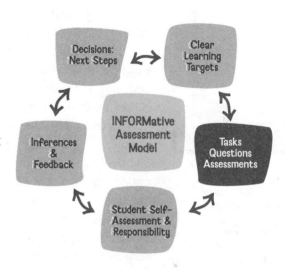

Overview

Conversations as Formative Assessment

One of the most powerful ways to implement INFORMative assessment is through our own classroom interactions, specifically, conversations. Conversations help us find out what students really know, and as has been discussed in previous chapters, students' knowledge is critical information for instructional planning. Hearing students explain why and how they arrive at a given response gives us as teachers a chance to recognize incorrect understanding as well as correct but incomplete understanding. For example, one question we might ask ourselves during a conversation is, "Are students reasoning in a valid way, or are they simply repeating steps in a procedure without understanding what those steps mean?"

Conversations also allow us to intervene before incorrect processes or incomplete understandings are "practiced wrong" and misconceptions are solidified. Often students operate with "rules" that are *almost* correct but contain flaws so that when students apply their "rules," their answers are sometimes correct and sometimes incorrect. When correct answers are rewarded (e.g., with a check mark or a grade), the inappropriate "rules" are unintentionally reinforced. When we as teachers are able to intervene before incomplete understandings or inaccurate ideas coalesce into inappropriate "rules," we are more likely to have students who become competent and confident in mathematics. Intervening in this way may especially help struggling learners, in part by providing positive interaction time with the teachers. In conversations, a teacher can provide assurance to students who feel that "no one cares" about whether they are learning or can help frustrated students begin to overcome that frustration.

A "conversation" may be spoken words or it may be an exchange of written words, symbols, and drawings. When we ask students for a written response to a task, we are engaging in a conversation on paper with students. Thinking about written work as an "asynchronous conversation" puts a different light on that work. This chapter focuses on the spoken format of a conversation; see Chapter 5 for a more in-depth look at INFORmative assessment based on students' written work.

Spoken conversations may occur during whole-class discussions, small-group discussions, partner talk, or one-on-one discussions between the

Assessment Tip ✓

When we as teachers are able to intervene before incomplete understandings or inaccurate ideas coalesce into inappropriate "rules," we are more likely to have students who become competent and confident in mathematics.

Learn More...

A "conversation" may be spoken words or it may be an exchange of written words, symbols, and drawings. For a discussion of the latter, see Chapter 5.

teacher and individual students. When teachers use conversation as formative assessment, they are *listening intentionally* to try to determine what students understand. In the following section, we take a closer look at what it means to listen intentionally when using conversations to formatively assess.

Strategy 1: Intentional Listening

In order to turn conversations into effective formative assessment, it is important to become an intentional listener. Intentional listening goes beyond focusing on whether answers are correct or incorrect. *Intentional listening* happens when a teacher is actively working to make sense of what students are saying. Sometimes this means attending to what students say, and sometimes it means attending to what students are doing (body language may speak louder than words). Either way, intentional listening requires teachers to attend to *students'* actual thinking rather than to how the *teacher* is thinking about the mathematics in a task. It means focusing on what students are saying rather than planning what we are going to say next.

Intentional listening also means making an effort to do less telling—*talk less, listen more.* When a question is posed, teachers who are intentional listeners are comfortable with silence as students are thinking, and they reinforce the need for silence during "thinking time" That silence allows all students time to think, not just the student who is expected to answer the question.

And teachers who are intentional listeners not only make an effort to listen more, they make an effort to ask more. Asking students to clarify or "say more" is an intentional listening strategy. As students respond, teachers decide if students are communicating their misunderstandings or miscommunicating their understanding.

Intentional listening does not just apply to whole-class conversations and observations; it also means observing and attending to conversations between students as they are working in partners or small groups. Consider this your ticket as a teacher to eavesdrop. Listening as students talk with a partner or in a small group often reveals information about the thinking of

Assessment Tip ✓

Intentional listening happens when we actively engage in a conversation with students to make sense of what they are saying.

Assessment Tip ✓

Talk less, listen more!

Learn More...

Chapter 7, pages 289–300, offers a more detailed look at partner and group work.

students who are too shy or are not confident to share with the class as a whole.

The use of intentional listening is easier if teachers have some ideas about what to listen for. That is, through reflection on what students have said or done previously, we develop active hypotheses about what students understand. For example, if a student says that the median of these data— 56, 86, 75—is 86, a teacher might assume that the student is identifying the "middle term" in the list as it exists rather than the list after the data have been ordered. Two possible hypotheses about this incorrect answer are (a) the student forgot to order the data and (b) the student does not know that it is important to order the data first. Questions are needed to help identify which of these hypotheses is more likely correct. A teacher might ask, "How would you define the median of a set of data?" or "What is the process for determining the median of a set of data?"

Intentional listening can also happen when teachers have no active hypotheses about a student's understanding. Sometimes, there is no good clue about what is behind a student's explanation. This may happen when students use incorrect terminology or vague terms (e.g., many pronouns without clear antecedents) or it may happen when students take an unexpected turn in carrying out a series of steps in a process. A conversation can provide enough information so that the teacher has a sudden "aha" moment about the sense that a student is or is not making of the mathematics.

We should always keep in mind that as teachers *we know* the mathematics and *students are learning* the mathematics. Students' thinking is going to be less sophisticated and less polished. We cannot simply impose our way of thinking on students; students have to develop their own understanding of key concepts and procedures, and we need to help them negotiate that meaning.

> **Learn More ...**
>
> "Teachers must acknowledge that what their students learn is not necessarily what they intended, and this is inevitable because of the unpredictability of teaching. Thus, it is essential that teachers explore students' thinking before assuming that students have understood something."
> —*Embedded Formative Assessment* (Wiliam 2011, 75)

Strategies for Becoming a More Intentional Listener

To become more focused and intentional in attending to students' thinking, consider doing the following:

- Prior to lessons, identify common misconceptions and errors that you will look and listen for (see Chapter 2 for more insights).

- Prepare questions ahead of time while making lesson plans or reviewing students' written work.

- Avoid "giving away" too much information in the wording of questions.

- Ask, then listen carefully more often; tell and direct less often.

- Ask why, how, and what—and then wait; don't rush students to respond.

- Note key ideas that indicate understanding.

- Establish an environment in which both correct and incorrect responses are questioned.

┌─ Learn More... ─┐

"Observing, questioning, and listening are the primary sources of evidence for assessment that is continual, recursive, and integrated with instruction."
—*Assessment Standards for School Mathematics* (National Council of Teachers of Mathematics 1995, 46)

→ A Closer Look

Ms. Rich's Intentional Listening with *Function Rules*

Ms. Rich wanted her eighth-grade students to learn "that a function is a rule that assigns to each input exactly one output." She posed this task:

Ms. Rich drew her learning target from the CCSSM standard "Understand that a function is a rule that assigns to each input exactly one output" (CCSS.MATH .CONTENT.8.F.A.1).

Task: Function Rules

What are the differences in the sets of points generated by these rules?

1. *Find all (x, y) points so that the sum of the coordinates is 1.*

2. *Find all (x, y) points so that the sum of the squares of the coordinates is 1.*

Ms. Rich knew that there were several differences that might be identified by students:

- Rule 1 generates a line; rule 2 generates a circle.

- Rule 1 includes all x and y values; rule 2 includes only x and y values between −1 and 1.

- Rule 1 can be shown with a linear equation ($y = 1 - x$); rule 2 cannot.

- Rule 1 has x and y values that are paired in a one-to-one fashion; rule 2 has two y-values for every x-value, and vice versa.

It was the last of these differences that Ms. Rich really wanted to focus on. Although each of the differences was identified by at least one student, not even a third of the students identified the last difference. She wanted to lead a discussion that would help her understand why so few students could see this important fact on their own. Since almost everyone sketched the two graphs correctly, she began by talking about the graphs.

Ms. Rich: If you graph the two sets of points, what do they look like?

Mattie: One is a line and the other is a circle.

Ms. Rich: What happens if you draw vertical lines through the two graphs?

Mattie: The lines cross the graphs.

Carlton: But they cross them differently. For Number One there is only one point where they meet but for Number Two there are two points.

Tiffany: Not always two points. If the vertical line hits the left or right side of the circle there is only one point. And if the vertical line is way to the left or right of the circle there aren't any points at all.

Ms. Rich: That's a lot to think about for Rule Two. Does a vertical line intersect the graph for Rule One differently, depending on where the line is?

Carlton: The line for Number One is infinite, so I think there is always one point where they meet.

Mattie: I agree with Carlton. There is always only one point where they meet.

Ms. Rich:	When you say "they," Mattie, what are you talking about?
Mattie:	The vertical line and the line for Number One.
Tiffany:	I agree. There is always one point of intersection for Number One and any vertical line.
Ms. Rich:	That is an important difference between the two rules.

The discussion continued as Ms. Rich further developed the key ideas; let's focus on this part and how it illustrates Ms. Rich's use of intentional listening.

First, Tiffany's comment about intersections with a circle was an opening for Ms. Rich to make one clear distinction between the two rules. She might have chosen to ask the class if they understood Tiffany's comment, but that might have led the discussion off task to properties of circles rather than a discussion about function rules. Instead, Ms. Rich chose to focus immediately on the relevant difference between the two rules. That is, she recognized the important mathematics ideas represented by Tiffany's comment and she steered the discussion to build on those ideas.

Second, Ms. Rich chose to ask Mattie about the antecedent for "they." In ordinary conversation, people often use many pronouns without being specific about the antecedents. In discussions of mathematics, it is important to be sure that antecedents are clear so that communication is precise. Ms. Rich could have asked Carlton earlier to clarify the antecedents in his comments, and we cannot be sure why she did not. Perhaps she "sensed" a bit of confusion on the faces of other students after Mattie's comment, and she wanted to be sure that Mattie's comment was understood correctly.

Listening carefully to students' comments and using them to highlight key mathematics ideas is a critical element of formative assessment that supports effective instruction. Ms. Rich learned that Tiffany had a good understanding of how vertical lines might intersect (or not intersect) a circle. Even though she does not know whether all students shared that understanding, she was able to use the comment to enhance the discussion. Listening intentionally for differences in the use of terminology or the use of pronouns becomes a clue to this evolution. It is important to listen for the meaning behind what is said rather than just the form (e.g., terminology) of a response.

> **Learn More …**
>
> Teachers of mathematics at all levels might consider their instructional goals as they weigh the advantages and disadvantages of introducing representations, contexts, and language of various types, both vague and precise.
> —"Ambiguity in Units and Their Referents: Two Cases in Rational Number Operations" (Rathouz 2010, 51)

Being Cognizant of Our Use of Pronouns

As teachers, we need to be cognizant of not only students' use of pronouns but also our own use of pronouns. It is relatively easy for students to think of the wrong antecedent of a pronoun and unintentionally learn incorrect mathematics. Rathouz (2010) created this example to illustrate, in a simple way, the difficulty that can arise: "*I just picked up a box of 4 dozen donuts at the shop. Do you want one?*" (43). The pronoun *one* could refer to one doughnut, one-dozen doughnuts, or one box of four-dozen doughnuts!

Intentional Listening: Observing Students

Observations go hand-in-hand with intentional listening. For example, students' body language gives us feedback that is helpful in adjusting the pace of discussions. Sometimes students' facial expressions indicate confusion or we see an "aha" moment that leads us to restructure some portion of the lesson. Observations provide real-time data that most teachers use to make moment-to-moment decisions.

As teachers we regularly "wander the classroom" while students are working at their seats or in small groups. During these observational wanderings we typically listen to students' conversations or glance at what students write in order to determine if a student is headed in the wrong direction or seems confused or has an error that might lead to an incorrect solution. We can then decide whether to intervene. Sometimes, individual students take advantage of our wanderings by asking questions, more or less in private, as we pass by. If so, we need to respond, but that response might be a question that helps students move down a productive path. Any conversation we have with students as we wander the classroom can be called a "roving conversation."

Assessment Tip ✓

"I believe the most powerful aspect of formative assessment is the ability to adjust instruction minute-by-minute. By having students explain their thinking, I am able to identify what a student already knows and any misconceptions he or she may have. Furthermore, I am able to instantly address the needs of that student through another question, specific analogy, or most powerfully, through an explanation by a peer."
—Samantha Benson, teacher

→ A Closer Look

Ms. Rideau's Observations of Students with *Cross-Sections of Three-Dimensional Shapes*

One of the ideas in geometry that students often struggle with is visualizing cross-sections of three-dimensional objects. Ms. Rideau introduces this idea each year by asking students to imagine cross-sections of a sphere and a right cylinder. The learning target is to compare and contrast the cross-sections. The task Ms. Rideau chose follows.

The CCSSM standard relevant to Ms. Rideau's learning target is "Identify the shapes of two-dimensional cross-sections of three-dimensional objects, and identify three-dimensional objects generated by rotations of two-dimensional objects" (CCSS.MATH .CONTENT.HSG .GMD.B.4).

Task: Cross-Sections of Three-Dimensional Shapes

Use the models of a sphere and a right cylinder to help you imagine the shapes of the cross-sections that can be made by cutting each model with a plane.

1. *For the sphere, imagine all possible cross-sections that can be made.*

2. *For the right cylinder, imagine the cross-sections for each of these cuts:*

   a. *parallel to the bases*

   b. *perpendicular to the bases*

   c. *diagonally through the lateral surface of the right cylinder*

3. *What is similar about the sets of cross-sections for these shapes? What is different?*

4. *Challenge: What other kinds of cuts of the right cylinder might yield different shapes?*

Ms. Rideau picked the sphere and right cylinder for several reasons. First, there is only one cross-section of a sphere—a circle. Intuitively, this happens because no matter how you turn a sphere, it always looks the same. This means that for any "cut" of the sphere by a plane, you can rotate the sphere and that plane so that the plane is horizontal. Ms. Rideau knew that some students would try to find other cross-section shapes by "slanting" the cross-section plane. She knew that she would have to be alert for this struggle among her students, so that if it happened, it could be discussed during the debriefing. She also knew that if no one visualized slanted cuts, then she would have to raise that issue herself.

Second, in contrast, there are several different cross-sections of a right cylinder, depending on the slant of the cross-section plane making the cut. Ms. Rideau asked students to visualize only three of those cuts to generate cross-sections: circle (horizontal cut), rectangle (vertical cut), and ellipse (slanted cut through the lateral surface). One other fairly easily imagined cross-section shape is a non-rectangular parallelogram (slanted cut through both bases), and a less easily imagined shape is a truncated ellipse (cut through one face and lateral surface). She opted to pose a challenge to ask students to find these two cuts.

Ms. Rideau: By the end of the day, I want you to be able to compare and contrast the cross-section shapes for a sphere and a right cylinder. What does "*cross-section shape*" mean?

Kayli: What it looks like if you cut it apart.

Ms. Rideau: What do you mean by "*cut it apart*"?

Kayli: Cut through it.

Felipe: It's what the end of a piece would look like if you cut one of the 3-D shapes with a plane. We actually cut apart foam shapes in eighth grade.

Ms. Rideau: That's a nice way of explaining what a cross-section is, though we're not going to be able to actually cut our models today. A cross-section is the shape on the end of a cut section if you imagine cutting a shape with a plane. How might we position the plane that is doing the cutting?

Kayli: It might be across, up and down, or slanted.

Ms. Rideau: We can use the terms *horizontal*, *vertical*, and *diagonal*. Here is the task I want you to work on. *(Displays the task on the board.)* I want you to work in your groups of four, just as you did yesterday. As a group, you can describe the cross-section shapes with words or pictures or both. And be sure to answer the questions in Number Three of the task. Write a description of how the two sets of cross-section shapes are alike and how they are different. I want one set of answers from each group, with your signatures at the bottom of the page to show me that you all agree on the answers. If there are no further questions, send one person from each group to pick up one model of each 3-D shape and then begin work.

Since the eight groups had worked together before, there was not much time lost in getting organized. Ms. Rideau observed that all the groups were quick to imagine a horizontal cut of the sphere through the center of the sphere, and they correctly labeled the cross-section shape as a circle. All the groups decided that they needed to imagine more horizontal cuts other than through the center of the sphere. Five of the groups imagined one such cut, and then they all realized that any horizontal cut not through the center would generate a circle, though of a smaller size. Three of the groups imagined three such cuts before reaching the same conclusion. Some students in those groups seemed surprised that all of the cross-section shapes from horizontal cuts were circles.

Each group then imagined a vertical cut, and none of the groups imagined that cut through the center of the sphere. It was quickly obvious to the students that any vertical cut also yielded a circle as the cross-section.

Five groups then began discussing diagonal cuts through the sphere. The other three groups began to discuss cuts to the right cylinder. Ms. Rideau observed this difference in the ways the groups proceeded and made a note to address the different approaches during the debriefing. The five groups spent different amounts of time on their discussions, but they all came to the realization that no matter what kind of slanted cut was made, the cross-section was a circle. Only one group explicitly concluded that the sphere and plane could be rotated together so that the plane was horizontal. Ms. Rideau knew that she would want this group to explain its thinking during the debriefing.

The group discussions of cuts to the right cylinder were similarly revealing for Ms. Rideau. All the groups fairly quickly realized that the horizontal and vertical cuts yielded circles and rectangles. Most of the groups explicitly realized that the circles were the same size no matter where the horizontal cut was made, but the rectangles could be of different sizes depending on where the vertical cut was positioned relative to the major axis of the cylinder. The other groups never even addressed the issue of size of the cross-section shapes. Ms. Rideau realized that she needed to ask about this during the debriefing.

The discussions of the slanted cut created more disagreement within groups. A few students insisted that a slanted cut would yield a circle, but most students realized that it would be a distorted circle. Some students called it an oval, and only a few thought it was an ellipse. Ms. Rideau did not hear any student offer a complete justification for "proving" that the shape was actually an ellipse. She realized that the students did not yet know enough about the mathematical properties of an ellipse to make a convincing argument. Some groups could not agree on what the cross-section shape would be for a slanted cut. The students thought that the shape would be different, depending on the degree of slant. By the time Ms. Rideau ended the task, one group still had not reached any consensus about what shape would result from a slanted cut.

Halfway through the period, Ms. Rideau had observed three categories of student performance:

Category 1: All correct
  a. sphere: circle
  b. right cylinder: circle and rectangle with disagreement about oval versus ellipse

Category 2: Mostly correct
  a. sphere: circle
  b. right cylinder: circle and rectangle with disagreement about the slanted cut

Category 3: Incomplete, but mostly correct
  a. sphere: circle
  b. right cylinder: circle and rectangle, but not enough discussion of the slanted cut

As Ms. Rideau watched the groups, she planned how to organize the debriefing discussion. Her observations of the students at work confirmed the careful planning and thinking that she had done as she organized the lesson. She knew some of the pitfalls that students might encounter, and she planned how she might deal with them. By the time she called the groups together, her observations had helped her create a plan for debriefing the task.

Intentional Listening: One-on-One Conversations

Conversations do not always have to be public in nature, such as whole-class discussions. It is also important to have (a) short, two- or three-minute private conversations with individual students who are experiencing difficulties or (b) scheduled interviews to explore a student's understanding. One-on-one conferences with students are often part of elementary school routines, but in middle and high schools, specifically planned conversations and scheduled interviews are not as common, even though such conversations can be helpful both to teachers and students. The number of students a secondary teacher interacts with during each day is the most frequently given reason for not using these kinds of interviews. Difficulty in scheduling a time when both teacher and student are free for a fifteen-minute private conversation is also a barrier. Following we take a closer look at both planned conversations and scheduled interviews and discuss ways to implement these.

Planned One-on-One Conversations

As teachers we can often use students' homework, questions asked in class, and lack of progress toward intended learning targets as a basis for identifying students who are struggling. We can then plan short conversations with these students during times when the class is otherwise engaged in individual or small-group work. The purpose of these conversations is to reveal a student's understanding about specific mathematics issues that the teacher thinks may be interfering with that student's learning. Before a planned conversation, identify specific questions to probe the student's reasoning, a proactive move that has potential to support the student's learning. The goal is to get enough information about a student's thinking so that either remediation can be provided or a decision can be made that such remediation is not needed.

> **Assessment Tip** ✓
>
> Be proactive when you see a student making mistakes; initiate a private conversation before the mistake becomes a habit.

Scheduled One-on-One Interviews

In schools where it is possible for interviews to take place before or after regular school hours, or in situations where teachers' planning periods are at the same time as students' study halls or lunches, scheduled one-on-one interviews can have payoffs for both teachers and the students. As teachers we are frequently surprised by students' mathematical intuitions or by the gaps in student understanding of mathematics content. Sometimes students' correct answers are based on procedures they have memorized but do not understand; only when their thinking is probed are these superficial understandings revealed. For example, a student may correctly compute $36 \times \frac{2}{3}$ but will not be able to explain how y and n are related when $y = n \times \frac{2}{3}$. If students understand the relationship represented by the equation, they should be able to explain some or all of these relationships:

- The ratio of y to n; that is, $\frac{y}{n}$; is $\frac{2}{3}$ (except, of course, when $n = 0$).
- If $n = 0$, then n and y are equal, since they are each equal to 0.
- If $n \neq 0$, then y is closer to 0 than n.
- If $n < 0$, then y is greater than n.
- If $n > 0$, then y is less than n.

Creating "if/then" statements like these demonstrates much more sophisticated reasoning than simply computing a result. We need to push students to reason about underlying mathematics ideas. Sometimes this kind of reasoning is best revealed in scheduled interviews during which students do not have to "perform" in front of their peers. We can push harder when probing students' arguments, ask "what if" questions, and determine more accurately the level of students' mathematical maturity.

This is not suggesting that teachers need to schedule individual interviews with all students. While this is ideal for planning instruction that challenges those who need challenges and assists those who need more clarification or experiences with specific content, it is not realistic for secondary school teachers. In high schools with senior projects or exit portfolio requirements, teachers may already be scheduling individual interviews with their homeroom students or those they are mentoring. Those interviews, however, serve a different purpose.

We do suggest that secondary teachers consider interviewing two or three students during each grading period to see for themselves the potential of interviews. Through interviews, teachers are better able to plan interventions for individual students who are having difficulties. If students performing at different levels are selected for interviewing, teachers are able to see the range of understanding of students in a class about particular topics. Identifying what information we are looking for and the mathematical thinking we want to probe is important for planning appropriate questions for either type of interview. Following are tips for responding to students' errors, especially during one-on-one conversations with students.

Tips for Responding to Students' Errors

- Acknowledge what is correct in the student's work.

- Frame questions to reveal the student's thinking.

- Focus on identifying underlying errors in logic or misunderstanding of big ideas.

- Support the student in self-correcting errors.

- When possible, avoid directing the student on what to do or what to think.

Remember, interviews are times to gather information, not teach. Probing an individual student's thinking may give hints about the effectiveness of whole-class instruction or may lead to individual remediation or enrichment.

Assessment Tip ✓

Interviews are times to gather information, not teach.

Strategy 2: Questioning for Different Purposes

Conversations as formative assessment are built on listening intentionally and effective questioning. Our questions, often created on the fly, need to respond to what students say or write. In this section we take a closer look at four different purposes for questioning during our conversations with students. These purposes are all related to formative assessment of students' thinking.

Learn More...

"In effective teaching, teachers use a variety of question types to assess and gather evidence of student thinking, including questions that gather information, probe understanding, make the mathematics visible, and ask students to reflect on and justify their reasoning."
—*Principles to Actions: Ensuring Mathematical Success for All* (National Council of Teachers of Mathematics 2014, 41)

Questioning for Different Purposes

Purpose 1: Engaging all students

Purpose 2: Clarifying and probing student thinking

Purpose 3: Eliciting student thinking when debriefing

Purpose 4: Highlighting mathematics ideas

Questions to Engage All Students

Any effective whole-class discussion has to begin with an *engaging question*; that is, a question that encourages all students to enter into the discussion. Engaging questions typically have more than one answer or more than one way to generate a single answer to the question. They are an invitation to further discuss the task, not an opportunity to give the answer. Engaging questions solicit multiple contributions from students.

Clearly, yes/no questions (e.g., Is 31 prime?) are not likely to engage students. Questions that ask for either an explanation (e.g., Why is 31 prime?) or a comparison (Why is 31 prime but 32 not prime?) are more likely to engage students and to reveal various aspects of their thinking. Similarly, "what if" questions (e.g., What happens if I add two prime numbers greater than 10?) may engage students in thinking about important mathematics ideas. Wiliam (2011, 86) used the term *reframed questions* to highlight how low-level questions might be rewritten to reveal more about students' thinking. (Some examples are given in Figure 4–1.)

Original Question	Reframed Question
A bicycle costing $96.00 is on sale at 25% off. What is the new price?	A bicycle costing $96.00 is on sale at 15% off. Chris has a coupon for another 10% off. Is the total discount 25%, more than 25%, or less than 25%? Explain.
Is $y = 3x$ a proportional relationship?	Why is $y = 3x$ a proportional relationship, but $y = 3x + 1$ is not a proportional relationship?
Find the y-intercept of $y = 3x - 2$.	How would you change the equation $y = 3x - 2$ so that the y-intercept is (0, 7)?
If $f(x) = 2x + 7$, find $f(x + 1)$.	If $f(x) = 2x + 7$, why is $f(x + 5) - f(x + 1)$ not 4?
Find all real solutions of $x^4 - 16 = 0$.	Why are there real solutions for $x^4 - 16 = 0$ but not for $x^4 + 16 = 0$?
Find the volume of a right circular cone if the height is 5 cm and the radius of the base is 4 cm.	If the height of a right circular cone doubles and the radius of the base is halved, how does the volume change, if at all?
If you roll a number cube twice, what is the probability that the sum of the two numbers is 5?	If you roll a number cube twice, how are the probabilities of the two events below related? a. The sum of the two numbers is 5. b. The sum of the two numbers is 5, given that the number on the first roll is 2.
A normal distribution has a mean of 53. What is the median?	For a normal distribution, why do the mean and the median have the same value?

FIGURE 4–1. Examples of Reframed Questions

When engaging questions are used to bring many students into the conversation while informally assessing the depth and breadth of their understanding at the beginning of a lesson, they are referred to as "range questions" (Heritage 2008a). These questions invite students' participation by allowing for more than one answer (e.g., Name two fractions that have a value between $\frac{1}{2}$ and $\frac{1}{10}$). They are relevant to the day's learning target (e.g., Explain how you could determine which fraction is greater $\frac{10}{21}$ or $\frac{15}{31}$) and serve as starting points for the lesson (Collins 2011).

Engaging questions might be part of warm-up tasks and can be prepared as part of lesson planning; other times an unexpected comment by a student triggers an engaging question. For example, in the midst of instruction on graphs of nonlinear equations a teacher might pose a warm-up task for pairs of students to complete.

> ### Assessment Tip ✔
>
> To engage students in a conversation, consider asking "range questions"—engaging questions that invite students' participation by allowing for more than one answer.

A Warm-Up Task

Which graph has the greater range over the domain interval [3, 6]? Be prepared to explain your reasoning. $y = \frac{1}{2}x^2$ *or* $y = \frac{1}{3}x^3$

One key purpose of asking range questions and discussing warm-up tasks is to get a quick "sense of the class" about how ready they are to engage effectively with the planned lesson. It may not be necessary to probe deeply into students' reasons for the responses they have for their solutions. But it might be helpful to try to determine which solution strategies are used by the majority of the students. Responses on whiteboards, with clickers, on index cards, or through a show of hands can give a "feel" for the class. Think about how your students might respond to the previous task. Then complete "Reflection 4–1: Questions to Engage All Students" (see page 162).

> **Reflection 4–1**
>
> Questions to Engage All Students
>
> Page 162

Questions to Clarify and Probe Student Thinking

Engaging questions are frequently paired with probing questions or clarifying questions. *Probing questions* are intended to reveal thinking that is not explicitly voiced by students. As teachers we know what needs to be said, but students sometimes do not say all that needs to be said. Probing questions can help reveal whether students know the mathematics and simply have omitted key elements or whether students either do not have complete understanding of those key elements or have a fundamental misunderstanding that is interfering with the learning of the targeted idea.

Clarifying questions are intended to help a student elaborate on ideas that are superficially or confusingly voiced. Clarifying questions encourage a student to rephrase a comment or make explicit the antecedent of a pronoun. This allows the explaining student to self-check her or his thinking, and it allows the rest of the class a chance to reflect on what was said and to decide how their own thinking relates to that explanation. Clarifying questions are probably most useful when you are fairly certain that a student understands the idea being learned, but the student's language is not precise or the explanation is not complete.

→ A Closer Look

Mr. Pennington's Questions to Clarify and Probe Student Thinking with *Solve a Quadratic Equation*

Mr. Pennington wanted to assess his students' skill at solving a quadratic equation. He asked them to solve a particular quadratic equation.

> *Task: Solve a Quadratic Equation*
>
> *Solve this quadratic equation:* $x^2 - x - 6 = 1$.

The most direct solution is to subtract 1 from both sides of the equation and then use the quadratic formula to find the roots. See Figure 4-2 for Carla's solution.

$$x^2 - x - 6 = 1$$
$$(x + 2)(x - 3) = 1$$
$$x + 2 = 1 \text{ and } x - 3 = 1$$
$$x = -1 \text{ and } x = 4$$

FIGURE 4–2. Carla's Response to *Solve a Quadratic Equation*

There are two points where Carla's work seems to go wrong. First, factoring the left side of the equation as it stands does not lead to a solution. Second, given the factoring, it is not correct to set each of the factors equal to 1. There are many questions that might be posed to try to reveal Carla's thinking. Before continuing to read, think about two or three questions that you would ask Carla. Following are a few questions Mr. Pennington considered, including a discussion on each.

- *Question 1: The factoring that you did is correct, but why did you factor the left side of the equation as the first step?*

This question acknowledges the correct work, yet also indirectly asks for the student to think about other "first steps" that might have been taken. This is likely to be viewed by the student as a positive approach and more helpful to Carla than asking *Why didn't you subtract 1 from both sides of the equation as the first step?* This question, while quite direct, may make Carla feel defensive. It carries the implicit message that even the first step of her work is incorrect and may send the message that she did not even know how to get started; that is, it may send the message that everything is wrong. It seems important to acknowledge that the factoring of the left side is correct, even though it is not very helpful.

- *Question 2: After you factored the left side, why did you set each factor equal to 1?*

While this question seems efficient at focusing on the relevant mathematics, it may give away too much about the error and thus not reveal sufficient information about Carla's thinking to identify her underlying error in logic.

- *Question 3: How do you know that x + 2 equals 1?*

  This question allows Carla to provide a rationale for her work; the question does not necessarily suggest that setting $x + 2$ equal to 1 is incorrect. Most students know that $1 \times 1 = 1$, so Carla may be thinking that each of the factors on the left would equal 1. On the other hand, she may believe that it does not matter what constant is on the right side; you simply set each factor equal to that constant, since this is what appears to happen when the right side of an equation is 0. Posing an alternate task—for example, *Solve* $(x + 2)(x - 3) = 6$—may help sort out Carla's logic. If she says that $x + 2 = 6$ and $x - 3 = 1$, this would be evidence of one kind of logic, but if she says that $x + 2 = 6$ and $x - 3 = 6$, this would be evidence of an alternate logic.

  The particular constellation of questions to ask Carla would depend on how she responded to whatever question is asked first. Remember that one purpose of questions or tasks is to identify a student's erroneous logic so that teachers can build instruction to help students reconceptualize their understanding.

Questions to Elicit Student Thinking When Debriefing

Another purpose of questioning is to elicit student thinking during debriefing. *Debriefing* refers to a discussion that happens, usually with the class as a whole, about the solutions to a problem and the ways that students created those solutions. We suspect that a large component of mathematics learning happens during debriefing, since that is when students can compare their own thinking to the thinking of their peers and the thinking that is highlighted by the teacher; that is, students have a chance to self-assess their progress. This self-assessment can go on "in private" in the students' minds, where there is no concern about "appearing stupid" in front of their peers. Students also have the opportunity during a debriefing to consolidate what they know (or are not sure of) as they listen to explanations.

When debriefing a task or problem that students have been working on, use probing and clarifying questions both to elicit students' thinking and to guide the conversation. Debriefing discussions can help students continue to develop their thinking when a variety of solutions are presented, but those solutions need to be carefully selected and sequenced during the debriefing discussion. Simply having "random solutions" presented may distract students from the relevant mathematics ideas. Allowing students to comment on a few different solutions will also elicit more information about the depth of their understanding. Smith and Stein identify five practices to help teachers manage discussions. "Instead of focusing on in-the-moment responses to student contributions, the practices emphasize the importance of planning" (2011, 7).

Assessment Tip ✔

The selection of solutions to display to the class and the order in which those solutions are displayed are important instructional considerations.

Five Practices for Orchestrating Productive Mathematics Discussions

1. *Anticipating* likely student responses to challenging mathematical tasks

2. *Monitoring* students' actual responses to the tasks (while students work on the tasks in pairs or small groups)

3. *Selecting* particular students to present their mathematical work during the whole-class discussion

4. *Sequencing* the student responses that will be displayed in a specific order

5. *Connecting* different students' responses and connecting responses to key mathematical ideas (Smith and Stein 2011, 8)

When students share their solutions, we develop a sense of how well the class as a whole understands the mathematics in a task, and we gather INFORMative assessment information that helps us make instructional decisions about the next task or the next lesson.

Maintaining a debriefing discussion that effectively elicits student thinking requires that teachers develop skill at posing critical questions on the fly. These questions need to help students build knowledge from the contributions that they have made to the discussion. Developing skill at posing questions not only takes experience but also reflection on the effectiveness of debriefing discussions across different kinds of content and with different kinds of students. As teachers we make many decisions based on what we hear during debriefing discussions, including "(a) moving on to new content . . . (b) trying a different approach . . . or (c) going backwards" to fill gaps (Heritage and Niemi 2006, 272).

Talk Moves

Teachers use talk moves to facilitate a class discussion in which the students' thoughts are the central focal point. When used frequently and strategically, the moves guide the students into using Mathematical Practice #3, which states that mathematically proficient students "construct viable arguments and critique the reasoning of others" (CCSS.MATH.PRACTICE.MP3). Talk moves can be found in the Math Solutions' publication *Classroom Discussions in Math: A Teacher's Guide for Using Talk Moves to Support the Common Core and More* (Chapin, O'Connor, and Anderson 2013); in a nutshell they consist of:

- Revoicing (So you're saying that . . .)

- Adding On (Who thinks they can explain why this is a good idea?)

- Waiting (Take your time, we'll wait.)

- Repeating (Can you repeat what [name] said in your own words?)

- Reasoning (Do you agree or disagree and why?)

As teacher Samantha Benson put it, "Sometimes, simply by my revoicing what the student said, 'So what I hear you saying is that . . . ,' my student can identify a problem in his or her own thinking. In my opinion, math talk moves are also math *think* moves because they require a personal, student-centered response, rather than a choral or rehearsed response. This year, I am challenging my students to use the talk moves on their own during daily class discussions and group interaction. Instead of waiting for me to ask a student if he or she agrees or disagrees, the student will state her mathematical thoughts just as she would state her opinion while having a conversation with a friend about going to the mall instead of to the movies."

→ A Closer Look

Ms. Bigney's Questions to Elicit Student Thinking with *Perimeter and Area Comparisons*

Ms. Bigney posed the following task in her high school geometry class, early in a unit on quadrilaterals. She used it to find out what students remembered about area, perimeter, and application of the Pythagorean Theorem.

> *Task: Perimeter and Area Comparisons*
>
> *Suppose a rectangle has a base of 5 cm and a height of 3 cm and a parallelogram with a 60° base angle has a base of 5 cm and a height of 3 cm. Which figure has the greater area? Which figure has the greater perimeter? Explain.*

Ms. Bigney expected students to first sketch the figures and then recognize that the "slanted sides" of the parallelogram are longer than the "vertical sides" of the rectangle, since each slanted side can be thought of as the hypotenuse of a right triangle with one of the legs being 3 cm long. So the perimeter of the parallelogram is greater, even though the areas are the same.

Ms. Bigney circulated as her students worked individually on the task. She stopped by Jenny's desk and asked, "What are you thinking?" Jenny responded that the areas and perimeters are equal since the dimensions are the same. Ms. Bigney realized that Jenny's response appeared to be based on the numerical information in the problem and did not account for the "geometric" differences in the shapes. Jenny may have been applying rules for calculating area and perimeter of a rectangle to both figures, even though the rules for perimeter are not correctly applied to the parallelogram.

Ms. Bigney thought of several questions she could ask next. Before you read on, think about how you might respond to Jenny, then complete "Reflection 4–2: Questions to Elicit Student Thinking When Debriefing" (see pages 163–164). This reflection shares other possible responses to the task from students in the same class.

Reflection 4–2

Questions to Elicit Student Thinking When Debriefing

Pages 163–164

Two questions that Ms. Bigney felt might elicit Jenny's thinking are given here; each is followed by discussion.

- Question 1: How could it help if you sketch the figures?

  This question is an alternative to simply directing Jenny to sketch the figures. The question highlights the need for a rationale for making sketches; it is intended to help her understand some advantages of making sketches. Asking this might have helped her generalize this strategy to other tasks.

- Question 2: Why are the areas equal?

  If Jenny were to respond correctly to that question, Ms. Bigney could then ask, "Why are the perimeters equal?" Of course, the incorrect part of Jenny's response concerns the perimeter, but if Ms. Bigney questioned that first, she might be revealing too much too soon about Jenny's work; namely, that the "perimeter part" is incorrect. Asking about the correct part of Jenny's response first might boost Jenny's confidence so that she would be willing to explain her thinking behind the incorrect part of her response. "Why" questions explicitly require explanations of the mathematics that supports an answer, so they are useful for revealing thinking, regardless of whether the answer being probed is correct or incorrect. In this case, if Jenny could not explain why the areas are equal, then Ms. Bigney would have learned that there is a greater deficit of knowledge than she might have expected. It is only by understanding students' thinking that teachers can provide feedback that will help students reconceptualize their mathematical understanding.

For more examples of questions that can be used effectively in debriefing discussions, see the Mathematics Assessment Project (MAP) Classroom Challenges (http://map.mathshell.org/lessons.php). In the MAP lesson *Interpreting Distance-Time Graphs*, part of the debriefing asks students to create a data table for the graph of "Tom's Journey." (See Figure 4–3.)

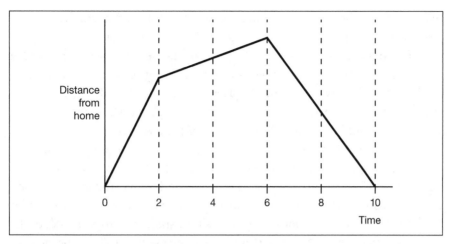

FIGURE 4-3. Graph of Tom's Journey
Source: From *Interpreting Distance-Time Graphs* (2015), http://map.mathshell.org/lessons
.php?unit=8225, © Shell Centre, The University of Nottingham.

Learn More...

Mathematics Assessment Project (MAP) Classroom Challenges reveal and develop students' understanding of key mathematical ideas and applications and offer questions that can be used effectively in debriefing discussions. For more lessons, see http://map.mathshell.org/lessons.php.

The following questions are suggested in the lesson outline and are intended to help students make connections between the graph and their suggested data. That is, these questions help to highlight important mathematics ideas.

Questions to Elicit Student Thinking When Debriefing the Task Tom's Journey

- Is Tom's speed slower or faster in this section compared to that section?

- How do you know from the graph? From the table?

- Is this speed constant? How can you tell? Do the figures in the table show a constant speed for this section of the journey?

- What units might these be measured in?

- Are the figures realistic?

Source: From *Interpreting Distance-Time Graphs* (2015), http://map.mathshell.org/lessons.php?unit=8225, © Shell Centre, The University of Nottingham.

Assessment Tip ✓

While students' thinking will likely be less sophisticated and polished than a teacher's thinking, giving students an opportunity to hear their peers' solutions provides opportunities for all students to examine and refine their own ideas.

Assessment Tip ✓

Exit cards after a debriefing discussion can encourage students to synthesize main points of the conversation.

Learn More...

Chapter 5, pages 191–193, takes a closer look at the use of exit cards. Student responsibility and self-assessment are addressed in Chapter 7.

Assessment Tip ✓

An important goal when formatively assessing is to find out the "why" of wrong answers rather than merely showing students that their responses are incorrect; it is equally important to create a classroom environment in which *both* correct and incorrect work are questioned.

Even students who are not participating directly in the discussion will benefit from thinking about the ideas highlighted in these questions.

Discussions like this can help students become better at taking advantage of debriefing as a means of reorganizing their understanding of mathematics. It may sometimes be useful at the end of a debriefing to ask students to complete an exit card or make notes about what they know and what they do not know related to the topic of the discussion.

Regardless of when questions are used, they provide an opportunity to observe and probe students' responses, ask for clarification of written work, pose "what if" questions, and focus on what individual students know and can demonstrate. An interaction may be a single question and response, or it may be a series of questions posed to a single student or some subset of the class. Clarification of students' thinking can be asked for at any point. Our task as teachers is not to convince students merely that an incorrect response is actually incorrect; we must help students understand *why* an incorrect response is incorrect.

It is also important to create a classroom environment in which *both* correct and incorrect work are questioned. In many classrooms, teachers ask questions only when an answer is incorrect, so students learn that if they are questioned, their work must be incorrect. The purpose of conversations as a formative assessment tool is to reveal the mathematical thinking behind a response. Sometimes a correct response is generated by incorrect or incomplete thinking. Failure to make that incorrect or incomplete thinking visible when a correct response has been generated can lead to future difficulties, especially in learning more complicated mathematics.

Questions to Highlight Mathematics Ideas

Sometimes in conversations it is appropriate to probe students' thinking in a generic way; for example, by asking *How did you get that answer?* or *Why did you decide to do that?* Generic clarifying and probing questions alone are not likely to be adequate for revealing the depth of a student's thinking, though they are a starting point for teachers just beginning to use conversations as formative assessment. These generic questions seem to probe the meaning that a student intended to communicate, but they lack the specificity that might be needed in some situations. More often, it is better to plan questions that highlight the specific mathematics that students are expected to learn. Some of these questions can be created during instructional planning, but some questions have to be created "on the fly" in response to specific comments that students make.

> **Assessment Tip** ✓
>
> Generic clarifying and probing questions are starting points for using conversations as formative assessment; progressing to more specific questions to highlight key mathematics ideas will reveal more about whether a student's incorrect responses are clear representations of a misunderstanding or misrepresentations of clear understanding.

→ A Closer Look

Mr. Salik's Questions to Highlight Mathematics Ideas with *Repeating Decimals*

Mr. Salik assigned the following task to his seventh-grade class. He wanted to explore decimal expansions of fractions,

> Mr. Salik derived this learning target from the CCSSM standard "Convert a rational number to a decimal using long division; know that the decimal form of a rational number terminates in 0s or eventually repeats" (CCSS.MATH .CONTENT.7.NS.A.2.D).

Task: Repeating Decimals

Both $\frac{7}{13}$ and $\frac{7}{130}$ have repeating decimal representations. Which one has more digits in the repeating pattern (or repeating cycle)? Explain.

Mr. Salik hoped that his students would realize that $\frac{7}{130} = \left(\frac{1}{10}\right)\left(\frac{7}{13}\right)$, understanding that the decimal expansion for $\frac{7}{130}$ is one-tenth as great as the decimal expansion of $\frac{7}{13}$. That is, the decimal expansion for $\frac{7}{130}$ is the same as the decimal expansion of $\frac{7}{13}$ except the decimal point is shifted one place to the left. The number of digits in the repeating cycle is the same for both fractions:

$$\frac{7}{13} = 0.5384615386461\ldots$$

$$\frac{7}{130} = 0.05384615386461\ldots$$

Mr. Salik also knew that many of his students would first reach for a calculator without much analysis of the mathematics of the task. They might simply write out the decimal expansions, but then they may not be able to explain why the number of repeating digits is the same. So Mr. Salik planned questions that might help his students focus on the relevant mathematics ideas. (See Figure 4–4.)

Question	Why Ask?	Possible Responses	Follow-Up Question	Why Ask?
How are $\frac{7}{13}$ and $\frac{7}{130}$ related?	to focus on the proportional relationship	$\frac{7}{13}$ is bigger	How many times bigger?	to highlight the need for understanding the proportional relationship
		$\frac{7}{13}$ is 10 times as large	What does that tell you about the two decimal expansions?	to call attention to the placement of the decimal point
How are the two calculator displays related?	to highlight the position of the decimal points	One has an extra zero after the decimal.	What does that extra zero tell you about the relative sizes of the fractions?	to help connect the decimal expansions to the sizes of the fractions
How do you know when a decimal expansion starts to repeat?	to assess students' understanding of fractions and their decimal expansions	You see repeating digits.	How many digits must be the same before you are sure you know how many digits repeat?	to help students avoid jumping to conclusions based on too little evidence

FIGURE 4–4. Questions to Highlight Students' Thinking About Fractions

Mr. Salik felt that many of his students might need considerable time to work out the relationships so that they could explain why the numbers of repeating digits in the two decimal expansions are the same. He felt it was important to check their understanding of the key mathematics ideas, so he chose a second task that would provide information quickly:

Task: Repeating Decimals Follow-Up

How many digits are there in the repeating cycle of $\frac{7}{1300}$ or $\frac{7}{13000}$?

Reflection 4-3

Questions to Highlight Mathematics Ideas: Decimal Expansions

Pages 165–166

There are several ways that Mr. Salik might have extended the mathematics ideas about decimal expansions. Before you read on, think about what tasks you might use and how challenging those tasks might be. Then complete "Reflection 4–3: Questions to Highlight Mathematics Ideas: Decimal Expansions" (see pages 165–166).

Highlighting mathematics ideas is also very important when debriefing problem-solving tasks. For the following task, the critical mathematical idea is that the area of a triangle remains unchanged if one of the vertices "moves" along a line parallel to the base opposite that vertex. An understanding of this idea can be developed with activities that involve triangles made on a geoboard, drawn on grid paper, or displayed using dynamic geometry software.

Assessment Tip ✓

When debriefing tasks, make a list for yourself of students whose responses indicate incomplete understanding.

Task: The Fence Problem

Two landowners, Mr. Green and Ms. Sanchez, agree to put up a new fence between their properties. Rather than replacing the fence as it now is (with a third fencepost), they want to put in a fence that is straight, thus requiring only the two endpoints.

Help them figure out where to position the new fence so that the areas of the two landowners' properties remain the same.

(continued)

(continued from page 157)

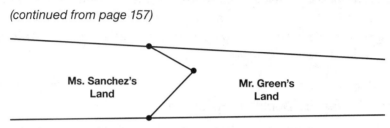

Source: Adapted from TIMSS 1999 Video Study (www.timssvideo.com/67).

Draw a diagram showing where the new fence should be placed and explain how you know the new placement has not changed the area of either piece of the properties.

As students work on this task, questions like the following might help students focus on the key mathematics ideas.

Assessment Tip ✓

One key to effective questioning is to refrain from being directive when helping students focus on relevant mathematics. We need to support students in focusing on key ideas without restricting students' thinking.

Questions to Elicit Student Thinking When Debriefing The Fence Problem

- What is important about the shape created by the two fences in the drawing?

- Are there any auxiliary lines that might help you find a solution?

- What properties of triangles will cause them to have the same area?

- What transformations to a shape leave its area unchanged?

Managing Discussions of Homework

One of the stereotypes of high school mathematics instruction is that the teacher begins class by going over the answers to homework and then asks, "Are there any questions?" This is often followed by students' questions of the form, "Can you work problem 14?" with the teacher then demonstrating one solution, probably the most efficient solution, for that problem. Unfortunately, efficient solutions may not connect with the ways that many of the students thought about the problem. Requests for the teacher to show a solution typically come from only a few students, while the rest of the class "tunes out." This "performance by the teacher" may go on for a large chunk of the class time. Then the teacher rushes through a demonstration of the mathematics for the intended lesson, assigns homework problems, and dismisses the class because time has run out. This scenario might not happen every day in every classroom, but it happens often enough that it has become the vision of high school mathematics instruction in the minds of many parents.

One unfortunate effect of asking, "Are there any questions on the homework?" is that it's a few students who determine what mathematics gets discussed. It is better for teachers to determine ahead of time which homework problems will be demonstrated or discussed in class. One criterion for making this decision is to choose homework problems that "set up" the students' thinking so that they are ready to learn the new mathematics ideas that are the focus of the lesson. For example, the chosen homework problems might cover prerequisite material for the lesson, illustrate ways of reasoning about the ideas, or begin the development of an overall perspective on the key mathematics ideas in the unit.

Creating and Maintaining Anecdotal Records

One major issue with observations and conversations is that there is no written record of what has transpired. It may be difficult for a student or the teacher to reflect accurately on what happened, since any reconstruction of a conversation, either by the teacher or the student, may be flawed. Keeping a few anecdotal records helps both teachers and students to reflect on students' progress over time. Anecdotal records are especially useful for English language learners, students involved in targeted interventions, or those with Individualized Education Plans (IEPs) that require documentation, since it is difficult to remember and reconstruct conversations.

Ideas for Creating Anecdotal Records

Class Printouts
Highlight information about students' errors related to specific mathematics on a class printout; use the printout to guide your planning of additional lessons on the topic.

Files
Create files with samples of individual students' work; refer to your files to guide targeted interventions.

Index Cards
Make notes on index cards; these can remind you to talk with a small group about a common misconception revealed in an assignment.

Sticky Notes or Mailing Labels
Record comments and things to watch for in subsequent lessons. You can put these notes in your planning book.

Technology
Use technology to keep notes that will help you plan not only for the current year but also in future years. Electronic notes would also be easy to share with colleagues.

Anecdotal records are a matter of personal choice—as the teacher, it's likely up to you to decide how, when, and whether to keep them. It is important to have a balance between encouraging students to keep records—for example, in journals—and expecting teachers to make notes about conversations. Keep in mind that making notes should never be "busy work"; we need to use anecdotal records to help us meet the needs of individuals as we work with all students in our classes.

Take a moment to think about the ways you create anecdotal records and then complete "Reflection 4–4: Creating and Maintaining Anecdotal Records" (see page 167). If you don't create and maintain anecdotal records, consider using this reflection to help you think about the benefit they might bring to your formative assessment journey.

Reflection 4–4

Creating and Maintaining Anecdotal Records

Page 167

INFORMing My Practice

Conversations, intentional listening, and questioning are critical components of *oral* formative assessments. They support our daily opportunities to learn more about our students' thinking and modify our instructional plans to promote greater opportunities for student learning. Making use of intentional listening and carefully planning how we will use questions allows us to quickly recognize student misconceptions, become better INFORMed, and make adjustments to our lessons. Think about the ideas in this chapter related to oral INFORMative assessments. We've provided "Reflection 4–5: INFORMing My Practice: Strategies to Support Oral INFORMative Assessments" (see pages 168–169) as a place for you to record your thinking.

Reflection 4–5

INFORMing My Practice: Strategies to Support Oral INFORMative Assessments

Pages 168–169

Reflection 4-1: Questions to Engage All Students

Read the following task. Think about how you would solve the task and then consider the questions that follow.

A Warm-Up Task

Which graph has the greater range over the domain interval [3, 6]? Be prepared to explain your reasoning. $y = \frac{1}{2}x^2$ *or* $y = \frac{1}{3}x^3$

---

1. List some ways that you think your students might solve this task.

2. Which of these questions would you choose as the lead-off question for discussion of the task? Explain your choice.

   How many of you chose the quadratic function? The cubic function?

   What is the range of a function?

   What is the range of a function over a domain interval?

   What characteristics of a function influence its range?

   How can you determine the range of a function over a domain interval?

Reflection 4-2: Questions to Elicit Student Thinking When Debriefing

Read and solve the following task. Then answer the questions for the two student work examples that follow.

Task: Perimeter and Area Comparisons

Suppose a rectangle has a base of 5 cm and a height of 3 cm and a parallelogram with a 60° base angle has a base of 5 cm and a height of 3 cm. Which figure has the greater area? Which figure has the greater perimeter? Explain.

Student Work Example A

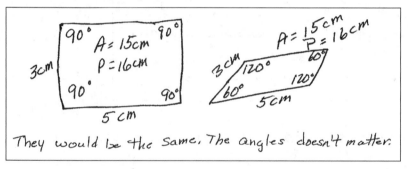

They would be the same. The angles doesn't matter.

1. What is the primary mathematical error or misunderstanding in this response?

2. Is this an appropriate sample to show during debriefing? Explain.

3. If so, what questions might you pose to help students understand the primary error?

(continued)

Reflection 4-2: Questions to Elicit Student Thinking When Debriefing (continued)

Student Work Example B

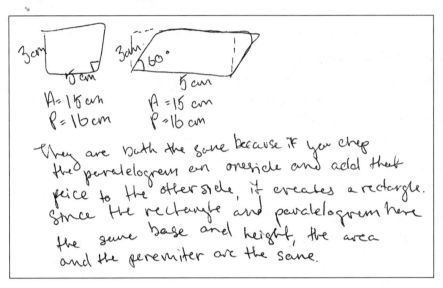

They are both the same because if you chop the paralelogram on one side and add that piece to the other side, it creates a rectangle. Since the rectangle and paralelogram have the same base and height, the area and the perimiter are the same.

4. What is the primary mathematical error or misunderstanding in this response? How does it compare to the error in Example A above?

5. What questions might you pose during the debriefing to help students understand the differences in the errors for Examples A and B?

Reflection 4-3: Questions to Highlight Mathematics Ideas: Decimal Expansions

Following are tasks related to the mathematics idea of decimal expansions. Solve the tasks and think about questions you might ask students to highlight the important mathematics ideas in these tasks.

Task 1

How are the decimal expansions of $\frac{1}{59}$ and $\frac{1}{5900}$ related?

(Hint: Don't try to find the decimal expansion of $\frac{1}{59}$.

$\frac{1}{59} = 0.01694915254237288135593220338983050847457627118$
    864406779661 . . .)

⌐ Learn More ... ⌐

See math.uconn.edu
/~kconrad/math3240f09
/decimalfil to find
decimal equivalents of
fractions, including the
expansion for $\frac{1}{59}$.

Task 2

a. *Solve for n (in fraction form):* $\frac{7}{33} = n \times \frac{7}{11}$

b. *The decimal expansion of $\frac{7}{11}$ is 0.63636363 . . . . Without using a calculator, use your solution for n to write the decimal expansions of $\frac{7}{33}$.*

Task 3

a. *Solve for n (in fraction form):* $\frac{7}{22} = n \times \frac{7}{11}$

b. *The decimal expansion of $\frac{7}{11}$ is 0.63636363 . . . . Without using a calculator, use your solution for n to write the decimal expansions of $\frac{7}{22}$.*

(continued)

Reflection 4-3: Questions to Highlight Mathematics Ideas: Decimal Expansions (continued)

1. How difficult do you think it would be for your students to solve these tasks?

2. What questions might you ask to highlight the mathematics ideas in these tasks?

3. What parts of students' solutions would you highlight during a debriefing of these tasks?

4. What generalization would you want students to internalize from solving these tasks?

Reflection 4-4: Creating and Maintaining Anecdotal Records

1. Do you create and maintain anecdotal records (informal notes made during class or when reviewing written work)? Why or why not? (If not, use this reflection to think about how implementing such might benefit you in formatively assessing.)

2. What are some of the ways you keep (or could keep) anecdotal records?

3. How do (or could) anecdotal records help you in planning for your class(es)?

4. How can anecdotal records be useful in supporting an individual student's learning?

Reflection 4-5: INFORMing My Practice: Strategies to Support Oral INFORMative Assessments

Think about the chapter you just read. How often do you use oral formative assessments, and in what ways? Use the following checklist to help you reflect on both your current uses of oral assessments and ways that you might use oral assessments in the future.

A Teacher's Self-Checklist: Using Oral INFORMative Assessments

Usually	Sometimes	Rarely	Never	Oral Formative Assessment Actions
				Talk less and ask more.
				Listen intentionally.
				Observe students as they work.
				Eavesdrop often.
				Use roving conversations.
				Use one-on-one conversations to probe thinking.
				Schedule one-on-one interviews.
				When planning lessons, also plan questions.
				Identify misconceptions and errors to listen for.
				Differentiate between misconceptions and incomplete understanding.
				Use questions to engage all students.
				Use questions to clarify and probe student thinking.
				Use questions to elicit student thinking when debriefing.
				Use questions to highlight mathematics ideas.
				Avoid imposing my thinking.
				Probe both correct and incorrect responses.
				Support students in self-correcting errors.
				Create and maintain anecdotal records.

(continued)

Reflection 4–5: INFORMing My Practice: Strategies to Support Oral INFORMative Assessments (continued)

Think about the chapter you just read. Use this space to record your ideas.

Ideas about the importance of oral INFORMative assessments:

Changes in my thinking about INFORMative assessment:

Ideas I envision becoming a more important part of my practice:

Questions I have:

Frustrations/concerns I have:

Strategies to Support Written INFORMative Assessments

In this chapter we continue the discussion of assessment strategies by focusing on written INFORMative assessments. Students create written work in response to tasks, questions, and assessments posed by teachers. Classwork, homework, quizzes, and major tests require students to demonstrate their understanding and use of mathematics facts, concepts, and procedures in writing. Some written work requires routine application of algorithms and procedures, while other tasks may require a solution to a problem or complex situation that involves multiple decisions and several steps to reach the solution. The visible record supports student self-assessment, allowing both teachers and students to make inferences about what students know and can do. This chapter specifically looks at two lenses— the diagnostic lens and the monitoring lens—through which we can examine students' written work.

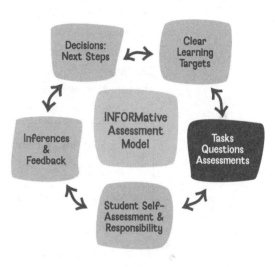

Overview

Formative Assessment of Students' Written Work

In addition to the oral assessments discussed in the previous chapter, examining students' written work is a powerful way to implement INFORMative assessment. As teachers we can make inferences about what students know and are able to do based on students' written work. We can ask ourselves, "When I look at students' written work, what do I learn about their thinking and reasoning?" There are two primary lenses through which teachers make inferences from students' written work: the diagnostic lens and the monitoring lens.

Two Lenses for Examining Students' Written Work

Diagnostic: inferences about what students already know

Monitoring: inferences about what students are learning

Diagnostic work is done in preparation for teaching; it is designed to determine what students know or do not know so that instruction can be better targeted to the needs of students. *Monitoring* is what happens on a day-to-day basis. It includes making inferences about what students know, determining what task might be posed next, and deciding whether reteaching is needed. In the following sections we take a closer look at what it means to examine student work through a diagnostic lens and a monitoring lens.

Strategy 1: Examining Students' Written Work Through a Diagnostic Lens

Diagnostic assessments are valuable for planning instruction of a new topic and for identifying the depth of understanding of content that students studied in previous years. The primary purpose is to generate information about students' thinking so that instructional planning can be better focused on the needs of those students. The following sections focus on several types of diagnostic assessments.

<table>
<tr><td>

Types of Diagnostic Assessments

- Pretests

- Homework for Diagnosing

- Writing Prompts for Diagnosing

</td></tr>
</table>

Assessment Tip ✓

When doing diagnostic assessments, use tasks to probe depth of student knowledge *prior* to setting up instruction.

Pretests

Often it is useful to develop a pretest of a few items—a diagnostic assessment—that can be given to students prior to new instruction on a topic. This can be administered in class or as homework, and use of notes (or the textbook) might or might not be allowed. The items should seek evidence of knowledge about mathematics ideas that support the learning targets. That means that the teacher has identified long-term goals, created clear learning targets, and determined the kinds of evidence that would demonstrate mastery of those targets. The items might be multiple-choice, open-ended, or a combination of the two, depending on the nature of the targets and the evidence of accomplishment.

┌ **Learn More...** ┐

Chapter 3 offers more information about identifying long-term goals and creating clear learning targets.

For diagnostic assessments to be practical, responses should be easily categorized in a way that does not consume too much planning time. For example:

1. If you ask students to sketch a parallelogram, you could categorize responses as (a) square, (b) rectangle not a square, and (c) parallelogram not a rectangle.

2. If you ask students to find the slope of $2y = 3x - 6$, you could categorize responses as (a) correct ($\frac{3}{2}$), (b) inverse ($\frac{2}{3}$), (c) y-intercept (3), or (d) other.

3. If you ask students to give the probability of rolling a 5 with two dice, you could categorize responses as (a) correct and unreduced ($\frac{4}{36}$), (b) correct and reduced ($\frac{1}{9}$), (c) failure to count repeats ($\frac{2}{36}$), (d) off by a count of 1 ($\frac{3}{36}$ or $\frac{5}{36}$), or (e) other.

The main purpose of categorizing responses is to assess areas of strength and weakness, both for individual students and for the class as a whole; that is, to make inferences about the depth of students' knowledge prior to instruction. This will help with planning for appropriate use of instructional time and will provide answers for questions such as the following:

Questions to Think About When Examining Students' Written Work on Pretests

- What ideas need to be emphasized?

- What ideas need explicit practice?

- What ideas can be lightly reviewed?

- Are there obvious misconceptions evident in students' work?

- Which extensions of ideas might help those students who enter the instruction with the best understanding?

Assessment Tip ✔

Use a diagnostic assessment such as a pretest to determine what students do or do not know, not to determine whether they have mastered the content.

Students should know that these items are not to be used in determining grades; after all, one purpose of a diagnostic assessment is to determine what students do or do not know, not to determine whether they have mastered the content. Scoring items will help identify particular students who are likely to need additional assistance as the instruction progresses, though no grade is associated with the score.

A Note About Grading

Teachers collect an enormous amount of information from students during the teaching of a course. Observations and conversations in the classroom and information from students' daily assignments, quizzes, and tests are all part of monitoring students' progress. Often students' work is graded, but teachers can also look beyond the grades for evidence of students' understanding.

As teachers we should be alert to the possibility that grading student work may be more likely to discourage students than to provide information for instructional planning. For example, one purpose of a diagnostic assessment is to uncover what students do not understand or understand incorrectly. Grading such an assessment defeats this purpose. Sometimes you want students to explore a task in order to get a "feel" for the underlying mathematics ideas. This work, too, should probably not be graded. Sometimes you pose a task for the purpose of helping students to self-assess their progress toward instructional goals. For example, when students respond to exit cards, grading defeats the purpose of the assignment.

Students' errors and mistakes provide information for instructional planning. We encourage teachers to think about going beyond mere grading to analyze students' thinking.

Learn More...
See Chapter 7 for more discussion of grading and what it represents.

The task that follows might be used as a pretest to provide information about students' understandings of linear functions. The information generated could assist teachers in planning instruction about functions.

Task: Relating Graphs

How are the graphs of $y = 2x + 7$ *and* $y = 2x - 5$ *related?*

Students should recognize that the graphs are lines that are parallel with y-intercepts that are 12 units apart. However, some students might say only that the two graphs are lines, without noting that they are parallel. Teachers would have to decide how much review of the properties of linear functions is needed. If most students simply look at the function rules and make correct statements about the graphs, then instruction can proceed at a rapid pace. If most students sketch graphs of the functions on grid paper (or graph them with technology tools), then the teacher might decide to provide additional instruction to help students relate the properties of the graphs with the elements of the function rules.

A diagnostic assessment should not be a "black hole" from which no information is ever shared with students. For a diagnostic assessment to be most effective, feedback about the performance of the class should be provided. Acknowledging what most students in the class seem to understand can support individual students in self-assessing their own understanding. A statement as simple as, *Almost everyone in the class seems to know the characteristics of equilateral triangles, so we won't need to spend time relearning that* is positive reinforcement for the knowledge that students bring to learning new content.

Look ahead to content you are planning to teach in the next few weeks and design a brief pretest to help determine what students already know about the learning targets. Use "Reflection 5–1, Examining Students' Written Work Through a Diagnostic Pretest" (see page 196) to help you with this process.

Reflection 5–1

Examining Students' Written Work Through a Diagnostic Pretest

Page 196

Homework for Diagnosing

Diagnostic assessments do not always need to be posed as a test; routine homework tasks can be used for diagnostic purposes. Even in that form, however, diagnostic assessment should happen prior to, or along with, instructional planning so that the information gathered can influence instruction. Following are several examples of homework tasks and the ways the corresponding student work can be used for diagnostic assessment.

→ A Closer Look

Mr. Hidalgo's Homework Assessment with *Modeling with a Graph*

Learn More…

Mathematics Assessment Project (MAP) lessons include pre-assessments that serve diagnostic purposes. For more on the lessons, see the Mathematics Assessment Project website, specifically http://map.mathshell.org.

Mr. Hidalgo has found Mathematics Assessment Project (MAP) lessons to be especially helpful in planning tasks for diagnostic assessments that can be given to students as homework. Many MAP lessons provide a pre-assessment that teachers can use to assess students' "entering knowledge." The pre-assessments are intended to be given to the entire class, often as a homework assignment, so that a sense of the class can be gained. The task that follows is part of the MAP lesson *Representing Functions of Everyday Situations*. Mr. Hidalgo selected this task to assess his students' knowledge of graphs of functions. He wanted to know how well his students could sketch graphs that are described in words.

Task: Modeling with a Graph

1. Sketch a graph to model the following situation. Think about the shape of the graph and whether it should be a continuous line or not.

Photographer

For each "shoot" a photographer charges a fixed fee for expenses, then a fixed amount for each hour (or part of an hour).

x = the time a "shoot" takes in hours

y = the total amount the photographer charges

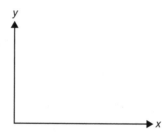

Source: From *Representing Functions of Everyday Situations* (2015), http://map .mathshell.org/lessons.php?unit=9260, © Shell Centre, The University of Nottingham.

When Mr. Hidalgo examined his students' responses to this task, he noticed some common issues revealed by their written work (issues like these are also noted in the corresponding MAP lesson plan):

- Students have a limited repertoire of graphs.

- Students draw continuous lines for all graphs.

- Students' graphs cut the axes at inappropriate places.

Mr. Hidalgo's analysis of his students' responses to this homework task allowed him to pinpoint mathematics ideas that should be the focus of his instruction. To help Mr. Hidalgo organize his inferences, he created a chart of potential errors and then recorded the names of students who made each error. (See Figure 5–1 on the next page.)

Error	Students
limited repertoire of graphs	Raoul, Alice, Derrick
draws continuous lines for all graphs	Scott, Pat
incorrect intercepts	George, Meghan, Lisa, Nadia

FIGURE 5–1. Mr. Hidalgo's Chart for Recalling Student Errors

The chart became a reference of errors for Mr. Hidalgo to address as he continued with his instruction. Teachers might also choose to debrief the pre-assessment directly or lead a wrap-up discussion at the end of the lesson.

 A Closer Look

Mrs. Samuelson's Homework Assessment with *Lines and Angles*

Mrs. Samuelson assigned the following task for homework the week before she began her lessons on proof of theorems about lines and angles.

Learn More...

Breyfogle and Lynch (2010), Fuys, Geddes, and Tischler (1988), and Usiskin (1982) provide detailed discussion of geometric thinking as organized in the van Hiele levels.

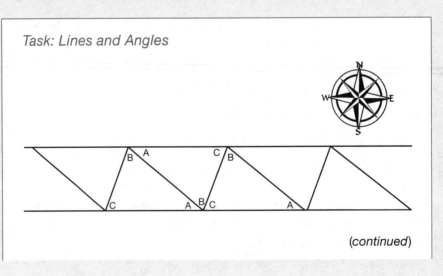

Task: Lines and Angles

(continued)

(continued from page 178)

- *What do you notice about the two horizontal lines?*

- *What do you notice about the line segments tilting from NW to SE?*

- *What do you notice about the line segments tilting from NE to SW?*

- *Highlight several pairs of alternate interior angles.*

Lines and Angles relates to the standard "Prove theorems about lines and angles. *Theorems include: vertical angles are congruent; when a transversal crosses parallel lines, alternate interior angles are congruent and corresponding angles are congruent; points on a perpendicular bisector of a line segment are exactly those equidistant from the segment's endpoints"* (CCSS. MATH.CONTENT.HSG. CO.C.9). The diagram specifically relates to the CCSSM standard "Use informal arguments to establish facts about the angle sum and exterior angle of triangles, about the angles created when parallel lines are cut by a transversal, and the angle-angle criterion for similarity of triangles. *For example, arrange three copies of the same triangle so that the sum of the three angles appears to form a line, and give an argument in terms of transversals why this is so"* (CCSS.MATH .CONTENT.8.G.A.5).

The task requires students to informally analyze the diagram. The diagram shows the three angles of a triangle, angles A, B, and C, appearing to form a straight line or straight angle along the bottom of the diagram. The questions posed provide opportunities for Mrs. Samuelson's students to tell what they know about the relationships illustrated in the diagram.

The written work Mrs. Samuelson received from her students provided data about what they remembered as well as evidence about their skill at writing coherent arguments, an essential skill for proof. Mrs. Samuelson used a chart to quickly categorize her students' work. (See Figure 5–2.)

Noted horizontal lines as parallel	Noted "tilted lines" as congruent and parallel
卌 |	卌　||||
Irrelevant comments (pull group)	*Explained why tilted lines are parallel and congruent (extensions needed)*
Julio, Margo, Katie, Joe	*Carmen, Edwardo*

FIGURE 5–2. Mrs. Samuelson's Chart for Recalling Student Errors

The task Mrs. Samuelson used is similar to those that help reveal students' geometric thinking as outlined by Pierre van Hiele. Knowing the van Hiele levels of geometric thinking can help in the planning of geometry assessment and instructional tasks.

A Closer Look

Mr. Gore's Homework Assessment with *Write a Division Problem*

Some concepts are so important that they arch over several grades. For example, we expect students in middle and high school to have a clear understanding of the meaning of division, but some students do not. Since there are numerous concepts that rely on this understanding, such as rational functions and division of polynomials, it is helpful to use diagnostic tasks to assess what students really know. Mr. Gore decided to do just this early in his algebra class so that his instruction on the arithmetic with polynomials could be targeted to match his students' level of understanding. He knew that most of his students could carry out relatively simple division computations, so he selected a task that focused on the understanding of what those computations mean.

Mr. Gore first assigned *Write a Division Problem* for his students to complete as homework. The task provides a window into the ways that students think about the meaning of division.

Assessment Tip ✓

Diagnostic assessments should target specific mathematics in order to inform instruction.

Task: Write a Division Problem

Write a whole-number division computation so that the answer is 34 r. 38. If it is not possible to do so, explain why not.

Mr. Gore hoped that his students would recognize that since the remainder is 38, the divisor must be greater than 38; that is, the remainder of a division problem is always less than the divisor. This understanding is an important outcome for division instruction in elementary grades, but it is an outcome that is often not achieved by students. (Sample division computations with quotients of 34 r. 38 are: 3438 ÷ 100 = 34 r. 38; 1364 ÷ 39 = 34 r. 38; 2248 ÷ 65 = 34 r. 38; and 41688 ÷ 1225 = 34 r. 38.)

Mr. Gore anticipated that in response to this pre-assessment task, some of his students would be uncomfortable because the remainder part of the quotient is larger than the integer part of the quotient, and they might say that the answer of 34 r. 38 is not possible. Other students might attempt to create an acceptable division problem by using trial and error, often trying "easy" divisors such as single-digit numbers. These attempts would be unsuccessful, since the divisor *must be* greater than 38.

Mr. Gore quickly reviewed the students' written work and tallied their responses. The responses included students who (a) gave an appropriate example and stated that the remainder is always less than the divisor, (b) said the answer is impossible, (c) believed that the answer is possible but couldn't identify a correct example, and (d) stated that problems with any divisor greater than 38 could result in a quotient of 34 r. 38.

Mr. Gore realized there are many possible questions he might ask to probe students' thinking about this task. The purpose of his questions is to better understand students' thinking—not lead them to a correct answer. Some questions Mr. Gore noted are:

- Why do you believe this answer is not possible?

- Why did you say the remainder always has to be less than the divisor?

- Why did you choose that divisor?

- What information does the remainder give you about the division problem?

- What is the relationship between the divisor and the remainder in division?

- How could you use the two parts of the quotient to help reconstruct the problem?

- Could the divisor be less than 25? How do you know?

- A student in another class used a divisor of 80. Do you think that is a good choice? Why or why not?

Students' lack of depth of understanding of division may be due to the fact that they probably have been only rarely asked to assign meaning to a division computation. They may have been only asked to carry out computations. But as we expose students to more sophisticated mathematics ideas in high school, the depth of students' conceptual understanding is critical. We want students to be able to think about "unusual" or "nonroutine" applications of those ideas as well as to complete traditional computations accurately. Choosing nonroutine, but still easily accessible, tasks—like Mr. Gore did—is one way of revealing depth of understanding.

Reflection 5–2

Homework for
Diagnosing
Students'
Understanding of
Multiplication of
Mixed Numbers

Page 197

Think about all the example tasks you just read, then turn to "Reflection 5–2: Homework for Diagnosing Students' Understanding of Multiplication of Mixed Numbers" (see page 197). In this reflection four items were used to diagnose students' understanding of multiplication of mixed numbers. There are similarities in the mathematical structure of multiplication of mixed numbers and the mathematical structure of multiplication of binomials. As you complete this reflection, explore the similarities and think about how you would use these items to diagnostically assess students' understanding.

Writing Prompts for Diagnosing

Sometimes teachers need to pre-assess students' understanding more quickly than a pretest or homework would allow; one such strategy is to use a writing prompt. Students might write on half pages or index cards, and they might or might not be asked to identify themselves. Since students are not likely to write much, especially if the prompt is used at the end of a class, it is possible to read through the responses quickly during instructional planning.

For example, prior to instruction on complex numbers, we might want to know what students remember about rational and irrational numbers. We could use the following writing prompt:

Is $\sqrt{2}$ rational or irrational? Explain how you know.

The following responses from four ninth-grade students may be representative of students' answers to this writing prompt. (See Figure 5–3.)

Based on these responses, students seem to have working definitions of rational and irrational numbers that need clarification and elaboration. Instruction will need to address the potential inaccuracies of students' thinking and help them refine and extend their understanding.

Reggie's Response	Kissie's Response
It is Irrational because it can't be written as a fraction	I think it is rational because it doesn't repeat.
Katie's Response	Jovan's Response
the square root of 2 is irrational because the decimal number doesn't terminate or repeat.	The square root of 2 is irrational because you cannot round the decimal point off to a fraction. The number goes on and on for a while.

FIGURE 5-3 Students' Responses to a Writing Prompt About $\sqrt{2}$

Strategy 2: Examining Students' Written Work Through a Monitoring Lens

As teachers we all monitor students' progress. Sometimes this is based mainly on counts of correct/incorrect responses or scores on quizzes or tests. Sometimes it is based on the amount of time students seem to need to complete a task. Sometimes it is based on the looks on students' faces as we explain an idea or work a problem. We have all seen that "deer in the headlights" look; noticing that expression on students' faces is often useful in assessing whether students are catching on to whatever idea is the focus of instruction.

When teachers use the *monitoring lens*, they are most often assessing the progress of the class as a whole in order to determine whether the instruction is "working" and progress is being made toward attaining the learning goals. This is somewhat different than assessing the thinking of an individual student. We are, of course, interested in the effects of instruction on individual students, but the monitoring lens is mainly about the effects

— Learn More...

"One of the starkest realities all teachers face is the fact that at any given moment, in any given class, more than half of our students are very likely not seeing, feeling, or processing the mathematics that we are teaching in the same way that we are seeing, feeling, and processing it. Call it 'learning styles' or 'alternative modes of learning'; it comes down to different brains work in different ways."
—*Accessible Mathematics: Ten Instructional Shifts That Raise Student Achievement* (Leinwand 2009, 102)

of instruction on the class as a group; information about the thinking of individual students will be revealed in the process.

Rather than waiting for a test at the end of an instructional sequence to determine the success or lack of accomplishment of students, a teacher thinking in monitoring-lens mode can analyze student work and "remediate" before remediation becomes necessary. Scoring should focus on classifying errors as conceptual, procedural, fact-based, or language-based. Through the same monitoring lens teachers differentiate among incomplete understandings, miscommunication of understandings, and incorrect conceptual or procedural approaches.

Questions to Think About When Examining Students' Written Work in Tasks for Monitoring

1. Are there problems that several students are missing? If so, do I have any ideas about why that is happening?

2. Are there obvious misconceptions that students are exhibiting?

3. What am I learning about students' thinking by examining the responses?

Learn More...

Chapter 6 addresses the issue of what mathematics a task requires versus what mathematics a task allows. This is an important distinction when choosing tasks for monitoring.

Assessment Tip ✅

When a large percentage of the students' responses surprise you, ask yourself (a) Did the assessment test what you taught? or (b) Did the instruction provide sufficient opportunities for students to make sense of the mathematics?

Tasks for Monitoring

Monitoring often requires more than one assessment item. Multiple sources of evidence (i.e., performance on more than one task) will increase the reliability of decisions. Although the monitoring lens can be applied to any task or daily assignment, tasks that are likely to show the depth of students' understanding are more effective in revealing errors that may need remediating. Following we explore several examples of monitoring tasks.

A Monitoring Task: *Determining Quartiles*

Consider the following standard, which deals with box plots: "Display numerical data in plots on a number line, including dot plots, histograms, and box plots" (www.corestandards.org/Math/Content/6/SP/B/4/). A critical idea that is prerequisite for successful creation of box plots is determining quartiles for a set of data. If students cannot do that, they will not be successful at creating accurate box plots, even though they may be successful at interpreting a correctly drawn box plot. As with many prerequisite skills, quartiles are not explicitly mentioned in most grade 6 standards. However, prior to assigning practice exercises about the creation of box plots, as teachers we might want to use monitoring tasks like the following one.

Task: Determining Quartiles

Find the quartiles for this set of data:

{1, 2, 3, 3, 4, 4, 4, 4, 5, 5, 5, 6, 6, 6, 12, 14, 14, 14, 17, 17, 17, 19, 19, 19, 36, 48, 48, 48, 50, 50}

Determining Quartiles relates to the standard "Display numerical data in plots on a number line, including dot plots, histograms, and box plots" (CCSS.MATH .CONTENT.6.SP.B.4).

The particular choice of a data set in this task raises two key issues:

- How do you find the median when there is an even number of data points?
- What values are included in each half of the distribution?

Finding out how students deal with these issues will suggest what instruction or review is needed about determining quartiles. Students need to understand how to compute a median for a data set with an odd number of data values and for a data set with an even number of data values. In the task just given, the median of the entire data set is the average of 12 and 14, and then students need to know whether this value (13) is to be included in either, both, or neither of the halves of the data (in this case, neither). Students need to understand that these are conventions developed over time by mathematicians; it is not information that students would be expected to discover or deduce.

A Monitoring Task: *End Behavior of Functions*

Choosing or creating tasks to monitor students' understanding means that as teachers we think about the mathematics in the task and the possible ways that students might reason to find a solution. We also consider the implications of wrong answers. For example, suppose instruction asks students to describe end behavior of functions. It is important to determine if students can generalize the understanding they have developed. The first question in the following task should be familiar to the students, but the second and third questions might test the depth of their understanding.

The learning target "show end behavior of functions" is addressed by a standard in the "Interpreting Functions" domain: "Graph polynomial functions, identifying zeros when suitable factorizations are available, and showing end behavior" (CCSS .MATH.CONTENT.HSF .IF.C.7.C). The use of fractional exponents goes beyond the scope of the standards in CCSSM, so it would not be fair to "test" students on a task like this; however, the questions serve as good monitoring or extension tasks.

> Task: End Behavior of Functions
>
> 1. Which function rises more steeply for large values of x: $y = x^5$ or $y = x^7$? Why?
>
> 2. Which function rises more steeply for large values of x: $y = x^{3.5}$ or $y = x^{3.7}$? Why?
>
> 3. Which function rises more steeply for large values of x: $y = x^{\frac{1}{5}}$ or $y = x^{\frac{1}{7}}$? Why?

At a simplistic level, the task asks students to focus on the power of x and imagine what the relative end behavior would be for two functions with different powers of x. The use of mixed numbers and fractions as exponents may confuse some students, however, so teachers need to monitor this to be sure that the level of frustration does not get too high. A simple comment like *If you are not sure what to do when the exponents are decimals or fractions, talk with someone in your group* may help alleviate some of the potential for frustration.

The third question in the task also involves knowledge of fractional exponents as a way to represent the "root" function—in this case, the fifth root and the seventh root. Lack of knowledge of this representational system may interfere with some students' success with this question. Also, students may not have graphed fifth- and seventh-root functions, but that is an advantage for this kind of task. It allows teachers to find out how students generalize in unfamiliar situations.

Assessment Tip ✓

At times it is important to find out how students generalize in unfamiliar situations.

Learn More...

"The gathering of evidence [of student learning] should neither be left to chance nor occur sporadically."
—*Principles to Actions: Ensuring Mathematical Success for All* (NCTM 2014, 53)

A Caution About Monitoring Tasks

Sometimes the examples that we as teachers include in instruction unintentionally share a property that we know is irrelevant but that students may *not* know is irrelevant. For example, diagrams of triangles with the three angle bisectors drawn in might all have "horizontal" bases. The intended point is that the angle bisectors of any triangle meet at a point, but students might mistakenly tie "having a horizontal base" to that generalization and might be unsure of whether a triangle in another orientation would share that property. We have to be careful in choosing examples to be sure we do not inadvertently embed an irrelevant common element. Examining students' work can sometimes reveal whether students have mistakenly focused on an irrelevant idea.

Student Self-Reflections

Helping students learn to reflect on and make judgments about their own understanding is a component of continuous monitoring. One strategy for encouraging this just prior to a unit test is to hand students a review sheet that lists the kinds of tasks that are similar to those that will appear on the test. (See Figure 5–4 on the next page.) Ask students to look at each task and (a) indicate that they are comfortable completing that task by drawing a smiling face or (b) indicate that they are unsure by drawing a frowning face. This will help students know what kinds of tasks they should review or study in preparation for the test.

Once students have completed their self-reflections, you could collect the papers and tally the number of smiling and frowning faces for each item. This will give you a sense of how confident students are about their learning of the key mathematics ideas in the unit. Then you could return the papers and ask students to actually solve the problems for homework as a self-check on their choices of smiling or frowning faces.

As teachers we also get useful information from students' responses. For example, on the self-reflection in Figure 5–4, if most students mark Item 3 with frowning faces but solve it correctly, that might indicate some confusion about the two units of measure. In contrast, if most students mark Item 3 with frowning faces and cannot solve it correctly, that might indicate serious misunderstanding either about the context or about the mathematical terminology of linear and exponential. This kind of task can provide useful information both to students (e.g., *What do I need to study?*) and to the teacher (e.g., *What appear to be areas of confusion?*).

Homework for Monitoring

Monitoring can occur during debriefing of homework assignments, provided that the assignment has been designed to reveal students' understanding of the key mathematics ideas in the instruction. When assigning homework

Assessment Tip ✓

Student indications of low levels of comfort and confidence with tasks (frowning faces) on a self-reflection review sheet highlight areas for further instruction.

Learn More …

Chapter 7 offers additional insights on student self-assessment.

Self-Reflection

Date _____

Student Name _____

Directions: Do not work the problems below. Instead, put a smiling face beside each problem that you are sure you can work correctly. Put a frowning face beside each problem that you are not sure you can work correctly.

☺ or ☹	The Problem
	1. Which is greater: $3^4 \times 4^4$ or 12^4?
	2. Imagine folding a sheet of paper in half 20 times. How many layers are there?
	3. A quart jar is put under a dripping faucet. It fills at a rate of 2 cups every 3 hours. How long will it take to fill the jar? Is this relationship linear, exponential, or neither?
	4. Does this table show a linear or exponential relationship? <table><tr><td>x</td><td>0</td><td>1</td><td>2</td><td>3</td><td>4</td><td>5</td></tr><tr><td>y</td><td>3</td><td>7</td><td>11</td><td>15</td><td>19</td><td>23</td></tr></table>
	5. Does this table show a linear or exponential relationship? <table><tr><td>x</td><td>0</td><td>1</td><td>2</td><td>3</td><td>4</td><td>5</td></tr><tr><td>y</td><td>64</td><td>32</td><td>16</td><td>8</td><td>4</td><td>2</td></tr></table>
	6. Sketch these graphs on a single set of axes. What are the points of intersection of pairs of the graphs? $y = 3x$, $y = 3x - 1$, $y = 2^x$, $y = 2^x - 1$
	7. Suppose a magic tree grows 50% taller each day. You plant it in your garden when it is 1 m tall. When will it be at least 50 m tall? 500 m tall? Write an equation to show the height (H) in terms of the number of days (D) since you planted it.

FIGURE 5-4. Sample Student Reflection Sheet for Linear Versus Exponential Relationships

for monitoring, consider first making a list of the errors that you anticipate might be revealed in students' responses. Then, when you collect students' assignments, you can quickly tally student responses by writing students' names next to the errors they appeared to make. A quick review of this list at the end of debriefing of the homework will suggest whether review of the instructional content from previous days is needed. Following is an example of a teacher's use of a monitoring task as homework.

→ A Closer Look

Ms. Davis's Monitoring of Students' Understanding with *Transformations of Familiar Shapes*

Ms. Davis gave the following task for homework the day before she discussed transformations in class. Her intent was to assess and help students recall information from their work in middle school. She used multiple terms for the transformations so that language was not a barrier to performance.

Transformations of Familiar Shapes illustrates the geometry standard "Given a rectangle, parallelogram, trapezoid, or regular polygon, describe the rotations and reflections that carry it onto itself" (CCSS .MATH.CONTENT.HSG .CO.A.3)

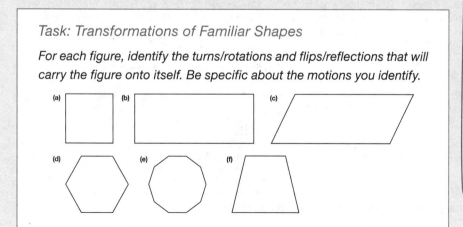

Task: Transformations of Familiar Shapes

For each figure, identify the turns/rotations and flips/reflections that will carry the figure onto itself. Be specific about the motions you identify.

Some teachers might choose to check all the answers for all the figures, but Ms. Davis knew that this would take a lot of class time. She suspected that students would be more successful describing flips than rotations, since most students had studied symmetric figures. She decided to debrief only the 2-by-5 rectangle and the regular hexagon. She created a document with the answers for the other figures, she emailed the document to all of the students, and she directed students to check *and correct* their work for homework the next night.

Ms. Davis was mainly interested in determining how students would identify the center of a rotation and whether the students recognized when a diagonal was, or was not, a line of reflection. If most students were successful at this, she would move quickly with instruction about formal definitions of rigid motions. Otherwise, she knew she would have to provide time with dynamic geometry software so that students could experiment with a wide variety of figures and rigid motions.

The discussion of reflections for the rectangle revealed that a few students identified four reflections, including diagonals. (See Figure 5–5.) The discussion of rotations suggested that some students used a vertex of the rectangle as

Question	Why Ask?	Student Responses	Follow-up Question for Monitoring	Why Ask?
How do you know that the diagonals are reflections?	to determine what strategies students were using	It just looks like they ought to be.	How could you prove that?	to determine if students tried to physically "flip" a copy of the rectangle or if they folded a copy
How did you choose the center point for your rotation?	to find out students' criteria for an acceptable center	I thought it had to be a point on the rectangle, so I picked a vertex.	If you pick a vertex, why is there only one rotation?	to determine if students know that any rotation other than 360 degrees will result in the rectangle *not* falling on itself
			Are there other points on the rectangle that work?	to determine if students recognize that any point on the rectangle would work for a 360-degree rotation
		The middle of the rectangle would let me spin it.	What do you mean by "spin it"?	to clarify the student's terminology
			What kinds of spins work?	to help relate "spins" to "rotations"

FIGURE 5–5. A Summary of the Monitoring Discussion in Ms. Davis's Class

the center of the rotation (for which only a 360-degree rotation works), while other students used the point of intersection of the diagonals (for which both a 180-degree and a 360-degree rotation works).

The discussion of reflections for the regular hexagon allowed Ms. Davis to focus students' attention on diagonals and the lines joining the midpoints of sides. She was able to contrast the properties of a regular polygon with those of a nonregular polygon. This discussion also helped set the stage for further instruction on reflections and rotations.

Discussions about monitoring tasks that have been assigned as homework also can help students become more comfortable voicing their incomplete understandings as particular tasks are debriefed. It is during the debriefing that monitoring can occur. When homework tasks are assigned with monitoring in mind, conversations rather than grades are likely to be more productive in engaging students in the mathematics of those tasks.

Proportional reasoning is critical knowledge for secondary school mathematics students. There are many ways to challenge students to think deeply about this important idea. "Reflection 5–3: Homework for Monitoring Students' Understanding of Proportional Thinking" (see pages 198–199) provides an example of how this might be done via monitoring tasks assigned for homework. Take a moment to complete this reflection and think further about homework for monitoring.

Writing Prompts for Monitoring

One form of writing prompt to use as a quick monitoring strategy is the exit card. Exit cards, often written anonymously, are short, written responses to questions posed by the teacher usually at the end of a class. Prompts are often given orally, and students may write responses on scratch paper since the responses are collected immediately. Exit cards prompt students to reflect on the day's lesson and encourage metacognition. Exit cards provide

---

Assessment Tip ✓

When homework tasks are assigned with monitoring in mind, conversations rather than grades are likely to be more productive in engaging students in the mathematics of those tasks.

Reflection 5–3

Homework for Monitoring Students' Understanding of Proportional Thinking

Pages 198–199

REPRODUCIBLE

feedback to teachers that can be quickly reviewed prior to the next lesson. Some examples of the types of statements teachers use for exit cards are shown here. The last two prompts show how specific content can be included in a prompt.

- Two things I have learned today are . . .
- Something that I need more help with is . . .
- I still have questions about . . .
- The solution strategy from today's discussion that I find most interesting is . . .
- What was the most important idea in today's lesson?
- What do you need for us to review before the test?
- Based on today's lesson, how would you define *proportional*?
- Give an example of the term *outlier* in a context that is different from today's lesson and explain why the term is appropriate in that context.

Teachers may also use exit cards to have students recall what they know about particular mathematics that will be the focus for the next week's instruction. Collected at the end of a class on a Friday, these student reflections can alert teachers to the need for review of background information for the upcoming learning targets or identify content already mastered so that time is not spent on ideas that students already understand.

Two important guidelines when using exit cards are (1) allow time for students to write, usually three to five minutes *before* everyone begins packing up to leave class and (2) respond in some way to individuals and/or the class about their statements on the cards. When information on the cards is ignored, students quickly learn there is no reason to be thoughtful in what they write. Following a class discussion about the meaning of 5^3, students created exit cards in response to the question, "Did the discussion about 5^3 help you?" (See Figure 5–6.)

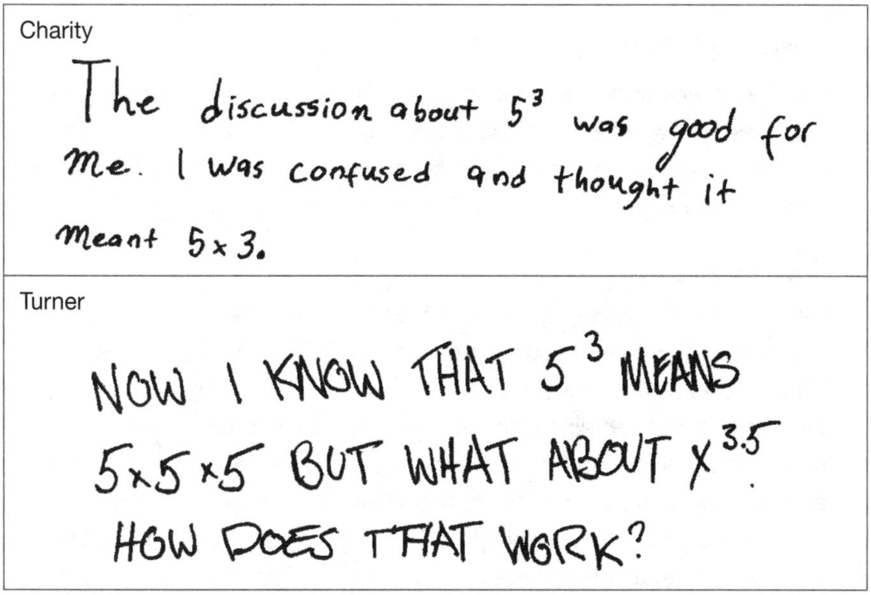

Charity

The discussion about 5^3 was good for me. I was confused and thought it meant 5×3.

Turner

NOW I KNOW THAT 5^3 MEANS $5 \times 5 \times 5$ BUT WHAT ABOUT $x^{3.5}$. HOW DOES THAT WORK?

FIGURE 5–6. Student Sample Exit Cards

Show Your Work

When teachers pose a task, they often ask students to *Show your work*. As teachers we have to be careful about the way this directive is phrased. There are subtle differences among the phrases *Show your work*, *Show the steps*, and *Justify your solution*. Each phrase can reveal useful information for monitoring students' progress as long as we are intentional about when we use it.

Show your work

Show your work seems to call for a recording of all the approaches that are attempted. Even approaches that lead to dead ends are, after all, part of the work that was done. Requiring students to use a pen instead of a pencil prevents erasures and assures that they show all their work.

(continued)

(continued from page 193)

On the other hand, students may interpret the directive *Show your work*, as "show only the good work" that leads to the answer. This interpretation requires that students make conscious decisions about what work to show and what work to eliminate from the record.

Show the steps

Students often interpret *Show the steps* as "show me [the teacher] the steps you know I want you to use." Sometimes we hear students say, "The teacher always wants me to do it her way." As teachers we need to be careful about deciding when to require specific approaches to doing mathematics and when to allow students to be able to use whatever approach is most meaningful to them. We encourage teachers to let students do what is most meaningful for them most of the time, but we acknowledge that different teachers can make different decisions about the degree of autonomy they allow students.

Justify your solution

Justify your solution asks for an explanation of both what was done and why it was done, so this goes beyond *Show your work* to include *Tell me why you did that*. This asks students for reasoning that supports their choice for a solution strategy along with an explanation of why the solution is correct. It is, however, something less than *Write a proof*. If students are less than facile at explaining what they did in words, they may focus more on just showing their work and ignore the implied directive to explain. Carefully crafted class discussions can help students develop better skill at explaining their thinking. When students listen to other students explain, and also hear the teacher paraphrase students' explanations, they have models to use in future attempts to explain their own thinking.

Learn More...

For more on classroom discussions, see Chapter 4.

Whenever you give a writing prompt to students, you must then analyze the responses that students provide. An example of a writing prompt for defining the variables in a word problem is given in Reflection 5–4, along with responses from four students. Complete "Reflection 5–4: Analyzing Responses to a Writing Prompt to Monitor Skill at Defining Variables" (see page 200), which asks you to interpret student responses in a way that will inform your instruction.

Reflection 5–4

Analyzing Responses to a Writing Prompt to Monitor Skill at Defining Variables

Page 200

INFORMing My Practice

We can learn a lot about students' thinking by applying INFORMative assessment ideas to our examination of students' written work. The information we gather will supplement what we learn from oral assessments. The two primary lenses for examining written work are the diagnostic lens (preparing to teach) and the monitoring lens (watching learning as it happens).

We can use pretests, homework assignments, and writing prompts to diagnose. Diagnosis happens *prior to* lessons on particular content. The mathematics focus of diagnostic lens techniques is typically on prerequisite knowledge or companion knowledge that is important for success during the planned lessons.

We can monitor learning by choosing tasks that reveal critical thinking by having students self-reflect or by homework assignments or writing prompts that reflect the critical ideas addressed in instruction. These techniques are used *along with* the planned instruction. They are not intended to measure mastery of the content, but rather, progress toward understanding of the content.

Of course, any of the techniques discussed in this chapter are built around asking students to complete mathematics tasks. The next chapter discusses "rich tasks" and the ways that they can reveal information about students' thinking.

Before leaving this chapter, turn to "Reflection 5–5: INFORMing My Practice: Strategies to Support Written INFORMative Assessments" (see page 201) and record your thoughts about written formative assessments.

Reflection 5–5

INFORMing My Practice: Strategies to Support Written INFORMative Assessments

Page 201

Reflection 5-1: Examining Students' Written Work Through a Diagnostic Pretest

1. Choose a standard that you will be teaching within the next month. Write it below.

2. Write a learning target that is suggested by this standard.

3. List one or two examples of prerequisite content that students need to know.

4. Create a diagnostic pretest containing two or three items to assess knowledge of the prerequisite content.

5. Administer the pretest to your students and score their papers. What strengths in understanding did you uncover? What misunderstandings did you uncover? Were you surprised at the results?

Reflection 5-2: Homework for Diagnosing Students' Understanding of Multiplication of Mixed Numbers

Sometimes when students multiply binomials, they do not keep track of all the partial products. The same difficulty sometimes happens in multiplying mixed numbers. Consider the following four items; these items might be used as homework to diagnose students' understanding of multiplication of mixed numbers.

1. $6\frac{1}{2} \times 8\frac{2}{3}$

2. $(6 + \frac{1}{2}) \times (8 + \frac{2}{3})$

3. $\begin{array}{r} 6\frac{1}{2} \\ \times\ 8\frac{2}{3} \\ \hline \end{array}$

4. $\begin{array}{r} (6 + \frac{1}{2}) \\ \times\ (8 + \frac{2}{3}) \\ \hline \end{array}$

1. Here are two students' answers to the above items. What can you infer about each student's understanding?

Chas	Kerry
1. 48 1/3	1. 48 1/3
2. 14 2/6	2. 56 2/3
3. 48 1/3	3. 48 1/3
4. 14 7/6	4. 56 1/3

2. How does this information inform your planning for the teaching of the FOIL method for multiplying two binomials?

Reflection 5-3: Homework for Monitoring Students' Understanding of Proportional Thinking

Students' misunderstanding of common fractions can sometimes interfere with their understanding of rational expressions and rational functions. First think about how you would solve the task and then use *Halfway in Between* (see the next page) to help you document your students' understanding of common fractions.

1. Choose one of your classes (at any grade level) and predict how your students would respond to the two tasks in *Halfway in Between*.

2. Administer the tasks to your class as homework, then collect and score the papers. Were you surprised by the results?

3. Plan to debrief the two tasks with your students in a whole-class discussion. One way to talk about the tasks is to note that the relationships among the whole numbers are additive, while the relationships among the fractions are multiplicative or proportional. How could you help students understand this important difference? What questions might you plan to ask during the debriefing?

(continued)

From INFORMative Assessment: Formative Assessment to Improve Mathematics Achievement by Jeane M. Joyner and George W. Bright. © 2016 by

Reflection 5–3: Homework for Monitoring Students' Understanding of Proportional Thinking (continued)

Date _____

Name _____

Task: Halfway in Between

Task 1

We know that 3 is halfway between 2 and 4. Is $\frac{1}{3}$ halfway between $\frac{1}{2}$ and $\frac{1}{4}$? Justify your solution.

Task 2

We know that 14 is halfway between 13 and 15. Is $\frac{1}{14}$ halfway between $\frac{1}{13}$ and $\frac{1}{15}$? Justify your solution.

Reflection 5–4: Analyzing Responses to a Writing Prompt to Monitor Skill at Defining Variables

Read the following writing prompt, created to help assess students' skills at defining variables for a problem. Then answer the questions that follow it.

Writing Prompt

Without solving this problem, how would you define variables to use in solving it?

Carlita is on the school basketball team. During yesterday's game, she made 4 more free throws than two-point shots. She scored a total of 13 points during the game. How many free throws did she make? How many two-point shots did she make?

---

1. Which of these student responses are correct? Which are incorrect?

   Tabatha: F = free throws, S = two-point shots

   Martina: F = number of free throws, S = number of two-point shots

   Harper: F = number of 1s, S = number of 2s

   Grace: F = ones, S = twos

2. What do the student responses tell you about the thinking of these four students?

Reflection 5-5: INFORMing My Practice: Strategies to Support Written INFORMative Assessments

Think about the chapter you just read. Use this space to record your ideas.

Ideas about the importance of analyzing students' written work:

Changes in my thinking about INFORMative assessment:

Ideas I envision becoming a more important part of my practice:

Questions I have:

Frustrations/concerns I have:

Strategies for Choosing Mathematically Rich Tasks for Instruction and Assessment

The process of choosing appropriate and effective tasks is a critical part of teaching and of assessing the depth of students' understanding. In this chapter, we talk about characteristics of tasks and the decisions we as teachers make for both choosing tasks for our lessons and using those tasks to support INFORMative assessment. Tasks can be routine or complex, they can be challenging or boring, and they can be effective or ineffective in supporting students' mathematical development. Each task has potential to be used as instruction or assessment or both. This chapter focuses on *mathematically rich tasks*; that is, tasks that engage students at different levels of sophistication, that move students' thinking forward toward attaining learning targets, and that help us reveal the depth of students' understanding of key mathematics ideas.

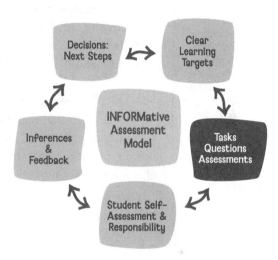

Overview

What Is a Mathematically Rich Task?

Mathematically rich tasks provide many opportunities for teachers to see "mathematics in action" as students work and discuss their solutions with peers. One of the ways that teachers learn about students' thinking is through observation of students as they work on a task. Students' work reveals information about their understanding and use of mathematics content and mathematical practices. Getting a broad picture of students' understanding helps teachers appreciate the variety of students' thinking—and the richness of a mathematically rich task.

Characteristics of Mathematically Rich Tasks

What defines a mathematically rich task, referred to by some as a "mathematically rich problem," varies among authors. We've chosen the characterization of Hsu, Kysh, and Resek, who provide the following list of key characteristics of a mathematically rich problem.

Learn More...

In *Adding It Up* (Kilpatrick, Swafford, and Findell 2001, 117), the diagram "Intertwined Strands of Proficiency" illustrates how content and practices are related.

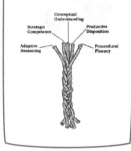

Key Characteristics of a Mathematically Rich Problem

1. The "mysterious" part of the problem is mathematical.

2. The problem has very little visible scaffolding.

3. There are many ways to do the problem.

4. Students of different skill levels can learn from this activity.

5. The problem has natural extensions.

6. The problem is hard.

7. The problem encourages getting your hands dirty with data.

8. The problem has interesting partial solutions (mileposts).
   (Hsu, Kysh, and Resek n.d., 7–12)

Characteristic 1: *The "mysterious" part of the problem is mathematical.*

A mathematically rich task encourages students to engage with important mathematics ideas. If a task is set in a real-world context, the "mysterious" part of the task should not be the context; rather, the "mysterious" part should be the mathematics ideas that underlie the task. This suggests that any context for rich mathematics tasks should be familiar or easily accessible to students, but there should be some "different twist" in the way that the mathematics ideas are embedded in the task.

Characteristic 2: *The problem has very little visible scaffolding.*

A mathematically rich task allows students to develop their own solution strategies. In particular, the task statement itself should not include directions on what approach to take. Too, teachers should not have to explain so much that the task no longer requires students to think deeply about the mathematics. Sometimes teachers give away too much information, either in presenting the task to students or in answering students' queries. When teachers do this, they are essentially replacing students' thinking with the teacher's thinking. It is important that students do the thinking. After all, if students are not thinking, they are not learning.

> **Learn More...**
>
> The kind of thinking that students do is sometimes called the "cognitive demand" of the task. The cognitive demand needs to be high, both in the statement of the task and in the implementation of the task in classrooms (Boston and Smith 2009, 2011; Jones and Tarr 2007; Stein et al. 2009).

> **Assessment Tip** ✓
>
> If students are not thinking, they are not learning.

Characteristic 3: *There are many ways to do the problem.*

A mathematically rich task is approachable in more than one way; for example, algebraic manipulation, graphing, mental imagery, creating a model, or using technology. Rich tasks are not solvable by an already-learned algorithm; if students just need to know an algorithm for determining a solution, the task is not likely to engage them very long or to challenge their thinking. Rather, rich tasks require that students struggle with choosing ways to approach the task. Teachers need to have suggestions, perhaps in the form of questions, ready to help students who struggle too much; for example, "Would a picture help?"

Struggling or Frustrated?

Struggle is OK, but frustration is not. Struggling students who resolve their struggles are learning. Students who are frustrated often give up. They may have tried strategies more or less at random; that is, without metacognitive planning. What teachers do to help a frustrated student depends on why the student is frustrated; for example, the student may be frustrated because he doesn't understand the words used in the task, thinks the context is not relevant, or doesn't know how to compute with fractions. Teachers might ask directly, "Are you struggling or are you frustrated?" It may be helpful for students to recognize the difference.

> Constructive struggling can happen when a skillful teacher gives students engaging yet challenging problems. Constructive struggling can take place when a teacher decides that one demanding, possibly time-consuming problem will likely provide more learning value than several shorter but more obvious problems. Constructive struggling involves presenting students with problems that call for more than a superficial application of a rote procedure. Constructive struggling occurs when an effective teacher knows how to provide guiding questions in a way that stops short of telling students everything they need to know to solve a problem. . . . As students engage in . . . constructive struggling . . . they learn that perseverance, in-depth analysis, and thinking are valued in mathematics as much as quick recall, direct skill application, and instant intuition. (Seeley 2015, 115–16)

Characteristic 4: *Students of different skill levels can learn from this activity.*

Students will not all have the same prerequisite knowledge, and different amounts and kinds of knowledge need to be useful for creating a solution. If the task requires sophisticated computation or symbol-manipulation skill, students who have not reached that level of mastery may not be able to begin. So a rich task should not depend exclusively on any particular skill level. Mathematically rich tasks allow students with varied backgrounds to engage with significant mathematics facts, concepts, and algorithms. They help students who have different kinds of skills and knowledge to deepen their mathematical understanding and develop connections among key concepts.

Sometimes it is difficult for us as teachers to imagine multiple solution strategies for a task; we are so comfortable with carrying out the steps in the solution process for some kinds of tasks that we find it challenging to think of any other way of proceeding. Yet students are very resourceful; they often think about mathematics ideas in ways that are different from our ways, and those unusual ways of thinking sometimes lead students to different, but equally correct, strategies.

Characteristic 5: *The problem has natural extensions.*

A mathematically rich task should support speculations—"what if" questions—that go beyond the specific solution to the task. Students should be encouraged to think about how their solutions might change if various elements of the task were changed. Thinking beyond a single task helps students organize and internalize their understanding of the key mathematics ideas.

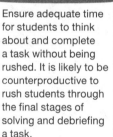

> **Learn More...**
>
> Characteristic 4 addresses the importance of supporting students at different levels to be able to access the task; in turn, this gives teachers a chance to access students' different levels of thinking. For more on implementing rich tasks for formative assessment, see page 219 in this chapter.

> **Assessment Tip** ✓
>
> Ensure adequate time for students to think about and complete a task without being rushed. It is likely to be counterproductive to rush students through the final stages of solving and debriefing a task.

Are Practice Exercises Mathematically Rich Tasks?

Practice exercises are not mathematically rich tasks; students already have been expected to learn the mathematics that is the focus of such exercises. The point of practice exercises is consolidating already-learned ideas, while the point of rich tasks is to learn or explore new mathematics ideas or make connections among ideas that have already been introduced. The speed and accuracy with which students work on practice exercises also provides teachers with an estimate of the confidence students have with previously learned content.

Characteristic 6: *The problem is hard.*

Hard is a relative term. What is "hard" for a seventh-grade student might be "easy" for an algebra student. A task that is "rich" for an eighth-grade student might be "routine" for a calculus student. Students who are learning about the mathematics may not be able to see the key ideas embedded in a task, so they may struggle to figure out how to begin or how to solve a task.

Mathematically rich tasks should also be at an appropriate level of abstraction for students. In order for a problem to be a problem, the mathematics needs to be slightly unfamiliar so that students have a challenge. That is, tasks should be in the "zone of proximal development" for students (Moll 1994; Schmittau 2004; Staples 2007). Teachers want students to be successful at solving tasks; however, the tasks should also push students to greater breadth or depth of understanding.

Characteristic 7: *The problem encourages getting your hands dirty with data.*

Often, students need to "play"—or "get their hands dirty"—with a task in order to understand the parameters in the task and to identify the mathematics ideas that are relevant for a solution. This frequently means generating data of some kind. The data might be computations, specific examples, models made with manipulatives or technology, or deductively generated mathematical statements. Looking for patterns in those data can be helpful to students in generating a solution and to teachers in understanding how students think.

Characteristic 8: *The problem has interesting partial solutions (mileposts).*

Working on the task should promote significant mathematics learning, whether or not a complete solution is created. Partial solutions or mileposts provide positive motivation for students and allow teachers to see how students' thinking is progressing as they work toward a complete solution.

> **Assessment Tip** ✓
>
> Mathematically rich tasks are not easy but they are possible.

Examples of Mathematically Rich Tasks

Now let's take the list of characteristics above and show how they are exemplified in mathematically rich tasks. This section shares two different tasks, *Restaurant Profits* and *Cevians*. Each of these tasks involves an aspect of problem solving that students should find challenging but accessible.

A Mathematically Rich Task: *Restaurant Profits*

The problem *Restaurant Profits* illustrates the characteristics of a mathematically rich task. Take a moment first to carefully read the task. (See Figure 6–1 on the next page.) The mathematical richness of this task allows it to be used in various grades. In middle school, students might be expected to solve the task as is; it seems particularly useful for helping students develop problem solving strategies such as organizing data, making a table, and finding patterns in data. In high school, the task might be reworded slightly to ask students to create a function that could be used to compute the profit based on the number of tables in the restaurant. The context of this task is also familiar enough so that it should not interfere with students' engagement with the ideas of maximizing profits. To help us think more about the mathematical richness of this task, read the rest of the chart, which looks at *Restaurant Profits* through each of the criteria for mathematically rich problems.

A Mathematically Rich Task: *Cevians*

A second example of a mathematically rich task is the geometry problem *Cevians* (paraphrased from Driscoll et al. 2007, 43). Take a moment first to carefully read the task. (See Figure 6–2 on page 211.) The definition of *cevian* is typically not included in middle and high school instruction, but it can be used across several grades and is easily accessible to all students. For example, the median of a triangle and the angle bisector of an angle in a triangle are special kinds of cevians. To help us think more about the mathematical richness of this task, read the rest of the chart, which looks at *Cevians* through each of the criteria for mathematically rich problems.

> **Learn More...**
>
> A *cevian* is a line segment that joins a vertex of a triangle with a point on the opposite side (or its extension). The condition for three general cevians from the three vertices of a triangle to concur is known as Ceva's theorem (http://mathworld.wolfram.com/Cevian.html).

Restaurant Profits highlights several aspects of the Standards for Mathematical Practice, including perseverance with problem solving (MP1: "Make sense of problems and persevere in solving them."), reasoning quantitatively (MP2: "Reason abstractly and quantitatively."), and making use of mathematical structure (MP7: "Look for and make use of structure.").

The Characteristics of a Mathematically Rich Problem	The Task: Restaurant Profits
	Each of the 20 tables in a local restaurant generates $500 per night in profit. The owner wants to put more tables in the restaurant, but she knows that because of the increased noise and crowdedness, some customers may stay away. She knows that the amount of profit per table will decrease by $15 per night for each additional table that is added to the restaurant. What is the maximum profit that the owner can generate?
1. The "mysterious" part of the problem is mathematical.	The task is a fairly typical "maximization" task of the type often seen in algebra or even calculus courses. It is simple enough computationally to be solved without the use of advanced techniques, though the specific mathematics needed to generate the solution is not immediately obvious.
2. The problem has very little visible scaffolding.	The task does not point students in any particular direction in terms of how to create a solution. Computation strategies would probably come to mind for most students.
3. There are many ways to do the problem.	Students might begin by trial and error or they might analyze the situation more thoroughly before they begin to create a solution. A spreadsheet would be particularly useful for either trial-and-error approaches or approaches that begin with careful analysis.
4. Students of different skill levels can learn from this activity.	Because computation is a way to begin, students at different skill levels can approach the task almost immediately. If students' computation skills are weak, consider providing calculators.
5. The problem has natural extensions.	Changes in either the initial number of tables or the effects on the restaurant's profit as each new table is added lead to natural extensions.
6. The problem is hard.	It may not even be obvious to some students that there is a maximum amount of profit. Some students may simply assume that adding more tables must result in greater profits.
7. The problem encourages getting your hands dirty with data.	Most students are likely to begin by generating data about profits with different numbers of added tables.
8. The problem has interesting partial solutions (mileposts).	Computations of profits for various numbers of added tables will provide students with a better sense of the variability inherent in this task. Teachers also will learn a lot about students' thinking as they watch students complete these computations.

FIGURE 6–1. The Mathematical Richness of *Restaurant Profits*

The Characteristics of a Mathematically Rich Problem	The Task: Cevians
	The triangle has three cevians drawn from a single vertex. What is the minimum number of angle measures that you need to know in order to determine all angle measures?
1. The "mysterious" part of the problem is mathematical.	The task combines application of knowledge about the sum of the angles for a triangle with analysis of whether any "solution" actually represents "the minimum" number of data values that are necessary.
2. The problem has very little visible scaffolding.	The focus on "minimum number of angles" might lead students to focus on imagining measuring two or three angles at a time, rather than on the implications of knowing the measure of a single angle.
3. There are many ways to do the problem.	The task does not suggest either which angles might be measured or in what order angles might be measured. For example, the four "small" angles at the vertex from which the cevians were drawn can be measured individually, in "pairs," in "triples," or altogether.
4. Students of different skill levels can learn from this activity.	The only prerequisite knowledge required is that the sum of the angles of any triangle is 180 degrees. Students in the middle grades might approach this problem mainly through examining specific examples and specifying more than the minimum number of angles as "known." High school geometry students might argue more deductively, for example, "If I know the measure of two of the angles in the leftmost triangle, then the third angle is determined, and the supplement of the 'inside angle' is also determined."
5. The problem has natural extensions.	Some students might begin by analyzing simpler cases; for example, a triangle with no cevians, a triangle with one cevian, and a triangle with two cevians. One extension is to find a pattern: *If a triangle has n cevians drawn from a single vertex, what is the minimum number of angle measures that you need to know in order to determine all angle measures?*
6. The problem is hard.	It is not obvious that the minimum number is constant, independent of the order in which angles are measured.
7. The problem encourages getting your hands dirty with data.	There are a lot of ways that students might imagine which angle measures are known. The "data" here would be the specifications of which angles are completely determined (without being measured directly) as each new measured angle is added to the mix.
8. The problem has interesting partial solutions (mileposts).	Students may create partial solutions that do not meet the criterion of "minimum number." Teachers might also learn a lot about students' reasoning as they watch students work on this task; students need to reason about the implications of specifying one or more angles as having been measured. Some students may say that this problem has no solution simply because they don't know any of the angle measures. Some students may try to use a protractor to measure all the angles. In either case, you would have useful information about the students' misunderstanding of the task itself or of the language used in the statement of the task.

FIGURE 6-2. The Mathematical Richness of *Cevians*

Cevians highlights several aspects of the Standards for Mathematical Practice; including perseverance with problem solving (MP1: "Make sense of problems and persevere in solving them."), reasoning abstractly (MP2: "Reason abstractly and quantitatively."), constructing viable arguments (MP3: "Construct viable arguments and critique the reasoning of others."), and looking for repeated reasoning (MP8: "Look for and express regularity in repeated reasoning.").

Reflect On Your Tasks: Are They Mathematically Rich?

There are degrees of richness for mathematical tasks; richness is not an all-or-nothing attribute of a task. Not every task we choose is likely to exemplify the eight characteristics of mathematically rich problems discussed previously. Reasoning and problem solving can happen either in mathematical contexts or in real-world contexts. Both kinds of contexts can help students learn how to apply their mathematics knowledge, and both kinds of contexts can be engaging for students. Using "moderately rich" tasks can be a transition stage for teachers as they learn to make sense of students' thinking. Moderately rich tasks can open up opportunities for students to develop and reveal their understanding of concepts, problem solving, and constructing viable arguments. Those tasks also provide an environment in which we can assess how well students are progressing toward developing important mathematical practices.

Sometimes it is difficult to look at our favorite tasks and problems objectively. But it is important to decide which of those tasks qualify as mathematically rich tasks. Complete "Reflection 6–1: Reflect On Your Favorite Tasks: Are They Mathematically Rich?" (see pages 240–241). This reflection gives you an opportunity to compare your favorite tasks to the list of characteristics of mathematically rich problems discussed earlier.

Remember that the main purpose of using a mathematically rich task is to engage students with the underlying mathematics ideas, not just to solve the task. It's important to imagine what mathematical understanding students will take away from a task. As teachers we should choose tasks that not only fit within our long-term goals and learning targets but also motivate students. In choosing motivating tasks, we rely on our expert content judgments and the interests and perseverance of our students.

Reflection 6–1

Reflect On Your Favorite Tasks: Are They Mathematically Rich?

Pages 240–241

What a Task Allows Mathematically Versus What a Task Requires

A critical part of selecting mathematically rich tasks is the identification of the mathematics that a task *requires* versus the mathematics that is *allowed* or *expected*. The required mathematics is the least mathematics that can be used to solve a problem, while the allowed or expected mathematics is the mathematics that teachers want students to use.

Many times teachers are surprised when students use simpler mathematics to solve a problem than the mathematics they expected students to use. For example, if students are asked to solve this equation, $3x - 7 = 23$, some students will simply observe that $30 - 7$ is 23, so $3x$ must be 30 and x must be 10. They will see no need to "write out the steps," and indeed will be confused by the teacher's expectation that students will "add 7 to both sides of the equation" as the first step. Students see $30 - 7 = 23$ as a fact rather than as a relationship that needs to be developed.

When a student uses simpler-than-intended mathematics, as teachers we cannot be sure that the student *does not know* the intended mathematics. Rather, we know only that the student *did not use* the intended mathematics. In this situation, we need to have probing questions (or follow-up tasks) ready that can be used to reveal information about students' knowledge of the intended mathematics.

Some teachers think that if a solution is not efficient or elegant it is not as correct as it might be. We argue, however, that as teachers we need to distinguish among correct, elegant, and appropriate-but-inelegant solutions. The following task can be used to illustrate this issue.

Assessment Tip ✓

The *required* mathematics is the least mathematics that can be used to solve a problem; the *allowed* or *expected* mathematics is the mathematics that teachers want students to use. A critical part of selecting mathematically rich tasks is the identification of the mathematics that a task *requires*.

Task: Perimeters of Shapes

Which figure has the greatest perimeter? Explain.

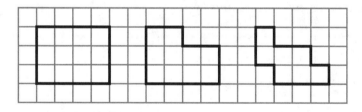

CCSS

Perimeters of Shapes supports the standard "Look for and make use of structure" (MP7).

Some students will simply count the number of line segments around the perimeter of each figure. This is an appropriate-but-inelegant solution. These students are likely to be surprised that the counts are all the same; after all, the figures look noticeably different. As teachers we want to have questions already in mind to push these students to find reasons why the counts are the same.

Simply counting units around the perimeter suggests that the students did not do much analysis of the problem before jumping in for a "simple" solution.

Other students will notice that the rectangle actually fits around each of the other two shapes. If you imagine doing that, you can imagine pushing out the pieces of the perimeters of those two shapes to match up with the perimeter of the rectangle. That is, the perimeters of the other two shapes can be rearranged to form exactly the rectangle. So the perimeters of the three shapes have to be the same, since they can all be rearranged to form congruent shapes. Many teachers would classify this solution as "elegant." Notice that the question does not ask for a measurement of the perimeter, only an identification of which figure has the greatest perimeter and an explanation of the response. This "elegant solution" shows that the perimeters are the same, even though it does not provide that value.

The second solution also reveals understanding of mathematical structure. The student has identified common structure in the three figures and has used that structure to create an argument to show that the perimeters are the same. As teachers we would want to acknowledge and support thinking like this, but we should not denigrate the thinking behind the first solution. Counting perimeter units when they are easy to count is certainly a correct way to approach this task.

Sometimes the solution strategy that a student selects strikes us as being more complicated that the solution we expect students to use. Consider the following *Proportional Reasoning* task.

Learn More...

"There are three features of tasks that are critical:
First, the situation must be one that students can treat problematically. . . .
Second, the tasks need to connect to something the students know and are able to do. . . .
Third, what is problematic about the task should be the mathematics of the situation so that what gets left behind is something of mathematical value."
—*Making Sense: Teaching and Learning Mathematics with Understanding* (Hiebert et al. 1997, 161)

Task: Proportional Reasoning

Find the length of the missing length:

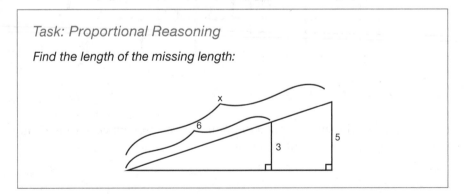

Incorrect solutions will almost always involve the use of mathematics ideas that were not intended. In the solution that follows, the student used additive reasoning rather than proportional reasoning. (See Figure 6–3.) As teachers we have to decide how to provide feedback on incorrect solutions.

5 is 2 more than 3, so x is 2 more then 6

$x = 8$

FIGURE 6–3. An Incorrect Solution

Sometimes students use mathematics ideas that are useful but are not absolutely necessary for a solution. For example, we expect that, in general, high school mathematics students would set up a proportion and then solve that proportion. This is a strategy that always works. (See Figure 6–4.)

$$\frac{3}{5} = \frac{6}{x}$$

$$3x = 30$$

$$x = 10$$

FIGURE 6–4. A Solution Using Proportions

In contrast, some students might use percentage-increase thinking. (See Figure 6–5.) We might see this as a more "complicated" kind of thinking, even though it is mathematically correct.

5 is 67% more than 3, so x is 67% more than 6

67% of 6 is 4 so x is 6+4 or 10

FIGURE 6–5. A Solution Using Percentages

The two solutions using proportions and using percentages are mathematically equivalent, but the tools for making the solutions are different. That is, students may not use proportions explicitly to solve the task, even though the underlying mathematical thinking is similar. We have to help students connect their thinking with the mathematics ideas that we may have intended to be used.

Choosing Mathematically Rich Tasks

Choosing mathematically rich tasks can be challenging and often takes considerable time. Because middle grades teachers and high school teachers typically teach multiple classes to large numbers of students, and because there is pressure on us to "cover content," it sometimes feels more efficient to rely heavily on textbook materials as the primary source of problems and tasks for lessons. However, there is an equally important goal of helping students learn, and sometimes this goal might be better accomplished by choosing tasks from other sources.

Assembling a collection of rich tasks is often a multiyear project, especially if we commit to choosing tasks from sources other than our existing text materials. However, there are many resources for good problems, some of which are easily accessible on the Internet. Mathematics Assessment Project (MAP) lessons certainly qualify as a source of mathematically rich tasks, in addition to other sources cross-referenced throughout this book. As you examine these resources, keep in mind that some of the same tasks we choose for instruction might also work as INFORMative assessment tasks. We want to choose tasks that not only engage students' thinking but also have the potential to reveal that thinking for us and other students to examine. The list of characteristics of mathematically rich tasks presented earlier in this chapter can be used to help us choose appropriate tasks.

Modifications That Make Traditional Tasks Richer

As discussed, the rich tasks we select should not only support students' learning and their engagement with mathematics but also provide opportunities for students to demonstrate what they understand about key mathematics ideas. This often means that the use of mathematically rich tasks requires more time for planning and preparing lessons, especially if we use tasks that are not in the textbook. Sometimes, however, it is possible to modify a "traditional task" to make students' engagement with that task richer. We can selectively use problems from the textbook and sequence those problems in ways that are likely to reveal students' thinking or raise issues we want to discuss with students; for example we can "re-create" them as explorations of mathematics ideas. Consider the following traditional tasks and examples of how to modify them.

> **Learn More...**
>
> Keep in mind this NCTM Teaching Principle: "Effective mathematics teaching requires understanding what students know and need to learn and then challenging and supporting them to learn it well."
> —*Principles and Standards for School Mathematics* (National Council of Teachers of Mathematics 2000, 370)

Modifying the Traditional Task *Integer Powers*

> *A Traditional Task: Integer Powers*
>
> *Compute the fourth power and the eighth power of 0.5.*

> *A Modification of the Traditional Task: Integer Powers*
>
> *What is the smallest integer power of 0.5 that is less than 0.1? Less than 0.01? Predict the smallest integer power of 0.5 that is less than 0.001 and check your prediction.*

Compare the above traditional and modified versions of the task. The traditional task is really a practice exercise; it is not likely to help students develop reasoning and analysis skills. Its modification, however, is more "open" and supports a variety of approaches. Students could simply compute a bunch of examples and then choose the one that fits the conditions, but we would want to encourage students to think about how the relative sizes of different powers of 0.5 relate. A debriefing discussion of students' work might be the best way to accomplish this goal.

Modifying the Traditional Task *Mean and Median*

> ### A Traditional Task: Mean and Median
> *Find the mean and median of this data set: 4, 8, 5, 3, 7, 2, 4, 3.*

> ### A Modification of the Traditional Task: Mean and Median
> *Create a data set of 8 numbers so that the mean is 4.5 and the median is 4.*

Learn More...

The question about the mean and median of the weights of dogs in Chapter 2 on page 36 illustrates how a nonroutine question can become a richer task.

Compare the above traditional and modified versions of the task. The modification has infinitely many solutions, so students might be asked to check one another's solutions; this would provide additional engagement with the key mathematics ideas. A debriefing discussion might focus on how the magnitudes of the data elements affect the values of the mean and the median. For example, the teacher might pose the following questions during the debriefing: *If 3, 4, 6, 8, and 10 are the five least values in a data set containing nine elements, what is the median? If the 10 were removed and replaced with a 7, would the median change? If so, how?*

Modifying the Traditional Task *Difference of Squares*

> ### A Traditional Task: Difference of Squares
> *Write $x^6 - y^4$ as the sum and difference of the same terms.*

> ### A Modification of the Traditional Task: Difference of Squares
> *What is similar about $x^2 - y^2$, $x^6 - y^4$, $x^6 - y^8$, and $x^{16} - y^6$? How does this similarity in structure help you factor each difference?*

Compare the traditional and modified versions of the *Difference of Squares* task on the previous page. In order to emphasize the fact that the difference of any two squares can be easily factored, we might pose the first traditional task. However, a richer task would be the second. Of course, changes in the values of the exponents would make this rich task easier or more challenging. A debriefing discussion might focus on the fact that each term in these expressions is a *perfect square*.

As you can see from these examples, sometimes we can turn traditional tasks into richer tasks by thinking about how the mathematics ideas can be used to create information about the task. Sometimes we can turn the task on its head and think about re-creating the task from its solution. Brainstorming with colleagues is sometimes a good way to develop skill at modifying traditional tasks to create richer tasks. Complete "Reflection 6–2: Modifying Traditional Tasks" (see pages 242–243), which provides an opportunity to modify some traditional tasks that we suggest and tasks that you identify from your curriculum materials.

> **Reflection 6-2**
>
> Modifying
> Traditional Tasks
>
> Pages 242–243

Using Mathematically Rich Tasks as Part of INFORMative Assessment

Whatever the source of tasks we choose, we always want to think carefully about why and how we are using them. Effective instruction will include mathematically rich tasks, though certainly not every task in an effective curriculum will be mathematically rich. Making decisions about when to use mathematically rich tasks is frequently challenging. Those decisions need to account for students' ever-increasing knowledge and understanding. INFORMative assessment can provide information that is critical for making these decisions, and the tasks themselves can serve as contexts for gathering additional assessment information.

Characteristics of Tasks for Formative Assessment

Some tasks are posed for instructional purposes, some tasks are posed specifically for assessment purposes, and some tasks are posed for both purposes. Mathematics tasks that engage students' thinking can be used to monitor that thinking in the moment while also playing a central role in instruction. It is not always necessary to pose assessment-only tasks, even though there are times when such tasks are important for revealing students' thinking.

Tasks that have formative assessment purposes generally share several characteristics as follows. Many instructional tasks may also share these characteristics. We want to keep in mind that the same quality tasks we choose for instruction we can also use for assessment. That is, instructional planning and INFORMative assessment are highly interrelated.

Characteristics of Tasks for Formative Assessment

1. The task aligns with the expectations described in the learning target(s).

2. The task engages students with mathematics content and/or practices.

3. The challenge of the task is neither too easy nor too complicated.

4. The task's solution(s) can be generated in multiple ways.

5. Partial solutions (mileposts) are possible.

6. The task should take a reasonable amount of time.

Characteristic 1: *The task aligns with the expectations described in the learning target(s).*

┌ Learn More ... ┐
Chapter 3 offers an in-depth look at learning targets.

An effective formative assessment task gives students opportunities to show what they understand and can do in connection with the learning target(s). Teachers gain evidence of students' growing competence and accomplishments related to the learning target(s).

Characteristic 2: *The task engages students with mathematics content and/or practices.*

Engaging with content or practices happens best when the situation in the task is motivating for students. Sometimes motivating tasks are real-world contexts (often called "applications") and sometimes they are mathematical contexts (such as puzzles or patterns).

Characteristic 3: *The challenge of the task is neither too easy nor too complicated.*

Students should be able to recognize that they know enough both to generate solutions and to explain those solutions. The explanations provide critical information for us in assessing students' understanding. This means that the size of the tasks will be neither so small as to be trivial nor so big as to be overwhelming. Sometimes variations of tasks may be needed, for example, by changing the numbers, to meet the needs of different levels of skill and knowledge in a class.

Characteristic 4: *The task's solution(s) can be generated in multiple ways.*

Some students may choose to approach the task by looking at examples, while other students may choose to use more generalized solution strategies. Use of different models and strategies (for example, pictures, technology, symbols) should be possible for the task. As we observe different strategies, we can adjust instruction to meet the needs of the class.

Characteristic 5: *Partial solutions (mileposts) are possible.*

Effective formative assessment tasks should not be "all or nothing"; there should be mileposts along the path toward a solution. One of the mileposts should be an easy start to the problem. As we observe which mileposts students reach, we can plan ways to help students move further or debriefing discussions that will highlight the differences.

Characteristic 6: *The task should take a reasonable amount of time.*

Of course, what is reasonable time for one group of students may be much less than what is reasonable time for another group of students. While instructional tasks may sometimes extend over multiple class periods, most tasks used for assessment purposes should likely be completed in a single period.

Implementing Mathematically Rich, Formative Assessment Tasks

Clearly, as teachers our judgments play a crucial role in identifying effective formative assessment tasks. We need to have a deep understanding of our students' levels of skill and knowledge. For this reason our choices of formative assessment tasks may not be as effective early in a school year, precisely because we do not yet know our students. However, as we learn about our students' thinking, we are able to choose tasks that are likely to reveal their depth of mathematical understanding. A key for choosing a rich task for both assessment and instructional purposes is careful planning. In this section we highlight ways to generate insight into student thinking (INFORMative assessment) while supporting student learning. Some of these actions we cover in depth in other chapters and hence have chosen to briefly revisit and cross-reference for your information.

Implementing Mathematically Rich, Formative Assessment Tasks

1. Link content and practice standards.

2. Use contexts to help students.

3. Choose tasks that reveal the *range* and *depth* of students' levels of understanding.

4. Use questions to amplify the effects of the tasks on learning.

Link Content and Practice Standards

When people think of mathematics standards, they often think first about content standards, which typically address algorithms, concepts, and so on. Not to be overlooked, however, are practice standards (sometimes referred to as "process standards"). It is important that mathematics instruction balance attention to developing understanding of facts, concepts, procedures, problem solving, justification of arguments, and others. It is through the practice (process) standards that students both learn content and demonstrate that learning.

Mathematically rich tasks provide an environment not only for development of the more sophisticated parts of instruction such as problem solving and constructing viable arguments, but also for assessing how well students are progressing toward developing these important mathematical practices. Being explicit about what to look for as evidence of learning while students are completing a task is an important component of planning that links instruction and assessment.

Learn More...

The Common Core State Standards for Mathematics include eight Standards for Mathematical Practice that "cut across" content areas and grades. These practices define some of the critical skills that allow students to use mathematics in a wide range of situations. For more on the Mathematical Practices, see Chapter 2, pages 45–46.

→ **A Closer Look**

Mrs. James's Exploration of Precision with *Identifying Units of Measure*

Mrs. James knew that her students were developing understanding of functions, but she did not know how deeply they understood the interpretation of functions that modeled real-world contexts. Such functions frequently represent measurements, which involve units of measure. To find out more about her students' thinking, she posed the following task. It addresses two of the issues raised in Mathematical Practice Standard 6: "Attend to precision"— namely, the correct use of the equals sign and with units of measure.

"Mathematically proficient students try to communicate precisely to others. . . . They state the meaning of the symbols they choose, including using the equal sign consistently and appropriately. They are careful about specifying units of measure . . . " (www. corestandards.org/ Math/Practice/MP6/).

Task: Identifying Units of Measure

The equation d = 5t + 7 describes the depth of water (in centimeters) in a jar when water is poured in a steady stream into the jar over t seconds (0 < t < 12). What are the correct units of measure for 7 and for 5 in the equation?

In this task, both sides of the equation must have centimeters as the unit of measure, so each term on the right side must also have centimeters (cm) as the unit of measure. Since 7 stands alone, it must have centimeters as its unit of measure. The term $5t$ is a bit more complicated. The variable, t, has seconds (sec) as its unit of measure, so the coefficient, 5, must have cm/sec as its unit of measure. That is, the unit of measure for 5 is rate or speed, and speed × time is distance or length or, in this case, depth. (The classic formula is $d = rt$.) Getting students to see this is not always easy.

Some students may say that "seven is the constant in the equation," without being able to attach a unit of measure. Other students will not be able to explain that the term $5t$ has *any* unit of measure; students have difficulty thinking about an abstract expression as having a unit of measure. Some students will see that the unit of measure for 7 is centimeters, but will be unable to separate the units of measure for t and 5. The following dialogue illustrates

Learn More...

"As with many abilities, the best way to learn precision—in communication, graphing, measurement, or computation—is to use it. "
—*Smarter Than We Think: More Messages About Math, Teaching, and Learning in the 21st Century* (Seeley 2014, 317)

how Mrs. James used questions to reveal students' understanding about how to determine units of measure. This discussion helped students develop a better sense of "precision."

Mrs. James: What is the unit of measure for d?

Uriah: The problem says centimeters.

Mrs. James: OK. That means the left side of the equation has centimeters as its unit of measure. Then what is the unit of measure for the right side of the equation?

Annalee: Since it is an equation, the right side must be centimeters, too.

Mrs. James: OK. Then what do you know about the units of measure for the two terms $5t$ and 7?

Annalee: The problem doesn't tell us.

Mrs. James: Could the units on terms that are added be different, say, inches and meters or inches and pounds?

Uriah: You can't add different units.

Annalee: You could convert meters to inches.

Uriah: But you can't convert pounds to inches.

Mrs. James: Yes, sometimes you can convert units so they are the same, but sometimes you can't. In this problem, would you expect $5t$ and 7 to have the same units or different units?

Uriah: The same.

Mrs. James: What would the common unit be?

Uriah: Centimeters.

Mrs. James: Then would the unit of measure for 7 be centimeters?

Uriah: Yes.

Mrs. James: And the unit of measure for $5t$?

Annalee: Centimeters, too.

Mrs. James: What is the unit of measure for t?

Felicia: Isn't it seconds?

Annalee: Yes, the problem says that.

Mrs. James: Can you work backward to figure out what is the unit measure for 5? The unit of measure for 5t is centimeters and the unit measure of t is seconds *(writes on the board: (5____) x t sec = Y cm)*.

Just focus on the units.

Uriah: Well, if we solve to 5 blank, we get Y centimeters over t seconds *(Mrs. James writes $\frac{Y\,cm}{t\,sec}$ on the board)*. That would make $\frac{Y}{t}$ centimeters over seconds.

Mrs. James: How can you read "centimeters over seconds"?

Annalee: I think it is centimeters per second.

Mrs. James: What kind of a unit is centimeters per second?

Felicia: It sounds sort of like miles per hour, which is speed.

Mrs. James: Right. Centimeters per second is a unit of speed; that is, distance per unit of time.

Mrs. James continued this discussion to help students understand the process of "working backward" with units of measure to determine the proper units of measure for values in an equation. This kind of thinking is sometimes referred to as "units analysis."

What did Mrs. James learn about the students' thinking? Early in the conversation, Annalee acknowledged that both sides of the equation had to use the same units of measure. Uriah built on this idea by commenting, "You can't add different units," followed by noting that 5t and 7 have the same units. This showed a developing understanding of aspects of precision. By the end of the discussion, the students developed the idea that $\frac{cm}{sec}$ is a unit of speed. This was a significant improvement over Annalee's first comment, "The problem doesn't tell us." Mrs. James was able to find out what the students understood ("You can't add different units") and then move the students' thinking forward toward attainment of the apparent learning target while also revealing different aspects of students' thinking. That is, the questions posed by Mrs. James helped students be more precise about what units should be attached to components of the function rule.

Reflection 6-3

Linking Content and
Practice Standards:
Understanding
a Mathematical
Practice

Page 244

In order to know how to help students learn to use Mathematical Practices, we as teachers have to understand those practices deeply. Complete "Reflection 6–3: Linking Content and Practice Standards: Understanding a Mathematical Practice" (see page 244), which provides an opportunity to delve into Mathematical Practice 3: "Construct viable arguments and critique the reasoning of others."

Use Contexts to Help Students

It is important to consider context when selecting tasks for formative assessment purposes. The choice of context can help us in gaining insight into students' thinking.

Experience with both applications and mathematics contexts is important for development of mathematical expertise; however, applications may be more motivating and engaging for students, provided students have a clear connection to the context of the applications. These connections can also help students better remember how they thought about the underlying mathematical ideas. In turn, this memory is useful when students need to recall the mathematics ideas for future problem solving and reasoning.

It is too simplistic to say, "Tasks are presented within contexts." Sometimes a context is set up so that many different tasks can be presented with that context; for example, computing costs for food bought at a grocery store, then computing the tax on that purchase, then computing the change received from a payment. Sometimes different contexts are used to illustrate the same mathematics.

Learn More...

See Chapter 3, "Problem Solving and Applications" (page 96), for discussion of two kinds of contexts: real-world contexts (often called "applications") and mathematics contexts.

Learn More...

"Finding the right context, choosing appropriate numerical values, ensuring that the relevant is obvious and that the irrelevant can also be identified as such, and making the whole situation accessible for students, requires a deep mathematical knowledge."
—"Choice and Use of Examples as a Window on Mathematical Knowledge for Teaching" (Chick 2009, 30)

→ A Closer Look

Ms. Luna Combines Mathematical Practices and Context with *Concentrations of Medicine*

Ms. Luna has several goals for her high school algebra students, including understanding recursion, developing problem-solving skills, and applying mathematics in applications. *Concentrations of Medicine* is a task she has used successfully to help students think about all these ideas in a single context. She has observed that when students focus on the details of a context rather than the details of a purely mathematics task, the mathematics ideas that lead to a solution sometimes are more obvious. Students are more likely to use a range of ideas and less likely to try to force the use of a particular algorithm.

Task: Concentrations of Medicine

A prescription says to take 400 mg of this medicine every 4 hours. If 67% of the medicine in a patient's body is filtered out every four hours, how much medicine is in the patient's body after 8 hours? After 24 hours? At what point will the amount of medicine in the patient's body reach a state of equilibrium? When equilibrium is reached, how much medicine is in the patient's body? Why is an equilibrium of medication important for the patient?

Ms. Luna chose this task as a way to help her students engage with context, content, and processes; there were also many opportunities in this mathematically rich task to assess her students' thinking. As she planned for the use of this task, she made a list of issues that she wanted to gather evidence about:

- Are students able to assign and use variables in a mathematical model?

- Can students connect aspects of the context with mathematics ideas and notations?

- Can students recognize an equilibrium point?

The introduction to the CCSSM high school "Functions" domain describes the importance of mathematical models that may include the use of recursive rules. "Because we continually make theories about dependencies between quantities in nature and society, functions are important tools in the construction of mathematical models . . . A function can be described in various ways, such as by a graph (e.g., the trace of a seismograph); by a verbal rule, as in, 'I'll give you a state, you give me the capital city'; by an algebraic expression like $f(x) = a + bx$; or by a recursive rule" (corestandards.org/ Math/Content/HSF/ introduction/).

- Will students recognize that once equilibrium is reached they can stop computing?

- Do any students model a recursive process? If so, will they find the equilibrium point?

- What false starts will students make because of the nature of the context?

Students must realize that the state of equilibrium happens when the amount filtered out is equal to the amount of the dose. The questions in the task typically prompt a great deal of discussion among students, and Ms. Luna encouraged this discussion by having students work in groups. Pat's group approached the problem through computations; they found that equilibrium is reached with the seventh dose. (See Figure 6–6.)

Dose #	Time	Amount of dose (in mg)	Amount at start of 4 hours (in mg)	Amount filtered out (in mg)	Amount remaining at end of 4 hrs (in mg)
0	12 pm	0	0	0	0
1	4 pm	400	400	268	132
2	8 pm	400	532	356	176
3	12 am	400	576	386	190
4	4 am	400	590	395	195
5	8 am	400	595	399	196
6	12 pm	400	596	399	197
7	4 pm	400	597	400	197
8	8 pm	400	597	400	197

FIGURE 6–6. The Computation Solution by Pat's Group

Marie's group used recursion to model the task, though developing the notation for recording their thinking proved a bit of a struggle. They used A_n to represent the amount of medication remaining at the end of the nth dose. (See Figure 6–7.)

$$A_1 = 400 - .67 * 400$$

$$A_2 = (400 + A_1) - .67(400 + A_1)$$

.
.
.

$$A_n = (400 + A_{n-1}) - .67(400 + A_{n-1})$$

FIGURE 6-7. Recursive Notation Developed by Marie's Group

Ms. Luna observed that Marie's group spent so much time on analyzing the task and developing the notation that they never identified the equilibrium point. She decided that she wanted to highlight the differences between the approaches of these two groups during the debriefing.

Ms. Luna: Pat, how did your group approach the task, and what solution did you get?

Pat: Well, we started with everything at zero and then we computed. The eighth dose is the same as the seventh dose, so that is the equilibrium.

Ms. Luna: Do you need to go beyond the eighth dose?

Pat: We computed up to the tenth dose, but it stayed the same.

Ms. Luna: Marie, what did your group do?

Marie: We thought that task showed a recursive process, so that's what we did. It took us a while, though, to figure out how to write what we were thinking.

Ms. Luna: How did you find the equilibrium point?

Marie: We never actually got that.

Ms. Luna: How would you use your work to get there?

Marie: I don't know.

Kimi: I think we should have also computed, but probably not like Pat's group. And we could have shown a simpler formula.

Ms. Luna: Come to the board and show us what you mean.

Kimi: We could have combined terms, since one minus point sixty-seven is point thirty-three *(writes $A_n = (400 + A_{n-1}) * .33$ on the board)*.

Ms. Luna: So you're using the distributive property to make the formula simpler. What does A_n mean?

Kimi: It is the amount of medicine left in the body after the nth dose.

Ms. Luna: And what would you have to compute to find the equilibrium?

Kimi: I think we would have to start with A_1. Let's see, that's point thirty-three times four hundred, or one hundred thirty-two. Then we'd find A_2 and A_3 and so on.

Ms. Luna: Do you know when you'd stop computing?

Marie: We should get the same solution that Pat's group got, but we'd have to do it to be sure.

Ms. Luna: OK. We won't do that now, though. Was the situation in the task easy for you to understand?

Jess: We had to talk about what *filtered out* meant, but once we did that it was okay. It seemed obvious to compute like Pat's group did. I'm not sure I ever would have thought of what Marie and Kimi's group did.

Helen: I agree with Jess. Can you get Kimi to say more about their stuff?

The discussion continued, with Ms. Luna probing students' thinking about how they connected aspects of the context with mathematics ideas that they had already learned. She revisited Pat's comment about stabilization after the seventh dose with this question: *Is it true or false to say that no matter how many doses beyond the seventh a patient is given, the amount of medicine in the patient's body remains the same?* She extended students' engagement with the task by posing this challenge for homework: *Would you reach equilibrium sooner if the amount of medicine in each dose were increased? Why or why not?*

Mathematically rich tasks set in a real-world context can be powerful for engaging students and helping them make connections among mathematics ideas. Ms. Luna's careful planning for how to use the task not only helped her make sense of students' thinking but also enhanced the effective implementation of the task.

Choose Tasks that Reveal the *Range* and *Depth* of Students' Levels of Understanding

As we discussed earlier in this chapter under Characteristic 4 of a mathematically rich task, such rich tasks provide opportunities for students with different levels of understanding to approach a task, even if some levels of understanding might not lead quickly to a solution. In turn, mathematically rich tasks, unlike some more directive tasks, give us as teachers a chance to reveal students' different levels of understanding. When we recognize those different levels of understanding, we can support students by posing questions to help clarify the implications of those different levels. For example, there are several "levels" of questions that might be posed about the relationship among the angles shown in Figure 6–8.

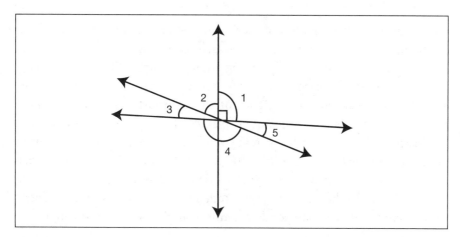

FIGURE 6–8. Relationships Among Angles

At a basic level, students could be asked to identify the different types of angles shown in the figure. Students would be expected to think beyond just identifying the individual angles that are numbered to thinking about "composite" angles, such as angle 1 + 2.

Questions, Set 1 (Basic Level)

- *Which angles are acute angles?* (angles 2, 3, and 5)

- *Which angles are right angles?* (angles 1, 2 + 3)

- *Which angles are obtuse angles?* (angles 4, 1 + 2, 1 + 5)

- *Which angles are straight angles?* (angles 3 + 4, 4 + 5, 1 + 2 + 3, 2 + 1 + 5)

Questions such as those in Set 1 can help to activate students' prior knowledge about angles, so questions such as the ones listed in Set 1 can launch a more advanced study of angle relationships. When asked, many students can recall the definitions of an acute angle and an obtuse angle, even though those students might not spontaneously use either of those terms or understand their meanings. Names of various angles are just not used regularly enough to be in many students' spontaneous vocabularies. When students activate prior knowledge, they are more likely to create rich cognitive structures that will support good problem-solving skills.

At a more challenging level, students could be asked to identify relationships among the angles. For example, angle 2 + 3 is a right angle.

Questions, Set 2 (More Challenging Level)

- *What do you know about the measures of these angles?*

- *If you know the measure of angle 2, what other measures can you compute?*

For the first question, students should know that the sum of the measures of angles 2 and 3 is 90 degrees, and angles 3 and 5 have equal measures. These two conclusions would generate the additional conclusion that the sum of the measures of angles 2 and 5 is also 90 degrees, even though they are not adjacent angles. Because these two angles are not adjacent, it might be difficult for some students to imagine the sum of their measures. For the second question, if you know the measure of angle 2, you can compute the measure of angle 3, then angle 5, and then angle 4. And, of course, we already know that the measure of angle 1 is 90 degrees. That is, if you know the measure of angle 2, you can compute the measures of all the other angles. Actually, if you know the measure of any angle other than angle 1, you can compute the measures of each of the other angles.

Questions posed with figures like the one shown in Figure 6–8 (see page 231) can be used across different grade levels to help students develop more, and more sophisticated, understanding. Revisiting situations with more sophisticated questions can help students connect previous knowledge to new knowledge. Equally important, these questions give us as teachers a chance to reveal students' different levels of understanding.

Many tasks have multiple mathematics ideas that can be highlighted, and every mathematics learning target can be approached through a variety of tasks. It is important to assess students' thinking across a variety of tasks so that we can choose tasks that will be most helpful for moving students' thinking forward. The students in a class will likely be at many different places in the journey to reach each learning target. Mathematically rich tasks can often be used to assess students' progress toward several learning targets simultaneously. Knowing the relative positions of students is an important part of being able to target instruction appropriately for that class. INFORMative assessment helps generate information that allows us to understand these relative positions. Our challenge is to select mathematically rich tasks that involve ideas (for example, concepts, algorithms) that are currently being taught or have recently been taught so that we can assess students' progress toward learning those ideas.

When students work on practice exercises, they are typically using a procedure that is specified for them, but when students work on significant problem-solving tasks, they have to decide what solution strategies to use. It is often only in this more complex activity that the depth of students' understanding is revealed—as well as gaps in their knowledge or flaws in their decision making. INFORMative assessment helps reveal *both* what students know and what gaps they have. In these situations we have opportunities to reveal common misconceptions or gaps in students' knowledge, especially related to practice standards, and then we can help students correct their understanding or fill in their gaps.

> **Assessment Tip** ✔
>
> Consider working together with teachers at different grade levels to promote the development of connections across grades.

Some tasks provide contexts in which students can reason in very different ways. Analysis of the mathematics that *might* be used is an important step in choosing a mathematically rich task to pose to students. This analysis requires us to try to imagine how some students might think. It is often difficult for us to forget what we know, but that is part of the fun of being a teacher! For example, the task that follows *seems* fairly routine, but in fact several issues need to be considered.

Task: Finding Dimensions

Find the dimensions of the box of greatest volume that can be cut out of a square piece of cardboard that measures 40 inches on each side. The box has no top.

The task leaves open whether the box model must be "foldable" from the cutout or whether the sides of the box can be taped together after they are cut out. It also leaves open the issue of whether each side of the box must be made of a single piece of cardboard or whether it can be formed from many different pieces. There is a restriction that the total surface area of the box cannot be greater than 1,600 square inches (the size of the cardboard), but there is no requirement that the dimensions of each side be whole inches. Because we are making a box (a rectangular prism), however, there is an implicit requirement that the dimensions of the sides "match" along the edges of the sides of the box. So this task has considerable potential to reveal many different aspects of the depth of students' thinking.

When planning instruction that includes rich tasks, we think about both the major strategies that students are likely to use in generating a solution and what the use of various strategies reveals about students' thinking. Recognizing the range of understanding in a class is critical for making decisions about whether to move on or to provide more experiences for the content in a lesson—to differentiate instruction.

Use Questions to Amplify the Effects of Tasks on Learning

Tasks do not stand alone. There are always interactions, not only between students and the teacher but also among students themselves. Sometimes those interactions are structured around questions posed by students to each other.

More often, questions are posed by the teacher, so it is important to consider the kinds of questions that might accompany mathematically rich tasks.

When we plan to use a mathematically rich task, we should think about probing questions we might pose that will reveal more information about students' thinking. Writing probing questions during instructional planning is a good way to "get your head around" the mathematics concepts embedded in a task. Each question should focus on some critical aspect of the task so that we are better able to reveal students' thinking. These questions can also have the effect of focusing students' attention on those critical aspects.

Learn More...

Chapter 4 contains more information on the use of probing questions to understand students' thinking.

→ A Closer Look

Mr. Poole's Probing Questions with *The Fair Game*

Mr. Poole wanted his students to think about conditional probability. He chose to use the context of whether games are fair or not fair. He asked his students to analyze *The Fair Game* task, shown below. He knew that some students would have difficulty with the changing probabilities caused by nonreplacement of the balls in the box.

Task: The Fair Game

A box contains 4 red balls and 8 yellow balls. Without looking, draw two balls from the box, one at a time, without replacement. If the balls are the same color, you win. If the balls are different colors, you lose. Is this game fair?

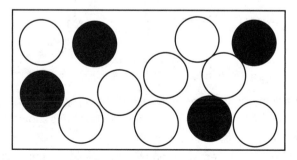

Conditional probability appears in the high school statistics standards in CCSSM. *The Fair Game* is aligned with the standards in the "Conditional Probability and the Rules of Probability" domain.

Making a determination of "fair or not fair" requires some theoretical analysis. Empirical results from playing the game will not be definitive because it is so close to being fair. Think about the task before you read on. How would you begin work on this task? Could you solve it confidently?

This task matches the characteristics of rich tasks we discussed earlier in this chapter. There is no algorithm that will lead students to the solution. Rather, students have to analyze the probabilities involved and then relate that analysis to the issue of fairness. Students who approach the task empirically might generate a partial or incomplete solution.

Mr. Poole asked his students to work on the task individually, then collected the work to examine overnight. He observed three different kinds of solutions, shown in the work of Martha, Jason, and Chris. (See Figures 6–9 through 6–11.) The thinking behind these solutions is somewhat different and he wanted to show these solutions and pose questions to help all the students in his class understand the differences in thinking.

$$rr \quad \frac{4}{12} \cdot \frac{3}{11} = \frac{12}{132}$$

$$ry \quad \frac{4}{12} \cdot \frac{8}{11} = \frac{32}{132}$$

$$yr \quad \frac{8}{12} \cdot \frac{4}{11} = \frac{32}{132}$$

$$yy \quad \frac{8}{12} \cdot \frac{7}{11} = \frac{56}{132}$$

Not fair but almost

$$rr + yy \quad \frac{12}{132} + \frac{56}{132} = \frac{68}{132}$$

$$ry + yr \quad \frac{32}{132} + \frac{32}{132} = \frac{64}{132}$$

FIGURE 6–9. Martha's Solution for *The Fair Game*

Martha solved the task correctly, even "elegantly" (see Figure 6-9). Some teachers might ask, "What is there to question? Doesn't this show that her thinking is good?" As noted earlier, it is important to create a classroom environment in which *all* thinking is reflected upon. Martha could probably answer all the questions that follow, but Mr. Poole knew that being able to explain one's work clearly is an important part of learning. Questioning her response also provided other students opportunities to hear Martha's reasoning. He listed the following questions to use during the discussion on the next day.

- *What do you mean by "almost"?*

- *Why did the denominators change in the fractions you multiplied?*

- *How did you determine the numerators for the fractions you multiplied?*

- *For the "ry" case, why did you multiply?*

- *Why did you add the fractions for the "rr" and "yy" cases?*

Assessment Tip ✓

Challenge students to justify their work even if their answers are correct.

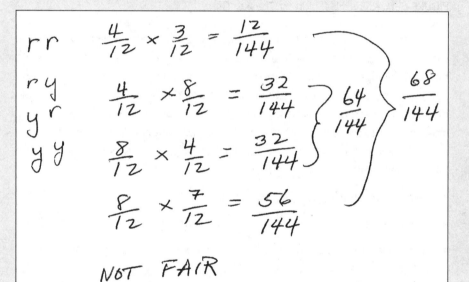

FIGURE 6-10. Jason's Solution for *The Fair Game*

Jason's solution suggests that he is on the right track (see Figure 6–10). He made one important error, however—not accounting for the reduction in the number of balls in the box after the first ball was drawn. Mr. Poole felt that Jason needed to be challenged to think through his solution and possibly to self-correct himself. Mr. Poole listed the following questions to use during the discussion on the next day.

- *How did you determine the denominators of the fractions you multiplied?*

- *For the "rr" case, why did you multiply?*

- *How did you find $\frac{64}{144}$ and $\frac{68}{144}$?*

- *For the "rr" case, why do the numerators change?*

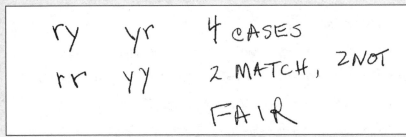

FIGURE 6-11. Chris's Solution for *The Fair Game*

Mr. Poole found that Chris's solution was somewhat difficult to interpret (see Figure 6-11). Listing the four combinations is a good start, and that should be acknowledged, but Chris's work then fails to account for the unequal, and changing, probabilities of drawing each color ball from the box. Mr. Poole decided he wanted to help the class see the errors in this response, but he knew he had to be careful not to put Chris on the defensive with the questions. Mr. Poole listed the following questions to use during the discussion so that the whole class could struggle with them.

- *Are the four combinations equally likely? How do you know?*

- *If we drew only one ball from the box, what is the probability that the ball is red?*

- *If we draw one red ball from the box, how many balls remain? What is the probability of drawing a second red ball?*

Asking probing questions is one way to integrate INFORMative assessment with the use of mathematically rich tasks. Martha's, Jason's, and Chris's solutions to *The Fair Game* task illustrate how we as teachers have to deal with a range of responses for tasks. Thinking of questions that reveal students' thinking is challenging. It is important, however, to weave those kinds of questions into the debriefing of a task, since questioning helps students reflect on their own understanding.

> **Learn More...**
> Chapter 4 offers more about the importance of debriefing.

INFORMing My Practice

Mathematically rich tasks play a critical part in mathematics instruction. These tasks both teach and provide information about students' thinking. Yet teachers may have to take some risks in learning how to use such tasks effectively and certainly will have to be diligent in finding mathematically rich tasks that match the learning targets in their lessons. Students must be helped to recognize that the extra work that rich tasks require of them will pay off in the amount that they learn. The journey toward this kind of instruction is worth the effort. We encourage all teachers to make a commitment to use mathematically rich tasks more extensively.

Before leaving this chapter, turn to "Reflection 6–4: INFORMing My Practice: Strategies for Choosing Mathematically Rich Tasks for Instruction and Assessment" (see page 245) and record your thoughts about mathematically rich tasks.

Reflection 6–4

INFORMing My Practice: Strategies for Choosing Mathematically Rich Tasks for Instruction and Assessment

Page 245

Reflection 6-1: Reflect on Your Favorite Tasks: Are They Mathematically Rich?

Think of one of your favorite problems to pose to students. Write your task at the bottom of the page for easy reference. Then, think about the task in relation to each of the characteristics of a mathematically rich problem (adapted from Hsu, Kysh, and Resek n.d.).

The Characteristics of a Mathematically Rich Problem	The Task
1. The "mysterious" part of the problem is mathematical.	
2. The problem has very little visible scaffolding.	
3. There are many ways to do the problem.	
4. Students of different skill levels can learn from this activity.	
5. The problem has natural extensions.	
6. The problem is hard.	
7. The problem encourages getting your hands dirty with data.	
8. The problem has interesting partial solutions.	

(continued)

Reflection 6-1: Reflect on Your Favorite Tasks: Are They Mathematically Rich? (continued)

1. Which of the criteria for mathematically rich problems does your task reflect the most? Explain.

2. Which of the criteria for mathematically rich problems does your task reflect the least? Explain.

3. How might you modify your task so that it fits more of the criteria?

Reflection 6-2: Modifying Traditional Tasks

For each traditional task below, write a modification of the task that will make it "richer." List the characteristics of a rich task (see page 204) that your modification addresses.

Traditional Task	Modification	Characteristics addressed
1. Which of these functions represents a proportional relationship? $f(x) = 3x - 1$ $f(x) = 3x$ $f(x) = 3x + 7$		
2. Find the volume of these 3-D shapes: cylinder: r = 5 cm, h = 5 cm sphere: r = 5 cm		
3. Solve this equation: $\sqrt{2 - x} = x$		

4. Choose a traditional task from your text and write it below.

(continued)

5. Answer these questions about the task you've chosen:

   a. What is the key mathematics idea addressed by the task?

   b. What is the traditional way to solve this task?

   c. What errors do students typically make in solving this task? What misunderstanding is associated with each error?

   d. What related mathematics ideas might help students solve this task?

6. Write a modification of the traditional task that might help students connect these related ideas.

Reflection 6-3: Linking Content and Practice Standards: Understanding a Mathematical Practice

To be able link content and practice (process) standards, it's important to be able to first really understand each practice standard. Following is an excerpt from the Common Core State Standards for Mathematical Practice 3. Read the excerpt, thinking specifically about the italicized words. Then answer the questions that follow.

> *3 Construct viable arguments and critique the reasoning of others.*
>
> Mathematically proficient students understand and use stated assumptions, definitions, and previously established results in constructing arguments. They make *conjectures* and build a *logical progression of statements* to explore the truth of their conjectures. They are able to analyze situations by breaking them into cases, and can recognize and use *counter examples.* They justify their conclusions, communicate them to others, and respond to the arguments of others. They *reason inductively about data*, making plausible arguments that take into account the context from which the data arose. (CCSS.MATH.PRACTICE.MP3; italics added)

1. How are *conjectures* different from *guesses*?

2. What does "*logical progression of statements*" mean?

3. How are *counter examples* different from *nonexamples*?

4. What does "*reason inductively about data*" mean?

Reflection 6–4: INFORMing My Practice: Strategies for Choosing Mathematically Rich Tasks for Instruction and Assessment

Think about the chapter you just read. Use this space to record your ideas.

Ideas about the importance of mathematically rich tasks:

Changes in my thinking about INFORMative assessment:

Ideas I envision becoming a more important part of my practice:

Questions I have:

Frustrations/concerns I have:

Section IV

How Can I Support My Students in Assessing Themselves?

Supporting Student Self-Assessment and Responsibility

How can we encourage, facilitate, and support students in taking greater responsibility for their learning? How can we guide them to learn and use techniques for self-assessment? This chapter focuses on strategies to help students become better at self-monitoring their learning. The strategies are grouped under two main headings, but in reality they overlap and could be organized in many different ways. Together, these strategies promote an atmosphere of mutual respect and shared responsibility for student learning.

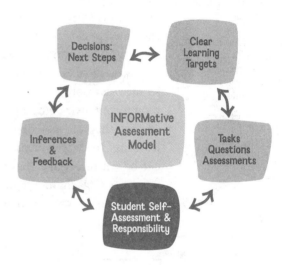

Overview

Creating a Positive Climate for Learning and Student Responsibility

Learn More...

Oxford Dictionaries provide one definition of *climate* as a "general attitude or feeling; an atmosphere or a situation which exists in a particular place." (oxforddictionaries. com/us/definition/ learner/climate)

Everyone agrees that classrooms should provide a positive climate for learning for all students. We work hard to make our classrooms comfortable, inviting places. Yet some secondary students do not see school as an enjoyable place to be, whether their perceptions are based on lack of academic success, their own personalities, not seeing the relevance of classes they must take, or circumstances outside of school beyond our control.

One goal of education is to nurture lifelong, independent learners, so the classroom climate must be structured to help students gain skills in monitoring their own learning. Students need to develop internal motivation so that they are not dependent on teachers or grades as an impetus for learning. In classrooms where students are motivated, students prove they can be self-directed and can take greater ownership for their learning. While we cannot teach motivation, we can create a positive climate conducive to students' development of internal motivation. Consider the following characteristics of a positive climate.

Characteristics of a Positive Climate for Learning

- The environment is open and positive.

- Students are treated with respect.

- Students know their ideas are valued.

- Students are involved in decisions.

- Students have choices.

- Students are encouraged to set goals.

- Learning, not grades, is emphasized.

- Mistakes are opportunities to learn.

- Teachers set high but realistic expectations.

- Teachers are enthusiastic about mathematics.

- There are many opportunities for success.

- Teachers provide feedback frequently.

- Students work with partners and in groups.

- Intense competition is avoided.

- Often tasks include real-world contexts.

- Applications and tasks are related to students' interests.

In this section we discuss five strategies that incorporate the characteristics of a positive classroom climate for learning into a "win-win" situation for students and teachers. Some strategies are subtle and at first may appear mundane. Other strategies challenge our traditional ways of teaching mathematics and consequently may also challenge our comfort level. Regardless, all the strategies discussed here require careful implementation.

Strategies for Creating a Positive Climate for Learning

1. Communicate clear expectations.

2. Establish respect for thinking.

3. Establish characteristics of quality student work.

4. Address issues of language and vocabulary.

5. Define what grades represent.

Learn More...

"Teachers establish and nurture an environment conducive to learning mathematics through the decisions they make, the conversations they orchestrate, and the physical setting they create."
—*Principles and Standards for School Mathematics* (National Council of Teachers of Mathematics 2000, 18)

The Research: A Climate to Support Student Learning

Research on teaching and learning mathematics with understanding identifies four features of classrooms that function as communities of learners:

1. Students' ideas and methods are respected and valued because they have the potential to contribute to everyone's learning.

2. Students choose and share with the class their methods of solving problems while recognizing that many strategies are likely to exist for solving problems.

3. Students appreciate the value of mistakes as opportunities for learning by examining reasoning, thus deepening everyone's analysis of the mistakes.

4. Students learn that decisions for whether something is correct and sensible lie in the logic and structure of mathematics rather than the status of the teacher or the popularity of the student making the argument.

Strategy 1: Communicate Clear Expectations

Being explicit about expectations is part of establishing a classroom climate in which all students can learn. Secondary students may have as many as five or six different teachers each day, and each teacher may have a different way of doing things and different expectations for student performance. Adolescents need to learn, as part of the transition to adulthood, that they are responsible for their actions. For this reason it's especially crucial that students know the "housekeeping" expectations of each class, including:

- what they do when they first enter the classroom,
- what materials they need to have ready when class begins,
- how their homework is handled, and
- how their papers should be organized.

When setting these housekeeping expectations, we encourage a focus on clear, specific directions for what to do rather than on what *not* to do; for example, *I want you to copy notes and the examples we put on the board into your notebook so you will have them as a reference.*

There are instructional expectations that go beyond housekeeping; for example, all students are expected to complete assignments and students will have opportunities to revise work that is incomplete or incorrect. In addition, students need to know that assistance is available to help them overcome their struggles. Assistance might include peer help to get started on a task, conversations with the teacher to clarify thinking, or use of additional tools (e.g, manipulatives, technology) to relieve the burden of making calculations or models.

Learn More...

"[I]n addition to selecting tasks with goals in mind and sharing essential information, the teacher's primary role is to establish a classroom culture that supports learning with understanding, thereby serving to motivate students to learn."
—*Adding It Up,* (Kilpatrick, Swafford, and Findell 2001, 345)

→ A Closer Look

Mrs. Kolb Creates a Climate of Clear Expectations with *Cori the Camel*

Mrs. Kolb, an experienced high school algebra teacher, knows it takes time and effort to establish an environment with clear expectations, so she begins working on expectations the first day of school each year. She starts her classes with an open-ended, nonroutine problem. Her primary focus is engaging all students in a rich task that challenges students but is accessible to all. The tasks she chooses do not have obvious solution paths and the possibilities for reaching a solution are usually intriguing. Because there is some ambiguity in the tasks and possible partial solutions, Mrs. Kolb uses her students' questions about the tasks as an opportunity to share her expectations:

- Every student will engage in mathematical thinking.

- Each student contributes when working with a partner or in a group.

- Mistakes are viewed as part of developing competence.

- Presentation of solutions is required.

- Discussions about thinking are the norm.

Cori the Camel (in Rachlin et al. 1992) is one of the tasks Mrs. Kolb uses. She explains, "I like to start off the year with nonroutine activities that are accessible to all students. My purpose is to spark students' interest and involvement in the process of problem solving, to encourage them to generate possible solutions and to have them learn how to challenge each other to find a 'better' answer. I give them my rules and make clear my expectation that everyone will participate. With tasks such as *Cori the Camel*, students always have questions and want me to scaffold the task for them. Instead I encourage them to talk with their partners and to be prepared to justify their solutions based on the parameters they establish. This level of openness is not appropriate for many tasks, so I use their different interpretations to talk about how justifying solutions goes beyond simply telling the steps they use to get an answer."

Take time to solve *Cori the Camel*. What kind of thinking could be useful in solving the task?

Task: Cori the Camel

Cori the camel is 1,000 miles from market. She has 3,000 bananas. She can carry a maximum of 1,000 bananas and eats one banana for each mile traveled. What is the maximum number of bananas she can get to market?

Though there are no Common Core State Standards directly connected to the *Cori the Camel* task, students do have opportunities to engage with several of the Standards for Mathematical Practice in solving this task, especially, "Make sense of problems and persevere in solving them" (MP1) and "Reason abstractly and quantitatively" (MP2).

The computations for this task are simple: basic addition and subtraction. There are numerous questions that are suggested by the task, for example:

- Does Cori eat the banana at the beginning of the mile, during the mile, or at the end of the mile? Does it matter?

- Can Cori carry 1,000 bananas at the start *and* eat a different banana or does the banana that is eaten on the first mile have to be one of the 1,000 she carries?

Mrs. Kolb encourages students to answer their own questions and form their own interpretations, but she cautions them to be prepared to justify their solutions.

Would a task such as *Cori the Camel* engage your students, encourage them to ask questions and make assumptions, and cause them to want to share their solutions? When a teacher's purpose is to establish a classroom climate that encourages discussion and engages students in solving nonroutine problems, it is OK for tasks to be somewhat ambiguous; justifying solutions is a major part of real-world problems.

Time invested in nonroutine tasks early in a course affords an opportunity to establish guidelines for participation and class discussions while reinforcing the idea that mistakes are opportunities for learning. As Mrs. Kolb comments, "In addition to establishing my rules for how students should work together, problems like this allow me to provide guidelines for how we will share solutions and the language that is acceptable for critiquing each other's reasoning."

Routines are part of classroom management that can help maximize learning. In Mrs. Kolb's classroom, students know they are expected to take out their homework as soon as they enter class and go through each question with others in their group. She moves around the room talking with individuals, listening to the conversations, and making notes. "This allows me to write down things I think we need to talk about as a group. It also allows me to talk with students who seem to be having difficulty. I might ask them, 'What do you think about the idea that [another student] has?' or 'Talk with me about why you used this approach.'" Mrs. Kolb points out that she spends time early in the semester talking with students about the value of hearing how fellow students think about problems. "I stress that if they do not do their homework, they are doing their group a disservice because they have nothing to talk about." While it would be a rare classroom in which every student is fully prepared every day, providing opportunities for students to voice their ideas is an important part of convincing them that there is value in being prepared. This classroom routine highlights three important expectations for students:

- Complete your homework.

- Be prepared to begin class with a discussion of your work.

- Consider and evaluate your peers' approaches to assigned tasks.

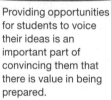

Assessment Tip

A nonroutine task is often helpful when you provide students with guidelines on how to share solutions, critique each other's reasoning, and more.

Assessment Tip

Providing opportunities for students to voice their ideas is an important part of convincing them that there is value in being prepared.

Clear expectations about the management of the classroom are only part of the equation. It is equally important to be sure that students know what mathematics they are to learn, how they are to complete assignments, and how they will show what they have learned. This information is especially important when lessons extend to more than one day; students need to remain explicitly aware of expectations for demonstrating learning.

Classroom routines can influence students' expectations and their thinking about characteristics of quality instruction. It is important for us to understand the kinds of expectations that students bring at the beginning of the year, so that we can help students adjust those expectations to match the classroom routines that we want to use. For example, one change in students' mind-set we want to foster is to go from thinking, "The teacher will give me the answer if I wait long enough" to "I need to figure this out for myself." Student expectations that we think are most productive include the following:

- Teachers will question both correct and incorrect responses.
- Teachers may not always give simple answers to students' questions.
- Assigned tasks will reflect a range of complexity.
- Students will often be asked to pose questions about assigned tasks.
- Students need to learn to explain their thinking; "opting out" is not acceptable.

Teachers may have to introduce these ideas to students (and parents!), but students must ultimately internalize them. Without changes in students' visions about instruction, teachers will face a serious uphill battle in changing instructional practices.

> **Learn More…**
>
> "[W]hen teachers hold high expectations and make students responsible for their own learning by requiring active participation in mathematically rigorous lessons, students get the message that teachers believe in their abilities."
> —"Mathematical Reasoning and Sense Making Begins with the Opportunity to Learn" (Stiff and Johnson 2011, 89)

→ A Closer Look

Mr. Ross Communicates Clear Expectations for Problem Solving with *Eric the Sheep*

Making sense of the problem, perseverance, and critiquing the reasoning of others are part of the classroom climate that can be emphasized with the task *Eric the Sheep*, which Mr. Ross uses with his students. Try to solve the task before you read on about Mr. Ross's experiences with it.

Eric the Sheep relates to many of the standards in the domain "Building Functions" as well as to the Math Practices "Make sense of problems and persevere in solving them" (MP1) and "Construct viable arguments and critique the reasoning of others" (MP3).

Task: Eric the Sheep

It's a hot summer day, and Eric the Sheep is at the end of a line of sheep waiting to be shorn. There are 50 sheep in front of him. Eric is impatient and every time the shearer takes a sheep from the front of the line to be shorn, Eric sneaks up two places in line. How many sheep will get shorn before Eric?

In this nonroutine algebraic task, Mr. Ross's students collect and organize data and then examine the data to look for and generalize patterns. He expects students to be clear about what they do to solve the problem and about explaining both their processes and their solution, and he knows he, in turn, has to be very clear about stating these expectations before students begin work on the task.

Mr. Ross: Are there any words in the problem that are unfamiliar to you?

Mark: What does *shorn* mean?

Mr. Ross: It means cutting the wool off the sheep. Who can explain what we are trying to figure out in this problem?

Letoya: The question is, "How many sheep get shorn before Eric does?"

Mr. Ross: Letoya, can you say that in your own words?

Letoya: There will be some number of sheep that get shorn before Eric, and we need to figure out how many. It might be one or two or it might be fifty. That is what we have to find.

Assessment Tip ✓

"Not all classroom discussions result in improved learning if we confine ourselves to looking for a particular response. Part of creating an environment that promotes sense making and reasoning is being open to students' unanticipated answers."
—Jason Haynes, teacher

Mr. Ross: What are some strategies that we might use to solve this problem? Please talk with you group to generate some ideas before you start to solve the problem. (*Circulates to listen to strategies being proposed and to maintain the focus of the conversation in each group.*)

Mr. Ross: I would like to ask Travis and Alisa to share the strategies proposed by their groups.

Travis: We decided to draw a picture.

Alisa: We are going to make a table showing the number of sheep shorn and the number in line ahead of Eric.

Mr. Ross: OK. Let's all work the problem. We will share strategies and compare answers and see if you come to the same conclusion.

Students' success in learning the process of generalizing, along with their success in learning the process of making convincing mathematical arguments, are important factors in how well they succeed in mathematics through high school and beyond. As part of our instruction, we need to invest in the time to establish and support the expectation that students will communicate their mathematical thinking coherently and clearly to peers, teachers, and others.

Strategy 2: Establish Respect for Thinking

One fundamental component of a positive climate for learning is an atmosphere of mutual respect. Mutual respect means not only respect for a person but also respect for the ability to think and reason logically. It is the latter—*respect for thinking*—that we focus on here. Respect for thinking is foundational to self-assessment, work with partners, and peer collaboration. Later in this chapter we discuss partner and group work in depth.

Establishing a positive climate for learning in which students feel safe to say what they are thinking rather than trying to guess what the teacher wants them to say does not happen in one or two lessons; it has to be negotiated by the teacher, working with students over time. Teachers know that they must pay attention to building trust while establishing ground rules for student interactions if students are to become resources for each other and be willing to assess their own mathematics knowledge thoughtfully. As teachers we can model respect for thinking in several ways; following we suggest a few.

Practices for Establishing Respect for Thinking

1. Emphasize that it is OK for students to express opinions.

2. Emphasize that it is OK for students to change their minds.

3. Give students "think time" before responding to a question.

4. Give students time to explain their thinking without interruption.

5. Encourage students to ask questions when ideas are unclear.

6. Encourage students as they make efforts to learn.

When these practices are adopted as classroom norms, students may need to be reminded of them occasionally. But over time, students will internalize them. Certainly, this process is easier if such norms are incorporated throughout the school, but even if this is not the case, individual teachers can create positive classroom climates for learning that establish respect for thinking. Following we take a more detailed look at each of the six practices for establishing respect for thinking.

Practice 1: Emphasize that it is OK for students to express opinions.
Differences of opinion are good—they indicate that students are thinking. While it is OK to disagree with an opinion, it is not OK to attack the person who expresses that opinion. When everyone's opinions are valued, there are opportunities for clarifying discussions about key mathematics concepts and relationships among concepts, as well as about interpretations of tasks. If students are able to join into conversations without being laughed at or feeling foolish, they are more likely to become risk takers who are willing to work to learn more challenging mathematics.

It's important for students to learn the difference between opinions and facts. Teachers have to be clear that it is OK for students to express opinions and that opinions will not be ridiculed, even if the teacher or other students disagree. Opinions are not necessarily based on facts (either mathematics facts or other kinds of facts), so it is acceptable for a wide range of opinions to be expressed without the need to resolve differences. Mathematics facts, on the other hand, are not based on opinions. Students' opinions, for example, about what constitutes adequate evidence for a proof or a convincing argument must be recognized and understood by teachers as part of assessing what students know and can do. Consider the following examples.

Examples of Student Misconceptions About What Constitutes a Convincing Argument

Geometry
Some students may say that the diagonals of a rectangle can never meet at a 90-degree angle because a rectangle is always longer than it is wide. That incorrect belief fails to recognize that a square is also a rectangle.

Statistics
Some students may say that since the mean of a set of data is 48, then half of the values are above 48 and half are below. This misunderstanding may represent a confusion between *mean* and *median*.

Algebra
Some students may say that the reciprocal of a number is less than the number, because $\frac{1}{3}$ is less than 3 and $\frac{1}{10}$ is less than 10. Making a generalization from too few examples is often an issue in generating a convincing proof.

Practice 2: Emphasize that it is OK for students to change their minds.

Since learning is all about incorporating new ideas and skills into what we already know, students must learn that it is OK to change their minds and that mistakes are natural components of learning. When students have a different idea from their first response, they need to be comfortable saying, "I was wrong because . . ." or "At first I thought . . . , but now I think. . . ." Even when a statement is clearly incorrect mathematically and needs to be corrected, respect dictates that the thinking behind the statement is not ridiculed.

Sometimes as teachers we pose a question in response to an incorrect answer. Providing time for reflection about an incorrect answer often helps students to self-correct, and learning how to self-correct is an important metacognitive skill. On the other hand, sometimes teachers pass over an incorrect response, since focusing on it may create a diversion that is counterproductive to the instructional goals for the lesson. This is OK; there is not always enough time to follow up on every student comment.

Practice 3: Give students "think time" before responding to a question.

Good questions almost always require more than one-number or one-word answers. Thinking takes time, and thinking is very important in mathematics lessons. Historically, "think time" is often called "wait time." Researchers found that when the wait time—a period of silence—between when a teacher poses a question and students respond was increased from the typical one and a half seconds to three seconds, the length and correctness of students' responses increased and teachers' questions became more varied. As the cognitive complexity of a question increases, we can expect that the amount of think time should increase correspondingly.

There should be think time after a teacher-posed question and also after a student gives a response to that question. It may feel awkward to pose a question and be met with total silence and little or no eye contact. Teachers also may feel pressure to move on because of the number of content expectations that have been prescribed for their course. However, uninterrupted silence after a teacher asks a question offers students opportunities to process information and think about an appropriate response.

Teachers use different approaches to providing think time. For example, rather than prefacing a question with a student's name, a teacher might pose a question, pause, and then call on a student to respond. Another approach for providing think time is to wait until at least a third of the students have raised their hands before calling on someone to respond. Teachers who want to increase think time sometimes count silently to five or ten before calling on a student for a response.

Learn More...

Metacognition is often informally defined as "students thinking about their own thinking." To read more about John Flavell and metacognition, go to lifecircles-inc.com/Learningtheories/constructivism/flavell.html.

Learn More...

Stahl's (1994) article, which can be found on the ERIC Digests Web site, offers more on the value of think time (or wait time) and using it skillfully in the classroom.

Practice 4: Give students time to explain their thinking without interruption.

┌─ **Learn More...** ─┐
See Chapter 4 for
a more detailed
discussion on
intentional listening.

Respect for thinking demands that we practice patience and intentional listening. Modeling intentional listening sends a message to the class that what each student has to say is important.

A student's explanation needs to be understood by both the teacher and the student's peers. When it is appears not to be understood, it is important to give opportunities for other students to ask clarifying questions. Everyone in the classroom must recognize that all students can learn, though not necessarily at the same pace or in the same way. Teachers have to balance the need for different pacing and different paths to learning with the demands of covering the curriculum. Sometimes there are teachable moments when instruction takes a slightly different track than was planned, and other times it is necessary for teachers to limit the discussion of alternate solutions to a problem even when some of those solutions might be particularly compelling to a few students. There may be some students who still need additional instruction on the mathematics. For example, a student's response to a question may reveal a misconception that needs to be addressed, especially if several students seem to "buy in" to that same misconception. If we interrupt students' explanations too quickly, we may not identify these kinds of misconceptions. When students' conversations or work indicates a lack of understanding, teachers might provide individual attention to those students or form a small instructional group for further investigations of the mathematics.

Practice 5: Encourage students to ask questions when ideas are unclear.

Allow students to ask questions. It is often the case that if one student asks a question that indicates a mathematical confusion, there are probably other students in the class with similar confusion. A question may seem trivial or silly to a teacher who understands the content, but for the novice who is just learning the content, the question may be very relevant. When it appears content is not understood, give opportunities for other students to ask clarifying questions. We have to be alert, however, to the possibility that one or two students will *always* ask clarifying questions, regardless of whether they personally do or do not understand the student's explanation.

We want to avoid allowing a few students to dominate discussions. All teachers have experienced the student who loves to hear himself (or herself) talk and who asks question after question. This kind of "question asking" has to be curtailed, but otherwise there should be a classroom norm that emphasizes that all serious questions are welcomed.

Practice 6: Encourage students as they make efforts to learn.
As teachers we should always communicate that if a student doesn't understand, there will be avenues for assistance, as long as the student *makes an effort to learn*. Students must understand that learning is a responsibility they share with the teacher and that there are consequences for their actions. Hard work and completed assignments will bring the reward of increased knowledge and the likelihood of improved grades, whereas failure to complete assignments will likely lead to poor grades and the failure to master the learning targets. In a positive climate for learning, students embrace the opportunity to improve and are able to believe that success is within their grasp.

> **Assessment Tip** ✓
>
> Honoring think time may mean preventing overly vocal students from immediately calling out ideas.

> **Assessment Tip** ✓
>
> "Sometimes I give a struggling student a special version of a test. It has the same content as the tests for other students, but there are fewer problems. No one knows this except the student and myself."
> —Matilda Godfrey, teacher

→ A Closer Look

Mr. Moser Establishes Respect for Thinking During Discussion with *Volume of a Cylinder*

In establishing a positive climate for learning, there are times when worthwhile tasks must be specifically chosen with dual purposes of addressing content standards and building respect for ideas and mathematical reasoning. Consider the following discussion in an eighth-grade classroom. The teacher, Mr. Moser, recognizes that some of his students are not clear about what happens to the volume of cylinders when one dimension increases. What does Mr. Moser do, rather than telling students what would happen or asking questions that lead students to a correct response?

Mr. Moser: (*Draws a cylinder on the board and labels height as 9 cm and radius as 2 cm.*) If I triple the height of the cylinder, will the volume triple?

Loren: Yes. It would be like three cylinders stacked on top of each other. (*Many students nod in agreement, but some look puzzled.*)

Mr. Moser: (*Takes out three same-sized cylinders.*) Loren, can you show the class what you mean?

Loren: (*Stacks the cylinders one on top of the other.*) Like this.

Mr. Moser: (*Calls on a student who looks puzzled.*) Jolene, can you explain why the volume would triple?

Jolene: It would be like three cans of tennis balls stacked on top of each other. If there are three balls in one can, there would be nine balls in the three cans.

Mr. Moser: Would this be true if I triple the radius of the cylinder? Will the volume of the cylinder triple?

Loren: Sure. It would be like these three cylinders bundled up together.

Carley: I don't think that is right. I think the volume would be greater because you are multiplying twice when you change the radius.

Mr. Moser: Loren, what do you think about what Carley is saying? Is there a question you want to ask her?

Loren: (*Speaking to Carley.*) I don't understand what you mean when you say you multiply twice. Oh wait, you mean you triple the radius number and then multiply by pi.

Mr. Moser: (*Writes on the board:* What happens to the volume of a cylinder when you triple the height? What happens to the volume of a cylinder when you triple the radius?) Think about what Loren and Carley have said. What did Carley mean by "multiply twice"? I want each of you to answer the questions on the board in your journals and justify your responses. Tomorrow we will discuss these questions.

Rather than imposing his interpretation about what Carley meant, Mr. Moser gave Loren the opportunity to ask Carley a question. Mr. Moser could have continued the discussion immediately, but he wanted all the students to think about and then perhaps visualize what happens to the volume when each dimension of a cylinder is changed. He felt that it was important for all students to understand why changing the height of a cylinder does not have the same effect on the volume as changing the radius. Through journaling, Mr. Moser encouraged the students to think about the conversation and clarify their own understanding of the situation. Then, by looking at their writing, Mr. Moser felt he would be able to see which students figured out the relationships. This would give him clues about the students' depth of understanding of volume of cylinders beyond applying the formula.

> **Assessment Tip** ✓
>
> When students critique each other's solutions, they have opportunities to engage in key mathematics ideas.

Strategy 3: Establish Characteristics of Quality Student Work

Knowing what is expected and what counts as quality work is critical if students are to take greater responsibility for their own learning. We need to be very explicit about what it means to work thoughtfully and productively on mathematics tasks. General descriptions that guide students in understanding the characteristics of quality responses can be elaborate or simple, and students come to recognize that mathematics learning involves more than just getting a correct answer to a problem. Following is a list of characteristics to discuss with students.

Characteristics of High-Quality Student Work

- Appropriate processes and/or tools are used.

- Computations and/or diagrams, graphs, charts, and representations are clearly labeled.

- Solution methods are clearly explained in words and/or numbers using appropriate mathematical vocabulary.

- All parts of the problem are attempted; progress is made toward a correct solution.

- Work completed so far is correct.

Descriptions of criteria are best brought to life for students by anchor papers or models of quality work. Class discussions about why a particular sample represents "quality" implicitly encourage students to compare their work to that sample to see what they can improve. During discussions, students might compare two quality responses or one strong sample and one that needs improvement. Of course, models of quality student responses are always linked to specific tasks. For conversations about samples to be helpful, students usually need to solve, or attempt to solve, the task and write their own answers first. Having two responses to the same problem also reinforces the idea that there are multiple ways to solve most problems and to explain thinking.

Strategy 4: Address Issues of Language and Vocabulary

Many students struggling with English face classroom challenges in listening, speaking, reading, and writing. Traditional assessments may not provide a true picture of the mathematics these students understand. Part of instructional planning is seeking tasks and using assessment strategies that are sensitive to the needs of these students. When assessments do not provide a clear picture of what students know and can do, those students may be inappropriately placed in groups or courses. In these situations students' instructional needs may not be met, their confidence in their own abilities may diminish, and they may be denied opportunities to learn challenging mathematics. In addition, when instructional and assessment strategies fail to engage students and appropriately evaluate their mathematical proficiency, students are more likely to "tune out" and thus compound the problem of failing to learn important mathematics.

Creating a Positive Climate When There Are Issues of Language and Vocabulary

Mr. Leiva, a Math I teacher, has the following to say about how to create a positive climate when there are issues of language and vocabulary.

"Because I grew up in San Salvador and moved to the United States in seventh grade, I am an English language learner myself. I know that students process in their native language first before reprocessing the information in English. When questions are posed, many students need more wait time.

"Also from experience, I know that English language learners may sometimes feel inadequate in the classroom; they realize that they are in need of extra help from the teacher to accomplish classwork, and consequently, their self-esteem plummets. In my classroom I try to build confidence in these students by celebrating their diverse backgrounds and inviting them to share ideas from their cultures. For example, a native Spanish-speaking student may use a comma instead of a decimal point in a number, which is not what is done in English. When a student shares this, I make an effort to point out how interesting it is. This in turn helps encourage the student to continue sharing and contributing to the classroom discussion.

"As another example, when we learn about the metric system and the U.S. customary system, I invite students whose native language is not English to explain the metric system and/or Celsius temperatures because they often know it well; therefore, they feel they can teach their peers something! Here again, they feel valuable as contributors to the classroom.

"I also enthusiastically share my experiences as a student whose language in the classroom was different from my native language. I help all students understand that it is OK to have differences and accept everyone's differences. It is wonderful to eventually see all students supporting each other's ideas."

It is difficult for students to engage in group activities, make sense of instruction, and participate in discussions if the words spoken by others in the class are not understood. Consider the simplest vocabulary challenges for students whose native language is not English: at home, *tables* hold dishes, not data, and *roots* are the part of a plant that is under the ground, not the location at which the value of a function equals zero. In mathematics *similar* figures have precise relationships and are not merely a collection of rectangles or other shapes that look alike in some way, and the *Law of Sines* is not something voted on by legislators.

Addressing your students' language and vocabulary needs may mean reducing the language demands wherever possible and using a variety of assessment strategies. Enright (2009) lists ten guidelines to help teachers identify and reduce the language demands of their instructions and word problems, making tasks more accessible to students.

Ten Guidelines to Reduce Language Demands

1. Use active voice at first.

2. Use simple verb tenses and constructions.

3. Use flow charts and graphic organizers.

4. Incorporate cognates (words that look or sound similar across languages).

5. Avoid introducing new concepts or processes and new vocabulary together.

6. Simplify sentence structure.

7. Delay use of pronouns.

8. Repeat patterns of language, then paraphrase.

9. Prioritize vocabulary.

10. Make the language of mathematics more demanding over time. (Enright 2009, 30–36)

Think through each of Enright's guidelines; in what ways do you incorporate each of them into your instruction? Think of some examples. For example, Guideline 7, *Delay use of pronouns*, illustrates how precise language, rather than a pronoun, can support understanding; consider saying, "The perimeter of ABCE equals *the perimeter* of ARST" instead of "The perimeter of ABCE equals *that* of ARST."

The following two tasks are paraphrased from an example in Enright (2009, 35). (See Figure 7–1.) Read each task; which one do you feel might be easier for a student struggling with English to understand? Why?

Task 1: Ratio of Areas 1

The perimeter of a square and the circumference of a circle are equal. What do you know about the ratio of their areas? Is the ratio independent of the actual value for the perimeter and circumference?

Task 2: Ratio of Areas 2

Think about a square and a circle for which the distances around have the same value. Would the ratio of the areas be constant, independent of the actual sizes of the figures?

FIGURE 7–1. Alternative Wordings for *Ratio of Areas*

Task 2 may be easier for students who are struggling with mathematics terminology (because they are still early in learning English). Task 1 is "more precise" mathematically, but that does not mean that it is easier to understand or "better." For either version of the task, many teachers would expect students to do some algebraic manipulation in order to compute the ratio of areas. We could scaffold the task directly by providing formulas and by identifying what values to compare in the ratio. (See Figure 7–2 on the next page.) Although this might help students solve the task, doing this runs the risk of reducing the cognitive demand of the task too much; that is, we would end up doing the thinking for the students. As teachers we have to decide when too much scaffolding actually interferes with students' learning. We would argue that the scaffolding in Figure 7–2 goes too far.

Suppose the perimeter of a square and the circumference of a circle are equal.

$P = 4s$, where s = length of the side of the squares

$C = 2\pi r$, where r = radius of the circle

So, $4s = 2\pi r$

What can you say about the ratio of their areas?

$A = s^2$, where s = length of the side of the squares

$A = \pi r^2$, where r = radius of the circle

What is the ratio, $\frac{s^2}{\pi r^2}$?

Is this ratio independent of the actual value for P and C?

FIGURE 7-2. Scaffolding That a Teacher Might Supply for *Ratio of Areas*

Consider Claudia's response to the task. (See Figure 7–3.) Skill with symbol manipulations may be independent of language skills, but skill at explaining why manipulations work is certainly influenced by those language skills. When asked to explain why she "squared both sides" in the second step, Claudia got confused. "I squared both sides, but this is not the square in the problem. I didn't make a square. I just multiplied. I'm not sure how to explain it." In addressing issues of language and vocabulary, as teachers we should be ready to ask questions or to suggest language that can improve explanations. For example, "What did you multiply each side by when you wrote the second step? How do you know that is the correct thing to do?"

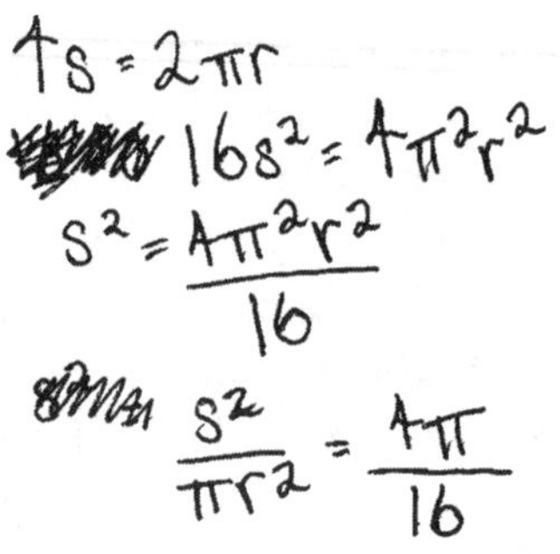

FIGURE 7-3. Claudia's Solution for *Ratio of Areas*

Dacey and Gartland (2009) suggest additional strategies including having students summarize tasks in their own words and trying out thinking in small groups before speaking in front of the class. Other strategies that teachers might use—such as teaching with multiple representations, planning collaborative activities, making explicit connections between and among mathematics topics, and demonstrating concepts concretely, pictorially, and symbolically—will benefit all students. By implementing these strategies, we further support students in gradually building the language skills they need to become independent in mathematics classrooms. It's important to point out as well that these strategies benefit *all* students, not just those with language issues.

Strategy 5: Define What Grades Represent

How grades are determined varies greatly; teachers' decisions about grades are influenced by their personal beliefs, the needs of students, the desires of parents, and the policies of the school district. The purpose here is neither to promote one grading routine versus another nor to advocate for classrooms without grades. Rather, it is to invite teachers to consider how their philosophy and grading practices impact positively or negatively on student persistence and learning.

For example, when feedback rather than a grade is given for some assignments and students have an opportunity to rethink a procedure or to review and revise incorrect solutions, students may become more motivated and further recognize the benefits of completing assignments. One consideration related to feedback or the lack of it is the message that students may internalize when items are marked as incorrect but there are no written comments or further discussion of the work. There are times when students misread a question and answer correctly a different question than the one the teacher intended. Because the answer is marked wrong, the student may think that the mathematics is incorrect when in reality the mathematics may be totally correct. The problem is that the answer does not match the intended question. This situation may be common for many students struggling with the English language, and for students who are poor readers.

There is a popular belief that grades are comparable across classrooms and that they provide an accurate reflection of students' understanding of

> **Assessment Tip** ✔
>
> Consider how your philosophy and grading practices impact positively or negatively on student persistence and learning.

> **Learn More ...**
>
> In Chapter 9, we discuss the idea that feedback to students can be an alternative to grading for some assignments.

mathematics. While many parents and the general public subscribe to this idea, most students and teachers recognize that grades may represent many different things. Criteria used to generate grades vary greatly, and the manner in which grades are combined into one score for a report card can vary from teacher to teacher even within the same school. There are potentially a number of factors that can influence grades. Some teachers consistently grade on a scale of 0 to 100 (percent correct), others score assignments and tests in comparison with the work of all students in the class (grading on a curve). Still other teachers focus on the achievement of goals and measure work against standards (criteria-based grading). Many teachers also consider factors such as attendance, effort, class participation, attitudes, or progress made across the grading period. Some teachers provide opportunities for students to earn extra credit. At the end of each grading period the manner in which grades from class activities, homework, quizzes, major tests, and projects are weighted by different teachers can result in the same set of numbers resulting in different grades on report cards, depending on the teachers' choices.

All teachers have to deal with students who fail to complete assignments. We agree that good grades can sometimes motivate students, but we also have to be concerned that poor grades may discourage students. Often failures to complete work are recorded in grade books as "zeros." Some students, especially some middle grades students, may not understand the consequences of those zeros. If students think that zeros "don't count," it is helpful for them to learn the effects of zeros on averages. For example, the means for {85, 75, 90, 80, 90, 100} and {85, 0, 90, 0, 90, 100} are very different. If these are test or major project scores, the first set represents a student who would pass the course, but the second set represents a student who may fail. If the scores represent test scores from the beginning to the end of the grading period, some teachers might argue that both students ended up knowing virtually the same amount. Strictly computing averages of scores for the end-of-term grade can put students out of the running for anything more than an F or D because of difficulties early in the grading period. Teachers have to ask, "What is my purpose in scoring every assignment? Is it important for students to demonstrate learning throughout the grading period, not just at the end? Should the final grade in a course represent what a student knows at the end of the grading period without regard to earlier assignments?"

Learn More...

Portfolios offer a more detailed view of students' learning, but they are not a replacement for grades. See the discussion of portfolios on pages 280–283 of this chapter.

Whatever guidelines are used in determining grades and however often feedback is given without a grade attached, an important step in creating a climate where success is possible for everyone is being explicit about grading practices. It is critical to communicate to students what is expected for written work, how and when they will have assistance, and what opportunities will be available to revise work that is incomplete or incorrect.

Before we can be explicit with students about guidelines for grading, we have to be clear in our own minds about what grades mean. How do you determine grades in your classes? How does your approach to grading influence students (pro or con)? Complete "Reflection 7-1: Defining What Grades Represent: My Beliefs About Grades" (see pages 303–304), which provides an opportunity to think about both your personal beliefs about grading and the impact that guidelines for grading might have on students.

> **Reflection 7-1**
>
> Defining What Grades Represent: My Beliefs About Grades
>
> Pages 303–304

How Does Creating a Positive Climate for Learning Benefit Teachers?

For all that students gain in a positive climate for learning, there are many benefits for us as teachers. One of the most important is that students are more likely to be engaged with their learning. Classrooms where students are involved in their work give us opportunities to:

- move around the room and observe students close at hand;
- engage in short but needed conversations with individual students;
- converse with students to better understand their thinking about the mathematics in their assignments;
- steer students to more productive paths if they are misinterpreting tasks; and
- discuss issues that relate to individual students rather than the class as a whole, such as improving a specific response, giving feedback when an answer is wrong, or nudging a student to attempt more complex problems.

> **Learn More...**
>
> Chapter 4 offers a more detailed look at individual conversations.

Very often the information we gather from several students provides a general view of where the class is in relation to the topic and helps us make decisions about our next instructional plans. Note that sometimes our conversations with individual students relate to management issues, such as staying on task, doing one's share of the work, and so on, which helps enforce the positive climate for learning.

Spending time up front to establish clear guidelines for working together ensures more successful collaboration. While a "no-talking" classroom does not facilitate intellectual growth, neither does a chaotic classroom. Our goal is to create a supportive environment in which students think about their own ideas and those of others. In every classroom, students sometimes work alone and many times with other students. Students may not recognize that this environment facilitates their learning, but we do. Our opportunities and our students' opportunities to monitor understanding and identify misunderstandings set the stage for everyone to believe success is within reach.

Supporting Expanded Roles for Students

In this section we look specifically at strategies for supporting expanded roles for students. These strategies are in addition to creating a positive climate for learning. As teachers we increase the likelihood of students' being successful in taking greater responsibility for their learning when we craft opportunities for students to engage more fully in mathematics lessons. We accomplish this by setting high expectations; encouraging students to do their best; allowing students' choices whenever possible; and planning lessons that involve higher-order thinking, collaboration, and active student participation (National Research Council 2004). We limit the amount of time students are expected merely to sit and listen.

> ### Assessment Tip ✓
> Classrooms that are effective in promoting high levels of student achievement are those in which an emphasis on learning is evidenced by the obvious engagement of students.

Strategies for Supporting Expanded Roles for Students

1. Encourage students to become self-assessors.

2. Support student reflection through the use of journals, portfolios, and rubrics and checklists.

3. Promote the development of positive peer interactions through partner and group work.

4. Facilitate students' rethinking about their mistakes.

Strategy 1: Encourage Students to Become Self-Assessors

Self-assessment is a reflective process in which students not only monitor and evaluate the quality of their performance but also identify discrepancies between the desired performance and their current work. Through self-assessment, students focus on their own thinking related to the mathematics in lessons and identify strategies that will help them improve their performance. Through self-assessment, students give themselves feedback *while* learning is taking place, rather than waiting for feedback *from* the teacher *after* instruction.

Self-assessments can help students engage with mathematics ideas and understand the reasoning behind their mistakes. Students are able to recognize what is correct as well as articulate for themselves that they need to know more. They learn that when assessments uncover mistakes, mistakes also highlight content that needs to be revisited—and that's a good thing. Self-assessments provide information to help students evaluate what they know, identify what they still need to learn, and refine their understandings.

Both students and teachers have roles in making student self-assessment a tool for learning. Students must learn to ask themselves questions like the following:

- What do I need to learn? (identify the learning target)
- What do I already know? (recognize prior knowledge)
- Where am I now in the process? (reflect on understanding)
- How do I get to the goal? (identify what else is needed)
- Do I know what constitutes success? (know characteristics of quality work)
- How will I know when I have accomplished the goal? (evaluate my work against quality work)

One important role for teachers is to help students become more confident and competent by serving as a coach, a facilitator, and a consultant, at first providing specific models and directions and gradually helping students take greater ownership of decisions. As teachers we provide support

> **Learn More…**
>
> "If formative assessment is to be productive, pupils should be trained in self-assessment so that they can understand the main purposes of their learning and thereby grasp what they need to do to achieve."
> —"Inside the Black Box: Raising Standards Through Classroom Assessment" (Black and Wiliam 1998, 143)

> **Learn More…**
>
> "Students need to self-assess to know when they are learning, how much effort they must expend for success, when they have been successful, when they are wrong, and which learning strategies work well for them."
> —"Student Self-Assessment: The Key to Stronger Student Motivation and Higher Achievement" (McMillan and Hearn 2008, 44)

for students in becoming self-assessors when we collaborate with students to establish goals and set criteria for success:

- Clearly communicate mathematics expectations (the learning targets).
- With student input establish criteria for quality work (models and examples).
- Model thinking about possible solutions to tasks and reflecting on work (metacognition).
- Provide opportunities—time and strategies—for students to self-assess (checklists, rubrics).
- Give students feedback on their self-assessments (goal setting).

We know students' beliefs about themselves as learners of mathematics affect their willingness (motivation) to take seriously opportunities to evaluate their work, so attention to tasks that are appropriately challenging are closely linked with the opportunities we provide for student self-assessment. Students need to perceive themselves as powerful learners of mathematics. Their perceptions are influenced by classroom interactions with teachers and peers as well as by reflections on their learning when they self-assess.

Learn More...

Chapter 6 addresses tasks that are appropriately challenging, and Chapter 9 addresses actionable feedback.

Learn More...

"Self-evaluation is defined as students judging the quality of their work, based on evidence and explicit criteria, for the purpose of doing better work in the future. When we teach students how to assess their own progress, and when they do so against known and challenging quality standards, we find that there is a lot to gain."
—*Student Self-Evaluation: What Research Says and What Practice Shows* (Rolheiser and Ross 2001)

Students' Perceptions Make a Difference

Students must believe that

- success in math is within their reach;
- they know what success looks like;
- assessment supports their learning;
- feedback can be helpful; and
- they will have chances for improving. (Bright and Joyner 2004a)

During a class period there are both planned and unplanned opportunities for students to self-assess. Indeed, there are a huge number of possible self-assessment strategies, and students who are good at self-assessing will likely invent new ways. For example, we might assign a journal prompt in which students are to justify a particular solution to a task, or we might spontaneously ask students to use a hand signal or whiteboard to indicate their level of confidence with their response to a task. When we provide a review sheet and direct students to identify which questions they are confident they can answer correctly and which ones they are uncertain about, students are engaged in self-assessment.

Consider the assessment opportunities described in "Reflection 7–2: Scenarios That Support Student Self-Assessment," pages 305–306. What suggestions would you make if you were advising a colleague on becoming better at supporting student self-assessment?

Learn More...

"Strategy 2: Establish Respect for Thinking" on page 258 in this chapter offers additional examples of student self-assessment strategies.

Reflection 7–2

Scenarios That Support Student Self-Assessment

Pages 305–306

Strategy 2: Support Student Reflection Through the Use of Journals, Portfolios, Rubrics, and Checklists

We recognize that if we want our students to be reflective learners, we must take responsibility for providing a positive classroom climate that encourages and supports students in reflecting on their learning. In this section, we focus on tools that may help students reflect. Journal prompts are tools that can be used with simple instructions from teachers. Students simply respond as they would to any mathematics task. The use of portfolios and rubrics may require a more substantial introduction and modeling in order for students to use them effectively. All these tools, however, encourage student responsibility. Students must be willing to use these tools to develop insights into both what they know and what they can do to enhance their performance. We offer a more detailed look at how journals, portfolios, and rubrics and checklists are important tools for supporting student reflection here.

Journals

Journal entries reflect what students have synthesized from investigations or lessons devoted to developing concepts. The entries are "artifacts" that students can use for reference. They are also an ongoing communication between the teacher and individual students that supports metacognition and can be crafted to help students become better at self-assessing.

Usually students are asked to write in their journals once or twice a week. For journaling to be effective, there must be time for students to write and for teachers to periodically review and respond to what students have written. This back-and-forth between the teacher and each student can turn journaling into an asynchronous conversation that can extend over the entire course.

If students are new to journaling, consider giving specific prompts and guidelines for journaling. Entries may be in response to open prompts such as the following.

Sample Open Journal Prompts

- Describe what you learned today.

- Write what you are confused about.

- How did the discussion at the beginning of the class help you complete the assignment?

- What part of today's lesson was easiest? Hardest?

- How could you use what you learned today?

- What did you already know that was useful in today's lesson?

- What was most enjoyable about today's lesson? Why was that fun for you?

- What do you want us to review before the test?

Learn More...

Chapter 5 provides more information on the use of writing prompts for monitoring student thinking.

Students may summarize what they have learned, describe progress they have made, and analyze mistakes they made (and, hopefully, corrected), or simply list examples of different solution strategies. Encourage students to include drawings and sample problems to illustrate their thinking.

Students who have opportunities to write about how they solved problems are likely to become more reflective in their thinking, more effective in responding to open-ended questions, and better able to justify their thinking. Often prompts are specific to the mathematics in a lesson, such as the following.

Sample Journal Prompts Specific to the Mathematics in a Lesson

- Why can't you divide by zero?

- How do the statistics support the award to the Statesville High School team?

- What guidelines would be helpful to a student who is just learning to graph functions?

- Describe a parallelogram in fifteen or fewer words.

- How are the terms *probability* and *chances* the same? Different?

- How do you know when two shapes are similar?

- How do you solve a quadratic equation?

- What happens to $y = \frac{1}{x}$ for large values of x? For values of x close to zero?

Assessment Tip ✔️

Other writing activities that can be part of mathematics instruction and assessment include writing a mathematics autobiography, writing a poem or letter about a mathematics idea, writing a paragraph using a list of vocabulary words, or editing a paragraph (or solution to a problem) that contains mathematics errors.

Students may need to be reminded to include the prompt in their journals before they respond since there is often a time lag between the journaling and the teacher's reading of the entries.

Journaling can be especially helpful for teachers during the first week or two of a course. Writing prompts such as *List two or three things from previous mathematics instruction that encouraged you to participate in class* and *List two or three things from previous mathematics instruction that caused you to become bored* can reveal what students believe is important for their learning. Of course, students' comments from these prompts or other private communications must be kept private so that students feel safe to express their opinions. However, the information from journals can be summarized anonymously and used in discussions about the classroom climate.

Once trust has been established, students sometimes use their journals to ask questions or make comments about their mathematical thinking that they would not be willing to reveal in front of their peers during class discussions. These entries can serve as monitoring tools to help teachers see progress (or lack of progress) toward achieving the learning objectives and can reveal important information about students' understanding or confusion.

Portfolios

A portfolio is a collection of student work that is carefully assembled to meet certain criteria. In assembling a portfolio, students think about the goals for learning as well as their progress toward reaching those goals. Students typically write reflections about some or all of the contents of a portfolio. Portfolios are not a replacement for grades; rather they offer a more detailed view of students' learning that in turn helps us as teachers provide actionable feedback and encourages students to self-assess. Portfolios are also good vehicles for student-teacher and student-parent conferences and provide opportunities for conversation about students' accomplishments and mathematical thinking. Teachers who have used portfolios successfully report that they are worthwhile because of the benefits to students—in particular, greater ownership of their learning and insight into what they understand and what they still need to learn.

Portfolios represent a significant investment of time on the part of students and teachers, so management decisions need to be addressed before students are required to create portfolios. To determine what is included and how the contents are organized in a portfolio, we must first define the audience and purpose. Portfolios are named in a number of ways with a variety of guidelines for their composition. Examples include showcase or display portfolios, working or progress portfolios, and assessment or pass-along portfolios. For a *showcase portfolio*, students choose assignments that represent their best work; for a *progress portfolio*, students choose examples that demonstrate how much they have learned across the course. For an *assessment* or *pass-along portfolio*, students include specified items (such as major tests) along with a few examples of their own choosing.

As teachers we need to consider purpose in having students create portfolios. Consider the following organizational questions to help make portfolio creation a positive experience.

Thinking About Portfolios: Organizational Questions

- Who is the audience for the portfolios?

- What is the time line for their creation?

- Will these be showcase portfolios or progress portfolios?

- Do the portfolios need to focus on specified learning targets and content (such as demonstrating students' understanding of slope) or can the portfolios address any aspect of mathematics chosen by the student?

- Are there some required work examples, such as specific tasks or tests?

- Will there be class time devoted to compiling the portfolio?

- Will students have feedback from the teacher or their peers in choosing their entries and work examples?

- How will the portfolio be judged or evaluated?

Students may need to get preliminary feedback about the appropriateness of their portfolios before the final portfolio is submitted; some students may want to include too many items; that is, more items than necessary for displaying their progress. Other students may write reflections that are too general and do not adequately describe their increased proficiency with mathematics. The opportunity for revision is important for helping students develop skill at analyzing their progress. Let's take a closer look at Ms. Hernandez's guidelines for a portfolio.

→ A Closer Look

Ms. Hernandez Gives Directions for *Creating a Portfolio*

Ms. Hernandez asks her pre-calculus students to create a portfolio that documents their progress. *Early in the course, I asked you to save your work so that you could create a portfolio of your progress across the semester. A portfolio is a collection of documents that you choose to provide evidence of what you have learned, changes in your mathematical thinking, and your accomplishments across the semester. I want you to finish this task by the end of the month.* She then distributes copies of the task, *Creating a Portfolio*.

Task: Creating a Portfolio

Create a portfolio with the components listed below. The new elements that you create (for example, Table of Contents, Reflections, and so on) should be typed; if not, please use very neat handwriting. Your work samples should not be recopied, and you do not have to rework any of your samples. Your portfolio should be organized neatly in a folder.

Table of Contents
Your portfolio should open with a table of contents that lists all your entries.

Entries
There should be *at least four entries* in your portfolio. Title each of your entries and include the work examples you've selected to support that entry.

   As you go back through past work, look for items that have been important to you. Examples may come from:

- *class activities,*   • *assignments,*

- *group work,*   • *readings,*

- *homework,*
- *labs,*
- *projects,*
- *quizzes,*
- *tests, or*
- *anything else you think is appropriate.*

Reflections

Accompany each entry with a reflection that is at least a paragraph long (four or five sentences). Each of your reflections should (a) identify specific mathematics topics or important connections that you made between topics and (b) explain why that work sample is important as part of your story. For example, one work example in an entry might be a homework assignment that helped you see a new way of thinking about mathematics; share your new way of thinking in your reflection! You might include an assignment you believed impossible that now seems easy—tell more about this in your reflection. You may include a test that was instrumental in changing your study habits for the better or caused you to make changes in the way you think about mathematics— share your changes. Maybe you choose to incorporate in one of your entries a group activity that helped you realize there were many different paths to the same idea. We have done a lot of work with assistance of technology; how has that changed the mathematics you are doing? There may be an assignment that was fun to do.

Summary

Think back to the person you were when you began to study pre-calculus. What is different? What are you proud of? What have you learned? This summary should reflect your opinion of your overall progress as a learner of mathematics in this course during the year.

Ms. Hernandez concludes by saying, *If you have questions or want my opinion on a particular entry, I will be happy to help you.*

→ A Closer Look

Mr. Rohner and Maxine Discuss Her *Progress Portfolio* Reflection

Mr. Rohner knew that creating a portfolio would help his ninth-grade Math I students recognize the progress they had made during the semester. He asked them to create a progress portfolio.

Task: Progress Portfolio

Create a portfolio of your work this year to show the progress that you have made in understanding the mathematics we have been studying. Include five samples of your work, and explain how they document your progress.

Maxine chose these five samples of her work:

(a) September quiz with a score of 75 from the first unit in the semester,

(b) October unit test with a score of 80,

(c) October journal entry, which her teacher had praised as "creative,"

(d) November homework assignment with all problems correct, and

(e) November unit test with a score of 95.

The reflection she first wrote is shown in Figure 7–4.

I chose these items because they show how my grades have improved during the semester. Of course the problems I worked were not the same on all of these papers, but my grades improved. I think grades are the best way to know whether you are learning.

FIGURE 7-4. Maxine's First Reflection for Her Progress Portfolio

Maxine asked her teacher, Mr. Rohner, to look at the entries she had chosen and to give her feedback. Mr. Rohner wanted to help Maxine have greater confidence in her decisions about what she included and to explain her choices more completely. He felt it was important for Maxine to realize that her developing understanding was not dependent on grades from an external authority. He began by asking Maxine to explain what she knew and did not know on each of the five pieces of work. As Maxine talked, Mr. Rohner encouraged her to identify how her understanding changed across time and pointed out that this information needed to be included in the reflection.

Maxine went to work at refining her reflections. With Mr. Rohner's feedback in mind, her reflections began to share more. (See Figure 7–5.)

On the September quiz, I didn't understand what it meant to solve an equation. And the computations with fractions on that quiz were hard, so I made computation mistakes. On the October unit test, I did a better job of showing my steps for solving an equation, but it took me too long to do that, so I didn't finish the test. By the time we began to study functions in November, I was more sure of myself, and I was faster at completing the problems.

FIGURE 7–5. Maxine's Refined Reflection for Her Progress Portfolio

Reflection 7-3

Portfolios: Opportunities for Self-Assessment and Sharing

Page 307

Teachers who use portfolios are quick to suggest that it is important to "begin small" and become comfortable with portfolios as evidence of learning. We encourage teachers to assign portfolios to a single class rather than instituting them in all classes so that there is opportunity to refine the guidelines (and avoid having a large number to read in a short period of time). Complete "Reflection 7–3: Portfolios: Opportunities for Self-Assessment and Sharing" (see page 307), which provides questions to help you frame the guidelines you might use for your own students.

Rubrics and Checklists

Rubrics and checklists help students make decisions about how to solve mathematically rich tasks and evaluate the quality and completeness of their responses and those of their peers. Rubrics are descriptions of various levels of performance that point out criteria for successful accomplishment of learning targets. *Holistic rubrics* focus on general descriptions of the quality of the work; the criteria are considered together with one scale for scoring. *Analytic rubrics* focus on different dimensions of tasks, such as how well students communicate and justify the process they used, how well they present evidence that shows their understanding, and how accurate and efficient their solutions are. Analytic rubrics may be more useful than holistic rubrics in guiding student learning. An example of a generic analytic rubric that might be used as the basis for a class discussion about quality work or modified to fit a specific assignment is presented here. (See Figure 7–6.)

Learn More...

A simple Web search should produce numerous examples of both holistic and analytic rubrics. Two websites that seem especially helpful can be found at http://tinyurl.com/lehu6lb and http://tinyurl.com/ovub9jl.

While rubrics help students reflect on their work, checklists help students be reflective about their responsibility as learners. We want students to learn, so we need to encourage them to focus their attention in ways that might actually have payoff for learning. Checklists can typically be used without much explanation for students. The two samples that follow focus on class participation and test preparation. (See Figures 7–7 and 7–8 on pages 288 and 289.) These checklists can help students evaluate whether the ways they spend their time are the best choices they could make.

	Solution Process, Computation	Knowledge of Core Concepts, Problem Solving, and Reasoning	Representations, Communication
4: Advanced	• Solution strategies are similar to those used at advanced levels. • Algorithms are carried out completely, appropriately, efficiently, and accurately; may suggest alternative approaches.	• Work demonstrates deep understanding of mathematical concepts in the task and shows connections to other situations. • Work has evidence of clear reasoning, valid arguments, and generalizations.	• Representations are accurate, appropriate, and complete. • Work clearly communicates reasoning and solution process and is organized in a logical manner with accurate labels and vocabulary.
3: Proficient	• Solution strategies are appropriate and efficient for grade level. • Algorithms are carried out appropriately and completely, but may have minor computational errors.	• Work shows understanding of mathematical concepts in the task and is completed using a workable strategy. • Work includes a clear argument and/or conjecture with some evidence of reasoning behind the conclusions.	• Representations are appropriate, but may have minor errors or lack complete details. • Work communicates general solution; uses appropriate terms and notations.
2: Progressing	• Solution strategies may be inefficient for grade level. • Algorithms are incomplete and have computational errors, or work is correct, but a solution is not reached.	• Work shows incomplete understanding of mathematical concepts in the task. • Work may begin with a strategy, but student cannot reach a solution.	• Representations are incomplete or are ineffective in communicating information. • Work does not clearly communicate process or solution.
1: Basic	• Solution strategies are inconsistent or not in evidence. • Algorithms are inappropriate or incorrect with multiple computational errors.	• Work shows little or no evidence of understanding of the task or of mathematical concepts involved. • Work shows difficulty setting up problem; answer is not reasonable.	• Representations are inappropriate for the situation. • Work lacks labels or explanations and is difficult to interpret; explanation does not match solution.
NA	• Work is nonexistent or unrelated to task.	• Work is nonexistent or unrelated to task.	• Work is nonexistent or unrelated to task.

FIGURE 7-6. Example of a Generic Analytic Rubric (Bright and Joyner 2005, 8)

Learn More...

"When students know the criteria against which their work will be evaluated [e.g., rubrics shared in advance], it can help them focus their learning."
—*Faster Isn't Smarter: Messages About Math, Teaching, and Learning in the 21st Century, 2nd ed.* (Seeley 2015, 241)

Learn More...

"[I]nvolving students in creating rubrics encourages them to think about the criteria of quality work and promotes ownership of the assessment process."
—"Rubrics at Play" (McGatha and Darcy 2010, 334)

Date _____

Name _____

How prepared are you for class? How likely are you to participate? Complete the following checklist to help evaluate yourself as a mathematics student.

	Always	Usually	Sometimes	Never
I complete assignments and bring them to class.				
I am ready to work when the teacher begins.				
I am attentive in class and listen carefully.				
I am polite and considerate of others.				
I participate in class discussions.				
I ask questions when I do not understand.				
I finish class assignments.				
When absent, I make up work that I missed.				
Overall, I use my time in class wisely.				

If you checked "Never" for a question, what could you do to change your habits so that your response would be "Usually"?

FIGURE 7–7. Student Checklist: Evaluating My Preparation and Class Participation

Date _____

Name _____

How do you prepare for tests? Complete the following checklist to help evaluate yourself as a mathematics student.

	Always	Usually	Sometimes	Never
I make certain I know what will be on the test.				
I review class notes and homework.				
I study with other students.				
I ask questions if I don't understand something.				
I have everything I need and am ready to begin when the test begins.				

How could you improve the way you get ready for tests?

FIGURE 7–8. Student Checklist: Evaluating My Test Preparation

Strategy 3: Promote the Development of Positive Peer Interactions Through Partner and Group Work

There are many different work environments that students might be immersed in after graduation. However, the lists of expectations that businesses have for their employees are fairly consistent across numerous occupations. These expectations include:

- being good problem solvers and creative thinkers;
- working well with others and being team players;

Assessment Tip ✓

Grouping flexibly— placing students in varying configurations for different tasks— allows students to thrive through opportunities to work with different classmates.

- being effective communicators who listen well and are able to share their ideas; and

- being dependable workers who are dependable, goal oriented, and willing to learn and share and who complete tasks on time.

In the classroom these same characteristics can define our aspirations for students and support the importance of peer interactions and collaboration. As teachers we should limit the amount of time students are expected to merely sit and listen to the teacher and increase the time students are actively listening, sharing, and working with others. We should craft opportunities for students to engage more fully in mathematics lessons, learn more mathematics, and take more responsibility for making sense of mathematics. In addition, we should use partner and group discussions to help students become resources for each other, benefit from their peers' thinking, compare the ideas of other students with their own, and minimize the tendency to turn to the teacher for assistance. Working with partners and in groups— and therefore contributing to the mathematical learning of others—can increase students' own independent thinking and communication skills. Through conversations with their peers, students learn from situations that may initially seem to be unsolvable, ambiguous, or challenging. Together, students can also learn to analyze what is correct and what is incorrect and then make decisions about how to proceed. In this section we take a more detailed look at how both partner and group work support student self-assessment and responsibility.

Partner Work

Having students turn and talk to a partner gives them opportunities to express their ideas and often brings quiet students into a conversation. For example, the traditional think, pair, share strategy can activate prior knowledge (*Tell your partner what you know about the diagonals of a parallelogram*) or help students "commit" to the answer they think is appropriate before being asked to respond in class. Turning to talk with one partner about a specific question can be a stepping stone toward working productively in a group— and establishing a positive learning climate.

Learn More...

As noted throughout the report *Engaging Schools* (National Research Council 2004), to create a positive learning environment (which we refer to as a positive climate for learning), teachers need to set high expectations, encourage students to do their best, allow students choices whenever possible, and plan lessons that involve higher-order thinking, collaboration, and active student participation.

Assessment Tip ✓

Having students turn and talk with their partner about a specific question can be a stepping stone toward working productively in a group.

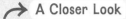

A Closer Look

Mr. Jordan Uses Turn and Talk with *The Knockout*

Mr. Jordan hoped that students would learn to work effectively with a partner while simultaneously calculating probabilities for compound events through the use *The Knockout*. (See Figure 7–9.) One of his reasons for selecting this task was to capitalize on many of his students' interests in sports. There is an implicit assumption in this task that past performance of the tennis players will be reflected exactly in future performance, even though many people would acknowledge that other factors (e.g., injury, tiredness) might also influence future performance in important ways.

> **Learn More...**
>
> See Chapter 6 for a detailed look at the characteristics of mathematically rich tasks.

The Characteristics of a Mathematically Rich Problem	The Task
	The Knockout This problem gives you the chance to ■ *figure out the probability of each person's winning a game of tennis* Rani, Tony, and Sarah have entered a tennis knockout competition. They have played each other before. **Rani** — So far against Tony, I have won 12 matches and lost 8 matches. **Tony** — So far against Sarah, I have won 10 matches and lost 20 matches. **Sarah** — I have won a third of the matches I have played against Rani. In the tournament, Rani will play Tony. The winner will then play Sarah. What is the probability of each person's winning the tournament? Show your reasoning and calculations as clearly as you can. *Source:* From BALANCED ASSESSMENT: HIGH SCHOOL ASSESSMENT PACKAGE 1 Copyright © 1999 by the Regents of the University of California. Reprinted by the permission of Pearson Education, Inc. All Rights Reserved.
1. The "mysterious" part of the problem is mathematical.	The "mysterious" part of the task involves conditional probability. This concept is often difficult for students to learn and to apply.

(continued)

(continued from page 291)

2. The problem has very little visible scaffolding.	There is no direction to students about how to proceed, but there are numerous options that might come to students' minds. As a first step, however, students have to make accurate interpretations of the words from Rani, Tony, and Sarah. This may be challenging for some students, depending on their levels of language skills.
3. There are many ways to do the problem.	Students can "act out" the tournament or use mathematical information about conditional probability.
4. Students of different skill levels can learn from this activity.	Students who have limited understanding of probability could begin by acting out the problem. Students with more understanding could begin by computing probabilities for winning a match for each student in each pair. These computations should be quite familiar to many students.
5. The problem has natural extensions.	The task could be extended by altering the numbers or by expanding the size of the tournament to include more players.
6. The problem is hard.	Students are not likely to "see" the solution immediately, so they will feel challenged. Students also have to recognize that the comment from each of Rani, Tony, and Sarah involves exactly two of the tennis players. This information is important for calculating the compound probabilities.
7. The problem encourages getting your hands dirty with data.	Because students can act out a solution, generating relevant data (probabilities of winning a match) is possible.
8. The problem has interesting partial solutions (mileposts).	Students might create a partial solution by translating the words in the "thought bubbles" into numerical relationships. In particular, Sarah's comment "looks" different from the other two comments; her data about wins and losses are not as explicit as the data Rani and Tony offer.

FIGURE 7–9. The Mathematical Richness of *The Knockout*

As students worked, Mr. Jordan circulated, observing and asking questions as needed. He spent some time with one pair of students, Karim and Deanna. He noticed that Karim and Deanna seemed to be somewhat off task; that is, his turn-and-talk direction wasn't working well for them. Mr. Jordan decided to have a conversation with them in hopes of focusing their attention on the ways that the probabilities represented by the comments could be used to answer the question. He also intended to use the conversation to help reveal how the partners were thinking.

Mr. Jordan: When Rani plays Tony, who wins more often?

Karim: Rani wins fifty percent more.

Mr. Jordan: Then what is the probability that Rani beats Tony?

Karim: Twelve-twentieths.

Mr. Jordan: What is the probability that Tony beats Rani?

Karim: It says only how often Rani beats Tony, not the reverse.

Deanna: I think if Rani loses to Tony, then Tony beats Rani. It's eight-twentieths.

Mr. Jordan: What is eight-twentieths?

Deanna: The probability that Tony beats Rani.

Mr. Jordan: What is the probability that Rani beats Sarah?

Karim: Well, since Sarah won a third of the time, she lost two-thirds, so it's two-thirds.

Mr. Jordan: What is the sequence of events that allows Sarah to win the tournament?

Deanna: Sarah plays the winner of the first game, so either Rani wins that game or Tony does.

Karim: Since she plays only one game, she'll probably win the tournament.

Mr. Jordan: Karim, would anyone who only played one game be more likely to win the tournament? Or does it depend on how good they are?

Karim: Well if Sarah lost every game she ever played, she wouldn't win.

Mr. Jordan: So it depends on the probabilities?

Karim: Yeah, I guess.

Deanna: So we have to use Sarah's winnings against both Rani and Tony to figure it out.

Mr. Jordan: See if you can finish the problem now. (*departs, allowing the partners to continue to work it out together*)

Mr. Jordan's conversation with partners Karim and Deanna seemed to help them get back on track toward finding a solution. Karim seemed to be "distracted" by the fact that tennis player Sarah plays only one game, while the winner of the Rani/Tony match has to play two games. This is important information for Mr. Jordan, since it helped him recognize the need to keep the discussion focused on computation of the probability of compound events before returning to the issue of who actually is more likely to win the tournament. Since Sarah has the greatest probability of winning this tournament, this might unintentionally reinforce Karim's "logic." Deanna talked less in this conversation, but she seemed to have a reasonable grasp of the underlying mathematics. This conversation might encourage her to be more proactive in using her knowledge. Mr. Jordan will have to decide later whether to follow up with a variation of the tennis task in which Sarah does not have the greatest probability of winning the tournament or to use a task in a different context.

Group Work

Group work, like partner work, helps students to make connections and to communicate their reasoning to their peers. Group work works especially well for helping students engage in "constructive struggling"; that is, engagement in tasks that have no obvious solution. For groups to be productive, however, all members need to assume responsibility for the group's work toward a common goal. In an effective group, students monitor themselves and each other, and no one "opts out." Within a group, students can be both independent and interdependent, assessing each other's ideas and communicating their own solution strategies.

When as teachers we first begin to incorporate group work into instruction, our initial efforts may not go smoothly. Noise is to be expected, and noise is OK if students are talking about, and working with, mathematics ideas. There may be times when conversations within a group go off track; as teachers we then need to help that group refocus on the task. Less-than-successful group work may reflect unclear expectations, directions for group work that are not explicit, or a task that is not sufficiently interesting and challenging for students.

> **Learn More...**
>
> Cathy L. Seeley's Message 17, "Constructive Struggling: The Value of Challenging Our Students," in *Faster Isn't Smarter* (2015, 113–119) highlights the benefit of having a classroom climate that engages students rather than frustrates them.

We can set the stage for group work by asking students to think individually about a task before talking with a partner or working in a group. This think time need not be long, but it is important for students to make sense of the task. When students begin to recognize that working with others includes receiving as well as giving help, they are more likely to participate with the group. As students discuss a variety of points of view and explore diverse approaches to solving a task, they are likely to find learning mathematics much more satisfying.

Some teachers will choose to add a procedure for what students should do if the group gets stuck; for example, giving each group "teacher help tickets" that can be used to ask for specific feedback or assistance in getting to a more productive path. Some teachers assign specific roles within the group such as a materials person, recorder, timekeeper, manager, and reporter. In some groups students have two jobs. One student may be assigned to read the task aloud to the group.

Guidelines for Group Work

Some students come to secondary classrooms with numerous experiences working with partners and in groups. Others have few collaborative experiences while learning mathematics. Providing guidelines is especially important in this latter situation. Let's take a more detailed look at each of the following guidelines.

Guidelines for Group Work

- Everyone contributes to discussions.

- Everyone recognizes the difference in critiquing and criticizing.

- Everyone works on the task and writes a solution.

- Everyone prepares to report the group's solution.

Everyone contributes to discussions. Students are expected to engage with the task in order to contribute ideas. They listen carefully to each other. They avoid interrupting, but make certain they understand suggestions and explanations. If there are vocabulary words a group member does not understand, others in the group explain. If unclear or incorrect mathematics vocabulary is used, others in the group ask for clarification. If some students are not very articulate in their explanations, others in the group probe rather than ignore the ideas.

Everyone recognizes the difference between critiquing and criticizing. Ideas are to be explored and solutions are to be justified, but individuals are not to be criticized nor their ideas ridiculed. Learning to disagree with dignity is important in the mathematics classroom, just as in the workplace. A critique should elicit reasoning and justification.

Everyone works on the task and writes a solution. Each student is responsible for completing all aspects of the task and answering questions individually; for example, if there is a worksheet to be completed, parts of the task are not divided up and each other's work copied. Getting and giving assistance are expectations for group work, but individuals remain responsible for engaging in work on all components of the task and for keeping their notebooks up to date. Work is not complete until the group has reviewed the task and guidelines and made certain that their solution answers the question posed in the task.

Everyone prepares to report the group's solution. The expectation is that all students are prepared to share how their group arrived at a solution, describe what conjectures were considered and eventually discarded, or explain, for example, the group's chart or display. Students can report about the questions the group asked as they worked on the task and the decisions the group made. Students sharpen their own mathematical reasoning and ability to communicate ideas when they know they must be prepared to represent the group.

- Learn More ...

Lessons that incorporate group work are hallmarks of the Mathematics Assessment Project (MAP). Based on the premise that students should expect mathematics to make sense, the concept lessons are planned to develop and reveal students' misconceptions and understanding of significant mathematical ideas, helping students to connect new content with their existing knowledge.

Group Tests

Group tests help students take greater responsibility for their own learning. In a group test students collaborate on solutions to problems, but students must create their own solutions after the collaboration. For example, if there are four students in the group and four problems on the test, the teacher scores a different problem on each student's paper in order to obtain the group's grade. Students do not know which problem the teacher will score on an individual's paper, so collaboration and discussion are very important. Group tests might be used for standards that are more complicated, such as modeling standards. The problems on group tests are often more difficult than problems on tests for individuals. Group tests do not replace individual assessments and might be used infrequently throughout a course, but they do support peers who are serving as resources for each other and reinforce the importance of cooperation during learning.

The Teacher's Role During Group Work

There are different roles for teachers before, during, and after the time students work in groups. As with any lesson, it is important to think about not only the learning targets that are supported by the group work but also what the task, along with the use of group work, has the potential to reveal about students' understanding. Planning for group work includes being sure that the physical arrangement of the class is conducive to discussion and determining which students will work together. Will friends be allowed to pair with each other? Are there some students who definitely should be separated? Grouping by convenience (for example, *You four are sitting close together so you make a group*) is not likely to be the most productive way to form groups. Will students with different performance levels be grouped into homogeneous or heterogeneous groups? Some teachers recommend creating groups of four, each group having one high-level student, two middle-level students, and one low-level student. Since there is no one right way to organize students into groups, consider configuring groups in response to the dynamics of the class and your personal preferences.

While students are working in groups, one important role for the teacher is to monitor and prod group interactions. Sometimes as teachers we need to ask students to elaborate on the ideas they are presenting to the group; other times we may ask a student to restate what a partner has explained or ask if the student is in agreement with the partner and why. There are times when one student may dominate a group's discussion and proceed to explain his or her solution without waiting for others in the group to present their ideas. Joining this group for a brief time is an opportunity not only to reiterate the expectation that everyone should participate in discussions but also to draw others into the conversation. Monitoring helps us gain information about how confident the class is with the task and whether groups are struggling with aspects of the mathematics.

Another role for the teacher is to be an intentional listener. By listening to groups' conversations, we can get a sense of what aspects of the task different groups find difficult. We may decide to address the difficulties as the groups debrief their work or to incorporate the issues in the next lesson. Sometimes as teachers we may decide it is important to stop the groups right away and provide information to the class or ask specific students to report on what their group has been discussing. As partners work, we question individual students about their ideas and conduct important "three-minute interviews." There are times when students can be nudged toward a more productive path by a single question or suggestion; for example, *Can you make a diagram that would help you explain whether or not two figures that are similar have to be congruent?*

Learn More...
Chapter 4 offers a detailed look at what it means to intentionally listen.

Debriefing Group Work

It's important to remember to debrief group work. When planning to debrief a group task, we need to decide the order in which groups will present their work and help establish the connections among mathematics ideas that need to be made explicit during the discussion. This planning takes place while students are still working in their groups. Debriefing group work takes many forms. Here are some possibilities for sharing groups' solutions.

Ideas for Debriefing Group Work

- *Group presentations to the class.* A representative of each group presents the solution. Deciding what order to have groups share is important, as well as planning what questions you, as the teacher, want to pose about each solution.

- *Exchanging and critiquing written work.* Pairs of groups come together to compare work and explain their solutions to each other. Students question each other.

- *Pairs share in new groups.* Pairs of students "travel" to other groups and present their solutions. Depending on the time available, pairs can meet with two or three different groups.

- *"Experts" move.* Students number off in their groups. At an appointed time, students with the same numbers regroup. Depending on the task, students with the number 1 may be asked to focus on one aspect of the task, students with the number 2 focus on a different aspect, and so on.

With each debriefing strategy, as teachers we monitor the learning that is taking place. Our roles during debriefing include summarizing when necessary, probing when ideas are confusing or incomplete, and identifying students who may need additional assistance. We also begin to make decisions about next lessons and questions for class discussions.

Informing Parents and Others About Group Work

In the real world, mathematicians share their work through reports, formal papers, and presentations. Student-led conferences serve a similar function. This is a popular formative assessment tool in elementary grades, and it can be implemented equally well in secondary schools. Student-led conferences provide opportunities for students to share what they are learning with parents or other significant adults. These conferences frequently involve compiling portfolios and require similar preparation to that of student presentations for

Learn More…

For a more detailed look at using portfolios, see page 280 in this chapter.

senior projects. Students describe their work, show examples to document what they have learned, and often identify future goals. One colleague in an eastern North Carolina high school sets aside two evenings each semester for student-led conferences. Using the media center, over the two evenings each class has a designated 45-minute time slot for students and parents to review the student's work. The teacher circulates among the tables but intervenes only if invited by the student. If parents have specific questions, she schedules a different time for that conference.

Strategy 4: Facilitate Students' Reflections About Their Mistakes

Learning from mistakes is one way that students can become better self-assessors. When students reflect about their mistakes and rework incorrectly worked problems to create (hopefully) correct solutions, they become more aware of the errors in their thinking. That is, they become better at self-assessment. Asking students to explain the error that they made can amplify this effect, and it can provide evidence that students have identified what was incorrect.

Less formally, some teachers mark incorrect answers on an assignment (without including a grade) and return the papers to students. Students work in pairs or small groups with students who answered those items correctly to get assistance in rethinking the work. For example, Jesse was asked to compute the sum, $-12\frac{1}{2} + 4\frac{1}{3}$. His answer was $-8\frac{2}{3}$. Before you read on, do you think you know what his error is?

Jesse's teacher asked him to talk with his partner and then to rework his computation. (See Figure 7–10.) Jesse's error is not uncommon. Students often forget that the negative sign in the mixed number, $-12\frac{1}{2}$, applies to both 12 and $\frac{1}{2}$; $-12\frac{1}{2}$ is between -13 and -12, so it is *less than* -12. This might be a lapse or it might represent a misunderstanding of the ways that mixed numbers less than 0 are written.

Circle Reason for Missing the Question	New Work and Answer Show work to receive credit	How Did You Get Your New Answer?	Need more instruction
• Thought I got the right answer • (Calculation error) • Reading error • Did not understand question • Rushed—made a careless mistake • Guessed	I added $\frac{1}{2} + \frac{1}{3}$ by mistake. $-12\frac{1}{2} + 4\frac{1}{3} = (-12 + 4) + (-\frac{1}{2} + \frac{1}{3})$ $= -8 + (-\frac{1}{6}) = -8\frac{1}{6}$	• Reviewed my notes/textbook • (Corrected a calculation error) • Corrected a reading error • Asked the teacher to explain • Asked a friend to explain	• Yes • (No)

FIGURE 7–10. Jesse's Reworked Computation

As students rework mistakes and provide assistance to each other, this "collaborative teaching" reinforces the importance of clear communication about mathematical concepts and processes. The students doing the explaining are often expanding their own understanding through their explanations, while those who are being taught have opportunities to ask questions they might hesitate to raise in a whole-class discussion.

What Are the Benefits of Supporting Expanded Roles for Students?

As has been shared thus far in this chapter, when we create a positive climate for learning, there are many benefits for students. These benefits enhance students' learning of content and accrue partly because of the change in roles for students. Let's recap some of our thinking; specifically, looking at the benefits that transpire when we support expanded roles for students.

We are asking students to self-assess. Seeing oneself as a self-assessor is a critical role. Self-assessments help students engage with mathematics ideas and enhance the potential for learning new content. Students become better at keeping themselves "on track" during times when the solution to a task seems far away. When students self-assess, they can see whether they are making progress toward a solution. Sometimes this means students need to change course or even reverse course as they analyze a task and attempt to find a solution. At other times this means students recognize that their work so far is correct, even if the solution seems temporarily out of reach.

We are asking students to become more reflective about what they know and to serve as resources for their peers. Expecting these roles from students in turn helps students become more confident about their ability both to learn and to be a contributor to group outcomes. These are important qualities of lifelong learners. When students believe that they can be successful, their motivation for engaging with challenging mathematics is likely to increase.

We are asking students to become better explainers of their thinking. This might happen during partner or group work, or in an individual conversation with the teacher, or in a class discussion. Exposing thinking is risky for many students, so it is critical that the classroom environment support students as they take these risks. We want each individual student to learn, an outcome supported by having students share their thinking with each other.

We are asking students to use their mistakes as well as their correct solutions as vehicles for learning. Everyone makes mistakes, and the truism that we should learn from our mistakes is certainly a byword of mathematics learning. School needs to be a safe place to make mathematical mistakes, and teachers can help students take advantage of those mistakes as a way to deepen learning.

Creating a positive climate for learning involves changes in both teachers' roles and students' roles. Modifying our daily routines may not be easy; but implementing strategies in which students are expected to and supported in taking more responsibility for self-assessing is critical for their long-term learning.

INFORMing My Practice

Throughout this book we hope that one message continues to be clear: INFORMative assessment and the decisions that we make on a day-to-day basis are integrally linked. Our decisions have a profound influence on students and their success in learning mathematics. This chapter has focused on ways to help students self-assess and take on more responsibility for learning. Self-assessment encourages students and the teacher to work together to assume responsibility for learning. Classrooms need to be alive with questions that are worth answering and discussions that are rich in opportunities to extend students' understanding of the mathematics they are learning. Teachers have a responsibility to communicate their personal enthusiasm for teaching and their excitement about helping students learn rich mathematics. We need to communicate our love of mathematics and the internal pleasure that comes from solving difficult problems. We also need to communicate the importance of assessing the quality of our own work as part of being a lifelong learner.

Consider actions you might take to provide more opportunities for student self-assessment in your own classroom. Answer the questions in "Reflection 7–4: INFORMing My Practice: Supporting Student Self-Assessment and Responsibility" (see page 308). Then continue reading as we discuss two more important issues related to INFORMative assessment in the next chapters. Chapter 8 focuses on making inferences about what students know. Chapter 9 focuses on the feedback we might provide that will help students learn more.

Reflection 7–4

INFORMing
My Practice:
Supporting Student
Self-Assessment
and Responsibility

Page 308

Reflection 7-1: Defining What Grades Represent: My Beliefs About Grades

Think about your approach to grading. Use the table to analyze each factor that potentially influences grades, then answer the questions that follow.

Factor	Degree of Influence (circle one)	Why do you choose to assign this weight?
Attendance	1 2 3 4 5	
Effort	1 2 3 4 5	
Participation	1 2 3 4 5	
Attitude	1 2 3 4 5	
Progress over time	1 2 3 4 5	
Homework completion	1 2 3 4 5	

(continued)

Reflection 7-1: Defining What Grades Represent: My Beliefs About Grades (continued)

1. In what way does each process below impact students (pro or con)? Explain.

    a. Grading on a 0 to 100 scale

    b. Grading on a curve

    c. Grading against a standard

2. How should the following be considered in determining report card grades?

    a. Weighting of homework, classwork, quizzes, tests

    b. Incomplete assignments and zeros

3. How do you determine grades for report cards? Does your grading system match your philosophy?

Reflection 7-2: Scenarios That Support Student Self-Assessment

Read each scenario and decide if it (a) definitely supports, (b) somewhat supports, or (c) does not support student-self-assessment. Then make suggestions as if you were advising a colleague on becoming better at supporting student self-assessment.

Scenario	Rating	Suggestions
1. Evan, an eighth-grade student who struggles in math, gets back a quiz on solving percent problems. His answers are marked with an "X" if they are incorrect. Out of the 10 questions, he got 3 correct. His teacher asks Evan to correct his mistakes for homework.	(a) Definitely supports (b) Somewhat supports (c) Does not support	
2. The teacher asks students to read and think about a problem. Students are instructed to write down any questions they have and potential strategies for solving the problem, without actually solving it. Students discuss their questions and strategies with partners and then solve the problem.	(a) Definitely supports (b) Somewhat supports (c) Does not support	
3. The teacher returns a graded assessment and assigns students to groups based on their grades. Students who made an A or B have an enrichment assignment and students who made a C have an assignment that reiterates the material on the assessment. The teacher personally goes over the assessment with students who made a D or F.	(a) Definitely supports (b) Somewhat supports (c) Does not support	
4. At the beginning of a unit; the teacher provides a list of "I Can" statements to students outlining the objectives that will be taught in the next unit. Students are asked periodically throughout the unit to reflect on the statements. For example, "I can determine the mean of a set of data." Or "I can compare and interpret data shown in two different box plots."	(a) Definitely supports (b) Somewhat supports (c) Does not support	

(continued)

5. Van turns in an assignment where most of the answers and explanations are incorrect. Because it seems he has misunderstood the concepts, the teacher returns it with a "Please See Me" note so she can discuss it with him. Two weeks later Van still hasn't come to see her and has now turned in another assignment with the same mistakes.	(a) Definitely supports (b) Somewhat supports (c) Does not support	
6. Students take an assessment on Monday. The teacher returns the papers on Tuesday and provides specific feedback to students. Students do not receive a grade; instead they are asked to rework the problems using the feedback provided by the teacher.	(a) Definitely supports (b) Somewhat supports (c) Does not support	
7. The teacher provides a task with student responses to review. One solution is identified as a good solution. Students determine criteria to judge the solutions to the task and discuss with partners possible feedback for improving the poor solutions.	(a) Definitely supports (b) Somewhat supports (c) Does not support	
8. Students take out their homework. The teacher reads the correct answers and then asks if anyone has a question. No students have questions. The teacher directs students to put their homework away and begins the new lesson.	(a) Definitely supports (b) Somewhat supports (c) Does not support	

Source: Scenarios are modified from *Partners for Mathematics Learning Project*, North Carolina, 2001, a Mathematics Science Partnership funded through North Carolina Department of Public Instruction.

Reflection 7-3: Portfolios: Opportunities for Self-Assessment and Sharing

Consider how you might plan to use portfolios in one of your classes; use the table to help you.

Question	My Decision
Who is the audience for the portfolio, and what is the time line for its creation?	
What is the purpose of the portfolio and how will it be used?	
Is there a specific content focus or can the portfolio address any aspect of mathematics chosen by the student?	
Are there some required pieces, such as specific tasks or tests?	
Is any class time devoted to compiling the portfolio?	
How will feedback be provided as students choose their entries?	
How will the portfolio be judged or evaluated?	

What changes would you make to the organizational questions provided in this chapter on page 281? How would those changes better reflect your instructional goals?

Reflection 7-4: INFORMing My Practice: Supporting Student Self-Assessment and Responsibility

Think about the chapter you just read. Use this space to record your ideas.

Ideas about the importance of student self-assessment and responsibility:

Changes in my thinking about INFORMative assessment:

Ideas I envision becoming a more important part of my practice:

Questions I have:

Frustrations/concerns I have:

Section V

How Can I Make Quality Inferences and Give Quality Feedback?

Making Inferences About What Students Know and Can Do

As has been noted so far, the first steps in improving our formative assessment skills are to become better at observing and listening to students. However, watching and listening are not enough; as teachers, we also need to make sense out of what we observe and hear—we need to make *inferences*—in particular, *inferences about students' understanding*. INFORMative assessment helps us make inferences that reflect the depth of our students' understanding of mathematical concepts, skills, and applications.

In this chapter we explore the importance of examining students' correct, incomplete, and incorrect answers in order to infer their level of understanding of mathematics ideas. Students typically have a logic for their answers; their responses are rarely truly random. So it is important that we try to identify that logic in order to pinpoint the causes of incorrect answers or inaccurate thinking.

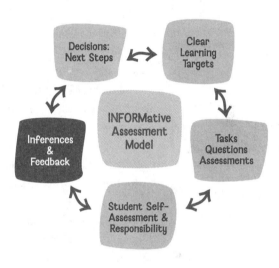

Overview

Making Inferences About What Students Know and Can Do

Learn More...

For a more detailed look at the idea of students' logic, see pages 330–334 in this chapter.

Inferences are conclusions we as teachers make about what students know and the ways they are thinking. That thinking is sometimes based on a "logic" that makes sense to the students but is incorrect when viewed from our "teacher perspective" of deeper understanding. Our interpretations of what students say and do should reveal their logic while also noting the discrepancy between that logic and correct understanding of mathematics ideas.

The best instruction typically happens when teachers make inferences about what students know and then use those inferences in instructional planning. Failure to make accurate inferences can lead to instruction that does not meet the needs of students or to a situation in which teachers provide feedback that does not connect with the thinking of the students. Unfortunately, students don't always communicate clearly what they know. This may be because their mathematical understanding is not complete, they do not use precise terminology, or English is not their first language. As teachers, we sometimes have to make inferences based on these vague communications. Inevitably, our inferences about what students are thinking are also influenced by our own experiences and understandings.

Assessment Tip ✔

The best instruction typically happens when teachers make inferences—conclusions about what students know and the ways they are thinking—and then use those inferences in instruction planning.

In general, we should make inferences conservatively; that is, underestimate rather than overestimate what students understand. Assuming too much may inadvertently put too big a burden on students to make sense of the instruction. If instruction assumes too much rather than too little about students' knowledge, students may internalize incorrect ideas. Sometimes, for example, as teachers we focus on the steps that are involved in learning a process and ignore the possible flaws in students' thinking that might lead students to make errors in carrying out those steps. It is important to create a classroom climate that supports mutual sharing of perspectives both among students and also between students and the teacher.

Learn More...

Chapter 7 offers a more detailed look at creating a positive classroom climate for learning and student responsibility.

In order to make inferences about students' thinking, we must think about the mathematics ideas underlying a task. Sometimes these ideas interact with an understanding of the context of a task. Following is an example of how that INFORMative assessment can help a teacher analyze and make sense of students' thinking about a task.

→ **A Closer Look**

Mr. Garcia Makes Inferences About Students' Understanding with *Race Cars*

Mr. Garcia posed a graphing task, *Race Cars*, to his eighth-grade students. This task was aligned most directly with the standards on graphing proportional relationships and had the potential to reveal students' thinking about proportional reasoning.

It is critical that students develop facility with proportional reasoning before they enter high school, so middle school students need to engage in a variety of proportional reasoning tasks that encourage use of different ways for representing proportional relationships. Mr. Garcia wanted to see how his students would deal with the mathematics issues that arise when they engaged with a simplified real-world situation appropriate for their level of thinking. Because he had used this task before, he knew it was a good task for generating information about his students' thinking and would let him make inferences about their understanding.

One CCSSM standard that can support teacher efforts to reveal student understanding about proportional relationship is "Graph proportional relationships, interpreting the unit rate as the slope of the graph. Compare two different proportional relationships represented in different ways. For example, compare a distance-time graph to a distance-time equation to determine which of two moving objects has greater speed" (CCSS.MATH .CONTENT.8.EE.B.5).

Task: Race Cars

The graph and the table show distances that two model race cars traveled. Each car traveled at a constant speed. Which car went faster?

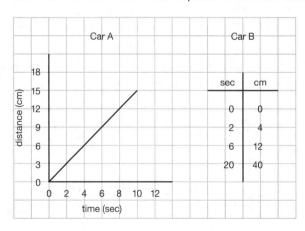

This task can be solved in multiple ways (e.g., proportions, graphing, computation) and shows speed in more than one way. It allows students to generate data (e.g., coordinates of points on the graph), and it suggests generalizations about how speed is represented in distance-time graphs.

There are several mathematics issues that Mr. Garcia's students had to address. First, there is an oversimplification of the actual behavior of cars; namely, that a car can reach a constant speed instantaneously. (Of course, since the designation of an origin point is arbitrary, one can imagine that the distance is being measured from some arbitrary point after the cars have reached their constant speeds.) Second, there are two representations that have to be compared. The graph for Car A is clearly continuous (in a mathematical sense), but the data for Car B may appear to some students to be discrete. Mathematically, any set of four points will "fit" onto infinitely many graphs, but the condition of "constant speed" stated in the task forces the graph to be linear.

Third, the graph for Car A clearly shows a proportional relationship, but the data for Car B is not so obviously proportional. Fourth, Mr. Garcia's students needed to compare unit rates for the cars (e.g., cm/sec). There are many ways to do this, so students had to make decisions about which ways to choose.

Students' choices could provide important INFORMative assessment information that would help Mr. Garcia decide what to do next with his students. Based on the information he gathered, he made inferences about what his students understood. Then he could use his inferences to make instructional decisions, such as (a) posing more tasks like this or (b) exposing students to different contexts that illustrate proportional reasoning.

As Mr. Garcia watched students work, he observed two apparently correct solutions that used different mathematical thinking: Randy's solution and Wendy's solution. (See Figures 8–1 and 8–2.) Before you read on, make your own inferences about what thinking is represented by each solution.

$$\frac{40}{20} = 2 cm/sec \leftarrow car B$$

$$\frac{15}{10} = 1.5 cm/sec \leftarrow car A$$

Car B is faster

FIGURE 8–1. Randy's Solution for *Race Cars*

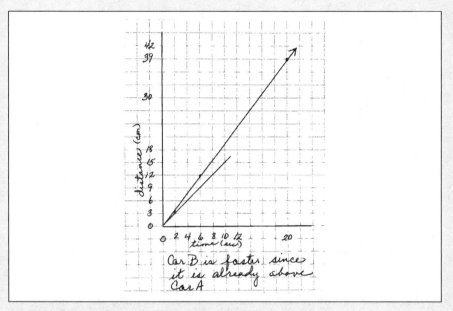

FIGURE 8-2. Wendy's Solution for *Race Cars*

Mr. Garcia wanted to help his students understand *why* Randy and Wendy's solutions were correct, so he decided to share them in a whole-class debriefing discussion. Mr. Garcia took Smith and Stein's *5 Practices for Orchestrating Productive Mathematics Discussions* into account in facilitating the discussion. In the dialogue that follows, Mr. Garcia's thinking is shown in parentheses.

Learn More...

In *5 Practices for Orchestrating Productive Mathematics Discussions*, Smith and Stein (2011) note the following practices: (1) anticipating, (2) monitoring, (3) selecting, (4) sequencing, and (5) connecting. These are discussed in Chapter 4.

Mr. Garcia: Randy, why did you compute forty-twentieths and fifteen-tenths? (to check whether Randy sees these as proportional situations)

Randy: Those show the speeds of the cars.

Mr. Garcia: Why does fifteen-tenths show the speed of Car A? (to verify Randy's reasoning)

Randy: Fifteen is the total distance and ten is the total time.

Mr. Garcia: How did you find the total distance from the graph? (to be sure Randy is reading the graph correctly)

Randy: The graph starts at zero zero so the distance is fifteen minus zero.

Mr. Garcia: Wendy, why did you graph Car B's points on the graph for Car A? (to find out why Wendy chose graphing to compare the cars)

Wendy: It is easier for me to see what's going on.

Mr. Garcia: Why did you connect those points? (to see how Wendy sees the structure of the data)

Wendy: Car B travels along a path, so I wanted to show that path.

Mr. Garcia: Why does Car B's graph being above Car A's graph show that Car B is faster? (to reveal details about Wendy's reasoning)

Wendy: Because the slope for B is greater. Slope is speed.

Mr. Garcia: Is the graph for Car B always above the graph for Car A? (to reveal details about Wendy's reasoning)

Wendy: Yes.

Mr. Garcia: Even at the origin? (to point out a limit on Wendy's observation)

Wendy: Well, not there. You got me on that one!

Mr. Garcia: Wendy, you and Randy both said that Car B was faster. How is your graph related to his computation?

Wendy: If two lines have different slopes, the line with the bigger slope will be above the line with the smaller slope.

Throughout the discussion, Mr. Garcia wove together the different perspectives of these two solutions. In the process, he highlighted his inferences about students' understanding. For example, his question "Even at the origin?" revealed information that supported his inference that Wendy had not realized that the graph of Car B was not above the graph of Car A at the origin. He suspected that she had overlooked the behavior at the end points of the graphs, and her response supported that inference.

Mr. Garcia led the discussion by successfully creating probing questions, seemingly "on the fly," in response to specific things that Randy and Wendy said and what he inferred about their thinking. Posing effective probing questions takes practice, but we can begin to develop skill by reflecting on instruction (e.g., *What should I have asked yesterday?*) or by talking with colleagues about questions that we might pose in response to students' written work. Brainstorming alternatives is part of the process of becoming better. The information we generate by asking probing questions will either support or refute the inferences that we make about students' understanding.

⌐ Learn More... ¬
See Chapter 4 for more discussion of probing questions.

Strategies for Making Quality Inferences

There isn't a "quick and dirty" algorithm for making inferences about what students know; however, there are some strategies that can help us make quality inferences about students' thinking. In this section we elaborate on several of these strategies. Of course, making sense of students' work is always dependent on the specifics of the tasks and the ways that the students respond to those tasks.

> **Learn More...**
> Mathematically rich tasks are discussed in Chapter 6.

Five Strategies for Making Quality Inferences

1. Differentiate Correct, Incomplete, and Incorrect Responses

2. Identify Possible Causes of Incomplete or Incorrect Answers

3. Examine the Logic Behind Incomplete or Incorrect Answers

4. Determine If Errors in Answers Reflect Substance or Presentation

5. Use Probing Questions and Follow-Up Tasks to Support Inferences

---

Strategy 1: Differentiate Correct, Incomplete, and Incorrect Responses

Virtually everyone who is learning new content goes through a stage during which the learning is incomplete. New ideas are typically not immediately internalized, and the connections among these new ideas and previously learned ideas often do not get developed quickly. So when we make inferences about students' responses, it is first important to try to separate out *incorrect* understanding from *incomplete* understanding. INFORMative assessment can help teachers make the distinction among correct understanding, incomplete understanding, and incorrect understanding.

> **Assessment Tip** ✓
> INFORMative assessment can help teachers distinguish among correct understanding, incomplete understanding, and incorrect understanding.

→ A Closer Look

Mrs. Nelson Categorizes Correct, Incorrect, and Incomplete Responses with *Fractional Exponents*

CcSS

Fractional Exponents relates to the standards cluster "Extend the properties of exponents to rational exponents," which is part of the domain "Number and Quantity: The Real Number System" (CCSS .MATH.CONTENTS. HSN.RN.A.1) The task is also supported by a standard in the "Number and Quantity: The Complex Number System" domain: "Use the relation $i^2 = -1$ and the commutative, associative, and distributive properties to add, subtract, and multiply complex numbers" (CCSS.MATH .CONTENT.HSN.CN.A.2).

Mrs. Nelson selected *Fractional Exponents* for monitoring students' understanding in a unit about complex numbers. She knew from previous use of the task that students were likely to give both correct and incorrect solutions, and she anticipated that she might also observe some incomplete solutions. Before you read on, solve the task yourself.

Task: Fractional Exponents

True or false: $((-4)^2)^{1/2} = ((-4)^{1/2})^2$ Explain.

Mrs. Nelson knew that there are two critical mathematics ideas in this task that might challenge students. First, on the right side, there is the issue of taking the square root of a negative number. This is possible only when complex numbers are allowed. Second, the expression on the left ends with taking a square root, so there ought to be two possible ending values, while the expression on the right ends with taking a square, so there ought to be only one possible ending value. (If students are operating within the convention that $\sqrt{x}$ or $(x)^{1/2}$ represents only the principal square root, then the second issue would not apply.) Figures 8–3, 8–4, and 8–5 show examples of students' answers for this task. Before reading Mrs. Nelson's insights, decide how you view each student's response—correct, incorrect, or incomplete?

$$\left((-4)^2\right)^{\frac{1}{2}} = (16)^{\frac{1}{2}} = \pm 4$$

$$\left((-4)^{\frac{1}{2}}\right)^2 = (2i)^2 = 4i^2 = -4$$

These are not the same, so FALSE

FIGURE 8–3. Jana's Response for *Fractional Exponents*

Mrs. Nelson determined Jana's response to be correct. (See Figure 8–3.) Jana seemed to think about the order in which the square root and the square are taken and used that information to generate computed values for the two sides of the equation. Jana evaluated the left side to ±4 and the right side only to −4 (i.e., $4i^2$). These two values are not the same, so the equation is false, as Jana noted. Mrs. Nelson knew that it would be sufficient for students to acknowledge that the left side evaluates to two values and right side to only one value, without specifying the particular values, but she expected students to specify the particular values, as Jana did.

If students do not know about imaginary numbers, they may say that $(-4)^{1/2}$ is impossible, since you can't take the square root of a negative number. They may conclude, therefore, that the equation is false—a correct answer with an incorrect, or at least incomplete, rationale. Depending on the level of mathematics course in which this task is used, this explanation might be viewed as acceptable. Remember, however, that "acceptable" is not always the same as "correct."

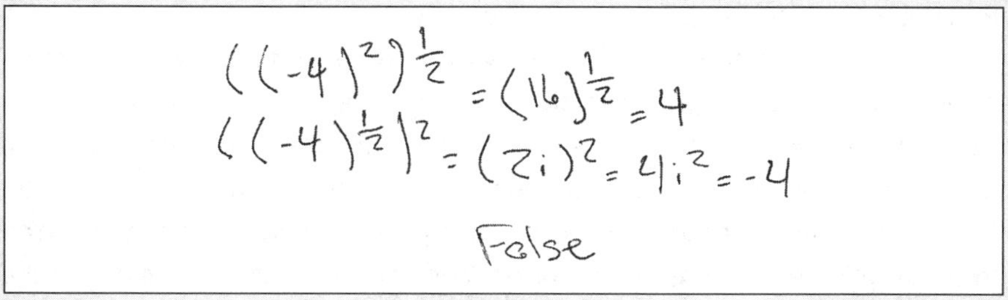

$$\left(\left(-4\right)^2\right)^{\frac{1}{2}} = \left(16\right)^{\frac{1}{2}} = 4$$
$$\left(\left(-4\right)^{\frac{1}{2}}\right)^2 = \left(2i\right)^2 = 4i^2 = -4$$
$$\text{False}$$

FIGURE 8-4. Hydar's Response for *Fractional Exponents*

Mrs. Nelson determined Hydar's response to be incomplete. (See Figure 8–4.) Hydar generated computed values for the two sides of the equation, but considered only the positive (principal) square root of 16. Mrs. Nelson had provided instruction to help students understand that both square roots should be considered, but Hydar apparently had not internalized this idea. Hydar is an example of a student who generates the correct response ("False"), but for the wrong reason. Mrs. Nelson knew that she needed to probe the incorrect computation, $(16)^{1/2} = 4$, to find out whether it represented a misconception or a misunderstanding.

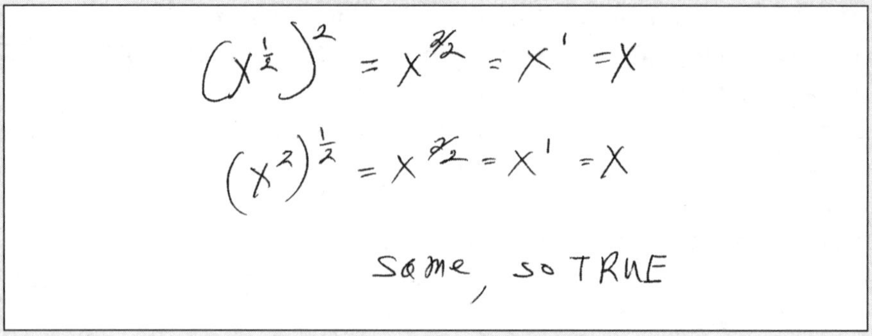

$$\left(x^{\frac{1}{2}}\right)^{2} = x^{\frac{2}{2}} = x^{1} = x$$

$$\left(x^{2}\right)^{\frac{1}{2}} = x^{\frac{2}{2}} = x^{1} = x$$

same, so TRUE

FIGURE 8-5. Rayan's Response for *Fractional Exponents*

Mrs. Nelson determined Rayan's response to be reasonable but incorrect. (See Figure 8–5.) Rayan began by "simplifying" the powers of the variable, and seemed to have reasoned that the square root of the square is the same as the square of the square root. This reasoning led to the conclusion that this relationship is true, since each side of the equation reduced to x. This response seemed to evolve from consideration only of the symbolic representations rather than understanding of the specific numbers.

Rayan's solution illustrates the need for students to know the limits on symbolic manipulations; for example, $5^3 \div 5 = 5^2$, but $x^3 \div x = x^2$ only when $x \neq 0$. As teachers we need to help students learn to determine when symbolic manipulations are appropriate and when those manipulations are inappropriate. In this case, the order in which roots and powers were taken matters. Yet, from Rayan's perspective, this incorrect solution seemed consistent with the knowledge gained from previous work with exponents. Mrs. Nelson knews that Rayan's understanding of exponents needed to be probed and probably needed to be refined. She categorized Rayan's incorrect response as a misconception that needed to be addressed.

Based on her categorization of these responses, Mrs. Nelson decided to have Jana and Hydar share their solutions with the class. She knew that a debriefing discussion would allow her to revisit the idea that there are two square roots of a number. She decided to delay discussion of the issues raised in Rayan's response; she felt that her students needed more work with actual computations before they would fully understand the limits of symbolic manipulations.

Becoming confident at categorizing students' responses takes time and experience. Complete "Reflection 8–1: Differentiating Correct, Incomplete, and Incorrect Responses" (see pages 349–350), which provides an opportunity for some of this practice.

Reflection 8–1

Differentiating Correct, Incomplete, and Incorrect Responses

Pages 349–350

Assessing Student Confidence

One key part of students' mathematics expertise is their confidence in being able to do mathematics. Confidence is difficult to assess. One technique is shared in Chapter 5 (page 188), which asks students to draw a smiling face or frowning face for each problem shown in a review sheet; these faces represent confidence, or lack thereof, at being able to answer the problem. Chapter 7 explores journal prompts to help students reflect on their understanding (see pages 277–280) and checklists to help students reflect on their metacognitive strategies (see pages 288–289). Another technique is shared in Chapter 9 (page 380)—the discussion of the alternative multiple-choice format.

Yet another means of assessing confidence is to ask students to write a task that they think they can solve easily and a similar task that they think they might struggle with. Giving students examples like the following will help communicate what you are asking them to do:

- A linear equation task with whole numbers versus the same equation task with fractions replacing the whole numbers.

- An area task with equilateral triangles versus a similar task with scalene triangles

- A data analysis task with one set of data versus a similar task with three sets of data.

The range of "easy" and "difficult" tasks will provide clues about what students are comfortable doing (i.e., confidence) versus what they feel not prepared to do (i.e., lack of confidence).

(continued)

(continued from page 321)

Because, as teachers, we interact with many students each day, it is not likely that we are able to make inferences about the *exact* level of confidence of each student. However, knowing when students lack confidence can provide opportunities both to have explicit discussions about the importance of confidence in learning and to pose tasks in which the main function is to help students develop confidence in their ability to learn mathematics. Consider these questions when thinking about students' confidence:

1. Why is it important to assess students' confidence?

2. What benefits are there for students if they understand their personal confidence levels?

3. How can you use your knowledge of students' confidence in instructional planning?

Strategy 2: Identify Possible Causes of Incomplete or Incorrect Answers

How we as teachers respond to incorrect answers depends on how we interpret the causes of those responses, so it is important to first seek out what caused a student to answer incorrectly. When seeking to understand the cause of an incorrect answer, we need to make sure our inferences are based on actual evidence about students' thinking. We need to be careful not to assume, for example, that the incorrect responses from "high-level" students are always carelessness and the incorrect responses from "low-level" students are always misconceptions.

We've found it helpful to think about causes of incomplete or incorrect answers through four categories: lapses, misunderstandings, misconceptions, and overgeneralizations. The labels are not as critical as the differences among the categories. The way we respond to an incorrect answer depends in part on which category we suspect it falls within. Let's take a more detailed look at each of these causes, one by one.

Assessment Tip ✅

Getting a student to change an incorrect response to a correct response by telling the student how to solve the problem "the right way" is not likely to resolve the underlying issue; instead we need to consider what *caused* the incorrect response.

Four Categories of Causes of Incomplete or Incorrect Answers

1. Lapses

2. Misunderstandings

3. Misconceptions

4. Overgeneralizations

Lapses

Sometimes students experience a *lapse* in using what they normally know; for example, being careless, recalling a fact incorrectly, or simply moving too fast and skipping over a step. Indicators of a lapse might be the incorrect placement of a decimal point or an order of operations error. Lapses are likely not a result of some fundamental misunderstanding, and often students can self-correct their work if teachers get them to slow down and rethink. Asking the student, "Does your answer make sense?" may prompt the student to self-correct. Unless we ask questions like this, we might mistakenly attribute incorrect responses to lapses, when actually those responses might reflect important cognitive issues that need to be addressed. An example of this is when students who normally score well give incorrect responses and we (mistakenly) decide that those are simply lapses. It's important to keep in mind that many incorrect responses are more than lapses.

Misunderstandings

A *misunderstanding* might occur because terminology is not well understood or because mathematical conventions are not firmly established. Sometimes in conversation students confuse sign and sine, and in written work they may confuse the long division symbol and the square root symbol. We

> **Assessment Tip** ✓
>
> Sometimes students experience a *lapse* in using what they normally know. Asking, "Does your answer make sense?" may prompt students to self-correct.

are likely all familiar with students who confuse perimeter and area or mean and median. If a student interprets $f(g(x))$ as the product of $f(x)$ and $g(x)$, the misunderstanding may be due to a lack of distinguishing between the symbolization for composition of functions and the symbolization for products of functions. For example, if $f(x) = 2x$ and $g(x) = x^2$, then $f(g(x)) = f(x^2) = 2x^2$ while $f(x) \cdot g(x) = (2x)(x^2) = 2x^3$. An incorrect response might suggest some underlying issues about the depth of understanding of composition of functions, but it may be due to a misunderstanding of the way that symbols are written.

Wiliam (2007b, 1070) noted that some items might not be ideal as test items but good as instructional tasks. His example is "Simplify (if possible): $2a + 5b$." He noted that students may assume that some work is required, just because the teacher posed the task. Students, then, may "do something" even though mathematically it is not possible to do any kind of simplification. That is, they may misunderstand the requirement of "simplify (if possible)." Using this as a test item, then, may yield results that are not an accurate reflection of students' understanding.

The very nature of a misunderstanding is that the student has mixed up something. Unlike when there is a lapse, teacher actions in response to a misunderstanding are more complicated than simply asking the question, "Does your answer make sense?" A misunderstanding might represent a fairly simple confusion or it might be a symptom of a significant misconception (discussed next). We have to make that determination before we can know how to respond.

Misconceptions

A *misconception* happens when mathematics ideas have been internalized incorrectly in a student's cognition. In a perfect world, misconceptions could be "unlearned" or "erased" and replaced with correct understanding. Unfortunately, it is more likely that misconceptions never completely disappear from the mental connections that students have created. Rather, teachers have to help students learn how to work around whatever residual, incorrect knowledge exists.

Assessment Tip ✓

Keep in mind that a *misunderstanding* is likely more complicated to diagnose than a lapse; a misunderstanding might represent a fairly simple confusion or it might be a symptom of a significant *misconception*.

Wiliam (2007b) noted that some students found it difficult to solve this set of simultaneous equations:

Task: Solving Equations

$3a = 24$

$a + b = 16$

Learn More...

Chapter 6 provides more information about choosing mathematically rich tasks and modifying traditional tasks to make them richer.

In part, this appeared to be the result of the fact that both $a = 8$ and $b = 8$, and students held a belief that since the variables a and b are different, their values should also be different. This highlights the need to reveal what students *believe* (or, perhaps, what they have overgeneralized) as well as what they *know*. Tasks need to be designed explicitly to do this.

A misconception is more than a misunderstanding or miscommunication, and misconceptions are often more critical for future learning than misunderstandings. Writing the square root of x as x^{-2} rather than $x^{1/2}$ may be more than just a "symbol-writing" issue; it may reflect faulty thinking about how exponents operate when those exponents are not positive integers. It is often difficult to get students to "fix" misconceptions. Misconceptions often reappear in unexpected ways when new content is being learned.

Assessment Tip ✓

A misconception is more than a misunderstanding or miscommunication, and misconceptions are often more critical for future learning than misunderstandings.

Overgeneralizations

Sometimes students *overgeneralize* an idea in a mathematically incorrect way; for example, $(x + y)^2 = x^2 + y^2$. (Of course, $(x + y)^2 = x^2 + y^2$ is *sometimes* correct; for example, when either $x = 0$ or $y = 0$.) Overgeneralizations may represent misunderstandings (e.g., confusion with $2(x + y) = 2x + 2y$) or misconceptions (e.g., mathematics is primarily additive in structure); we cannot know without probing students' thinking. Overgeneralizations may result when students focus on only one part of a teacher's or other student's comments. In response to an overgeneralization, a teacher may caution the student about its applicability or invite examples to show when it would not be true.

Assessment Tip ✓

An overgeneralization may represent a misunderstanding or misconception; we cannot know without probing students' thinking.

→ A Closer Look

Ms. Ertenberg Identifies Possible Causes of Incomplete and Incorrect Answers with *The Photocopier*

Ms. Ertenberg knows that scoring answers as correct or incorrect is not as important as uncovering the causes of incorrect answers. She considers the categories—lapses, misunderstandings, misconceptions, and overgeneralizations—as a way to think about students' incorrect answers. Her inferences about the causes of incorrect responses influence the feedback she then gives to the student. Having a sense of these causes helps her know what kinds of feedback might be helpful to students in reorganizing their thinking.

Ms. Ertenberg applied her thinking in reviewing students' responses to *The Photocopier.* Before you read on, solve the task yourself.

> **Learn More...**
> Chapter 9 offers a detailed look at actionable feedback.

Task: The Photocopier

When a photocopier enlarges an image, all dimensions are enlarged equally. A photocopier was used twice to create the larger circle from the smaller circle. This photocopier had a maximum enlargement capability of 140%. For example, a line segment 1 inch long could be enlarged, at most, to create an image that was 1.4 inches long. So the photocopier had to be used twice to create the larger circle. If the same enlargement factor was used both times, what enlargement setting was it?

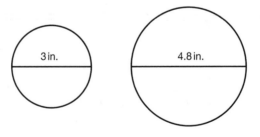

Following are five student responses for *The Photocopier.* (See Figures 8–6 to 8–10.) Before you read Ms. Ertenberg's insights about each, ask yourself what would you infer as the cause of each incomplete or incorrect answer?

The difference is 1.8 so
do .9 twice.

FIGURE 8-6. Liam's Response to *The Photocopier*

Ms. Ertenberg sees from Liam's response that he computed the difference in the diameters, and apparently used that difference as if it were the enlargement factor. (See Figure 8–6.) His thinking seems to represent a common misconception about proportional reasoning situations; namely, operating with additive reasoning rather than proportional thinking.

$$4.\frac{8}{3} = 1.6 \text{ or } 60\% \text{ bigger}$$

do 30% up each time

FIGURE 8-7. Zoey's Response to *The Photocopier*

Ms. Ertenberg sees from Zoey's response that Zoey computed the appropriate ratio, but then simply split the 60-percent enlargement factor into two equal parts. (See Figure 8–7.) Zoey seems to be operating at a transitional level between additive and proportional reasoning. She computed the 60-percent enlargement correctly, but then acted as if that enlargement factor could be split into equal additive parts.

$$\frac{4.8}{3} = 1.6 \text{ or } 160\%$$

do 130% twice

FIGURE 8-8. Emma's Response to *The Photocopier*

Ms. Ertenberg views Emma's response as conceptually the same as Zoey's. (See Figure 8–8.) However, Emma recognizes that an enlargement factor is greater than 100 percent. This may indicate marginally better thinking, even though her thinking also seems to represent a similar confusion between additive and proportional reasoning.

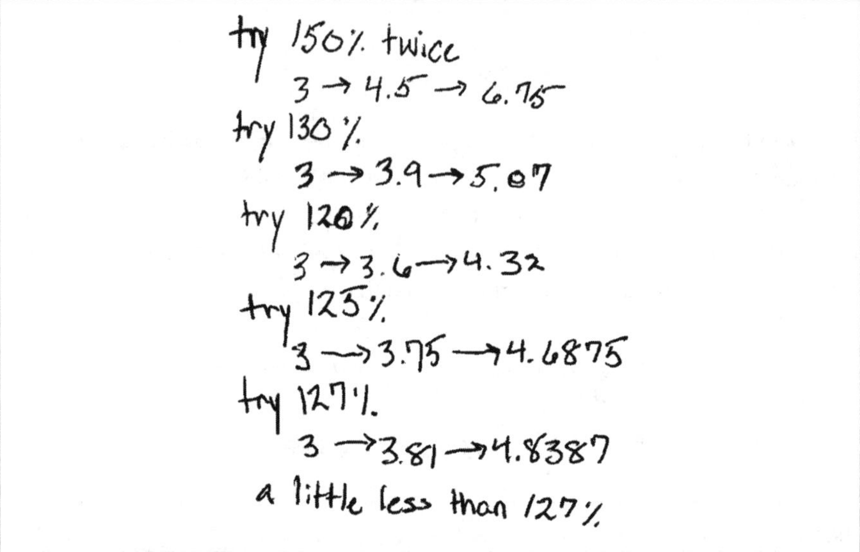

FIGURE 8–9. Lucas's Response to *The Photocopier*

CCSS

Lucas's use of so many decimal places may represent an inability to "communicate precisely to others", reflected in the standard "Attend to precision" (CCSS .MATH.PRACTICE.MP6).

Ms. Ertenberg recognizes that Lucas got close to a solution with his use of trial and error. (See Figure 8–9.) Lucas appears to have used a calculator to generate several decimal places in each of the computations, even though the large number of decimal places may not be appropriate for the context of this task. Ms. Ertenberg knows that many teachers would probably view Lucas's solution as acceptable, but it is not a solution strategy that would generalize easily to other tasks. If there is anything "incorrect" here, it is the number of relatively meaningless decimal places in some of the computations. His calculations might constitute a misunderstanding of what is appropriate precision rather than a misconception.

Ms. Ertenberg acknowledges that Juan created a mathematically correct solution to the task, at least within the computational precision supported by calculator use. (See Figure 8–10.) She might probe his thinking to find out what the value 1.6 means for the context of the task (*Why did you compute 4.8 divided by 3 and what does the quotient, 1.6, mean?*), and she definitely wants

$$\frac{4.8}{3} = 1.6$$

Need Enlargment so that

$$3 \cdot E \cdot E = 4.8$$
$$E \cdot E = 1.6$$
$$E = \sqrt{1.6} = 1.2649111$$

about $126\frac{1}{2}$ %

FIGURE 8–10. Juan's Response to *The Photocopier*

to ask him to define the variable, *E*, for his work (*What does* E *represent?*), but his thinking seems fairly clear and accurate mathematically for the task.

Lucas's solution, while correct, is less "elegant" than Juan's. As a result, some teachers might view Juan's solution as "more correct" than Lucas's. However, a lack of elegance does not necessarily mean a lack of understanding of the underlying mathematics ideas. Lucas and Juan appear to have used very similar thinking, though Juan's thinking is more abstract and certainly more succinct. Ms. Ertenberg decides to have Lucas and Juan share their solutions with each other in hopes that doing so might enhance the thinking of both students. Lucas's approach may be just a simpler application of the same kind of reasoning that Juan used.

Assessment Tip

Our inferences about the causes of incorrect or incomplete responses influence the feedback we then give to students.

When planning how to respond to incomplete or incorrect answers, it is helpful to be explicit about what we think are the causes (lapse, misunderstanding, misconception, or overgeneralization). Dealing with lapses is often easier than dealing with misunderstandings, misconceptions, or overgeneralizations. With experience we can become more accurate at identifying whether a lapse, misunderstanding, misconception, or overgeneralization is driving an incorrect response. Turn to "Reflection 8–2: Identifying Possible Causes of Incomplete or Incorrect Answers" (see page 351) and think about what may be the cause of several more incorrect or incomplete solutions.

Reflection 8–2

Identifying Possible Causes of Incomplete or Incorrect Answers

Page 351

Strategy 3: Examine the Logic Behind Incomplete or Incorrect Answers

Assessment Tip

Students rarely respond randomly; there is almost always some logic behind a student's solution to a task or response to a question that, as teachers, we need to try to find out.

Students rarely respond randomly; there is almost always some "logic" behind a student's solution to a task or response to a question. That logic may be mathematically correct, incomplete (perhaps because the student gave up in frustration), or incorrect. Understanding a student's logic may reveal that the student has rich cognitive connections that go beyond the requirements of the task, or it may help reveal gaps in his or her background knowledge that we can then deal with directly. As teachers we should be most concerned with the latter, when a student's logic is faulty. Sometimes the incorrectness is all we can see in a student's work, so it is important to try to find out the logic behind incomplete or incorrect answers.

Assessment Tip

Interpreting students' responses to questions requires a deep understanding of both the relevant mathematics ideas and the ways that students develop that understanding.

It takes time and experience to become proficient at identifying students' logic. This skill begins with questioning, but interpreting students' responses to questions requires a deep understanding of both the relevant mathematics ideas and the ways that people develop that understanding. That deep understanding grows with teaching experience, and it is a journey that never really ends.

An incorrect response that occurs because of faulty underlying logic is called an error; errors may represent misunderstandings or misconceptions. For example, sometimes students "distribute" inappropriately. (See Figure 8–11.)

These incorrect responses are mathematically significant. Students may have become so used to distributing that they do not stop to examine whether a particular situation is appropriate for the application of that property. Students may overgeneralize distributivity to encompass too many situations.

Assessment Tip

An incorrect response that occurs because of faulty underlying logic is called an error; errors are often mathematically critical.

Example A: $(3 + 4)^2 = 3^2 + 4^2$

Example B: $\sqrt{(x^2 + y^2)} = x + y$

Example C: $\sin(x + y) = \sin x + \sin y$

FIGURE 8–11. Three Examples of Faulty "Distributing"

→ A Closer Look

Mrs. Locklear Examines Students' Logic with *Computation* $12 \div \frac{2}{3}$

Mrs. Locklear asked her students to compute $12 \div \frac{2}{3}$. She knew that her students should have been able to complete this computation successfully; however, she also knew that it was likely some students would respond incorrectly.

Mrs. Locklear looked specifically at two incorrect responses and considered the logic behind each response. (See Figures 8–12 and 8–13.) Before reading Mrs. Locklear's insights, look at each student's response. What logic would you infer is happening?

$$12 \div 2 \div 3 = 6 \div 3 = 2$$

FIGURE 8-12. Spike's Response to *Computation* $12 \div \frac{2}{3}$

Mrs. Locklear saw that Spike gave an answer of "2." (See Figure 8-12.) When asked to explain, he correctly said that the fraction bar is like a division sign, he wrote the problem (incorrectly) as $12 \div 2 \div 3$, and he then applied order of operations correctly (when there is a single operation used repeatedly) to do the computations from left to right. The answer is mathematically incorrect because Spike forgot (or misunderstood) that the fraction bar is also a grouping symbol, so the correct expression is $12 \div (2 \div 3)$, and the division in parentheses must be completed first. In this case, Spike's logic seems incomplete rather than incorrect; that is, there is incomplete understanding of what the fraction bar means.

$$12 \div \frac{2}{3} = \frac{1}{12} \times \frac{2}{3} = \frac{2}{36} = \frac{1}{18}$$

FIGURE 8-13. Raven's Response to *Computation* $12 \div \frac{2}{3}$

Mrs. Locklear recognized that Raven reasoned that when you divide by fractions, you invert one of the numbers and multiply. (See Figure 8-13.)

When Raven inverted the 12 to get $\frac{1}{12}$, the product became $\frac{2}{36}$ or $\frac{1}{18}$. This was more than simply forgetting which number to invert; it reflected a lack of understanding about the meaning of division. In this case, Raven's logic seemed incorrect.

It seems reasonable to infer that the both students were operating mainly on the symbols of the computation. Embedding the computation in a context, such as, *It takes $\frac{2}{3}$ of an hour to draw a poster for the prom. How many posters can be drawn in 12 hours?* might have helped them rethink their work. Clearly, neither "2 posters" nor "$\frac{1}{18}$ poster" would be a reasonable answer. Unfortunately, although using a context might have convinced the students that their answers were not correct, use of a context might not provide any clue to the students about what erroneous thinking led them to their incorrect answers. Mrs. Locklear might also have asked the students to draw a picture to model the meaning of the computation; students' modeling often reveals a great deal about their thinking.

Students' errors in computation when dealing with fractions have clear implications for later work with algebraic fractions and rational functions. Thus, it is important to look for the logic behind students' answers and provide opportunities for students to examine the reasonableness of their answers and their own reasoning.

Assessment Tip ☑

Students' modeling often reveals a great deal about students' thinking. For example, these diagrams model $12 \div \frac{2}{3}$:

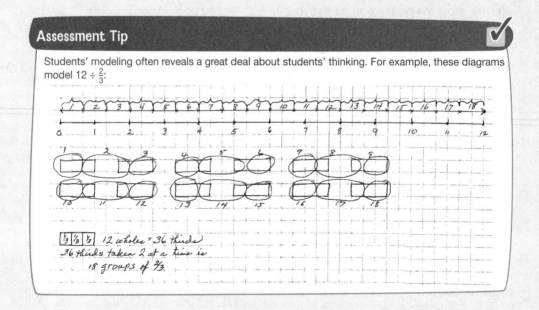

$\boxed{\frac{1}{3}}\boxed{\frac{1}{3}}\boxed{\frac{1}{3}}$ 12 wholes = 36 thirds
36 thirds taken 2 at a time is
    18 groups of ⅔

→ A Closer Look

Mr. Herje Examines the Logic Behind Incomplete and Incorrect Answers with *Water in the Bucket*

Mr. Herje asked his students to complete *Water in the Bucket*. He uses this task to explore students' logic in a problem-solving task. When he introduces the task, he does a quick review with the class to help them get started; in this case, a review of what the unit, kilogram, actually measures (i.e., mass, rather than volume). Students also frequently confuse mass and weight. Mr. Herje has found that talking with the science teachers has given him strategies for helping students understand the difference. Saying that the mass of the bucket is 1 kilogram simply means that the bucket is made of a relatively light material, say, aluminum. The *volume* of the bucket is a different attribute than its *mass*.

The first three parts of the task are related to standards for proportional reasoning in middle grades, while the fourth part is related to understanding rational functions in high school. Before you read on, solve the problem yourself.

The cluster of standards in the seventh grade "Ratios and Proportional Relationships" domain of the CCSSM that serve to "Analyze proportional relationships and use them to solve real-world and mathematical problems" support the first three parts of *Water in the Bucket* (CCSS.MATH .CONTENT.7.RP.A.1), while the high school algebra standard "Create equations and inequalities in one variable and use them to solve problems. *Include equations arising from linear and quadratic functions, and simple rational and exponential functions*" relates to the fourth part of the task (CCSS.MATH.CONTENT .HSA.CED.A.1).

Task: Water in the Bucket

A 1 kilogram bucket contains 99 kilograms of water.

1. *What percent of the total mass of the water and the bucket is water?*

2. *If 5 kilograms of water is removed, what percent of the combined mass of the remaining water and the bucket is water?*

3. *How many kilograms of water must be removed from the bucket so that the remaining water is 50% of the combined mass of the water and the bucket?*

4. *Suppose W is the amount of water removed and R is the percentage of water in the combined mass of the remaining water and the bucket. Write an equation that shows the relationship between W and R.*

(Bright and Joyner 2004a, 151; adapted from
Bush and Greer 1999, 118)

Mr. Herje specifically looked at three students' responses to *Water in the Bucket*. (See Figures 8–14 to 8–16.) As you review each, ask yourself the following questions:

- What can I infer about the logic behind each student's answer?

- How will my inferences influence possible instructional decisions?

1. $\frac{1}{99} = 0.0101\ldots = 1.01\%$

2. $\frac{1}{94} = 1.06\%$

3. $50\% = \frac{1}{2}$ so you have to remove 97 kg since there needs to be 2 kg of water left

4. $R = \frac{1}{(99-W)}$

FIGURE 8-14. Mateo's Response to *Water in the Bucket*

Mateo seems to have interpreted the amount of water as the "referent" amount; that is, he did not include the mass of the bucket in the total mass of the water *and* the bucket. (See Figure 8-14.) Mr. Herje thinks this error could represent a misreading (or superficial reading) of the problem or a lapse in understanding of the context (i.e., the total mass must include both the bucket and the water inside the bucket). Mateo used this interpretation consistently across all four parts of the problem, so Mr. Herje hoped that helping him correct his understanding of the context would have a "ripple effect" across all four parts of his response.

① $1/99 = 0.0101\ldots = 1.01\%$

② $1/94 = 1.06\%$

③ If you remove 50% of the water, you remove 49.5 kg

④ $R = (99 - W)/99$

FIGURE 8-15. Kita's Response to *Water in the Bucket*

Mr. Herje noticed that in the first two parts, Kita responded the same way as Mateo, but her focus shifted for the last two parts. (See Figure 8-15.) She seemed to consider only the water, without considering the mass of the bucket. This is a significant misunderstanding of the context, though her use of percentages and ratios suggests that she understands how to use proportional reasoning.

$$1. \frac{1}{100} = 1\%$$
$$2. \frac{1}{95} = 1.05\%$$
3. 50% is $\frac{1}{2}$, so the amount of water remaining must be 1 kg, so the amount removed must be 98 kg
$$4. R = \frac{(99-W)}{(100-W)}$$

FIGURE 8-16. Sergei's Response to *Water in the Bucket*

Sergei responded correctly, but the task did not specifically ask for an explanation of his thinking about the appropriate equation. (See Figure 8-16.) Mr. Herje planned to probe his thinking during the debriefing of this task by asking, "How did you determine that the amount of water remaining must be 1 kg?" since his reasoning for this solution was not explicitly provided. Probing Sergei's thinking about his correct responses would validate those solutions and allow others in the class to hear the logic behind his answers.

Water in the Bucket is a rich task that can be mined for more understanding, both about the task itself and about students' responses to it. Complete "Reflection 8–3: Examining the Logic Behind Incomplete or Incorrect Answers for *Water in the Bucket*" (see pages 352–353), which provides an opportunity for you to increase your understanding of the task as well as the logic behind students' responses.

Learn More... Chapter 4 offers detailed information about probing questions.

Reflection 8–3 Examining the Logic Behind Incomplete or Incorrect Answers for *Water in the Bucket* Pages 352–353

Strategy 4: Determine If Errors in Answers Reflect Substance or Presentation

As discussed thus far, errors can be triggered by misconceptions or misunderstandings. For example, when asked to evaluate 2(4) + 3, some students will write 2(4) = 8 + 3 = 11. This string of equations is mathematically incorrect (i.e., it is an incorrect response), but the thinking, or logic, behind the work

Learn More... In our book *Dynamic Classroom Assessment* (Bright and Joyner 2004a), we talk about the difference between the substance of an idea and the presentation of understanding of an idea.

Learn More...

The substance of an idea is the mental understanding of the idea; the presentation of an idea is the way one's understanding of the idea is communicated. An error of substance is probably a misconception; an error of presentation is probably a misunderstanding. For more on the connections among misconceptions, misunderstandings, substance, and presentation, see the work of David Pimm (1987, 1995).

Learn More...

Chapter 3 offers more discussion on conceptual and procedural knowledge.

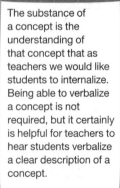

Assessment Tip ✓

The substance of a concept is the understanding of that concept that as teachers we would like students to internalize. Being able to verbalize a concept is not required, but it certainly is helpful for teachers to hear students verbalize a clear description of a concept.

is likely correct. Sometimes this is interpreted as "stream of consciousness" thinking; students just write down what they are thinking as they think it. It is important to acknowledge this thinking while helping students correct the way that thinking is communicated. This is where determining the difference between the *substance* of an idea (that is, the mental understanding of an idea—what a student knows) and the *presentation* of understanding of an idea (that is, the way that one's understanding is communicated—what a student shows) is helpful, especially when making quality inferences. As teachers we have to decide if a student's incorrect responses reflect some flaw in thinking (i.e., an error of substance) or a flaw in the way they've communicated that thinking (i.e., an error of presentation). If we connect this to the terminology *misconception* and *misunderstanding*, an error of substance is likely a misconception while an error of presentation is likely a misunderstanding. To better understand the distinction between substance and presentation, in the following sections we consider how they play out for both conceptual knowledge and procedural knowledge.

As a reminder, conceptual knowledge includes the big ideas in mathematics, and procedural knowledge deals with the way we do things. For example, students should enter algebra with an understanding of proportional reasoning. This is a big idea—conceptual knowledge. These same students also need to know how to solve proportions in a variety of ways. This is a way to do things—procedural knowledge.

Substance and Presentation for Conceptual Knowledge

The *substance of a concept* and the *presentation of a concept* are two different aspects of a concept. The *substance of a concept* is the understanding of that concept that we would like students to internalize. This might be a visual image (e.g., knowing what a square looks like) or a way of describing the concept (e.g., the mean of a set of data is the number that results from equal sharing among the data values). Evidence that a student is acquiring the substance of a concept might be that the student can identify examples and nonexamples, even if the student cannot give a definition or an exact description. Being able to verbalize a concept is not required, but it certainly is helpful for teachers to hear students verbalize a clear description of a concept. Without some kind of verbalization, it is almost impossible to know what is in a student's head.

The *presentation of a concept* is the way an internalized idea is communicated to others. Students might use words, symbols, pictures, or technology to let us know what is in their heads. Students may try to use the teacher's terminology without really understanding what those words mean. Students may use lots of pronouns, such as *it* or *they*, to cover up a lack of detailed understanding. Teachers often interpret the meaning of those pronouns in ways that provide mathematically correct meaning; that is, teachers tend to imbue students' words with the correct meaning. But when students' thinking is probed, we may discover that students do not have clear meaning for those pronouns; that is, they lack deep mathematics knowledge. The chart in Figure 8–17 shows how these ideas play out for *Conceptual Knowledge for Area of a Rectangle*.

> **Assessment Tip** ✓
>
> The presentation of a concept is the way an internalized idea is communicated to others. Since students can use words, symbols, pictures, or technology to explain what they have in their minds, it's important as teachers to attend to the way students communicate the ideas they have internalized.

	Substance (What a Student Knows)	Presentation (What a Student Shows)
Concept	Understands that area is the covering of a plane surface; knows that a region can be cut apart and reassembled into different shapes without changing the area	Shows the area of a figure by covering the surface with equal-size units (or pointing to the unit squares), leaving no gaps and having no overlapping pieces

FIGURE 8–17. A Substance/Presentation Chart for *Conceptual Knowledge for Area of a Rectangle*

The substance of conceptual knowledge includes (a) applying a definition, (b) calling up prototypical examples and nonexamples, (c) providing descriptions of the idea at different levels of specificity, or (d) recognizing when a concept does or does not apply in a given situation. The presentation of a concept includes using various representations (e.g., words, symbols) of the concept or having clear language for describing characteristics of examples and nonexamples.

Substance and Presentation for Procedural Knowledge

As students learn procedures, they frequently focus on the manipulation of symbols and try to learn rules for the "steps" rather than try to understand the mathematical ideas behind these steps. For the equation $2x + 5 = 19$, students should understand that 5 could be subtracted from each side (or negative 5 could be added) so that an equivalent equation is created ($2x = 14$). This is the "substance part" of that step in the procedure. Some students may say instead that when they move the 5 across the equals sign they have to change its sign; that is, they simply manipulate symbols. This verbalization would indicate a focus on the "presentation part" of the procedure.

The *substance of a procedure* is the internalization of how a procedure "works." Students may or may not be able to carry out the procedure; they may simply know when it is being carried out correctly by others. Teachers want students both to carry out the procedure and to explain how each step follows from previous steps.

The *presentation of a procedure* is the way that a procedure is represented. Students may be able to carry out the steps (e.g., write down the symbols) without knowing exactly what those symbols mean or why they are written in a particular order. For example, students can compute the sum of several multidigit decimal numbers by aligning the digits vertically, adding the digits in each column, and putting the "carry or regrouping marks" in appropriate places. They may be generating the correct sum without understanding how the steps are justified through place-value ideas. If students develop this habit of learning without meaning, they may come to believe that learning mathematics just means memorizing what the teacher says. The chart that follows shows how these ideas play out for *Procedural Knowledge for Area of a Rectangle*. (See Figure 8–18.)

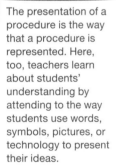

Assessment Tip ✓

The substance of a procedure is the internalization of how a procedure "works." As teachers, we want students both to carry out the procedure and to explain how each step follows from previous steps.

Assessment Tip ✓

The presentation of a procedure is the way that a procedure is represented. Here, too, teachers learn about students' understanding by attending to the way students use words, symbols, pictures, or technology to present their ideas.

	Substance (What a Student Knows)	Presentation (What a Student Shows)
Procedure	Knows that multiplying the length and width of a rectangle generates the number of units needed to cover that rectangle	Multiplies the length and width of a rectangle to find the area because that is the rule

FIGURE 8–18. A Substance/Presentation Chart for *Procedural Knowledge for Area of a Rectangle*

The substance of procedural knowledge includes knowing why the procedure works, how to derive the procedure, or having a rationale for each step in the procedure. The presentation of procedural knowledge is knowing what the steps are and carrying them out efficiently; for example, by following directions for what to do or applying the procedure to a particular example.

Summarizing Ideas About Substance and Presentation

The following chart summarizes the ideas about substance and presentation. (See Figure 8–19.) The entries in the chart characterize the differences among the four combinations of substance/presentation with concept/procedure.

	Substance (What a Student Knows)	Presentation (What a Student Shows)
Concept	Understanding an idea and knowing examples and nonexamples	Communicating an idea or recognizing different representations of it
Procedure	Understanding why the steps in a procedure work	Carrying out the steps in a procedure

FIGURE 8–19. Guidelines for Creating a Substance/Presentation Chart (adapted from Bright and Joyner 2004b, 86)

These ideas are most useful when they are applied to a specific mathematics idea. The chart that follows is a completed substance/presentation chart for *Area of a Rectangle*. (See Figure 8–20.)

	Substance (What a Student Knows)	Presentation (What a Student Shows)
Concept	Understands that area is the covering of a plane surface; knows that a region can be cut apart and reassembled into different shapes without changing the area	Shows the area of a figure by covering the surface with equal-size units (or pointing to the unit squares), leaving no gaps and having no overlapping pieces
Procedure	Knows that multiplying the length and width of a rectangle generates the number of units needed to cover that rectangle	Multiplies the length and width of a rectangle to find the area because that is the rule

FIGURE 8–20. A Substance/Presentation Chart for *Conceptual Knowledge and Procedural Knowledge* for *Area of a Rectangle*

Equation solving is another important idea for secondary school mathematics. The next chart is a completed substance/presentation chart for equation solving. (See Figure 8–21.) Sometimes in solving an equation, students have to rewrite $10 = x$ as $x = 10$ before they are sure that the value of x is 10. This is not really an error, but it does reveal lack of understanding of equivalent equations. In this case students seem to be distracted by the way the equations are written; that is, by the presentation of the solution process.

Learn More...

Distinguishing between substance and presentation for both concepts and procedures is an activity only for teachers, *not* for students.

	Substance (What a Student Knows)	Presentation (What a Student Shows)
Concept	Knows that two equations are equivalent when their solution sets are identical	Explains why two equations are, or are not, equivalent
Procedure	Knows what kinds of steps are acceptable and what kinds are not (i.e., might generate extraneous solutions)	Writes down steps to solve an equation

FIGURE 8–21. A Substance/Presentation Chart for *Conceptual Knowledge and Procedural Knowledge* for *Equation Solving*

Distinguishing between substance and presentation for both concepts and procedures is an activity only for teachers, *not* for students. Making these distinctions provides us as teachers with a context within which we can make more accurate inferences about the logic behind students' thinking. We can make these distinctions because we have mature knowledge of mathematics ideas. Students who are just learning about concepts and procedures do not typically have enough knowledge to make such sophisticated distinctions. Complete "Reflection 8–4: Creating a Substance/Presentation Chart" (see pages 354–355), which provides you with an opportunity to think about what a chart for *mean of a set of data* would look like and what it signifies for the context: *Each student in a class counts the number of people in his or her family.*

Reflection 8–4

Creating a Substance/ Presentation Chart

Pages 354–355

Strategy 5: Use Probing Questions and Follow-Up Tasks to Support Inferences

Probing students' thinking is a critical aspect of INFORMative assessment and effective mathematics instruction. In this section we revisit some of the ideas of questioning, only now within the discussion of how questioning helps us as teachers make inferences about students' thinking. Those inferences are based on information that we gather through the use of both probing questions and follow-up tasks.

Probing Questions to Support Inferences

As discussed thus far, incorrect responses are signals to the teacher that something may be wrong with students' understanding, most critically when an incorrect response appears to be triggered by a misconception. It is important to identify what might be causing incorrect responses before jumping in with remediation. Remediation needs to be targeted toward the causes of incorrect responses, not just toward getting students to change their responses. Inferences about possible causes for incorrect responses can come from analyzing information generated by the use of probing questions.

Similarly, correct responses, especially correct responses that are not adequately explained, can be confusing to other students. When we use probing questions to explore the thinking behind correct responses and then make accurate inferences about that thinking, we can use those inferences to accomplish two things. First, we can help students understand their own thinking better. Second, we can help students become better at communicating their reasoning. Both understanding and communicating are critical for students' mathematical development.

The use of probing questions for supporting inferences can be illustrated best by examining questions that might be used to probe students' responses to a specific task. The task that follows, *A Dog Food Sale*, focuses on unit rates. This is a critical idea not only for middle grades students but also for beginning algebra students. Solve the task yourself before you read on.

> **Learn More …**
> Questioning is further discussed in Chapter 4.

> **Assessment Tip** ✓
> Target remediation toward the causes of incorrect responses.

Task: A Dog Food Sale

Cuddly Dog pet store has two sizes of Happy Dog brand dog food on sale. The 7-pound bag costs $7.70 and the 3-pound bag costs $5.35. Which bag is the better buy?

Jacob's answer to this task is not the expected solution. (See Figure 8–22.) Sometimes students' responses seem confusing to us because their thinking does not match our way of solving the problem. In such a case, we may need to use questions to determine if those students grasp the mathematics that is critical to the task. Before you read on, try to reason through what Jacob did. What preliminary inferences would you make about his thinking?

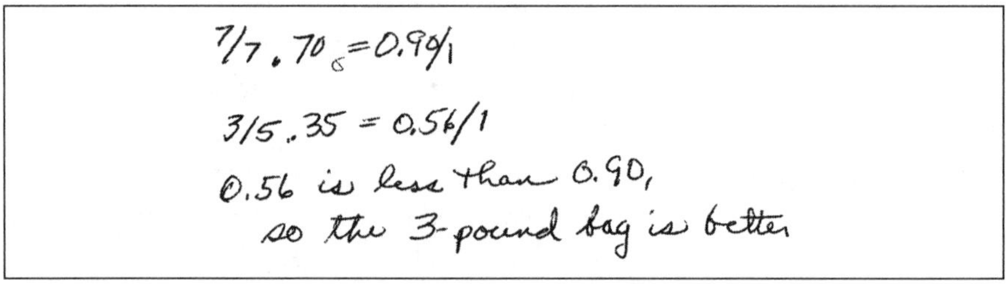

$$7/7.70 = 0.99/1$$

$$3/5.35 = 0.56/1$$

0.56 is less than 0.90,
so the 3-pound bag is better

FIGURE 8-22. Jacob's Response to *A Dog Food Sale*

Most teachers would expect students to compute the cost per pound for each bag; that is, the amount of money paid for each pound of dog food. Jacob computed the amount of dog food that each dollar will buy. That is, he computed the inverse of what most teachers would expect, so a correct conclusion from his computations would be that the greater quantity of dog food per dollar is the better buy. Since he did not label the quantities in his solution, it is not clear what he thinks the computations represent. However, he seemed to apply the "less is better" criterion to the computations to generate an incorrect conclusion.

There are several probing questions that we might pose to Jacob to help us understand his thinking and to help him analyze his work:

- *What are the units of measure for each of the numbers you used?*
- *What is the unit that applies to each quotient?*
- *Why did you divide 7 by 7.70?*
- *What does 7 over 7.70 tell you about the 7-pound bag?*
- *How did you decide that the 3-pound bag was the better buy?*

The goal of these probing questions is not to get Jacob to do it "our way." Rather, the goal is to help us understand his thinking and to help him interpret his work in a way that is appropriate for the task. Jacob's computations *could* lead to a correct solution to this task, but the lack of precision in his work (e.g., the omission of labels) seems to be related to a fundamental error in his logic.

Let's look at another example. The pre-assessment for the Mathematics Assessment Project (MAP) lesson *Evaluating Statements About Enlargements* includes questions to help clarify errors and reveal students' logic for their answers. These questions might serve as models for how to formulate effective questions about specific content. What we are calling *Pizza* is from the lesson's pre-assessment task, *A Fair Price*. Students' completion of this task will provide information for the teacher to use in planning instruction that responds to their understanding.

Task: Pizza

A large pizza has a diameter of 12 inches. A small pizza has a diameter of 6 inches.

(Diagram not to scale.)

"I get the same amount of pizza from three small pizzas as from one large pizza."

Is Jasmina correct about the pizzas?

If you think Jasmina is correct explain why.

If you think she is incorrect replace the statement with one that is correct. Explain why your statement is correct.

....

....

....

If the price for a small pizza is $3, what is a 'fair price' for a large one? Explain your answer.

....

....

....

Source: From *Evaluating Statements About Enlargements* (2015), http://map.mathshell.org/lessons.php?unit=9320, © Shell Centre, The University of Nottingham.

Learn More...

Pizza is from the MAP lesson *Evaluating Statements About Enlargements* (map.mathshell.org/lessons.php?unit=9320). Each MAP lesson includes questions that are intended to reveal students' thinking and logic about the particular tasks in that lesson. For more on MAP lessons and their value for formative assessment, see map.mathshell.org.

The MAP lesson plan that *Pizza* is part of lists several errors and probing questions. (See Figure 8–23.) These questions can help us identify what particular kinds of logic students are using.

Potential Error	Probing Question
Assumes the diagrams are accurate representations	*How can you use math to find out if the pictures are accurate?*
Fails to mention scale	*How can you figure out the scale of increase in area using your answers?*
Focuses on nonmathematical issues	*Are three small pizzas equivalent to one big one? How do you know?*
Makes a technical error	*What does r in the formula represent?*
Triples the price of the pizza	*Do you really get three times as much pizza?*

FIGURE 8-23. Potential Errors and Probing Questions for *Pizza*

Source: Evaluating Statements About Enlargements, © Shell Centre, The University of Nottingham, map.mathshell.org/lessons.php?unit=9320

Follow-Up Tasks to Support Inferences

In addition to probing questions, we might choose a follow-up task to help understand the logic behind students' incomplete or incorrect answers. Note that even students who have responded correctly can benefit from follow-up tasks and sometimes do not respond correctly to a follow-up task. Correct solutions can sometimes create a mind-set that may not generalize easily. The task that follows illustrates these issues. Before you read on, solve the task yourself.

Task: The Garden Problem

Hank has a vegetable garden that is 12 ft. by 20 ft. He wants to put a mulch path 2 ft. wide around the garden. In order to buy enough mulch he needs to find the area of the path. What is the area of the path?

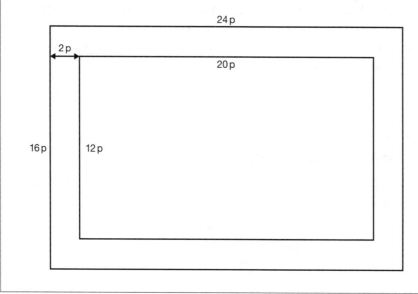

Now consider Darlene's answer to this task. (See Figure 8–24.) Try to reason through what Darlene did. What follow-up tasks might you give Darlene to help her understand the logic behind her answer?

two strips 24 x 2 ft = 48 ft²
two strips 12 x 2 ft = 24 ft²
                              72 ft²
                          x 2
                          144 ft²

FIGURE 8–24. Darlene's Response to *The Garden Problem*

Assessment Tip ✓

Discussions of multiple solution strategies provide students with ideas for solving similar follow-up tasks if their own solution strategy does not generalize easily.

Darlene decomposed the path into four strips. The two horizontal strips are 24 feet long and 2 feet wide; the two vertical strips are 12 feet tall and 2 feet wide. Decomposition of a shape into pieces for which area formulas easily apply seems like an effective way to solve the task.

The next follow-up task, *The Target*, may help Darlene think more deeply about her strategies. Decomposing each area here is not particularly helpful, so this task would encourage Darlene to think differently. Her solution to *The Garden Problem* may have created a mind-set that may be difficult for her to overcome.

Follow-Up Task: The Target

Here is a picture of a target for a darts game. Find the area of the bull's-eye and each ring in the target.

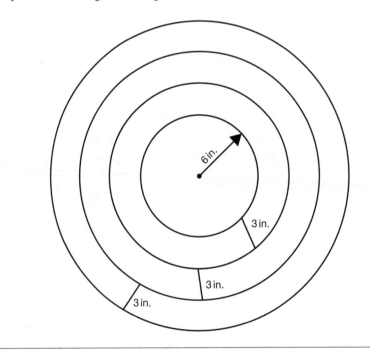

Now consider Peter's answer to *The Garden Problem*. (See Figure 8–25.) Try to reason through what Peter did and how Peter might approach the follow-up task *The Target*.

Outer rectangle 24 × 16 = 384
inner rectangle 20 × 12 = 240
_____
144

FIGURE 8–25. Peter's Response to *The Garden Problem*

Peter, in contrast to Darlene, visualized the path as a "ring" around the garden. He computed the areas of the outer rectangle and the inner rectangle. The area of the path is the difference in these areas. Unfortunately, Peter did not label the numbers in his solution, so we cannot be completely confident that he is thinking about area. Both Peter's and Darlene's solutions are correct, but they do not generalize in the same ways. Peter's strategy would generalize to *The Target* more directly than Darlene's, and posing *The Target* for Peter might also help him think more deeply about his strategies. It might encourage him to be more explicit about his understanding of area and the labeling of quantities.

Creating probing questions and follow-up tasks is an important skill for teachers as they implement INFORMative assessment. Often this has to be done "on the fly"; however, it's important to take time to think about the questions and tasks you might use. Complete "Reflection 8–5: Creating Probing Questions to Support Quality Inferences" (see page 356), which provides an opportunity to think more deeply about questions that might reveal the logic behind students' answers.

Learn More...

"Items [e.g., tasks or probing questions] that reveal unintended conceptions—in other words that provide a 'window into thinking'—are not easy to generate, but they are crucially important to improve the quality of students' mathematical learning."
—"Keeping Learning on Track: Classroom Assessment and the Regulation of Learning" (Wiliam 2007b, 1069)

Reflection 8–5

Creating Probing Questions to Support Quality Inferences

Page 356

INFORMing My Practice

Throughout this resource, but especially in this chapter, we emphasize that the inferences we make as teachers need to be as accurate as possible because they are the basis for our decisions about teaching. The heart of INFORMative assessment is the gathering of information that allows us to make inferences about what students know and can do.

There is no algorithm for accomplishing this challenging instructional task, though thinking of inferences through the five considerations discussed will help:

Strategy 1: Differentiate correct, incomplete, and incorrect responses

Strategy 2: Identify possible causes of incomplete or incorrect answers

Strategy 3: Examine the logic behind incomplete or incorrect answers

Strategy 4: Determine if errors in answers reflect substance or presentation

Strategy 5: Use probing questions and follow-up tasks to support inferences

As teachers we need to develop expertise by engaging in the process, discussing our successes and failures with colleagues, and evaluating the effects of inference making on both instructional decision making and students' learning.

Consider how your thinking in making inferences about students' thinking has changed and answer the questions in "Reflection 8–6: INFORMing My Practice: Making Inferences About What Students Know and Can Do" (see page 357). Then continue reading. Chapter 9 focuses on feedback and how feedback can be structured once teachers have made inferences about what students know or about the level of their confidence.

Assessment Tip ✓

One of the best ways to develop expertise as a teacher in making inferences is by engaging in the process.

Reflection 8–6

INFORMing My Practice: Making Inferences About What Students Know and Can Do

Page 357

Reflection 8-1: Differentiating Correct, Incomplete, and Incorrect Responses

Consider the task *Find the Center of a Paper Disk*, shown below and followed by three solutions. Think about how you would solve the task. Categorize each solution as correct, incomplete, or incorrect.

Task: *Find the Center of a Paper Disk*

Describe a procedure for locating the point that is the center of a circular paper disk. Use geometric definitions, properties, or principles to explain why your procedure is correct. Use the disk provided to help you formulate your procedure. You may write on it or fold it in any way that you find helpful, but it will not be collected.

Student Answer	Classification (Correct, Incomplete, or Incorrect?)
fold in half and in half again	
fold the disk in half so it looks like this fold it in half again so it looks like this	
Draw a square around the circle then put a cross from the corners. That intersection is the center.	

(continued)

Reflection 8-1: Differentiating Correct, Incomplete, and Incorrect Responses (continued)

NAEP scoring for some of the responses shown is noted below.

Student Answer	Classification (Correct, Incomplete, or Incorrect?)
fold in half and in half again	The first student response is scored by NAEP as "partial." We anticipate most teachers will score it as "incomplete."
fold the disk in half so it looks like this *fold it in half again so it looks like this*	The second student response is scored by NAEP as "satisfactory." We anticipate most teachers will score it as "correct."
Draw a square around the circle then put a cross from the corners. That intersection is the center.	NAEP scored the third student response as "minimal." We anticipate most teachers will score it as "incomplete" or "incorrect."

Source: U.S. Department of Education, Institute of Education Sciences, National Center for Education Statistics, National Assessment of Educational Progress (NAEP), 2013 Reading Assessment. Based on a released NAEP item, grade 12, 1996-12M10, #10.

Reflection 8-2: Identifying Possible Causes of Incomplete or Incorrect Answers

Recall the task *Fractional Exponents*, which Mrs. Nelson used in her class. Think about how you would solve the task. The task is also shown below, followed by two incorrect solutions. Categorize each solution as either a misunderstanding or misconception. Explain your thinking.

> *Task: Fractional Exponents*
>
> *True or false:* $((-4)^2)^{1/2} = ((-4)^{1/2})^2$ *Explain.*

Student Answer	Categorization (Misunderstanding or Misconception?) and Explanation
$((-4)^2)^{\frac{1}{2}} = (16)^{\frac{1}{2}} = 4$ $((-4)^{\frac{1}{2}})^2 = (2i)^2 = 4i^2 = -4$ False	
$(x^{\frac{1}{2}})^2 = x^{\frac{2}{2}} = x^1 = x$ $(x^2)^{\frac{1}{2}} = x^{\frac{2}{2}} = x^1 = x$ Same, so TRUE	

Reflection 8-3: Examining the Logic Behind Incomplete or Incorrect Answers for *Water in the Bucket*

Revisit the *Water in the Bucket* task, which was used by Mr. Herje. The task is also shown below. Think about how you would solve the task and then answer the questions that follow.

Task: Water in the Bucket

A 1 kilogram bucket contains 99 kilograms of water.

1. *What percent of the total mass of the water and the bucket is water?*

2. *If 5 kilograms of water is removed, what percent of the combined mass of the remaining water and the bucket is water?*

3. *How many kilograms of water must be removed from the bucket so that the remaining water is 50% of the combined mass of the water and the bucket?*

4. *Suppose W is the amount of water removed and R is the percentage of water in the combined mass of the remaining water and the bucket. Write an equation that shows the relationship between W and R.*

(Bright and Joyner 2004a, 151; adapted from
Bush and Greer 1999, 118)

---

1. Solve the task and write a short explanation of your solution.

2. What pictures or diagrams might be helpful for students as they work on this task?

(continued)

Reflection 8-3: Examining the Logic Behind Incomplete or Incorrect Answers for *Water in the Bucket* (continued)

3. For the third part of the task, Kita said to remove 49.5 kg of water (see page 334—Kita's response is shown below). Would you classify this incorrect response as a misunderstanding or misconception? Explain. What questions might you ask to verify your classification?

① $\frac{1}{99} = 0.0101... = 1.01\frac{2}{8}$

② $\frac{1}{94} = 1.06\%$

③ If you remove 50% of the water, you remove 49.5 kg.

④ $R = (99-30)/99$

Kita's Response to *Water in the Bucket*

4. Sergei's response (see page 335—Sergei's answer is shown below) might have been created essentially without any computation or symbol manipulation at all. What additional questions might you ask to reveal his reasoning?

1. $\frac{1}{100} = 1\%$

2. $\frac{1}{95} = 1.05\%$

3. 50% is $\frac{1}{2}$, so the amount of water remaining must be 1 kg, so the amount removed must be 98 kg

4. $R = \frac{(99-W)}{(100-W)}$

Sergei's Response to *Water in the Bucket*

Reflection 8-4: Creating a Substance/ Presentation Chart

Revisit the guidelines for completing a substance/presentation chart, initially shared on page 339 of this chapter and shown below:

	Substance (What a Student Knows)	Presentation (What a Student Shows)
Concept	Understanding an idea and knowing examples and nonexamples	Communicating an idea or recognizing different representations of it
Procedure	Understanding why the steps in a procedure work	Carrying out the steps in a procedure

Now consider the following completed substance/presentation chart for solving linear equations:

	Substance (What a Student Knows)	Presentation (What a Student Shows)
Concept	Knows when two linear equations are equivalent	Explains why two linear equations are equivalent
Procedure	Knows what steps (e.g., adding the same number to both sides) are acceptable to generate a solution	Manipulates symbols without giving reasons (e.g., changing the sign of a value when "moving" it from one side to the other)

Use the above charts plus the questions that follow to help you think about a substance/ presentation chart for *mean of a set of data* and what it signifies for the context: *Each student in a class counts the number of people in his or her family.*

1. List ideas that relate to the *conceptual* part of *mean*.

2. List ideas that relate to the *procedural* part of *mean*.

(continued)

Reflection 8-4: Creating a Substance/ Presentation Chart (continued)

3. Complete the following substance/presentation chart for *mean of a set of data* and what it signifies for the context: *Each student in a class counts the number of people in his or her family.* (Remember, creating charts like this is *only* a teacher activity intended to help in analyzing student responses. Students should not be expected to do this.)

	Substance (What a Student Knows)	Presentation (What a Student Shows)
Concept		
Procedure		

4. Explain why some sections are easier to complete than others. Which section did you find most challenging?

An example completed substance/presentation chart for *mean of a set of data*.

	Substance (What a Student Knows)	Presentation (What a Student Shows)
Concept	Understands that if all the family members were distributed equally among all of the students, the mean represents the number of people that each of the students in the class would have in her or his family	Given Unifix cubes for each student's family members, redistributes the cubes equally to show the mean
Procedure	Knows to add all the numbers of family members and then divide by the number of students in the class, because this shows how to redistribute family members among the students in the class	Adds the number of family members and divides by the number of students since that is the rule

Answer Key

355

Reflection 8-5: Creating Probing Questions to Support Quality Inferences

Consider the task *Understanding Equations*. Think about how you would solve the task. Write two or three different responses you would accept as correct.

Task: Understanding Equations

A store sells pens at $2 and notebooks at $5.

n = *number of notebooks sold*

p = *number of pens sold*

The following equations are true:

$4n = p$

$5n + 2p = 39$

What do the equations mean?

---

2. Dan said, "The first equation means that the store sells four times as many notebooks as pens." What misunderstanding or misconception seems to be evident in Dan's statement? What probing questions might you ask Dan?

3. Emma said, "The second equation means that the store sold 5 notebooks and 2 pens." What misunderstanding or misconception seems to be evident in Emma's statement? What probing questions might you ask Emma?

Source: Solving Linear Equations in Two Variables, © Shell Centre, The University of Nottingham, map.mathshell.org/lessons.php?unit=9235

Reflection 8-6: INFORMing My Practice: Making Inferences About What Students Know and Can Do

Think about the chapter you just read. Use this space to record your ideas.

Ideas about the importance of making inferences about what students know and can do:

Changes in my thinking about INFORMative assessment:

Ideas I envision becoming a more important part of my practice:

Questions I have:

Frustrations/concerns I have:

Actionable Feedback to Help Students Learn

As discussed thus far, INFORMative assessment provides a way for teachers to understand students' mathematical thinking so that this instruction can be targeted to help students learn. In previous chapters we have talked about how to gather information about students' thinking—creating clear learning targets, using oral and written assessments, using questioning and intentional listening, choosing rich tasks, and supporting students' self-assessment—and how to use that information to make inferences about what students really understand. Making inferences about students' thinking, however, doesn't help students learn. Action must be taken in response to the knowledge gained from those inferences.

In this chapter we discuss *actionable feedback* as a way to leverage those inferences into student learning. Actionable feedback helps students understand what parts of their work are correct, what parts need work, and how changes in their thinking might happen. Actionable feedback is a critical part of effective instruction, and it is the natural product of effective INFORMative assessment.

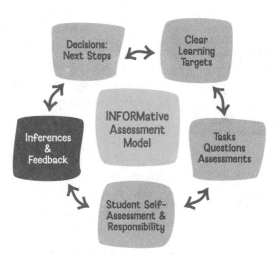

Overview

What Is Feedback?

Feedback is information teachers provide to students about their work. The goal of feedback is to help students improve their understanding of mathematics and their future interactions with mathematics tasks. Feedback is not a new idea, and it comes in several varieties, most frequently feedback that is motivational, directive, or actionable.

The stereotypical kind of motivational feedback is praise, such as "good job" or "nice work." It is intended to encourage students, but it provides no guidance about what aspects of students' work are good and which parts need improvement. Grades are also too general to provide useful information to students about how to deepen their understanding or to perform better in the future. If all a student knows is that he or she scored 83 out of 100, the student has no information related to how to improve. Research indicates that if feedback is focused on self-image and self-esteem (grades and praise), it may make performance worse.

Directive feedback is specific to a task and may be viewed by students as an attempt to replace their thinking with the teacher's approach about what to do next; for example, *To find the median, you have to order the data first, not just take the middle number of the list as it appears in the book.* Giving directive feedback runs the risk that students will do what the teacher says but will not understand either why that approach works or how it might be used in other similar situations. In the example just given, students might generate data and still think that the middle number of their unordered list is the median.

Assessment Tip ✓

"The formative assessments that I collect in class are really important. I always struggle with whether the cause of a student's misunderstanding is the student's inability to sufficiently explain in writing or the lack of true understanding. I should say I struggle if I have to put a 'grade' on it. As a true formative assessment it shouldn't be a struggle, since I can easily write a question on the paper to give back to the student, or ask the student to clarify his or her thinking. This is a goal of mine—to commit to using formative assessments to help students grow, not to have a grade in the grade book."
—D'Shawn Martinez, teacher

The feedback that is best for enhancing learning is about students' work, not about the students themselves. It focuses on addressing the logic behind students' thinking that has led to mistakes, incomplete responses, or even correct solutions. When feedback is effective, students will understand the mathematics more deeply and they will be able to perform better in future situations. High-quality feedback helps students develop confidence and stimulates their thinking. It also helps them become better at self-assessment so that they can make connections among mathematics ideas.

Actionable feedback, as opposed to motivational or directive feedback, is descriptive and gives students enough information so that they have an idea about what they need to rethink or how they might improve. Actionable feedback is the kind of feedback that seems most useful to students, and hence is the kind of feedback we focus on in this chapter.

Focusing on Actionable Feedback

Actionable feedback can be viewed as the interaction between our understanding of what students know and the strategies we as teachers use to guide students along productive paths. That is, actionable feedback points students in the direction of doing better. Actionable feedback should identify *what is good*, *what needs to change*, and *how the changes might happen*.

Actionable feedback, then, begins with a teacher's making inferences about students' understanding from their work. The quality of those inferences influences the quality of the feedback. Inferences include judgments about what students truly understand, such as the depth of their knowledge, what they misunderstand, and their confidence about that knowledge. These inferences are frequently based on information gained from planned assessments (i.e., tasks specifically selected to provide information about students' thinking); however, homework, day-to-day tasks, observations, and conversations can also provide information about what students understand.

Actionable feedback takes place when teachers use their inferences to make suggestions in a way that helps students correct the current situation and do better next time. Sometimes this feedback addresses a critical

> **Assessment Tip** ✓
>
> It's important to keep in mind that feedback is about students' work, not about the students themselves.

> **Assessment Tip** ✓
>
> Actionable feedback should identify *what is good*, *what needs to change*, and *how the changes might happen*.

> **Learn More...**
>
> Making inferences is discussed in depth in Chapter 8.

misunderstanding, while at other times it helps students become more proficient in communicating their mathematical understanding. Regardless, the goal is not to move students quickly to the correct answer, but rather to support their development of mathematical competence.

Students respond in different ways to the feedback their teachers give, so it's important to be observant about what seems most productive for any particular group of students. As we learn more about our students during the school year, the process of sharing can be refined so that students can use the information to become better mathematics learners.

> Although there is a clear set of priorities for the development of feedback, there is no "one right way" to do this. The feedback routines in each class will need to be thoroughly integrated into the daily work of the class, and so it will look slightly different in every classroom. This means that no-one can tell teachers how this should be done—it will be a matter for each teacher to work out a way of incorporating some of these ideas into her or his own practice. However, the size of the effects found in the experiments . . . and in the other research reviewed by Black and Wiliam, suggests that changing the kinds of feedback we use in mathematics classrooms could have more effect than all the government initiatives put together. (Wiliam 1999, 11)

Often, asking probing questions is a form of actionable feedback. For example, in response to a student's interpretation of a graph, a teacher might ask, *How does the graph provide evidence for your conclusion?* By posing such questions, teachers initiate student "action" even though there is no specific direction to the student. Actionable feedback might also be a simple comment that refocuses attention on some aspect of the mathematics that students seem to have ignored. Sometimes this kind of comment might be given to the class as a whole, to call attention to a key mathematics idea, even though perhaps not all students actually ignored the relevant mathematics. At other times teachers may provide actionable feedback to particular students or to groups of students who make similar kinds of responses. When there is a cluster of students making the same error, there are opportunities for small-group work. Pulling students into a small group allows us to help several students simultaneously refocus their thinking. Sometimes peer feedback between students is appropriate through judicious use of discussions or rubrics. With experience, we learn to balance feedback to the class with feedback to individuals.

Let's consider several classroom examples (see the following four "A Closer Look" sections) to help clarify what qualifies as actionable feedback and how teachers think about making actionable feedback helpful while avoiding simply telling students exactly what to do.

→ A Closer Look

Mr. Frye's Actionable Feedback with *Relations and Functions*

Mr. Frye chose the task that follows to assess students' understanding of the definition of function. He posed the task at the beginning of a class to activate prior knowledge, though it could also have been given as homework. As he observed students' responses, he realized both that some responses required additional probing and that feedback needed to "fit" individual responses. The examples that follow illustrate the need for planning to make feedback effective.

Task: Relations and Functions

The table shows all the ordered pairs (x, y) that define a relation between the variables x and y. Is y a function of x? Give a reason for your answer.

x	y
−2	3
−1	0
0	−1
1	0
2	3
3	8

Source: U.S. Department of Education, Institute of Education Sciences, National Center for Education Statistics, National Assessment of Educational Progress (NAEP). Based on a released NAEP item, grade 12, 2009, algebra, item 2009-12M2 #7.

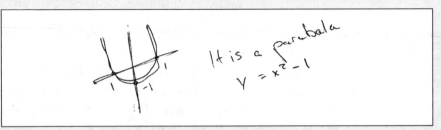

FIGURE 9-1. Aki's Response to *Relations and Functions*

Aki's response to the functions problem was "yes." She then provided the explanation. (See Figure 9–1.) Of course, the function, $y = x^2 - 1$, is only *one* of the possible functions that can be drawn through the (x, y) pairs given. Thus, the claim that it *is* a parabola is incorrect. The claim is consistent with the data, but it forces the data to fit a particular pattern.

Mr. Frye decided that his feedback to Aki should acknowledge her recognition that the data fit a relatively simple function, but challenge the underlying assumption that the relation is more than the pairs listed in the table. He decided to say, "I agree that the (x, y) pairs fit the function you wrote, but how are all the other points on the graph connected to the relation given in the problem?" This feedback identifies what is good in Aki's work (i.e., the (x, y) pairs fit the function), focuses on the part of the response that needs to be rethought (i.e., all those *other* points on the graph), and suggests a way to begin that rethinking (i.e., whether to connect those other points to the given relation). Mr. Frye's question nudges Aki's thinking in a productive direction without directing her to the "correct answer."

yes, since no two x values are the same

FIGURE 9-2. Sherise's Response to *Relations and Functions*

Mr. Frye felt that Sherise's solution showed some understanding of the difference between a relation and a function. (See Figure 9–2.) He realized that some teachers might accept this response as adequate, though it is incomplete. Having no two x-values the same in the set of (x, y) pairs in a relation is sufficient to guarantee that a relation is a function, but this response does not show that Sherise understands that a relation is a function when none of the (x, y) pairs have the same x-values but different y-values. She *might* know this, but Mr. Frye cannot be sure. The response seems to focus more on the way the values are given in the table rather than on the attributes that distinguish a function from nonfunction relations.

Sherise's response may be a lapse (e.g., she just did not say all she knows), a misunderstanding (e.g., she thought the question was asking *only* about the values in the table), or a misconception (e.g., she does not understand that applying the definition of *function* requires attending to both x-values and y-values). Feedback for these situations would be somewhat different, so Mr. Frye decided to probe her thinking before actually choosing feedback to provide. In creating a probing question, Mr. Frye also thought about the types of responses Sherise might give. (See Figure 9–3.) Mr. Frye's probing question sets up actionable feedback by acknowledging the part of her comment that is useful mathematically.

Learn More...
Chapter 8, pages 322–325, takes a closer look at lapses, misunderstandings, and misconceptions.

Mr. Frye's Probing Question	I agree that having no two x-values the same is helpful information, but why does that make this relation a function?
Student Response Suggesting a Lapse	This guarantees that no x-value will have two y-values paired with it.
Student Response Suggesting a Misunderstanding	In the table, the only two identical y-values have different x-values.
Student Response Suggesting a Misconception	You only have to look at x-values for it to be a function.

FIGURE 9–3. Possible Responses to Mr. Frye's Probing Question Prior to Setting Up Feedback

Assessment Tip ☑

Sometimes as teachers we move too directly and too quickly to focusing on the incorrect elements in students' responses. Students need reinforcement of what they "got right" as well as feedback about what they "got wrong." Simply saying, "I agree with you" or "I understand what you did" can be powerful motivators for reinforcing correct thinking. Then clarification can be sought about elements of a response that are unclear or ambiguous or mathematically incorrect.

Yes, because when placed as in a
Function you can solve for one
of the variables

FIGURE 9–4. Gabriela's Response to *Relations and Functions*

Gabriela's response seems to focus on the form of function notation. (See Figure 9–4.) It is not unexpected that students might focus on solving equations for unknowns, but this is not a part of the definition of function. Helping Gabriela reconceptualize her understanding of *function* might take considerable time. Mr. Frye decided to begin a conversation with Gabriela by asking, "What do you mean by 'placed in a function'?" Her language here is unconventional, and he needs more information about what these words mean to her before he can formulate actionable feedback.

Mr. Frye realized that his students collectively showed a wide range of understanding. His choices for the next few tasks would have to take this range into account. Those choices would have to be made to allow him to tailor his feedback to the needs of individual students.

→ A Closer Look

Ms. Denton's Actionable Feedback with *Order of Operations*

A second example illustrates how actionable feedback can be woven into a whole-class discussion. Ms. Denton asked her seventh-grade students to "compute 3 more than 2 times 7." Order of operations is part of grade 6 standards, but she wanted to be sure that her seventh-grade students remembered that information. The mathematical issue Ms. Denton looked at in the following dialogue is the way Cody recorded his work.

Ms. Denton: Cody, please write what you did on the board.

Cody: (*Writes* 2 x 7 = 14 + 3 = 17.)

Ms. Denton: Now, please explain what you did.

Cody: Two times seven is fourteen and plus three is seventeen.

Ms. Denton: Why did you multiply first?

Cody: Order of operations.

Ms. Denton: What do you mean?

Cody: Order of operations says you multiply first, even though this problem says add first.

Ms. Denton: So is the problem wrong?

Cody: No, you tried to trick us. (*Ms. Denton and several students chuckle.*)

Ms. Denton: Well, I really wanted to see if you remembered the correct order of operations. Now, does anyone have a comment about what Cody *wrote*? (*Emphasizes the word* wrote.)

Olivia: It looks wrong. Two times seven is not equal to fourteen plus three.

Cody: But it shows what I did.

Ms. Denton: I agree, Cody, that what you wrote matches what you said. But if you cover up the middle part, is the equation still true?

Cody: (*Puts his fingers over* 14 + 3 *to leave* 2 x 7 = 17 *showing.*) Well, no. But it shows what I did.

Ms. Denton: Can anyone suggest what Cody might have *written* differently? (*Emphasizes the word* written.)

Kris: He could do two equations. First, two times seven equals fourteen and then fourteen plus three equals seventeen.

Ms. Denton: Kris, please come write those on the smart board.

Kris: (*Writes* 2 x 7 = 14 *and* 14 + 3 = 17 *underneath.*)

Ms. Denton: Is this correct? Does it still use the order of operations correctly?

Olivia: Yes, and they are both correct equations.

Following an order of operations demonstrates the sixth-grade CCSSM standard that says students can "Evaluate expressions at specific values of their variables. Include expressions that arise from formulas used in real-world problems. Perform arithmetic operations, including those involving whole-number exponents, in the conventional order when there are no parentheses to specify a particular order (Order of Operations)" (CCSS .MATH.CONTENT .6.EE.A.2.C).

Some teachers would label Cody's number sentence a "run-on equation," analogous to a run-on sentence. Cody's "number sentence" is mathematically incorrect, since 2×7 is not equal to 17, so feedback is certainly called for. Ms. Denton had seen this kind of error before, so she was prepared to deal with it. During her lesson planning, she had thought about several ways to respond, but even with careful planning, she had to make a decision "on the fly" about exactly what feedback to provide.

Ms. Denton highlighted the correct part of Cody's explanation; namely, the use of order of operations. Then she gave Cody an opportunity to self-correct what he wrote. If his response was a lapse, we might expect him to self-correct his work. Unfortunately, he did not pick up on the clue in Ms. Denton's voice. Olivia seemed to do so, but Cody continued to defend his recording as an accurate representation of what he was thinking.

Ms. Denton then had Cody focus on the first and last parts of his equation to help him see why his recording scheme was not correct. He finally conceded the point, but added one more defense of his approach. So we might infer that Cody's error really was a misunderstanding, rather than a misconception, about how to record computations correctly. Kris was able to demonstrate a way of writing the work in a mathematically more acceptable way. The dialogue does not show how Cody responded to Kris's strategy, so we have to assume that he finally acknowledged the flaw in his technique. We hope that this was enough feedback so that he will make not the same error in the future.

Ms. Denton guided the discussion of Cody's work through a combination of questions and comments. She acknowledged the consistency between his thinking and his recording scheme while also helping him, and other students, see that the results of his recording were mathematically incorrect. One comment in particular shows her use of actionable feedback, phrased as a question: "I agree, Cody, that what you wrote matches what you said. But if you cover up the middle part, is the equation still true?" The comment helped Cody see how his written work did not reflect accurate mathematics. Ms. Denton also implicitly suggested a way to deal with the issue. By calling attention to pieces of the run-on equation that are incorrect when they are shown together, she implicitly challenged Cody and other students to find the pieces of the run-on equation that could be combined correctly. Kris picked up on Ms. Denton's comments to generate two correct equations that could replace Cody's single run-on equation.

In general, learning is more likely to happen if students correct their own work rather than expecting the teacher to tell them what to do. Actionable feedback should help students rethink their work with implicit suggestions but without specifying exactly what they should do. Complete "Reflection 9–1: Focusing on Actionable Feedback: Multiple Interpretations of a Task" (see page 388). This reflection prompts you to examine students' responses that reflect different interpretations of a computational task, make inferences about the thinking that might be behind each interpretation, and suggest actionable feedback for each student.

> ┌─ Reflection 9–1 ─┐
> Focusing on
> Actionable
> Feedback: Multiple
> Interpretations
> of a Task
>
> Page 388

→ A Closer Look

Mrs. McDaid's Actionable Feedback with *Greater Volume*

Luis, a high school geometry student, was working on the following task in Mrs. McDaid's class.

> ### Task: Greater Volume
>
> *Which is greater, the volume of a sphere with diameter 2 cm or the volume of a cube 2 cm on an edge? How much greater is it?*

Luis's work illustrates how important it is to make an inference about the nature of errors. (See Figure 9–5 on the following page.)

Before reading further, study Luis's response. Ask yourself:

- What is Luis's mistake and how can I help him understand that mistake?

- Do his errors appear to be lapses, misunderstandings, or misconceptions?

Determining which of two different solid figures has the greater volume reflects the CCSSM standard, "Use volume formulas for cylinders, pyramids, cones, and spheres to solve problems" (CCSS.MATH .CONTENT.HSG .GMD.A.3).

$$\text{Sphere: } \frac{4}{3}\pi 2^3 = \frac{32}{3}\pi = 10\frac{2}{3}\pi \approx 34$$

$$\text{Cube: } 2^3 = 8$$

Sphere is greater by 24^3 cm

FIGURE 9–5. Luis's Response to *Greater Volume*

Reflection 9–2

Focusing on Actionable Feedback: Luis's Response to *Greater Volume*

Page 389

Sometimes students, like Luis, fail to label measurements as they work, perhaps because they think those labels are not necessary or are implicitly understood. As teachers we have to decide when we want to call attention to the lack of labels and when we choose to focus on more fundamental errors in students' work. Before reading further, complete "Reflection 9–2: Focusing on Actionable Feedback: Luis's Response to *Greater Volume*" (see page 389). The reflection prompts you to suggest actionable feedback that might help Luis rethink his work to correct his errors. When you are finished, continue reading to learn how Mrs. McDaid used actionable feedback with Luis.

Mrs. McDaid noticed one error in Luis's work—his use of the diameter (2 cm) instead of the radius (1 cm) to compute the volume of the sphere. Many teachers would look at his work and probably assume that this error is a lapse in his thinking rather than a misunderstanding or a misconception. His work is direct, without false starts, so it seems to reflect a fairly solid understanding of the mathematics. Mrs. McDaid was careful, however, not to assume too much about Luis's thinking.

Mrs. McDaid knew that she could tell Luis about the error and ask him to recompute the volume of the sphere; this, however, would be directive feedback. Actionable feedback, on the other hand, would first acknowledge that Luis used the correct formulas. Mrs. McDaid could then pose a question: *The formulas are correct, but how did you decide what numbers to substitute in the formulas?* Mrs. McDaid's acknowledgment does not give away exactly where the error is, or even whether there is an error. The hope is that if Luis has to be explicit about his thinking, he will identify his mistake. Indeed, sometimes just asking students to explain their thinking is enough of a push

Assessment Tip ✓

In the example here, directive feedback would be to tell Luis about the error and ask him to recompute the volume of the sphere. Actionable feedback, however, would first acknowledge that Luis used the correct formulas and then perhaps pose a question. A question, rather than a "do this" statement, gives students opportunities to evaluate their answers and reorganize their thinking.

to help them reconstruct a more correct strategy. A question, rather than a "do this" statement, gives students opportunities to evaluate their answers and reorganize their thinking.

Luis's error might be more critical, however. Mrs. McDaid realizes that it's possible that Luis does not know the difference between diameter and radius of a sphere. When teachers assume too much about students' work and tell them exactly what to do, the result often has the effect of doing students' thinking for them. Calling attention to his error rather than telling him how to get the correct answer is a way to probe his thinking in order to determine if the assumption of his solid understanding is accurate.

Mrs. McDaid also noticed a second error in Luis's work: his lack of labels in the computations for the sphere and cube. Fortunately, he does use a label for the final answer, so Mrs. McDaid inferred that there is no error here. However, it would be worthwhile to probe his thinking just to be sure that he knows that the volumes are measured in cubic centimeters.

→ A Closer Look

Ms. Behr's Actionable Feedback with *Percentage Problem*

Considering one more task further illustrates how actionable feedback can be constructed—in this case, feedback about explanations—to probe individual student thinking while providing information to the class as a whole. Ms. Behr presented this task to her class as part of a set of lessons emphasizing how percentages are needed in real-world applications.

Task: Percentage Problem

If the price of a stock goes up by 50% on Monday and down by 50% on Tuesday, how is the final price related to the original price? Explain how you determined your answer.

Reflection 9-3

Focusing on
Actionable
Feedback:
Percentage Problem

Pages 390–391

Percentage Problem addresses an area of concern in the CCSSM for grade 7 students—the ability to understand and apply proportional relationships: "Students extend their understanding of ratios and develop understanding of proportionality to solve single- and multi-step problems. Students use their understanding of ratios and proportionality to solve a wide variety of percent problems, including those involving discounts, interest, taxes, tips, and percent increase or decrease" (corestandards.org/Math/Content/7/introduction/).

Feedback is always in response to something that a student writes or says. Before reading further, complete "Reflection 9–3: Focusing on Actionable Feedback: *Percentage Problem*" (see pages 390–391), which includes questions for you to consider as you examine student work. This will help you think about formulating actionable feedback for different situations. When you are finished, continue reading to learn about Ms. Behr's use of actionable feedback with her class.

As Ms. Behr watched students work (i.e., monitoring students' responses), she identified two examples that she wanted shared for the class (i.e., selecting particular students to present their work), and decided which of the two students would go first (i.e., sequencing the student responses). She knew that she would have to be sure that the discussion helped all students to connect the mathematics ideas in these two solutions.

Ms. Behr decided to show Tyler's work first. He had responded that the ending price was the same. (See Figure 9–6.)

PRICE + 50% - 50% = PRICE

IT'S THE SAME AT THE END

FIGURE 9–6. Tyler's Response to *Percentage Problem*

Ms. Behr wanted Brooke's response to be shown after Tyler's. Brooke had responded that the ending price was lower, though she computed only three examples. (See Figure 9–7.)

$100 —up 50%→ $150 —down 50%→ $75

$500 ————→ $750 ————→ $375

$8 ————→ $12 ————→ $6

The end is lower

FIGURE 9–7. Brooke's Response to *Percentage Problem*

Ms. Behr first asked Tyler, then Brooke, to display their work for the whole class. Both responses remained on display for the class to see. A discussion followed.

Learn More...

Recall the 5 Practices for Orchestrating Productive Mathematics Discussions (Smith and Stein 2011): (1) anticipating, (2) monitoring, (3) selecting, (4) sequencing, and (5) connecting. These are discussed in Chapter 8.

Ms. Behr: Tyler, how did you get your answer?

Tyler: Since it went up and down the same amount, it didn't change.

Ms. Behr: Why is fifty percent an *amount*? (*emphasizes the word* amount)

Tyler: Fifty percent of something is an amount.

Ms. Behr: Is fifty percent the same as fifty percent of *something*? (*Emphasizes the word* something.)

Tyler: Sure.

Ms. Behr: Is fifty percent of ten the same as fifty percent of twenty?

Tyler: (*pause*) Um, not really. One is five and one is ten.

Ms. Behr: So if you don't know the *something*, do you know how much fifty percent is?

Tyler: I'm not sure anymore.

Ms. Behr: Brooke, how did you get your answer?

Brooke: I can only think with numbers, so I tried some numbers.

Ms. Behr: Why did you pick those numbers?

Brooke: Well, one hundred was easy, and I wanted a bigger number and a smaller number.

Ms. Behr: What happened?

Brooke: The end price was always lower.

Ms. Behr: Do you think it would always be that way?

Brooke: I think so, but since you asked me about that, I'm not so sure.

Tyler: Brooke used actual dollars for her computation, and I used only percents.

Ms. Behr: Tyler, why are those two things different?

Tyler: Dollars are something.

The importance of being precise is articulated by Mathematical Practice 6: "Attend to precision." Ideas about constructing arguments are emphasized in Mathematical Practice 3: "Construct viable arguments and critique the reasoning of others."

Ms. Behr: We can say that "dollars" is a unit of measure. (*Uses "air quotes" when saying the word* dollars.) In the real world, a unit of measure lets us know how much of something we have.

Brooke: Since stock prices are always in dollars, how many prices should I check?

Ms. Behr: Could you check them all?

Brooke: No, there are too many to check them all.

Ms. Behr: Can someone summarize and tell us how the final price is related to the original price and how to justify this relationship?

One of the key elements of actionable feedback is helping students see some way to "do better." The conversation gives two examples of this. First, Ms. Behr helped Tyler distinguish a percent from a percent of something. She ultimately tied this to the use of units of measure. This is an important conceptual distinction, and it also relates to the Mathematics Practice "attend to precision" (MP6). The discussion should have helped Tyler reconceptualize this part of his mathematical understanding. Second, she helped Brooke realize that three examples do not constitute a proof. This is important for knowing how to construct arguments (MP3). Brooke seemed ready to adjust her thinking ("how many prices should I check?"), so this conversation seems well timed to help her be more precise in her thinking.

Learn More…

"Helping students succeed is as much about how we teach as what we teach."
—Cathy Seeley (2014, 344)

Ask Questions or Give Examples?

Through our use of actionable feedback, we learn when to ask a question and when to give examples. For instance, it may be less helpful to provide multiple examples than it would be to provide only one example and ask students to write about that example. Nonexamples can also be useful as part of feedback to students. It is sometimes said that we don't know what something really *is* until we know what it *is not*. When examples are used too often, without also some use of nonexamples, students may not develop a deep understanding of the mathematics.

Reflecting on Actionable Feedback

As discussed thus far, actionable feedback is the way that a teacher translates understanding of students' thinking, however flawed, into conversation or suggestions that help students rethink and reconceptualize their understanding of mathematics ideas. In this section we look at two strategies for using actionable feedback to help students learn.

> *Two Strategies for Using Actionable Feedback*
>
> 1. Refine Inferences
>
> 2. Provide Feedforward

Learn More …

"Effective feedback should make more explicit to students what is involved in a high-quality piece of work and what steps they need to take to improve."
—"Working Inside the Black Box: Assessment for Learning in the Classroom" (Black et al. 2004, 19)

Strategy 1: Refine Inferences

It is important that our inferences about students' understanding be accurate, so we often need to refine what we think we know about students' thinking; that is, we need to refine our inferences. Inferences about students' understanding are always preliminary; we must constantly test them against students' future work and keep in mind that no student will ever write down all he or she knows. Sometimes students' work is correct because of the particular task or the particular numbers in a task, but if the task is tweaked only a little, students may not be able to reach a satisfactory solution. For example, if fraction tasks posed to middle school students involve only halves and fourths, many students will succeed just because halves and fourths are "friendly" fractions. But if similar tasks are posed with thirds and sixths (or sevenths and fourteenths), some of those successful students will no longer be successful. At the high school level, students might be successful at proving theorems about rectangles, but have a more difficult time proving similar theorems involving general parallelograms.

Learn More …

Chapter 8 offers an in-depth look at inferences.

As discussed thus far, once we make inferences about students' understanding, we can formulate actionable feedback. The success of that feedback in helping students improve their learning is highly dependent on the quality of those inferences. In general, as teachers we should be conservative in making inferences; that is, if students' work seems to support inferences about deep understanding or not-so-deep understanding, we should probably choose the not-so-deep option. We've learned that it is better to assume too little about students' thinking than too much.

↱ A Closer Look

Mr. Thomas Refines Inferences About Students' Thinking with *Similar Triangles*

Mr. Thomas posed the following task to his high school geometry students.

Cc,S'

With *Similar Triangles*, students practice proving similarity in triangles. The task connects to the Common Core standard "Use congruence and similarity criteria for triangles to solve problems and to prove relationships in geometric figures" (CCSS.MATH. CONTENT.HSG. SRT.B.5).

Task 1: Similar Triangles

Lines l and m are parallel. Prove that triangles ABC and EDC are similar.

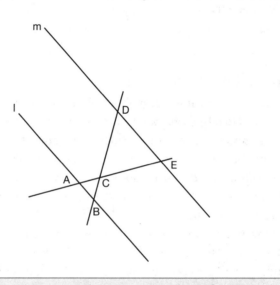

Juanita created a proof that these two triangles are similar by showing that the corresponding angles are congruent. (See Figure 9–8.)

∡CAB congruent to ∡CED   (alternate interior ∡s)
∡CBA ≅ ∡CDE   (same)
∡ACB ≅ ∆DCE   (vertical ∡s)
∆ ACB similar to ∆ECD   (AAA)

FIGURE 9-8. Juanita's Response to *Similar Triangles*

Mr. Thomas felt that Juanita had a good understanding of when angles are congruent and why two triangles are similar; however, the task addresses only part of the mathematics of similar triangles. The task did not ask for students to reveal any understanding about the scale factor of two similar triangles. Mr. Thomas knows that it is important to think about what a task reveals and what it leaves hidden about students' thinking.

Some teachers might think that because Juanita's proof is so elegant, she probably understands that the corresponding sides of similar triangles must have the same scale factor. Mr. Thomas, on the other hand, saw no evidence in Juanita's proof about whether she knew this. He was simply in the dark about whether she had understood this part about similar figures. As teachers, we should be careful about inferring too much about what students know. It is better in the long run to infer too little than to infer too much. Inferring too much may lead us to pose tasks or ask questions that go far beyond what students actually know.

Mr. Thomas knows that part of the process of deciding what actionable feedback to provide is determining whether he has enough information about a student's thinking to make accurate inferences. With this in mind, Mr. Thomas decided to pose a second task, *Length of Line Segment*.

Assessment Tip ✓

It is better in the long run to infer too little than to infer too much. Inferring too much may lead us to pose tasks or ask questions that go far beyond what students actually know.

Task 2: Length of Line Segment

Lines l and m *are parallel. Find the length of segment DE.*

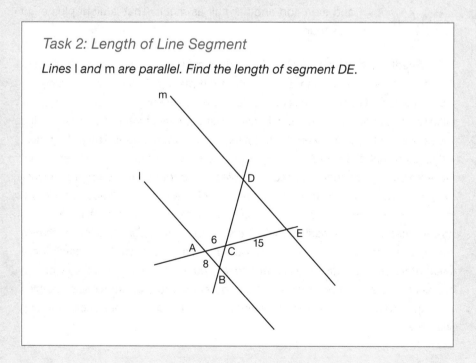

Mr. Thomas hoped this task would provide information about Juanita's understanding of scale factor, which was simply missing from the information provided by the first task. Mr. Thomas asked Juanita to explain her solution orally rather than in writing.

Juanita: We already know that the triangles are similar, with angles CDE and CBA as congruent alternate interior angles. So sides AC and EC are corresponding sides.

Mr. Thomas: Why are they corresponding sides?

Juanita: Because they are opposite the congruent angles. Side AC has length six and side EC has length fifteen. The ratio of these sides is two and a half to one. Side BA and side DE are corresponding sides, too, so the length of DE must be two and a half times the length of side AB. Eight plus eight plus four equals twenty. So the length of DE is twenty.

Mr. Thomas: Why did you add eight, eight, and four?

Juanita: Two and a half times means add the amount to its self and then add another half as much. That is eight plus eight plus four.

Feedback can be useful in helping students know which parts of their work to retain and which parts to discard. For example, Mr. Thomas recognized the correctness and succinctness of Juanita's proof in the original task; however, he also wanted to find out what she knew about the scale factor of corresponding sides. He might have asked, "What else do you know about similar triangles, other than that the corresponding angles are congruent?" This probe might have helped her connect congruent angles and common scale among corresponding sides in her own mind. Instead, he chose to pose a second task and engage in conversation with her about that task. It is important for learners to repeatedly ask themselves, *What else do I know about this mathematics idea? How can I connect all the individual pieces of information I have about each of the mathematics ideas that I am supposed to learn?* Juanita's work on the second task showed that she did understand more about similar triangles than the proof indicated, and it convinced Mr. Thomas that her understanding was deep.

Correct, Incomplete, or Incorrect?

It's nearly impossible for students to build deep mathematical conceptualizations from incorrect understanding, so it is critical that we also help them identify the good in their work. Students need to know when their response is correct, incomplete, or at least, acceptable, and often they are not able to make this determination solely on their own. It is equally important to help students identify the aspects of their work that are not correct or that might lead them astray. Students need to know how to circumvent the reasoning that may have led them off track. Actionable feedback should, at least some of the time, guide students to this information.

Learn More...

Chapter 7 offers more about student self-monitoring through the discussion on self-assessment. Chapter 8 offers more about the distinction of correct, incomplete, and incorrect responses.

In many instances, students are partly correct and partly incorrect (or incomplete). Our actionable feedback can acknowledge the progress that students have made while simultaneously providing some guidance about how to make further progress. Emphasizing the positive aspects of partially correct work may improve students' motivation and self-monitoring. Learning how (and when) to emphasize positive aspects of students' work takes practice. As teachers we want to become better at pointing out the good in students' work and in providing useful feedback to help students make changes, but we also want to avoid taking over students' thinking. Conversations with colleagues about this issue can be helpful.

Strategy 2: Provide Feedforward

While feedback responds to students' work, another actionable feedback strategy that helps students make connections is what we like to call *feedforward*. As teachers our experiences help us identify what students are likely to forget and help us predict when students may have difficulty. We often try to head off some of the common misconceptions that seem to occur each year.

Learn More...

Chapter 2 takes a closer look at activating students' prior knowledge.

Assessment Tip ✓

Sometimes students rush into work without fully understanding the goal of that work. Feedforward can be as simple as asking students to revoice directions to give them an opportunity to process what they need to do.

Feedforward includes statements to alert students to what needs attention (*Remember to label your diagram*) as well as to activate students' prior knowledge—reminding them of what they already know related to new content being taught. Feedforward might also include suggesting rules of thumb to serve as entry points for beginning to solve a problem; for example, *When solving quadratic equations, one strategy you might try is to make the right side equal to 0*. Of course this suggestion does not indicate what happens next, but it might help students avoid a common error like the following:

$$x(x + 1) = 4, \text{ so}$$
$$x = 4 \text{ and } x + 1 = 4$$

We need to be careful that providing feedforward does not turn into providing shortcuts that may ultimately interfere with learning. Many so-called shortcuts work in a limited domain (e.g., positive whole numbers) but fail in broader domains (e.g., all integers). For example, all middle grades and high school teachers have seen students overgeneralize the shortcut about cross multiplying as the first step in solving a proportion. Students often cross multiply when it is not appropriate, such as in the following *incorrect* multiplication:

$$\frac{2}{3} \times \frac{4}{5} = \frac{10}{12}$$

Feedforward is not going to be universally effective, but it is important to try to help prevent the development of misconceptions. Feedforward is especially helpful when struggling students get started on a task.

Using Alternative Multiple-Choice Format

Learn More...

In *Dynamic Classroom Assessment* (Bright and Joyner 2004a), we have written more extensively about the alternative multiple-choice format.

We can modify common instructional strategies to gather more information so that feedback can be more effective; one of these modifications is the *alternative multiple-choice format*. The alternative multiple-choice format encourages students to reflect on their understanding as well as on their level of confidence about that understanding. Reflection helps students provide feedback to themselves. At the same time it gives the teacher important information about students' thinking. Students use a recording sheet to indicate their understanding of the mathematics in each multiple-choice item. (See Figure 9–9 on page 382.)

Reteaching Versus Actionable Feedback

Providing feedback to the class is *not* the same as reteaching. Actionable feedback is designed to help students perform better individually; reteaching helps a class revisit an idea they did not master the first time around. Actionable feedback helps students reorganize their thinking and move forward to deeper understanding. Reteaching focuses on reacquainting students with some idea (or process) that was not internalized correctly the first time it was introduced. Typically, this happens when students overlook a critical element or when the teacher doesn't emphasize it enough in the initial instruction, or if something that students already know interferes with the intended learning.

Actionable feedback can be given to an individual student, whereas reteaching is almost always provided for a whole class or some subset of the class. One component of reteaching may be providing feedback to the group being retaught. Last but not least, feedback is often provided for individual tasks (or parts of tasks) or small groups of students whereas reteaching may not happen until a teacher realizes (e.g., in response to the results of a pop quiz) that many students did not learn (or did not remember) something that the teacher thought they had learned.

Sometimes an extension of the mathematics ideas can accompany reteaching. For example, reteaching about weighted averages might also introduce the idea of center of mass (or center of gravity) in physics. However a teacher decides to reteach, it is critical that reteaching be designed so that all students—those who responded correctly and those who responded incorrectly—are engaged with the mathematics content in the reteaching event. It is never sufficient simply to show the same examples and talk louder and slower. It is critical to choose different examples that will highlight the mathematics ideas that appeared not to have been learned the first time. Sometimes adding a new context in which the ideas are useful can help a variety of students.

Student Name:			Quiz Name:	
Problem Number	Circle Known Wrong Answers		Correct Answer	Are You Sure About the Correct Answer (circle)?
1	a b c d e			Yes No
2	a b c d e			Yes No
3	a b c d e			Yes No
4	a b c d e			Yes No

FIGURE 9–9. An Alternative Multiple-Choice Recording Sheet

On the recording sheet, for each item, students mark answer choices they believe are incorrect as well as choose the correct response. Then they indicate how confident they are about what they have marked. The purpose of this recording sheet is to encourage students to spend more time both analyzing multiple-choice items and reflecting on their confidence about their understanding. Using this recording sheet affords students a check on how well they know the mathematics (i.e., student self-assessment) and gives teachers important information for planning. In particular, it provides valuable information for making decisions about feedback to individuals and the need for reteaching. Suggested scoring guidelines make use of all the information on the recording sheet. (See Figure 9–10.)

Scoring Guidelines for Alternative Multiple-Choice Recording Sheet

Each problem is worth 4 points.

1. Correct answer marked in Known Wrong Answers column earns 0 points. No other points may be given for the item.

Otherwise,

2. Correct answer with "yes" in Sure column earns 4 points.

3. Correct answer with "no" in Sure column earns 3 points.

4. Incorrect answer with "yes" in Sure column earns 0 points.

5. Incorrect answer with "no" in Sure column earns 1 point for each incorrect answer marked in Known Wrong Answers column.

FIGURE 9–10. Scoring Guidelines for Alternative Multiple-Choice Recording Sheet

Teachers who use these guidelines have reported that scoring the recording sheets takes a bit more time initially but becomes easier after the first few times the marking system is used. Some teachers, however, score only the choices in the Correct Answer column. Carson's responses are shown on the recording sheet for a short quiz. (See Figure 9–11.)

Student Name: Carson		Quiz Name: Analyzing Election Data	
Problem Number	Circle Known Wrong Answers	Correct Answer	Are You Sure About the Correct Answer (circle)?
1	a b © ⓓ e	b	Yes No
2	ⓐ b © d e	d	Yes No
3	a b c d e	c	Yes No
4	a ⓑ c d e	a	Yes No
5	ⓐ ⓑ c ⓓ ⓔ	c	Yes No
6	ⓐ ⓑ c ⓓ ⓔ	d	Yes No

FIGURE 9–11. Carson's Responses Using an Alternative Multiple-Choice Recording Sheet

As noted, Carson's responses to multiple-choice problems 1 and 4 are incorrect. The fact that Carson was confident about the incorrect answer for item 1 suggests the possibility of a misconception that needs to be addressed. Of course, there is always the possibility that his work here was only a lapse in performance. Fortunately, "a" was the correct answer here, and at least he did not mark that as a Known Wrong Answer. His uncertainty about Problem 4 suggests that he needs a bit more instruction or practice with that content. All of this analysis can help his teacher decide what kind of feedback to provide.

This recording sheet is also useful for thinking about whole-class performance. The next task addresses a mathematics idea that is often confusing for students. It might be posed to middle grades students or high school students, though their approaches to the task will likely be different.

Before you read on, identify the reasoning that would lead to each of the choices provided as multiple-choice options.

Task: Weighted Average

In a school fund-raiser, one group of 10 students sold an average (arithmetic mean) of 4 boxes of cookies. A different group of 15 students sold an average of 9 boxes. What was the average number of boxes of cookies sold by the 25 students?

A. $\frac{13}{25}$

B. 1

C. $6\frac{1}{2}$

D. 7

E. $13\frac{6}{13}$

Source: Adapted from U.S. Department of Education, Institute of Education Sciences, National Center for Education Statistics, National Assessment of Educational Progress (NAEP). Based on a released NAEP item, grade 12, 2005, data analysis, statistics, and probability, item 2005-12M3 #13.

By examining the data from two classes' responses, we can make effective instructional decisions, specifically whether to provide feedback to individuals or to reteach. The correct answer for the *Weighted Average* problem is "D." Let's first study Figure 9–12, which shows the compilation of responses from students in Class A.

Half of the students in Class A chose the correct response, with C as the second most popular choice (C is the simple average of 4 and 9). It is interesting that no student chose C as a Known Wrong Answer. We might want to probe why this happened; it is perhaps because $6\frac{1}{2}$ is "close" in value to 7. Some teachers might reasonably decide that feedback individually to Students 3 and 5 might be the best use of time, both for the teacher and for the students. However, a whole-class discussion of options C and D might also be appropriate to help everyone develop better understanding of how to compute a weighted average.

Now let's consider Figure 9–13, which shows the compilation of responses from students in Class B. The students in Class B answered less

Student	Known Wrong Answers	Correct Answer Choice	Sure?
1	A, B	D	Yes
2	A, E	D	Yes
3	B	A	No
4	A, B, E	C	Yes
5		B	No
6	A, B, E	C	Yes
7	A, B, E	D	No
8	B, E	C	No
9	A, B	D	Yes
10	A	D	Yes

FIGURE 9–12. Alternative Multiple-Choice Recording Sheet Responses from Class A

Student	Known Wrong Answers	Correct Answer Choice	Sure?
1	B	A	No
2	A, B, C	D	No
3	A	E	No
4	B, E	C	Yes
5		C	No
6	A, B	C	Yes
7	A, E	B	No
8		A	No
9	A, B, E	D	Yes
10	E	C	No

FIGURE 9–13. Alternative Multiple-Choice Recording Sheet Responses from Class B

correctly than students in Class A, with less confidence, and with fewer choices of Known Wrong Answers.

Class B's pattern of responses suggests that there may be some confusion about the underlying mathematics; there seems to be a need for reteaching for this class. The students may not be proficient at computing a mean or they may not understand how to use the summary data like those given in the task. Part of the process of reteaching should be to reveal the sources of the students' confusion.

Reflection 9–4

Reflection 9–4: Use of the Alternative Multiple-Choice Recording Sheet with a Proportional Reasoning Quiz

Pages 392–393

Now complete "Reflection 9–4: Use of the Alternative Multiple-Choice Recording Sheet with a Proportional Reasoning Quiz" (see pages 392–393), which provides an opportunity to make inferences about students' understandings based on their responses to a multiple-choice quiz. In scoring students' work teachers consider simultaneously what they might infer about students' understanding and what kind of feedback will best move help move the students' learning forward.

Teachers report that the first couple of times they use the alternative multiple-choice format for a quiz, they have to review the directions with students. However, they also report that using the format gives them more information and encourages most students to think more carefully about their answers. Try the alternative multiple-choice format with your students. Then record your experience in "Reflection 9–5: Using the Alternative Multiple-Choice Recording Sheet" (see pages 394–395).

Reflection 9–5

Reflection 9–5: Using the Alternative Multiple-Choice Recording Sheet

Pages 394–395

INFORMing My Practice

In summary, INFORMative assessment provides a way for teachers to gather the information needed to make inferences about what students know and can do. Those inferences are the basis for teachers' decision making about how to provide actionable feedback to students.

As discussed, the goal of actionable feedback is to move learning forward by promoting student thinking rather than by telling students exactly what to do. For actionable feedback to be effective, we need to provide ways for students to make connections, determine what is correct about their understandings, and decide what to change in their thinking. By prompting students toward productive pathways, we encourage the

What we know . . .	Therefore, what we do . . .
Actionable feedback helps improve student achievement.	We make a concerted effort to provide frequent feedback to individuals and to the class.
Actionable feedback is most beneficial when it identifies what is correct or incorrect about work.	We comment on the work or pose questions rather than assigning a grade.
Feedback is most beneficial when it suggests actions students can take to improve.	We communicate what is most critical for students to address by questions or comments.
Feedback is most beneficial when it is timely so that students have an opportunity to address issues sooner rather than later.	We constantly observe our students at work and interact daily about their homework or classwork.
Feedback is most likely to support student self-assessment when students can compare their work to rubrics or models of quality.	We make learning targets, expectations, and criteria for success clear to all students and provide opportunities for peer evaluation.
Students view feedback through the lens of their own experiences, understandings, and self-concepts.	We are thoughtful about what we write or say and work to create environments in which mistakes are seen as opportunities for learning.
Actionable feedback affects motivation and can reinforce high expectations.	We provide opportunities for students to judge where they are and provide time for them to improve their work.

FIGURE 9-14. A Focus on Actionable Feedback Translates into Positive Teacher Actions

development of metacognition and help students become owners of their understandings. Armed with knowledge about students' thinking, teachers decide how best to help students move to deeper understanding of key mathematics ideas.

Consistently crafting quality feedback to students is challenging; reflecting on the quality of the feedback we give every day is one way to help us improve. Videotaping lessons and reviewing them, either alone or with a colleague, also provides an opportunity for our own self-assessment. As you craft your feedback, use the chart in Figure 9–14 to stay focused on positive actions.

Last but not least, complete "Reflection 9–6: INFORMing My Practice: Actionable Feedback to Help Students Learn" (see page 396) to help you further reflect on and organize your thoughts around actionable feedback.

Reflection 9–6

Reflection 9–6: INFORMing My Practice: Actionable Feedback to Help Students Learn

Page 396

Reflection 9-1: Focusing on Actionable Feedback: Multiple Interpretations of a Task

Students do not always "hear" what a teacher says. Ms. Denton asked, "Compute 3 more than 2 times 7" (see page 366). Students Pat, Karl, and Ming each heard different things. Complete the chart below.

Teacher Says: "Compute 3 more than 2 times 7."	Pat computes 35.	Karl computes 20.	Ming computes 12.
What do you infer about the thinking that might have led to each student's answer?			
What actionable feedback might you give as a teacher?			
Explain why your feedback qualifies as actionable feedback.			

Reflection 9-2: Focusing on Actionable Feedback: Luis's Response to *Greater Volume*

Following is a task originally presented on page 369. First read the task and think about how you would solve it.

> *Task: Greater Volume*
>
> *Which is greater, the volume of a sphere with diameter 2 cm or the volume of a cube 2 cm on an edge? How much greater is it?*

Following is Luis's response to the task. Study Luis's response. Ask yourself:

- What is Luis's mistake and how can I help him understand that mistake?
- Do his errors appear to be lapses, misunderstandings, or misconceptions?

Sphere: $\frac{4}{3}\pi 2^3 = \frac{32}{3}\pi = 10\frac{2}{3}\pi \approx 34$

Cube: $2^3 = 8$

Sphere is greater by 24^3 cm

Luis's Response to *Greater Volume*

Now answer the following questions.

1. Luis failed to use measurement labels in some of his computations. Why are measurement labels important?

2. Luis's work generated an incorrect answer for the task. What actionable feedback would you give Luis? Explain why your feedback qualifies as actionable feedback.

Reflection 9-3: Focusing on Actionable Feedback: *Percentage Problem*

Read the following task, originally presented on page 371, and think about how you would solve it. Then answer the questions to help you think further about the task.

Task: Percentage Problem

If the price of a stock goes up by 50% on Monday and down by 50% on Tuesday, how is the final price related to the original price? Explain how you determined your answer.

---

1. What would be a good explanation?

2. What thinking would be represented by that explanation?

3. What computation(s) might we expect to see a student carry out?

4. What common errors in tasks like this have you seen in the past? What actionable feedback might you give about those errors?

Now study Fran's response and answer the questions that follow.

$$50\% - 50\% = 0$$
There is no change.

Fran's Response to *Percentage Problem*

5. What inferences can you make about Fran's understanding of the problem?

(continued)

6. What questions might you ask Fran?

7. What feedback might you give Fran?

Now study Derrick's response and answer the questions that follow.

If it starts at 20, it goes to 30, and then to 10. It is lower.

Derrick's Response to *Percentage Problem*

8. What is correct in Derrick's work?

9. What errors did Derrick make?

10. What questions might you ask Derrick to clarify his understanding of the percentage of something?

11. What feedback might you give Derrick?

12. What instruction about percentages might you plan for both Fran and Derrick?

Reflection 9-4: Use of the Alternative Multiple-Choice Recording Sheet with a Proportional Reasoning Quiz

First read through the following proportional reasoning quiz.

Proportional Reasoning Quiz

1. The Happy Animal Zoo keeps records on the daily intake of food and the mass of the animals at the zoo. Four of the animals are listed below:

   tiger: 197 kg eats 6 kg of food each day

   elephant: 4012 kg eats 179 kg of food each day

   panda bear: 115 kg eats 12 kg of food each day

   hamster: 107 g eats 11 g of food each day

   Which animal eats the greatest proportion of its body mass each day?

A. tiger	B. elephant
C. panda bear	D. hamster

2. John and Chris ride their bikes equally fast in practice laps around a track. John started first. When John had biked 9 laps, Chris had biked 3 laps. When Chris completed 15 laps, how many laps had Josh biked?

A. 45 laps	B. 24 laps
C. 21 laps	D. 6 laps

3. These four players are the best hitters on the community softball team:

Shaniqua: 6 hits out of 26 at bats	Carlita: 7 hits out of 32 at bats
Janice: 4 hits out of 17 at bats	Gaia: 7 hits out of 29 at bats

   Which player has the best batting average?

A. Shaniqua	B. Carlita
C. Janice	D. Gaia

(continued)

Reflection 9-4: Use of the Alternative Multiple-Choice Recording Sheet with a Proportional Reasoning Quiz (continued)

Consider the Correct Answer responses below to the proportional reasoning quiz, compiled from four students' completion of an Alternative Multiple-Choice Recording Sheet. Then answer the questions that follow.

Student	Item 1	Item 2	Item 3	Score
Hughes	C	C	D	3
Jeneen	C	A	D	2
Lani	C	C	C	2
Justin	D	A	B	0

1. Which students understand proportional reasoning well?

2. What is the difference between Hughes's understanding and Jeneen's?

3. What feedback would you give to Jeneen? Justin?

4. Taken as a group, what do these students know?

5. What might you do to help the group move forward in developing their understanding?

Reflection 9-5: Using the Alternative Multiple-Choice Recording Sheet

1. What are the advantages and disadvantages to using the scoring guide suggested in Figure 9–10 (page 382) versus scoring only the answers?

2. As you introduce the Alternative Multiple-Choice Recording Sheet included with this reflection, ask students to work with a partner to describe what they can learn about the mathematics in the question-and-answer choices and about their own thinking as they complete the Known Wrong Answers and Are You Sure? columns. What value did your students identify in using the Alternative Multiple-Choice Recording Sheet?

3. Use the Alternative Multiple-Choice Recording Sheet for a quiz. What did you learn about your students' understanding that you might not have known if students only circled a lettered answer?

(continued)

Reflection 9–5: Using the Alternative Multiple-Choice Recording Sheet (continued)

Alternative Multiple-Choice Recording Sheet

Student Name:		Quiz Name:	
Problem Number	**Circle Known Wrong Answers**	**Correct Answer**	**Are You Sure About the Correct Answer (circle)?**
1	a b c d e		Yes No
2	a b c d e		Yes No
3	a b c d e		Yes No
4	a b c d e		Yes No
5	a b c d e		Yes No
6	a b c d e		Yes No
7	a b c d e		Yes No
8	a b c d e		Yes No
9	a b c d e		Yes No
10	a b c d e		Yes No

Reflection 9-6: INFORMing My Practice: Actionable Feedback to Help Students Learn

Think about the chapter you just read. Use this space to record your ideas.

Ideas about the importance of actionable feedback:

Changes in my thinking about INFORMative assessment:

Ideas I envision becoming a more important part of my practice:

Questions I have:

Frustrations/concerns I have:

Section VI

What Are the Next Steps in an INFORMative Assessment Journey?

Moving Ahead with INFORMative Assessment

This concluding chapter pulls together the ideas explored throughout *INFORMative Assessment*. It features the final "A Closer Look" in which we see how two teachers work together to use these ideas to make instruction more effective and help students consolidate their learning. Their efforts help you think about not only how the parts of the INFORMative model interact but also how you are thinking about your own use of the INFORMative assessment process.

We have found that as teachers gain insight into students' mathematical thinking, they often find greater reward in teaching, in part because they are better able to see students' understanding change over time. Insights into learning help teachers become more facile at managing strategies that help students learn. This increases a sense of success, both for teachers and students, and it helps teachers move forward in their development as instructional leaders.

Decisions: Next Steps ↔ Clear Learning Targets

INFORMative Assessment Model

Inferences & Feedback

Tasks Questions Assessments

Student Self- Assessment & Responsibility

Overview

Looking Back to Plan Ahead

Assessment Tip ✓

"For teaching to have the greatest impact on the learner, teachers must be thoughtful in their planning, flexible in their delivery, and relentless in their focus on what students are understanding. The formativeness of teaching means that teachers are constantly planning, implementing, and revising their lessons and instruction. Teachers choose lesson goals and plan activities; they anticipate student responses and possible misconceptions. When they implement lessons, teachers look for evidence that students are making sense of the mathematics. The formativeness of teaching occurs within the classroom as teachers immediately react to their students' needs and outside the classroom as they reflect upon what they might do differently to strengthen future lessons."
—Katherine Mawhinney, Appalachian State University

As has been emphasized in all the chapters, formative assessment should be intertwined with instruction. As we teach, we assess; and as we assess, we teach. Students' conversations and written work provide evidence for us to use to INFORM us about what they know and can do. That evidence feeds the INFORMative assessment process to help us make instructional decisions that guide our students' learning.

Our journey toward implementation of INFORMative assessment has included an exploration of several key ideas. Instruction and assessment should be merged (Chapter 1) so that students remain fully engaged. There are many decisions that have to be made (Chapter 2) in the process of creating that merger. An early step in instructional planning is identifying and communicating clear learning targets (Chapter 3) as a way to guide teaching and learning. We can gather information about students' thinking from oral (Chapter 4) and written (Chapter 5) work. It is critical to know what students understand, what they misunderstand, and what they still need to learn. Choosing rich tasks (Chapter 6) helps provide opportunities for students both to learn mathematics and to demonstrate that learning. Along the way toward learning, students need to develop self-assessment skills and to take responsibility for learning (Chapter 7). As we learn more about students' thinking, we become better at making inferences about their thinking (Chapter 8) and providing actionable feedback (Chapter 9) that helps students see what is good about their work and proceed in a successful direction.

Becoming a fully effective user of formative assessment is a lengthy journey. Our use of formative assessment strategies will also continue to change in response to changes in mathematics standards, in the use of technologies for teaching, and in what students bring to the classroom. This chapter takes an in-depth look at two teachers working together to learn how to implement INFORMative assessment in their teaching. It also provides abundant cross-references and connections to help you come full circle in reflecting on your current understanding of INFORMative assessment.

The Formativeness of Teaching

Covey (1989) has written about the habits of highly effective people. While he was not describing teachers who use INFORMative assessment in their classrooms, the habits he advocates serve us well—especially being proactive, beginning with the end in mind, and seeking first to understand and then to be understood. As teachers we continually search for ways to become "better educators" and to create environments in which all our students will learn with understanding and confidence. This ongoing quest for excellence can be thought of as the "formativeness of teaching." Teachers are truly lifelong learners. We are willing to examine our current practices and venture into new arenas that we may not be able to clearly envision. We are eager to become better at gathering information about our students' thinking, observing how close they are to achieving the learning targets we have established, and making adjustments in our instruction to intervene as needed.

With these thoughts in mind, here is a proposed list of "Habits of Highly Effective Teachers of Mathematics." Each habit is important in its own way, and increased expertise in any one of these areas contributes to our ability to help our students learn with understanding.

> **Learn More…**
>
> "The Formativeness of Teaching" is based on a similar discussion in *INFORMative Assessment* (Joyner and Muri 2011).

Habits of Highly Effective Teachers of Mathematics

1. Continue to deepen mathematics content knowledge.

2. Hone classroom management skills.

3. Sharpen skills at using questioning and choosing rich tasks.

4. Develop knowledge of students' mathematics thinking.

5. Create environments that support student learning.

6. Use formative assessment to improve planning and delivery of instruction.

7. Provide actionable feedback to students.

8. Reflect on teaching experiences and practices.

Putting Our Beliefs into Action

Every day in our classrooms some students appear to have mastered the learning targets, others are "on the way" but need more instruction, and still others have misconceptions that need to be addressed specifically. Establishing a climate in which all students are supported in self-assessing their progress and in talking about their thinking takes time and energy. As we become more intentional listeners and more attentive to what students' work reveals about their thinking, we are likely to have more, rather than fewer, "decision points" about follow-up instruction. Becoming skilled at implementing INFORMative assessment does not mean our jobs will be easier—just more rewarding!

Think about how your beliefs have changed over time. Compare your changes with those you identified in Reflection 1–1 when you read Chapter 1. Use "Reflection 10–1: My Changing Beliefs About Teaching and Learning" (see page 422) to help you organize your thoughts.

The table "Where We've Been . . . Where We're Going" compares traditional classrooms with ones in which there is a focus on INFORMative assessment. (See Figure 10–1.) On the left side of the chart, we list traditional classroom practices. The middle column identifies the corresponding chapters that address ways to move these practices toward INFORMative assessment. The right side lists classroom practices for long-term success in using INFORMative assessment; each of these practices is named so that we can cross-reference them in the dialogues that follow. As teachers we do not become experts at implementing these practices with two or three tries. The practices require planning and reflection; they require us to be flexible and open to feedback on our teaching. In other words, we must be willing to engage in the formativeness of teaching.

Think about how well you are implementing the practices listed in the right-hand column of the table. Remember that implementation is not an all-or-nothing situation; there will be degrees of implementation. Use "Reflection 10–2: Moving Toward INFORMative Assessment Practices" (see page 423) to help you organize your thoughts.

Reflection 10-1

My Changing Beliefs
About Teaching
and Learning

Page 422

Reflection 10-2

Moving Toward
INFORMative
Assessment
Practices

Page 423

Moving From . . .	Chapter	Moving Toward . . .
Covering textbook content chapter by chapter in a fixed time line	Chapter 2	**RESPONSIVE DECISIONS** Making decisions about what and how to teach based on what students already know and how they respond to instruction
Planning lessons based on general goals and the next topic in the textbook	Chapter 3	**LEARNING TARGETS** Clearly defining learning targets with criteria for their achievement and communicating these to students
Using quizzes and chapter tests as the primary assessment of learning	Chapter 4 Chapter 5	**INTENTIONAL LISTENING** Using intentional listening and questioning to monitor student progress and help identify achievement of learning targets
Assessing at the end of the week or the end of a unit and using the results primarily to assign grades	Chapter 4 Chapter 5	**ASSESSING REGULARLY** Assessing daily throughout instruction to uncover student thinking and make decisions about instruction
Using practice exercises and routine tasks as primary instructional strategy	Chapter 6	**RICH TASKS** Using modified routine tasks and mathematically rich tasks for both instruction and assessment to move students' thinking forward
Providing whole-class instruction with students working individually on the tasks	Chapter 7	**GROUPING FLEXIBLY** Having students work on tasks as a whole class, alone, or with partners
Identifying correct answers with little discussion of solution strategies	Chapter 7	**STUDENT PARTICIPATION** Establishing clear expectations for participation by all students and respect for different ways of thinking

FIGURE 10–1. Where We've Been . . . Where We're Going (continued on next page)

Assessment Tip ✓

Although it is often possible to practice some aspects of formative assessment (e.g., asking probing questions) individually, it is important to keep in mind that our ultimate goal is the implementation of the entire process as an integral part of planning and delivery of instruction. This is analogous to the observation that while some mathematics ideas (e.g., solving linear equations) can be practiced in isolation, the ultimate goal is for students to develop deep, connected mathematics understanding.

Moving From . . .	Chapter	Moving Toward . . .
Expecting students to know how to improve their work	Chapter 7	**SELF-ASSESSMENT** Creating a climate that promotes reflection, self-assessment, and responsibility through class discussions, models, and rubrics
Showing and telling students the most efficient way to solve problems or to compute	Chapter 5 Chapter 6 Chapter 7	**SHARING THINKING** Encouraging students to share multiple solution strategies and facilitating class discussions that move students toward efficient algorithms
Marking students' answers as correct or incorrect in order to assign a grade	Chapter 8	**STUDENTS' LOGIC** Examining the logic behind students' incomplete, incorrect, and correct answers
Asking questions that are primarily recall or yes-or-no questions	Chapter 4 Chapter 8	**PROBING QUESTIONS** Asking questions to engage students in a task or discussion and using questions to probe students' thinking
Scoring student responses as "right" or "wrong" and giving feedback primarily in the form of grades	Chapter 9	**ACTIONABLE FEEDBACK** Scoring student work for both the process and the answer and providing actionable feedback to inform the student on how to improve performance
Defining successful teaching as having a large percentage of the class score well on tests	Chapters 1–10	**SUCCESSFUL TEACHING** Defining successful teaching as having students who reason mathematically, exhibit perseverance in solving problems, communicate their ideas, and develop long-term knowledge and skills in using mathematics

FIGURE 10–1. Where We've Been . . . Where We're Going (continued)

→ A Closer Look

Mrs. Torres's and Ms. Brown's Joint Planning to Incorporate Formative Assessment in Instruction

The following vignette illustrates how the INFORMative assessment process might play out for particular instruction. Throughout the vignette there are cross-references that highlight the classroom practices just reviewed in the Moving Toward column of Figure 10–1. The two teachers involved in joint planning are an eighth-grade teacher, Mrs. Torres, and a high school teacher, Ms. Brown. The planning occurred in a summer meeting during which pairs of teachers (one middle school teacher and one high school teacher) developed lesson plans to use the following year. They also agreed to revise those lessons and post the revisions on a district Web site. Mrs. Torres and Ms. Brown volunteered to work on lessons to help students understand the concept of functions. Both teachers knew that linear functions would be the focus of one or more lessons at each of their grades, though at different times during the year. Ms. Brown wanted a task to use early in the unit on functions to assess how much her students remembered about linear functions before she moved into quadratic functions, while Mrs. Torres wanted a task to use later in the year as she helped students develop their thinking about linear functions. Let's take a closer look at how their planning—and consequently their use of formative assessment—transpires through the following phases:

- Identifying Standards

- Establishing Expectations

- Choosing a Task

- Planning for Use of the Task

- Mrs. Torres's Use of the Task

- Ms. Brown's Use of the Task

- Reflecting on How the Task Worked

- Summarizing the Process

Identifying Standards

Mrs. Torres and Ms. Brown teach in a district that uses Common Core, so they first looked up relevant standards for linear functions. Both teachers knew that modeling was a challenge for many students, so they focused on standards that addressed this content. (See Figure 10–2.)

Establishing Expectations

Ms. Brown raised the following concern: "What evidence will be acceptable to indicate attainment of these standards?" She continued, "We need some data for a linear relationship. Students should graph those data accurately and use

Grade 8 Standard	High School Functions Standards
Use functions to model relationships between quantities	**Interpret functions that arise in applications in terms of the context**
Construct a function to model a linear relationship between two quantities. Determine the rate of change and initial value of the function from a description of a relationship or from two (x, y) values, including reading these from a table or from a graph. Interpret the rate of change and initial value of a linear function in terms of the situation it models, and in terms of its graph or a table of values.	For a function that models a relationship between two quantities, interpret key features of graphs and tables in terms of the quantities, and sketch graphs showing key features given a verbal description of the relationship. *Key features include: intercepts; intervals where the function is increasing, decreasing, positive, or negative; relative maximums and minimums; symmetries; end behavior; and periodicity.*
(CCSS.MATH.CONTENT.8.F.B.4)	(CCSS.MATH.CONTENT.HSF.IF.B.4)
	Build a function that models a relationship between two quantities
	Write a function that describes a relationship between two quantities.
	(CCSS.MATH.CONTENT.HSF.BF.A.1)
	Determine an explicit expression, a recursive process, or steps for calculation from a context.
	(CCSS.MATH.CONTENT.HSF.BF.A.1.A)

Learn More...

To refresh your thinking on IDENTIFYING STANDARDS, see Chapter 2, pages 42–46.

FIGURE 10-2. Standards Identified by Mrs. Torres and Ms. Brown

that graph to find the slope and y-intercept. I want them to use these values to create a function rule in symbolic form. I know they will struggle with explaining their thinking during all of this. My students' use of terminology sometimes reveals confusions between domain and range. And they often don't know how to use patterns they see in a graph, like constant change, to write a symbolic expression."

Mrs. Torres responded, "My goals are mainly to get students to choose the independent and dependent variables and then see patterns in a graph of the data. I don't expect most of my students to be able to write the symbolic forms on their own. It takes some direction from me to get them to make the connections between a graph and a symbolic function rule. It seems, though, we both want students to relate the data to some underlying concepts for functions. So let's figure out a situation that could lead to data we could present."

Choosing a Task

Mrs. Torres and Ms. Brown talked for quite a while about real-world situations that might be modeled with a linear function. They considered some often-used situations, such as cell phone plans that involve a base charge plus a small charge per minute. They agreed that students had seen the cell phone example so many times that they might be tired of it. So Mrs. Torres and Ms. Brown decided to look for a less common application. Mrs. Torres finally commented that as a member of a Ping-Pong club that had sponsored a regional tournament, she and her teammates had to verify that the Ping-Pong balls they used were actually consistent with the tournament standard requiring each ball to have a mass of 2.7 grams. "We had to weigh a sample of the balls, but since they tended to roll off the scale, we had to weigh multiple samples inside a bowl. We used a plastic one because it was lightweight. I think we might be able to develop a task around the idea of how much a Ping-Pong ball weighs."

Both teachers agreed that they would really like to have students weigh Ping-Pong balls, but that there was not enough equipment or time to do this in class, so they decided to provide data from measurements and have students develop the mathematical model for these data. They got a small plastic bowl and some Ping-Pong balls and used a scale from the science lab to measure the mass of the bowl plus Ping-Pong balls as they added more balls. Then they wrote a task that incorporated their data.

Learn More...

LEARNING TARGETS help both teachers and students understand the mathematics learning expectations for a lesson. To refresh your thinking on establishing expectations, see Chapter 3.

Learn More...

Tournament standards for Ping-Pong balls can be found on The Laws of Table Tennis Web site at ittf.com/ittf_ handbook/hb.asp?s_ number=2.

Task: Mass of a Ping-Pong Ball

Mrs. Torres and her Ping-Pong club organized a tournament last summer. As part of the preparation, they had to verify that the balls had an acceptable mass. They picked a sample of 10 Ping-Pong balls. Then they weighed 1 ball, then 2 balls, then 3 balls, etc., until they had weighed the entire sample. They used a bowl to hold the Ping-Pong balls so each measurement (in grams) included both the bowl and the balls that were inside the bowl. Here are their data:

Number of Balls	Total Mass (g)
1	182.6
2	185.2
3	187.8
4	190.4
5	193.0
6	195.6
7	198.2
8	200.8
9	203.4
10	206.0

Graph these data and create a function to model the data. Interpret the parts of that model in terms of the measurements of Ping-Pong balls. Were the Ping-Pong balls acceptable for the tournament standard mass of 2.7 g?

Learn More...

RICH TASKS allow students to begin work on a task at different levels of sophistication; they encourage students to make connections among ideas. To refresh your thinking on choosing mathematically rich tasks, see Chapter 6.

Both Mrs. Torres and Ms. Brown knew that a graph of these data would be a straight line, with the slope being the mass of one Ping-Pong ball and the y-intercept being the mass of the bowl. They hoped that students would see the connection between this line and the function $y = 180 + 2.6x$, where x is the number of Ping-Pong balls and y is the total mass of the bowl plus the balls. Ms. Brown noted, "It is interesting that our Ping-Pong balls are a bit light."

As Mrs. Torres and Ms. Brown discussed the task, they noticed that the standard form, $y = mx + b$, suggests that this equation should be $y = 2.6x + 180$. However, the equation $y = 180 + 2.6x$ more closely mirrors the situation of adding Ping-Pong balls (each with a mass of 2.6 grams) to the bowl (with a mass of 180 grams). This version of the equation might help students connect the context to the model. However, since the two versions are mathematically equivalent, either would be acceptable as a model for the data.

Planning for Use of the Task

Mrs. Torres asked, "How do you get students to understand that the slope is the mass of one ball and that the y-intercept is the mass of the bowl holding the balls?"

Ms. Brown responded, "Sometimes it helps to remind them that slope is rise over run; that is, the amount of increase in the y-value for each unit increase in the x-value. I would have to help them connect the fact that x-values are the number of Ping-Pong balls. It takes time for some students to remember that x is not something magical. It is a number, and that number has meaning in the context of the problem."

Mrs. Torres replied, "I think it will be somewhat confusing that the bowl is so much heavier than the Ping-Pong balls. I often find that a large difference in values can grab students' attention in and of itself. And we'll have a chance to talk about mass versus weight. Some of the students won't even remember what grams are. The science teachers will like that we address this issue in math class."

Ms. Brown noted, "In my class we'll also talk about why the mass is written as 193.0 grams rather than 193 grams. For many students, the use of significant digits seems like an arbitrary process. I want them to appreciate what writing 'zero tenths' tells them about the accuracy of the measurement."

Mrs. Torres's Use of the Task

Mrs. Torres used the task early in the second semester of the year. She had previously reviewed how to compute the slope and y-intercept for linear equations, and she had introduced students to the vertical line test for graphs of different kinds of functions. She had introduced the terms *dependent variable* and *independent variable*, but she wasn't sure if these ideas had been mastered. Her students easily graphed the data. (See Figure 10–3 on the next page.)

> **Learn More...**
>
> Planning for RESPONSIVE DECISIONS helps teachers know what thinking to look for as students engage in a task. To refresh your thinking on teachers' decisions, see Chapter 2.

Learn More...

This section and the next feature dialogues between each of the two teachers and their students. The dialogues illustrate how Mrs. Torres and Ms. Brown implemented elements of the INFORMative assessment process. Some elements are called out specifically via cross-references in the margin. Think about what other elements (for example, assessing regularly) can be identified when you reflect on each dialogue in its entirety.

However, Mrs. Torres's students struggled over interpreting the meaning of the graph within the context of the task.

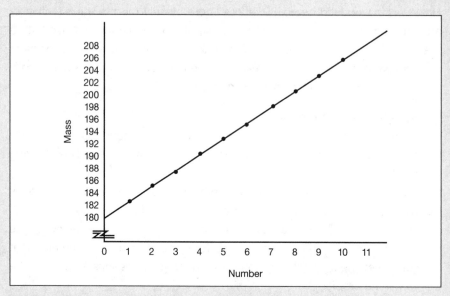

FIGURE 10-3. Student Response to *Mass of a Ping-Pong Ball*

Learn More...

PROBING QUESTIONS help teachers monitor the development and retention of learning. To refresh your thinking on questioning, see Chapter 4.

Learn More...

STUDENT PARTICIPATION can be encouraged by inviting particular students to join a conversation. To refresh your thinking on engaging questions and classroom discussions, see Chapter 4.

Mrs. Torres: How would you describe the shape of the graph?

Nora: It is a straight line, but it doesn't go through the origin.

Mrs. Torres: What do you know about a graph that goes through the origin versus one that doesn't?

Roi: If it goes through the origin, it's a proportion, so this one is not.

Mrs. Torres: So the data do not represent a proportional relationship, but the graph *is* a straight line. What term can we use to describe the relationship?

Ouida: Since it is a line, could we say, "linear"?

Mrs. Torres: Can we call it a linear function? How do we know when a relationship is a function?

Ouida: There is a line test. Or should I say, "linear" test?

Mrs. Torres: I think you mean the vertical line test. Can anyone tell me what that is? Samir?

Samir:	All vertical lines cannot hit the graph in more than one point.
Mrs. Torres:	Why is that important?
Nora:	A function can have only one *y*-value for each *x*-value, so if it hit in more than one point, that would make it *not* a function.
Mrs. Torres:	What is the "it"?
Nora:	Oh. The vertical line. So if any vertical line hits the graph in more than one point, that would make the graph *not* a function.
Mrs. Torres:	Okay. I understand that. So we can talk about this graph as a linear function. How did you choose what to show with *x*-values and what to show with *y*-values in your graph?
Roi:	Since the mass is measured, that would be the dependent variable. The number of Ping-Pong balls isn't measured.
Mrs. Torres:	Why isn't counting a measurement?
Roi:	There are no units.
Mrs. Torres:	So if I say, "seven Ping-Pong balls" then "Ping-Pong balls" (*uses "air quotes"*) isn't a unit of measure?
Ouida:	I'm not sure, but it certainly isn't a standard unit.
Mrs. Torres:	True, it's certainly not a standard unit. Let's keep thinking about what makes something a unit of measure. So, you have mass as the *y*-variable and number of Ping-Pong balls as the *x*-variable. What is the slope of the line and what is the *y*-intercept?
Samir:	We found the slope as two point six and the *y*-intercept as one hundred eighty.
Mrs. Torres:	How did you find those values?
Samir:	We used two points and found the change in *y* over the change in *x* for the slope. The *y*-intercept is where it crosses the *y*-axis.
Mrs. Torres:	How did you find the *y*-intercept?

Learn More...

PROBING QUESTIONS can help clarify the antecedent of a pronoun. To refresh your thinking on this, see Chapter 4.

Learn More...

STUDENTS' LOGIC can be revealed by asking students to explain the choices they make as they work on any task. To refresh your thinking on making inferences, see Chapter 8.

Learn More...

ACTIONABLE FEEDBACK is provided when teachers identify what is "good" in a response and how that response can be made "better." To refresh your thinking on actionable feedback, see Chapter 9.

Samir: Well, if you stretched the line back to the left, the intercept is where it crosses.

Roi: It is where that line would cross the y-axis.

Mrs. Torres: Okay. I see that. Now what does the *slope* tell us about the situation in the task?

Nora: It is the change in y over the change in x.

Mrs. Torres: Yes, that is how we compute it, but what can you say to show how the change in y and the change in x relate to the context of the task?

Nora: The change in y is the change in weight and the change in x is the change in the number of Ping-Pong balls.

Mrs. Torres: Now, what does the *slope* tell us about the Ping-Pong balls?

Nora: It would be the weight of a Ping-Pong ball.

Roi: Actually it would be *mass* per Ping-Pong ball.
(*students chuckle*)

Mrs. Torres: Okay, Roi, what is the difference between mass and weight?

Roi: Mass is the amount of stuff and weight is the force of gravity pulling on that stuff.

Mrs. Torres: You all can check that with Mr. Compton at your next science class. For now, we will just deal with the measurements in grams. How did you find the slope? How did you calculate it?

Ouida: I subtracted two y-values and the two corresponding x-values and then divided.

Mrs. Torres: What did you divide?

Ouida: I divided the y-differences by the x-differences. I got two point six.

Mrs. Torres: I think you mean two and six-tenths, but two and six-tenths what?

Ouida: Two and six-tenths grams?

Mrs. Torres: Is that correct?

Roi: I think it is two and six-tenths grams per ball. (*class giggles, but Mrs. Torres ignores it*)

Mrs. Torres: Is that correct?

Nora: I think that is right.

Mrs. Torres: Which one is right—grams or grams per ball?

Nora: Grams per ball.

Mrs. Torres: How would we write that?

Nora: I think it is *g over ball*. (*stifled laughter from a few students*)

Roi: We can say, "grams per ball."

Mrs. Torres: Maybe we can say, "grams per Ping-Pong ball." (*records $\frac{g}{\text{Ping-Pong ball}}$ on the board*) So the slope is the mass of a Ping-Pong ball. What is the *y*-intercept and what does that tell you?

Samir: It is one hundred eighty. That is where the line would cross the *y*-axis if we extended it.

Mrs. Torres: One hundred eighty what?

Samir: Grams per ball?

Mrs. Torres: How did you figure that out?

Samir: Wouldn't it be the same as the slope?

Nora: I think it is different. The *y*-intercept is just a value on the *y*-axis, and those numbers represent mass. So I think it is one hundred eighty grams.

Mrs. Torres: Samir, what do you think of Nora's explanation?

Samir: I'm not sure about what the *y*-values show. Why would they show mass?

Nora: The second column of the data table is grams. Those are the *y*-values.

Learn More…

SHARING THINKING happens when students engage in discussion of mathematics ideas. To refresh your thinking on debriefing discussions, see Chapter 4.

Learn More…

Admitting a lack of confidence is evidence of SELF-ASSESSMENT by a student. To refresh your thinking on student self-assessment, see Chapter 7.

Samir: Oh, I guess that's right.

Mrs. Torres: Let's look at the data and the graph in a slightly different way. If we extended the line to the left, what value of x would be associated with the y-value of one hundred eighty?

Roi: Since the line would cross the y-axis, the x-value would have to be zero; x is always zero on the y-axis.

Mrs. Torres: How many Ping-Pong balls would be in the bowl when the x-value in the model is zero?

Roi: None. Zero balls.

Mrs. Torres: So what in the context of the task is represented by the y-intercept of one hundred eighty grams?

Learn More...
ACTIONABLE FEEDBACK includes feedforward that points students in productive directions. To read more about this see Chapter 9.

Roi: It would be the empty bowl. Zero balls. I hadn't thought of it that way.

Mrs. Torres: Remember that we've looked at the form $y = mx + b$ for linear equations, with m as the slope and b as the y-intercept. So what equation could we write for these data?

Nora: It would be "y equals two and six-tenths x plus one hundred eighty."

Mrs. Torres: (Mrs. Torres records this on the board: $y = 2.6x + 180$.) But what might the equation look like if we think of filling an empty bowl with Ping-Pong balls?

Roi: Since the one hundred eighty is the empty bowl, we could start with that and then fill it up with Ping-Pong balls. It would look like "y equals one hundred eighty plus two and six-tenths x." (Mrs. Torres records $y = 180 + 2.6x$ on the board underneath the previous equation.)

Mrs. Torres: These two equations are equivalent, so either one would be correct. But the second one might model the context a bit better.

Mrs. Torres helped her students begin to develop an understanding of how a linear function could be used to model actual data. She used the students' understanding of graphs to make connections to functions presented in algebraic form. That is, she identified what students knew and helped them build on that knowledge. She had already taught them to graph functions like $y = 2x + 7$, so she focused on how to think about the connections between a graph and a symbolic representation. Sometimes she ignored students' imprecise language (i.e., two point six) because she wanted to focus on more important mathematics concepts.

Mrs. Torres returned several times to the issue of how to calculate slope. She wanted to be sure that students understood the process, and she wanted to help them focus on how the slope connected with the context of the task. It is also noteworthy that she used the same question ("Is that correct?") twice in succession—once in response to an incorrect answer and once in response to a correct answer. Questioning in this way helps students learn that being asked a question is not, in and of itself, a signal that the answer is incorrect. Developing a classroom norm that questioning is "normal" helps to create a positive climate for learning.

Ms. Brown's Use of the Task

Ms. Brown used the task early in the unit on functions as a way to gauge what her students remembered about linear functions. Her students had some experience with functions, but she wanted to check on what they remembered. The concepts of domain and range had been discussed, as well as the difference between relations and functions, but she suspected that students had not mastered those ideas. She also saw this task as an opportunity to discuss the meaning of the term *significant digits*. She asked her students to work in small groups to solve the task. They easily graphed the data and identified the slope and *y*-intercept of the line connecting the data points, but they seemed to struggle with writing a function in symbolic form.

> **Learn More...**
> GROUPING FLEXIBLY is a way that teachers encourage verbal interactions among students. To refresh your thinking on grouping, see Chapters 6 and 7.

Ms. Brown: Do the data represent a function?

Samantha: We think it is a linear function. The points are all in a line, and we can extend the line to the left and the right.

Ms. Brown: How far can the line go to the left and right?

Lily: To the right, forever, but to the left, only to the *y*-axis, since you can't have negative Ping-Pong balls.

Ms. Brown: So what is the domain of this function?

Lily:	From zero to infinity. Well, maybe not that far, since you can't have an infinite number of Ping-Pong balls, especially in a small bowl.
Ms. Brown:	Are all positive numbers acceptable for the domain?
Mack:	The x-values have to be whole numbers, since you have to count the number of Ping-Pong balls as whole numbers. But the line joining the data points covers all numbers on the x-axis. It's just that the situation won't allow numbers like "three and a half" Ping-Pong balls.
Ms. Brown:	Thanks, Mack. That describes the domain, both for the situation and for the model that we will develop. Raul, what did you get for the slope and y-intercept?
Raul:	The slope is two point six and the y-intercept is one hundred eighty. (*Ms. Brown records this on the board:* slope = 2.6 and y-intercept = 180.)
Ms. Brown:	What labels should we put on these numbers?
Raul:	I don't understand what you mean.
Ms. Brown:	Who can help Raul and his thinking?
Lily:	I think it is grams per ball and grams.
Ms. Brown:	How did you figure that out?
Lily:	Well, the slope is change in y-value over change in x. The y-values are grams, and the x-values are number of balls, so the slope is grams over balls and we could think of this as grams per ball or the mass of a single ball. The y-intercept is just a y-value, so that is just grams.
Ms. Brown:	Speaking of the y-values, why is the total mass for five Ping-Pong balls written as "one hundred ninety-three and zero tenths" rather than just "one hundred ninety-three" grams, without a zero after the decimal point?
Samantha:	Maybe you wanted to use the same form for each measurement.

Learn More...
PROBING QUESTIONS help reveal students' thinking. To read more about this, see Chapters 4 and 8.

Ms. Brown: That is probably important, but what does the use of "zero tenths" tell you about the measurement?

Raul: It shows the same accuracy for each measurement. We talked about that in science.

Ms. Brown: When you say, "same accuracy," Raul, what do you mean?

Raul: Each measurement is accurate to the nearest tenth of a gram.

Ms. Brown: Is it really the nearest *tenth* of a gram?

Mack: I think it is half of that—the nearest half of a tenth of a gram.

Ms. Brown: Why is it to the nearest half of a tenth of a gram? And what would half of a tenth of a gram be?

Mack: Well, if it were more than half of a tenth, we'd round up, and if it were less than half, we'd round down. So is it to the nearest five milligrams?

Ms. Brown: What do we call a *tenth of a gram*? (*provides wait time, but there is no response*) Anyone? (*provides more wait time, but still no response*) Maybe you don't know that term. A tenth of a gram is a decigram, but that unit is not often used. Usually people use only kilograms, grams, and milligrams to measure mass. How many milligrams are there in a gram?

Wanda: One thousand, so a tenth of gram is one hundred milligrams, and half of a tenth of a gram would be fifty milligrams.

Ms. Brown: Yes, so the measurements are correct to the nearest fifty milligrams. The way the measurements are written communicates that information implicitly. Now back to the issue of modeling the data. How can we use the information from the graph to make a function in symbolic form?

Samantha: If the slope is two point six and the *y*-intercept is one hundred eighty, we could write, "*y* equals two point six times *x* plus one hundred eighty." (*Ms. Brown records* $y = 2.6x + 180$ *on the board.*)

Learn More...

ACTIONABLE FEEDBACK happens when teachers acknowledge an incomplete contribution and point to a way to make that contribution more complete. To refresh your thinking on actionable feedback, see Chapter 9.

Learn More...

INTENTIONAL LISTENING helps teachers identify what to probe in a student's thinking. To refresh your thinking on intentional listening, see Chapter 4.

Ms. Brown: To be more precise, let's say two and six-tenths, but what are the measurement units on the two numbers, two and six-tenths and one hundred eighty?

Wanda: Lily said the units for the two and six-tenths is grams per ball and the units for one hundred eighty is grams.

Ms. Brown: If we add the units we'd have an equation that looks like this. (*Writes* $y = 2.6$ g/ball $x + 180$ g *on the board underneath the earlier equation.*) Which one makes more sense to you?

Jahan: I like the first one better. The label on "two and six-tenths" is confusing. There is an "x" after it, but it is not really clear what to do with that. In the first one, it is clearer that we multiply by x.

Wanda: Okay, that makes sense. Write it without the units but know what the units are.

Ms. Brown: What label would we put on x and what label would we put on y?

Mack: Well, x shows the number of Ping-Pong balls and y is the total mass of the bowl and the balls inside it. So the label on x is "number of balls" and the label on y is "grams."

Ms. Brown: Now that you have written the function and know what the variables represent in the context, how would you answer the last question in the task? Were the Ping-Pong balls acceptable for the tournament standard mass of two and seven-tenths grams? How would you answer that?

Lily: These Ping-Pong balls are a little light, but we don't know if the difference is enough to make them unacceptable.

Ms. Brown: How do we know what the mass of the Ping-Pong balls is?

Wanda: It's the slope.

Mack: The slope is two and six-tenths grams per Ping-Pong ball, and that is the mass of one ball.

Ms. Brown: Does that mean the balls are too small?

Mack: We'd have to find out more about the rules for Ping-Pong. How much "off" is too much? We don't know for sure.

> **Learn More...**
> ACTIONABLE FEEDBACK reminds students of what is important. To read more see Chapter 9.

Ms. Brown helped her students explicitly connect the slope and y-intercept from the graph with the symbolic representation of the function. She used a whole-class discussion to raise some important issues that have particular relevance for the task; namely, labels for derived measurements (i.e., slope) and the information communicated by significant digits in measurements. This kind of debriefing helps students make connections among mathematics ideas that may not seem obviously related. Ms. Brown would need to use future opportunities to probe how well those connections were cemented in the students' minds. Like Mrs. Torres, Ms. Brown also sometimes ignored students' imprecise language; developing understanding of the role of units was more critical.

Ms. Brown encountered a situation in which students seemed to lack some understanding of metric units of mass. She chose *not* to pursue further probing of that lack of understanding, since it was not central to the focus of the task. However, she made a mental note to pursue that issue at a later time. The students seemed to understand the concept of *slope*; indeed, they used the term repeatedly in correct ways. Ms. Brown, unlike Mrs. Torres, did not feel the need to probe students' understanding of this term. Although there was a discussion of the domain of the function, there was no discussion of the range, so Ms. Brown got no information about students' understanding of that concept. Their thinking about range would need to be explored at a later time.

Reflecting on How the Task Worked

Before Mrs. Torres and Ms. Brown posted the task *Mass of a Ping-Pong Ball* on the district Web site, they came together to share what happened in each of their classes. They wanted to be sure to discuss how the task helped students learn about modeling.

Ms. Brown began the conversation. "I think the task worked pretty well. The students stayed engaged with it, and it didn't take too long to complete. They wrote the equation pretty easily; that's encouraging. They were not sure whether to show the labels in the equation, so I finessed that by encouraging them just to remember what the labels should be. I was surprised that they did not know all the metric measurements; I might want to alert the science teachers about this. I was *not* surprised, however, that they were not clear about how the significant digits in the measurements show implicitly the level of accuracy of the measurements. I was pleased that they recognized that the y-intercept had meaning for the context of the task. It is important to push them to make connections between math ideas and real-world situations."

Learn More...
SUCCESSFUL TEACHING can be identified by reflecting on what happened during a lesson. Reflecting with a colleague is often very helpful. Consider using the Reflections provided throughout this resource with a colleague or as part of professional development sessions that your school or district might organize.

Mrs. Torres picked up on some of Ms. Brown's comments. "I helped them see how to label the slope and *y*-intercept, but I didn't push it very far. My students were unsure about the difference between mass and weight, but I didn't want to let the discussion get distracted about that issue, so I cut off the discussion. I let Mr. Compton know about this, and he said he would address it in science. They did know where to put slope and *y*-intercept in the linear-equation format, but I'm not sure how much the really understood. Any help you could give me on how to clarify these ideas would be gratefully accepted."

Summarizing the Process

Mass of a Ping-Pong Ball was chosen so that students would focus on critical aspects of the function concept and the teachers could use the discussion of the task to understand their students' thinking. Each teacher seized opportunities to understand the thinking of their students. Questioning was at the heart of this INFORMative assessment; choosing appropriate tasks was also a critical step. Sometimes the questioning was to check on previous learning (e.g., Mrs. Torres's question about proportional relationships) and sometimes it was about currently developing understanding (e.g., Ms. Brown's discussion about the importance of 0 in the value 193.0). The discussions also encouraged students to explain their thinking, even if that thinking was incomplete (e.g., Ouida's comment, "I'm not sure"). While we have only a brief glimpse into each classroom, it seems apparent that each teacher has established a classroom climate that supports opportunities for explanations without fear of ridicule, an important step for successful implementation of INFORMative assessment.

> **Learn More ...**
>
> Chapter 7 offers more insights on establishing a positive classroom climate for successful implementation of INFORMative assessment.

> **Reflection 10-3**
>
> Mentoring a Teacher
>
> Page 424

As you read the dialogues, you probably had some thoughts about how you would have interacted with the teachers as they planned and then debriefed their experiences. Complete "Reflection 10–3: Mentoring a Teacher" (see page 424), which gives you an opportunity to reflect on discussions you might have with one of the teachers.

INFORMing My Practice

In this chapter we've looked back on what we've learned thus far to further illustrate the interconnectedness of the parts of the INFORMative assessment process. However, as teachers we must look ahead toward integrating formative assessment into our regular instructional routines. This means that we have to take stock of where we are now in that process, where we want to be a few years from now, and how we can bridge between today's skills and future skills in this area. This bridge can be viewed as a solution strategy for the task of reaching personal long-term goals.

Learn More...

Consider reading some of the resources provided in the References as you continue in your INFORMative assessment journey.

Thoughtful implementation of INFORMative assessment means taking seriously the notion of reflecting frequently on what students understand and do not understand as well as on the logic behind students' answers. Incorporating formative assessment seamlessly into instruction is not a short-term event. Rather, it is a process that involves the use of a collection of strategies that engages teachers and students in becoming partners for supporting students' learning. We are confident that your journey will lead you to richer interactions with your students. Allowing students to INFORM your instructional decisions will allow you to lead your students to more powerful learning experiences and long-term success in mathematics.

"The most important type of assessment for guiding instructional decisions and supporting student learning is formative assessment, or the day-to-day monitoring of what students are learning. Knowing how to assess student learning well should be a major goal of a teacher's own career-long professional growth. As in other aspects of improving teaching, focusing on analyzing student work provides an excellent foundation for a teacher or group of teachers to advance their understanding of learning and testing. Ideally, a skillful teacher will regularly analyze student work using a range of informal and formal tools to determine what students are learning and how they are developing as mathematical thinkers. From interviews and observations, to quizzes and tests, to project reports and class work, to portfolios, students can come to see assessment as part of their daily learning experience in mathematics. The breadth of information a teacher can gain from using different types of measures allows the teacher to determine when misconceptions might be starting and when a student has developed an unexpected, but productive, approach to solving a problem. As teachers incorporate increasingly sophisticated ways of monitoring and guiding student learning, it becomes indistinguishable whether tests are driving teaching or the other way around."
—*Faster Isn't Smarter: Messages About Math, Teaching, and Learning in the 21st Century, 2nd ed.* (Seeley 2015, 232–33)

Reflection 10-1: My Changing Beliefs About Teaching and Learning

1. Look back to the three fundamental beliefs about teaching and learning you identified in the first reflection in Chapter 1 (Reflection 1–1). How have your ideas changed?

2. For each of these changes, give an example of how it is reflected in your classroom.

3. Today, how well do your classroom practices reflect your beliefs?

Reflection 10-2: Moving Toward INFORMative Assessment Practices

Rate yourself: 1 = Not Yet   2 = Sometimes   3 = Usually   4 = I do this!

Moving Toward These Classroom Practices	Self-Assessment
RESPONSIVE DECISIONS: Making decisions about what and how to teach based on what students already know and how they respond to instruction	1 2 3 4
LEARNING TARGETS: Clearly defining learning targets with criteria for their achievement and communicating these to students	1 2 3 4
INTENTIONAL LISTENING: Using intentional listening and questioning to monitor student progress and help identify achievement of learning targets	1 2 3 4
ASSESSING REGULARLY: Assessing daily throughout instruction to uncover student thinking and make decisions about instruction	1 2 3 4
RICH TASKS: Using modified routine tasks and mathematically rich tasks for both instruction and assessment to move students' thinking forward	1 2 3 4
GROUPING FLEXIBLY: Having students work on tasks as a whole class, alone, with partners, and in flexible groups	1 2 3 4
STUDENT PARTICIPATION: Establishing clear expectations for participation by all students and respect for different ways of thinking	1 2 3 4
SELF-ASSESSMENT: Creating a climate that promotes reflection, self-assessment, and responsibility through class discussions, models, and rubrics	1 2 3 4
SHARING THINKING: Encouraging students to share solution strategies and facilitating class discussions that move students toward efficient algorithms	1 2 3 4
STUDENTS' LOGIC: Examining the logic behind students' incomplete, incorrect, and correct answers	1 2 3 4
PROBING QUESTIONS: Asking questions to engage students in a task or discussion and using questions to probe students' thinking	1 2 3 4
ACTIONABLE FEEDBACK: Scoring student work for both the process and the answer and providing actionable feedback to inform the student on how to improve performance	1 2 3 4
SUCCESSFUL TEACHING: Defining successful teaching as having students who reason mathematically, exhibit perseverance in solving problems, communicate their ideas, and develop long-term knowledge and skills in using mathematics	1 2 3 4

Reflection 10-3: Mentoring a Teacher

Choose one of the teacher-student dialogues (Mrs. Torres's, page 410, or Ms. Brown's, page 415) and reread that teacher's dialogue. Then answer the questions below.

1. What questions would you ask the teacher about her class and/or her lesson?

2. What foundational ideas (conceptual, factual, and procedural knowledge) did the teacher emphasize adequately? Which ideas were perhaps not emphasized enough?

   Adequate emphasis:

┌─ **Learn More...** ─┐
To refresh your thinking on conceptual, factual, and procedural knowledge, see Chapter 3, pages 77–103 and Chapter 8, pages 336–340.

   Inadequate emphasis:

3. What student errors/mistakes might you have called attention to that the teacher did *not* call attention to? Why do you think it would be important to highlight these errors?

4. The teacher called attention to the units of measure that are attached to the slope and *y*-intercept of the equation. Would you have chosen to make that point? Why or why not? How do you think emphasizing the units of measure might help students understand modeling?

5. If you were mentoring this teacher, what overall feedback might you give the teacher about the quality of her discussion with students?

References

Akatugby, Ayo, Harriet Wallace, and John Wallace. 1999. "Mathematical Dimensions of Students' Use of Proportional Reasoning in High School Physics." *School Science and Mathematics* 99 (1): 31–41.

Anderson, Lorin W., and David R. Krathwohl, eds. 2001. *A Taxonomy for Learning, Teaching, and Assessing: A Revision of Bloom's Taxonomy of Educational Objectives.* New York: Longman.

Black, Paul, and Dylan Wiliam. 1998. "Inside the Black Box: Raising Standards Through Classroom Assessment." *Phi Delta Kappan* 80 (2): 139–44, 146–48.

———. 2009. "Developing the Theory of Formative Assessment." *Educational Assessment, Evaluation, and Accountability* 21: 5–31.

Black, Paul, Christine Harrison, Clare Lee, Bethan Marshall, and Dylan Wiliam. 2004. "Working Inside the Black Box: Assessment for Learning in the Classroom." *Phi Delta Kappan* 86 (1): 9–21.

Bloom, Benjamin S., ed. 1956. *Taxonomy of Educational Objectives: The Classification of Educational Goals; Handbook I: Cognitive Domain.* New York: David McKay.

Boston, Melissa D., and Margaret S. Smith. 2009. "Transforming Secondary Mathematics Teaching: Increasing the Cognitive Demands of Instructional Tasks Used in Teachers' Classrooms." *Journal for Research in Mathematics Education* 40 (2): 119–56.

———. 2011. "A 'Task-Centric Approach' to Professional Development: Enhancing and Sustaining Mathematics Teachers' Ability to Implement Cognitively Challenging Mathematical Tasks." *International Journal on Mathematics Education* 43 (6–7): 965–77.

Brahier, Daniel J. 2001. Assessment in Middle and High School Mathematics: A Teachers' Guide. Larchmont, NY: Eye on Education, Larchmont.

Breyfogle, M. Lynn, and Courtney M. Lynch. 2010. "van Hiele Revisited." *Mathematics Teaching in the Middle School* 16 (4): 232–38.

Bright, George W., John G. Harvey, and Margariete Montague Wheeler. 1985. "Learning and Mathematics Games." *Journal for Research in Mathematics Education Monograph Number 1* (whole volume). Reston, VA: National Council of Teachers of Mathematics.

Bright, George W., and Jeane M. Joyner. 2004a. *Dynamic Classroom Assessment: Linking Mathematical Understanding to Instruction in Middle Grades and High School: Core Program: Facilitator's Guide.* Book, CD-ROM, and video. Vernon Hills, IL: ETA/Cuisenaire.

———. 2004b. *Dynamic Classroom Assessment: Linking Mathematical Understanding to Instruction in Middle Grades and High School: Core Program: Participant's Guide.* Vernon Hills, IL: ETA/Cuisenaire.

———. 2005. *Dynamic Classroom Assessment: Linking Mathematical Understanding to Instruction in Middle Grades and High School: Revisiting Students' Self-Assessment: Participant's Guide.* Vernon Hills, IL: ETA/Cuisenaire.

Bush, William S., and Anja S. Greer, eds. 1999. *Mathematics Assessment: A Practical Handbook.* Reston, VA: National Council of Teachers of Mathematics.

Chick, Helen L. 2009. "Choice and Use of Examples as a Window on Mathematical Knowledge for Teaching." *For the Learning of Mathematics* 29 (3): 26–30.

Clements, Douglas H., and Julie Sarama, eds. 2003. *Engaging Young Children in Mathematics: Standards for Early Childhood Mathematics Education.* Mahwah, NJ: Lawrence Erlbaum.

———. 2004. "Learning Trajectories in Mathematics Education." *Mathematical Thinking and Learning* 6 (2): 81–89.

Collins, Anne M. 2011. *Using Classroom Assessment to Improve Student Learning: Problems Aligned with Curriculum Focal Points and the Common Core State Standards.* Reston, VA: National Council of Teachers of Mathematics.

Confrey, Jere. 2005. "The Evolution of Design Studies as Methodology." In *The Cambridge Handbook of the Learning Sciences,* edited by Keith Sawyer, 135–51. Cambridge. UK: Cambridge University Press.

Covey, Stephen R. 1989. *The 7 Habits of Highly Effective People: Powerful Lessons in Personal Change.* New York: Simon & Schuster.

Dacey, Linda, and Karen Gartland. 2009. *Math for All: Differentiating Instruction: Grades 6–8.* Sausalito, CA: Math Solutions.

Driscoll, Mark, Rachel Wing DiMatteo, Johannah Nikula, and Michael Egan. 2007. *Fostering Geometric Thinking: A Guide for Teachers, Grades 5–10.* Portsmouth, NH: Heinemann.

Enright, Kerry Anne. 2009. "Mathematics Instruction and Academic English: Adapting Problems for Varying English Proficiencies." In *Mathematics for Every Student: Responding to Diversity: Grades 9–12,* edited by Alfinio Flores and Carol E. Malloy, 29–38. Reston, VA: National Council of Teachers of Mathematics.

Franke, Megan, Thomas P. Carpenter, Linda Levi, and Elizabeth Fennema. 2001. "Capturing Teachers' Generative Change: A Follow-Up Study of Professional Development in Mathematics." *American Educational Research Journal* 38 (3): 653–89.

Fuys, David, Dorothy Geddes, and Rosamond Tischler. 1988. "The van Hiele Model of Thinking in Geometry Among Adolescents." *Journal for Research in Mathematics Education Monograph 3* (whole volume), Reston, VA: National Council of Teachers of Mathematics.

Gabel, Dorothy L., and Robert D. Sherwood. 1983. "Facilitating Problem Solving in High School Chemistry." *Journal of Research in Science Teaching* 20 (2): 163–77.

Hattie, John A. C. 2009. *Visible Learning: A Synthesis of over 800 Meta-analyses Relating to Achievement.* New York: Routledge.

Heritage, Margaret. 2008a. "Formative Assessment." Paper presented at the annual meeting of the Association of State Supervisors of Mathematics, Salt Lake City, Utah, April 5.

———. 2008b. "Learning Progressions: Supporting Instruction and Formative Assessment." Paper prepared for the Formative Assessment for Teachers and Students (FAST) State Collaborative on Assessment and Student Standards (SCASS) of the Council of Chief State School Officers (CCSSO).

Heritage, Margaret, and David Niemi. 2006. "Toward a Framework for Using Student Mathematical Representations as Formative Assessments." *Educational Assessment* 11 (3–4): 265–83.

Hiebert, James, Thomas P. Carpenter, Elizabeth Fennema, Karen C. Fuson, Diana Wearne, Hanlie Murray, Alwyn Olivier, and Piet Human. 1997. *Making Sense: Teaching and Learning Mathematics with Understanding.* Portsmouth, NH: Heinemann.

Hsu, Eric, Judy Kysh, and Diane Resek. n.d. Using rich problems for differentiated instruction. math.sfsu.edu/hsu/papers/HsuKyshResek-RichProblems.pdf.

Jones, Dustin L., and James E. Tarr. 2007. "An Examination of the Levels of Cognitive Demand Required by Probability Tasks in Middle Grades Mathematics Textbooks." *Statistics Education Research Journal* 6 (2): 4–27.

Joyner, Jeane M., and Mari Muri. 2011. *INFORMative Assessment: Formative Assessment to Improve Math Achievement, Grades K–6.* Sausalito, CA: Math Solutions.

Kahl, Stuart. 2005. "Where in the World Are Formative Tests? Right Under Your Nose!" *Education Week* 25 (4): 11.

Kahneman, Daniel, and Amos Tversky. 1972. "Subjective Probability: A Judgment of Representativeness." *Cognitive Psychology* 3: 430–54.

———. 1973. "On the Psychology of Prediction." *Psychological Review* 80 (4): 237–51.

Kilpatrick, Jeremy, Jane Swafford, and Bradford Findell. 2001. *Adding It Up: Helping Children Learn Mathematics.* Washington, DC: National Academy Press.

Kingston, Neal, and Brooke Nash. 2011. "Formative Assessment: A Meta-analysis and a Call for Research." *Education Measurement: Issues and Practice* 30 (4): 28–37.

Leinwand, Steve. 2009. *Accessible Mathematics: Ten Instructional Shifts That Raise Student Achievement.* Portsmouth, NH: Heinemann.

Mager, Robert F. 1962. *Preparing Instructional Objectives.* Palo Alto, CA: Fearon.

Mathematics Assessment Project. 2015a. *Evaluating Statements About Enlargements.* Mathematics Assessment Project Classroom Challenges: A Formative Assessment Lesson. map.mathshell.org/download.php?fileid=1754.

———. 2015b. *Interpreting Distance–Time Graphs.* Mathematics Assessment Project Classroom Challenges: A Formative Assessment Lesson. map.mathshell.org/download.php?fileid=1680.

———. 2015c. *Representing Functions of Everyday Situations.* Mathematics Assessment Project Classroom Challenges: A Formative Assessment Lesson. http://map.mathshell.org/download.php?fileid=1740.

———. 2015d. *Solving Linear Equations in Two Variables.* Mathematics Assessment Project Classroom Challenges: A Formative Assessment Lesson. map.mathshell.org/download.php?fileid=1730.

McGatha, Maggie B., and Peg Darcy. 2010. "Rubrics at Play." *Mathematics Teaching in the Middle School* 15 (6): 328–36.

McLeod, Saul A. 2007. "Zone of Proximal Development." Retrieved from simplypsychology.org/Zone-of-Proximal-Development.html.

McMillan, James H., and Jessica Hearn. 2008. "Student Self-Assessment: The Key to Stronger Student Motivation and Higher Achievement." *Educational Horizons* 87 (1): 40–49. eric.ed.gov/?id=EJ815370

McNamara, Julie, and Meghan M. Shaughnessy. 2011. "Student Errors: What Can They Tell Us About What Students DO Understand?" *NCSM Spring Newsletter* 41 (3): 28–30.

Mokros, Jan, and Susan Jo Russell. 1995. "Children's Concepts of Average and Representativeness." *Journal for Research in Mathematics Education* 26 (1): 20–39.

Moll, Louis C. 1994. *Vygotsky and Education: Instructional Implications and Applications of Sociohistorical Psychology.* New York: Cambridge University Press.

National Council of Teachers of Mathematics. 1980. *An Agenda for Action.* Reston, VA: National Council of Teachers of Mathematics.

———. 1989. *Curriculum and Evaluation Standards for School Mathematics.* Reston, VA: National Council of Teachers of Mathematics.

———. 1995. *Assessment Standards for School Mathematics.* Reston, VA: National council of Teachers of Mathematics.

———. 2000. *Principles and Standards for School Mathematics.* Reston, VA: National Council of Teachers of Mathematics.

———. 2014. *Principles to Actions: Ensuring Mathematical Success for All.* Reston, VA: National Council of Teachers of Mathematics.

National Research Council. 2004. *Engaging Schools: Fostering High School Students' Motivation to Learn.* Washington, DC: The National Academies Press.

Pimm, David. 1987. *Speaking Mathematically: Communication in Mathematics Classrooms.* New York: Routledge.

———. 1995. *Symbols and Meanings in School Mathematics.* New York: Routledge.

Rachlin, Sidney L., Barbara Dougherty, Annette Matsumoto, and Debra Perkowski. 1992. *The Hawaii Algebra Trainers Manual.* Honolulu: Curriculum Research and Development Group, University of Hawaii.

Rachlin, Sidney L., Annette Matsumoto, Li Ann Wada, and Barbara J. Dougherty. 2001. *Algebra I—A Process Approach.* 2d ed. Honolulu, HI: Curriculum Research and Development Group, University of Hawaii at Manoa.

Rathouz, Margaret. 2010. "Ambiguity in Units and Their Referents: Two Cases in Rational Number Operations." *For the Learning of Mathematics* 30 (1): 43–51.

Rolheiser, Carol, and John A. Ross. 2001. *Student Self-Evaluation: What Research Says and What Practice Shows.* Center for Development and Learning. cdl.org/resource-library/articles/self_eval.php/.

Ross, John A. 2006. "The Reliability, Validity, and Utility of Self-Assessment." *Practical Assessment Research and Evaluation* 11 (10): 1–13.

Schmittau, Jean. 2004. "Vygotskian Theory and Mathematics Education: Resolving the Conceptual-Procedural Dichotomy." *European Journal of Psychology of Education* 19 (1): 19–43.

Schoenfeld, Alan, Hugh Burkhardt, Phil Daro, Jim Ridgway, Judah Schwartz, and Sandra Wilcox. 1999. *Balanced Assessment for the Mathematics Curriculum: High School Assessment Package 1.* White Plains, NY: Dale Seymour Publications.

Schuster, Lainie, and Nancy Canavan Anderson. 2005. *Good Questions for Math Teaching: Why Ask Them and What to Ask, Grades 5–8.* Sausalito, CA: Math Solutions.

Seeley, Cathy L. 2014. *Smarter Than We Think: More Messages About Math, Teaching, and Learning in the 21st Century.* Sausalito, CA: Math Solutions.

———. 2015. *Faster Isn't Smarter: Messages About Math, Teaching, and Learning in the 21st Century.* 2d ed. Sausalito, CA: Math Solutions.

Shaughnessy, J. Michael. 1981. "Misconceptions of Probability: From Systematic Errors to Systematic Experiments and Decisions." In *Teaching Statistics and Probability: 1981 Yearbook*, edited by Albert P. Shulte and James R. Smart, 90–100. Reston, VA: National Council of Teachers of Mathematics.

Shavelson, Richard J., Gail P. Baxter, and Jerry Pine. 1992. "Performance Assessments: Political Rhetoric and Measurement Reality." *Educational Researcher* 21 (4): 22–27.

Shute, Valerie J. 2008. "Focus on Formative Feedback." *Review of Educational Research* 78 (1): 153–89.

Siegel, Alan. n.d. "Telling Lessons from the TIMSS Videotape: Remarkable Teaching Practices as Recorded from Eighth-Grade Mathematics Classes in Japan, Germany, and the U.S." cs.nyu.edu/faculty/siegel/ST11.pdf

Sierpinska, Anna. 1994. *Understanding in Mathematics* (Studies in Mathematics Series #2). Bristol, PA: Falmer Press, Taylor & Francis.

Simon, Martin A. 1995. "Reconstructing Mathematics Pedagogy from a Constructivist Perspective." *Journal for Research in Mathematics Education* 26 (2): 114–45.

Smith, Margaret Schwan, and Mary Kay Stein. 2011. *5 Practices for Orchestrating Productive Mathematics Discussion*. Reston, VA: National Council of Teachers of Mathematics.

Stahl, Robert J. 1994. *Using "Think-Time" and "Wait-Time" Skillfully in the Classroom* (Eric Digest ED370885). Bloomington, IN: ERIC Clearinghouse for Social Studies/Social Science Education. http://ericdigests.org/1995-1/think.htm

Staples, Megan. 2007. "Supporting Whole-Class Collaborative Inquiry in a Secondary Mathematics Classroom." *Cognition and Instruction* 25 (2–3): 161–217.

Stein, Mary Kay, Margaret Schwan Smith, Marjorie A. Henningsen, and Edward A. Silver. 2000. *Implementing Standards-Based Mathematics Instruction: A Casebook for Professional Development*. New York: Teachers College Press and Reston, VA: National Council of Teachers of Mathematics.

———. 2009. *Implementing Standards-Based Mathematics Instruction: A Casebook for Professional Development*. 2d ed. New York: Teachers College Press.

Stiff, Lee V., and Janet L. Johnson. 2011. "Mathematical Reasoning and Sense Making Begins with the Opportunity to Learn." In *Focusing in High*

School Mathematics: Fostering Reasoning and Sense Making for All Students, edited by Marilyn E. Strutchens and Judith Reed Quander, 85–100. Reston, VA: National Council of Teachers of Mathematics.

Stiggins, Rick, and Jan Chappuis. 2006. "What a Difference a Word Makes." *Journal of Staff Development.* 27 (1): 10–14.

Swan, Malcolm, Alan Bell, Hugh Burkhardt, and Claude Janvier. 1985. *The Language of Functions and Graphs.* Nottingham, UK: Shell Centre for Mathematical Education. mathshell.com/publications/tss/lfg/lfg_masters.pdf.

Sztajn, Paola, Jere Confrey, P. Holt Wilson, and Cynthia Edgington. 2012. "Learning Trajectory Based Instruction: Toward a Theory of Teaching." *Educational Researcher* 41 (5): 147–56.

Tversky, Amos, and Daniel Kahneman. 1971. "Belief in the Law of Small Numbers." *Psychological Bulletin*, 76 (2): 105–10.

———. 1973. "Availability: A Heuristic for Judging Frequency and Probability." *Cognitive Psychology* 5 (2): 207–32.

———. 1974. "Judgment Under Uncertainty: Heuristics and Biases." *Science* 185 (4157): 1124–31.

Usher, Alexandra, and Nancy Kober. 2012. *Student Motivation: An Overlooked Piece of School Reform.* Washington, DC: Center on Education Policy. cep-dc.org.

Usiskin, Zalman, 1982. "van Hiele Levels and Achievement in Secondary School Geometry: CDASSG Project." University of Chicago. ERIC Document Reproduction Service #ED 220 288.

Weiss, Iris R., Joan D. Pasley, Sean Smith, Eric R. Banilower, and Daniel J. Heck. 2003. *Looking Inside the Classroom: A Study of K–12 Mathematics and Science Education in the United States.* Chapel Hill, NC: Horizon Research.

Whitman, Carmen. 2011. *It's All Connected: The Power of Proportional Reasoning to Understand Mathematics Concepts, Grades 6–8.* Sausalito, CA: Math Solutions.

Wiliam, Dylan. 1999. "Formative Assessment in Mathematics: Part 2: Feedback." *Equals: Mathematics and Special Educational Needs* 5 (3): 8–11. eprints. ioe.ac.uk/1148/1/Wiliam1999Formativepart2_8.pdf.

——. 2006. "Formative Assessment: Getting the Focus Right." *Educational Assessment* 11 (3–4): 283–89.

——. 2007a. *Five "Key Strategies" for Effective Formative Assessment: Research Brief.* Reston, VA: National Council of Teachers of Mathematics. nctm. org/Research-and-Advocacy/research-brief-and-clips/Strategies-for-Formative-Assessment/

——. 2007b. "Keeping Learning on Track: Classroom Assessment and the Regulation of Learning." In *Second Handbook of Research on Mathematics Teaching and Learning*, edited by Frank K. Lester, Jr., 1051–98. Reston, VA: National Council of Teachers of Mathematics.

——. 2011. *Embedded Formative Assessment.* Bloomington, IN: Solution Tree Press.

Wiliam, Dylan, and Marnie Thompson. 2007. "Integrating Assessment with Instruction: What Will It Take to Make It Work?" In *The Future of Assessment: Shaping Teaching and Learning*, edited by Carol A. Dwyer, 53–82. Mahwah, NJ: Lawrence Erlbaum.

Wilson, Linda Dager, and Patricia Ann Kenney. 2003. "Classroom and Large-Scale Assessment." In *A Research Companion to Principles and Standards for School Mathematics*, edited by Jeremy Kilpatrick, W. Gary Martin, and Deborah Schifter, 53–67. Reston, VA: National Council of Teachers of Mathematics.

Index

About the Authors

Jeane M. Joyner is the Director of Meredith College's Mathematics and Science Institutes, has been the President of the North Carolina Council of Teachers of Mathematics, has written numerous teacher resource materials, and has more than 50 years in education, preK through college. She is a coauthor of the first book in this series, *INFORMative Assessment, Grades K–6*.

George W. Bright has more than 30 years of experience working with preservice and inservice mathematics teachers, from Northern Illinois University and University of Calgary to Emory University, University of Houston, and University of North Carolina at Greensboro. He has published extensively and has coauthored several resources with Jeane, including *Dynamic Classroom Assessment*.